LADIES OF LASCARIS

Christina Ratcliffe and The Forgotten
Heroes of Malta's War

This book is dedicated to all the girls and ladies who worked in the RAF Headquarters in Valletta, Malta, during the Second World War and especially those within No 8 Sector Operations Room, Lascaris.

LADIES OF LASCARIS

Christina Ratcliffe and The Forgotten
Heroes of Malta's War

Paul McDonald

PEN & SWORD
HISTORY

AN IMPRINT OF PEN & SWORD BOOKS LTD.
YORKSHIRE - PHILADELPHIA

First published in Great Britain in 2018 by
PEN AND SWORD HISTORY
an imprint of
Pen & Sword Books Ltd
Yorkshire - Philadelphia

HB ISBN 978 1 52674 545 3
PB ISBN 978 1 52675 170 6

Typeset in Times New Roman 10/13 by
Aura Technology and Software Services, India

Printed and bound in India by Replika Press Pvt. Ltd.

Pen & Sword Books Limited incorporates the imprints of Atlas,
Archaeology, Aviation, Discovery, Family History, Fiction, History, Maritime,
Military, Military Classics, Politics, Select, Transport, True Crime, Air World,
Frontline Publishing, Leo Cooper, Remember When, Seaforth Publishing,
The Praetorian Press, Wharncliffe Local History, Wharncliffe Transport,
Wharncliffe True Crime and White Owl.

For a complete list of Pen & Sword titles please contact

PEN & SWORD BOOKS LIMITED
47 Church Street, Barnsley, South Yorkshire, S70 2AS, England
E-mail: enquiries@pen-and-sword.co.uk
Website: www.pen-and-sword.co.uk

Or
PEN AND SWORD BOOKS
1950 Lawrence Rd, Havertown, PA 19083, USA
E-mail: uspen-and-sword@casematepublishers.com
Website: www.penandswordbooks.com

Contents

Acknowledgements

People across three continents have offered help in writing this book, from Europe, North America and Australia, as well as New Zealand. But the story could not have been told without the earlier writings of a girl from Cheshire and another from Yugoslavia. Christina Ratcliffe and Tamara Marks' individual tales reflect something quite rare: female perspectives at the heart of military conflict. It is unusual to come across such narratives, let alone two, especially when the lives of both ladies, eye-witnesses to trauma and tragedy, were not just connected but interwoven for a critically important period at the height of the siege of Malta in the Second World War. Neither lady would have described themselves as heroic, certainly not Tamara, but they both were; two very genuine heroes among many who found themselves at the centre of what fell from the skies upon Malta. And rarely have such personal accounts been so well-written, both ladies having a gift for descriptive writing.

There is immediacy about Tamara's words, written within months of the events she endured. She is open and honest to the point of sharing her pain and anguish, her inner-most feelings. Christina's colourful narratives were written later, but she has a rare knack of being able to create vivid and vibrant atmosphere. Her words instantly transport a reader back to join the Whizz-Bangs; then on to a hectic underground operations room to stand adjacent the 'chaps-in-the-gods' looking down on the ladies of Lascaris with their wooden cues moving tracks and blocks on the plotting table depicting the close-run air battle being fought out high above.

Tamara was evacuated to Egypt in 1942. She told her story in *A Woman in Malta,* published in Cairo in November 1943. We know nothing else of her, which is a great shame. Christina began writing after the Second World War. She never finished her story. Some gaps have now been filled, including the touching but ultimately tragic story of her and Warby.

Neither Christina nor Tamara could ever have imagined their experiences and the very words they used would be of interest to others some seventy-five years after the events in which they were involved. That we are able to share their world at war is down to Frederick Galea who unearthed their writings and reproduced them in *Carve Malta on my heart and other wartime stories* (2004), and *Women of Malta* (2006).

ACKNOWLEDGEMENTS

Frederick is a Second World War historian and writer. For many years he was Honorary Secretary of the National War Museum Association of Malta, to which Christina donated her British Empire Medal as well as scrapbooks, notes, photographs and other memorabilia. Frederick is also a founder member of the Malta Aviation Museum at Ta' Qali where he remains active. I am most grateful for Frederick's support with my books, for his permission to quote from his, and for making so many photographs available. Interestingly, Frederick and his wife Valerie have long had a connection with Christina and are important characters in any story about her. It is thanks to them that she rests in a manner appropriate to her contribution to Malta's victory.

Very few girls who worked within the RAF headquarters in Valletta left accounts of their experiences. I was privileged to meet and talk often with one of that gallant band: Marion Childs, née Gould. Now 92-years-old and living on her own, Marion's is an adventure story in its own right. I am particularly grateful to my friend and former RAF colleague Richard Kimberley for introducing me to Marion. Thanks also to Marion's daughter Margaret Biggs in New Zealand for her help.

Marion is from one of three extraordinary families in this story. The others are the Longyears and the Cuells. Michael Longyear is the youngest son and last survivor of his wartime family. At 86 years of age, he has been a key contributor to this book and a great help. I owe him sincere thanks for allowing me to quote from his writings and for telling me so much about his family and his sister Pauline, perhaps the youngest girl ever to serve at Lascaris at only 14 years of age. Michael also did me a great kindness in reading through an early draft and offering valuable advice.

Jane Passmore is the daughter of Betty Cuell, the oldest of three sisters from Casalpaola who were all aircraft plotters - Betty, Helen and Joan. Jane and her husband John put me in touch with the one surviving son, Eddie, of the wartime Cuell family living in Australia. Eddie is also 86-years-old and he and his daughter Kathleen Williams could not have been more helpful in adding details to their family history and in providing photographs. Jane's husband, John, also contacted Adrian Hide, son of the youngest of the Cuell sisters, Mona, whose husband Gordon worked for the RAF and GCHQ at Lascaris. The information Adrian offered was timely and very useful.

At the end of April 2018, I was contacted by Cara Egerton, daughter of the late Wing Commander Bill Farnes, OBE. Bill was the RAF senior controller on D Watch at Lascaris (Christina's Watch) for the most critical part of Malta's air war. I spent a fascinating afternoon with Cara, and her brother Nick Farnes, and they provided an invaluable insight into their father. I am very grateful for their time, and for the wealth of material Nick had painstakingly copied and made available. Included were the original gallantry certificates for their father's Mention in Dispatches and OBE, both earned for his service at Lascaris.

On 11 June 2018 I was contacted by Elle Duddell who recognised her grandmother Gladys Duddell, née Aitken, on the book's jacket. Elle put me in touch with her Aunt, Sandra Patterson, Gladys' eldest daughter. Sandra has provided a great deal of information and material about her late mother and her late Aunt Mary, Gladys' younger sister, both ladies of Lascaris. I am very grateful for the help Sandra so willingly offered.

I am also grateful to Diana Mackintosh, neé Tonna, for sharing her wartime memories of Malta and of the 'utterly charming, handsome young man with slightly crooked front teeth' she was walking out with in 1940. His name was Adrian Warburton.

Two other airmen of the period also offered first-hand recollections: the late Jack Vowles was 92-years-old when we first met. I spent many hours with Jack. His memories of Malta and of Warby were vivid and I very much enjoyed talking to him. Lieutenant General (Ret'd) William Keir 'Bill' Carr, RCAF, is now 94-years-old. I am grateful for his permission to quote from his written work.

Very special thanks to Miriam Farrugia for her fond memories of the beautiful lady who befriended her when she was a child in Bugibba, and whom Miriam met for the last time in the 1980s. After five years of contact, it was a great pleasure to meet Miriam and Ronnie in May 2018. The new material Miriam provided fills an important gap and is an essential part of Christina's story.

I am particularly grateful to Salvu Muscat for the information he provided about the Christina he knew between 1980 and 1987. Salvu was one of the last to know Christina. Also thanks once again to my good friend and constant support, Eman Bonnici. The archives at *Santa Maria Addolorata* cemetery are in very good hands. Thanks also go to Fiona Vella, and to Ingrid Scerri who allowed me access to the roof of her Floriana apartment to see for myself the views Christina described when she moved there in 1940.

Many who attended Warby's funeral in 2003 have also been extremely helpful: Tim Callaway, Heidi Burton née Cox, Glynn Strong, and Sue Raftree. Thanks also to Martin Ratcliffe, Christina's nephew, for sharing his memories of his aunt. I am also grateful to Dr Chris Joy, former archivist at Manchester High School for Girls for making available extracts from school records and magazines. Her successors, Gwen Hobson and Pam Roberts, also ensured my information about Christina's academic achievements was accurate. Thanks also to the RAF Museum for allowing me access to unpublished material, photographs and scrapbooks. Some documents quoted in this work are contained within official British government records held at the National Archives in Kew. These are Crown Copyright and their use is in accordance with the Open Government Licence. In Malta, thanks to Mario Farrugia, Chairman and Chief Executive Officer of the Malta Heritage Trust (*Fondazzjoni Wirt Artna*) for his help and support.

I am especially grateful to Anne Dowie for her continuing support and for the help of her relatives and friends: in Malta, Lora Dimech, Tess Gatt, and the Buhagiar

ACKNOWLEDGEMENTS

families; in the UK, Ruth Johnston and the Rose family, and to Brian Crook, a former colleague from XIII Squadron. Thank you all very much. My sincere thanks also go to my good friend Steve Pepper for his painstaking proofreading and continued encouragement.

Special thanks go to Laura Hirst of Pen and Sword Books who recognised the endeavours of the ladies who worked for the RAF in Malta were deserving of a stand-alone story. I am most grateful to Laura for giving me the push to get me started. Thanks also to Ken Patterson for his painstaking work in editing all three of my books, and to all at Pen and Sword.

In 2016 I was contacted by the playwright Philip Glassborow. Intrigued by Christina's story, he had the germ of an idea of putting together a musical play about her. *Star of Strait Street* was born. It had its world premiere in *Strada Stretta* in Valletta in April 2017. Starring Polly March, Larissa Bonaci and Geoff Thomas, the short musical was an instant success and has been on tour, playing to packed houses ever since, just like the Whizz-Bangs all those years ago. Well done Philip for translating your idea into a beautifully crafted musical stage play and for your personal encouragement. And congratulations to Polly, Larissa and Geoff for their sensitive and moving interpretation of a touching love story.

I would also like to say a special thank you to Polly, a font of connections of her own. One is the accomplished photographer Justin Mamo, who kindly provided all the publicity and dress rehearsal images. They add such colour to this story bringing it very much alive. Thanks also to the writers and journalists Veronica Stivala, André Delicata, Sarah Carabott, Philip Leone-Ganado and Teodor Reljic for allowing me to use and quote from their excellent articles and reviews. And thanks also to Edward Mercieca and Len Moscrop for their personal reflections on the play. A special thank you also goes to the actor John Rhys-Davies.

I am also deeply grateful to my late aunt, Detta Nicholson. This is the third of three manuscripts she avidly read. But without three vital and supportive personal connections - my wife Jackie and our children Matthew and Hannah - there wouldn't have been any books at all.

Paul McDonald
York
May 2018

Note: The provenance of some images is uncertain. If there are errors we apologise and will make appropriate acknowledgements in future editions. Some are Crown Copyright and are used under the Open Government Licence.

Foreword

By

John Rhys-Davies

One of modern cinema's most recognisable character actors, John was presented the BAFTA Special Award for Outstanding Contribution to Film and Television in 2017. He is best-known worldwide for his portrayal of Gimli in the Lord of the Rings *trilogy:* The Fellowship of the Ring, The Two Towers, *and* The Return of the King. *His many other performances include Sallah, the loyal sidekick to Indiana Jones in* Raiders of the Lost Ark. *His television credits include* The Naked Civil Servant *with John Hurt, and the BBC-TV series,* I, Claudius, *which earned him an Emmy nomination.*

John has made several extended visits to Malta when filming. He portrayed King Priam in Helen of Troy, *and was one of the stars in the acclaimed mini-series* Reilly Ace of Spies *starring Sam Neill. In 2014, he played Caiaphas in* Saul: The Journey to Damascus.

FOREWORD

Like Paul McDonald, I feel a connection with this magical island. I first came in 1953 on (I think) the SS *Madura* from Dar es Salaam to school in England. Later I filmed here. My late father-in-law, Surgeon Captain E.A.G. Wilkinson was a frequent visitor to Malta from the 1890s to after the First World War. I never met him but treasure what he wrote, a paean of praise for the people and the place. Like him and like Paul I am in awe of its history, its beauty and these wonderful people; generous, shy - but so warm and welcoming.

I came back to the island in March 2017 to document the musical play *Star of Strait Street* written by my good friend Philip Glassborow. Based on Paul's earlier work, the play had its world premiere in Valletta on 4 April 2017. By then I was familiar with Paul's writing: authoritative yet eloquent, well researched but carefully crafted, and a celebration of love in time of war, of great courage and of sacrifice.

The characters in *Ladies of Lascaris* came to Malta for a variety of reasons and from many different countries. Some, like Christina Ratcliffe, were simply stranded; Yugoslavian Tamara Marks was the wife of an RAF squadron leader. Many others were born on the island. Yet whatever their origins they all united in adversity and what they helped achieve encouraged millions of people across the world to hope when Allied fortunes were at their lowest ebb.

This story describes well many aspects of Malta's war but at its heart is a group of women, mostly unknown to us, many incredibly young, who were truly inspiring. But very few of us know their story. When their RAF work was done, most of the girls Paul describes simply got on with the rest of their lives, and rarely looked back; but all had been touched by what they saw. Thankfully two of them, Christina and Tamara, wrote of their experiences and Paul picked up on their tales some years after they were published by Frederick Galea.

The full story of what those ladies accomplished, and what they endured, is long overdue. And in Paul, we are lucky to have a natural storyteller. He takes us back through his own fascinating and personal connections with Malta, connections which set him on a quest to uncover more.

For Christina, her love for Warby, who was the love of her life, and her love for the island she describes as 'carved on my heart' was deep and enduring. Yet she suffered years of loneliness and her death was desperately sad.

I share with Paul the deep affection he has for the island and its magical people, and his admiration for those who lived through Malta's twentieth century siege. The result of his efforts is true drama, drama about people and what became of them. He has skilfully interwoven their words and his own and wrapped them up within Malta's story. *Ladies of Lascaris* has all the ingredients of a Shakespearian play - drama, heroism, love and tragedy. Without the heroism of the people of Malta, Britain might have been defeated. Read their story, and never forget the debt we owe.

The closing chapters of this fine work are poignant to the point of tears with Paul's quest ending next to Christina's grave in Paola. But that is not the end of the story. Paul immediately lifts up our spirits as we see Christina smiling once more and from where she always wanted to be, on the stage. The description of how the gem of a musical came together is fascinating and fast-paced. It is the encore Christina Ratcliffe was denied in life.

Paul's easy writing style makes this tribute to those unsung heroines of Lascaris a joy to read. I most strongly recommend it. Visit the island. And if you have the opportunity, go and see Christina's encore: *Star of Strait Street*.

John Rhys-Davies
Isle of Man
May 2018

Chapter 1

Connections

Valletta, Malta, Friday, 2 December 1988

The bank teller was worried, not for himself, but for a customer. He had only ever known her as 'Miss Christina', someone he served, not someone he had ever talked to, except over the counter. She only ever came into his branch of the Bank of Valletta on *Triq ir-Repubblika* in Malta's capital on the first of every month to cash her pension. She had done so for years, regular as clockwork. Yet she missed September, October and November with no word, which was very unusual. Now with only minutes to go before closing, she was again overdue.

This was most unlike Miss Christina. Some years earlier she hadn't collected her pension for a while but the bank had been informed and other arrangements made. Someone said she had fallen down the stairs and broken her leg. That was probably why she walked with a stick. He thought she was a lonely lady.

Now it was nearly three months since she had picked up her pension and there was no word. The bank teller was increasingly worried about Miss Christina. She still wore her distinctive hair to the shoulder and it continued to turn heads, although now it was completely white. She would have turned many more heads when she was younger, he thought. Not for the first time he wondered whether she drank too much. Did that cause her to fall? Yet she always raised a smile for him. He hadn't seen her small Scottie dog with the tartan ribbon for a long time.

Miss Christina was always polite. She also used some words of Malti which was rare for an English lady. *Grazzi ħafna* she would say. He thought her use of his language a huge compliment to his small country, the country she had made her home. She lived in Floriana in an apartment on Vilhena Terrace and had been there since the war apparently. Other than that he knew little except what George Darmanin, the chief cashier when he first began work at the bank over twenty years earlier had told him. Apparently, in the small cafés and bars on the island old men spoke about Miss Christina and a dashing RAF pilot. They said they were symbols of Maltese resistance and of suffering too. Both were heroes they said. He always thought it slightly odd how one particular English pilot could be held in such adulation, especially as a lot of pilots served on the island in the Second

1

World War. What was so special about him? And what happened to him? No one seemed to know. And what had Miss Christina done to merit being called a hero?

He was concerned something untoward had happened. He had to act; he owed her that much. He mentioned it to his manager who suggested telephoning the Pensions Branch at the British High Commission. He phoned immediately and spoke to an official, Mr Joseph Pace, who said he would investigate.

Joseph gave the matter some thought and then decided to contact the police. By then, it was Friday evening and Joseph was at his home in Kappara. How could he ensure action was taken immediately rather than it being left until Monday to be dealt with by the local Floriana police as something routine? He had an idea.

At 7.00 pm Joseph formally notified the Maltese Divisional Police by telephone that a British national, Miss Mary Christina Ratcliffe of Flat 3, 7 Vilhena Terrace, Floriana, had not been seen since August. Joseph said he was concerned there may have been foul play. That did the trick. Action was immediate. Inspector Zammit, along with Sergeant Ellul, Sergeant Muscat, Constable Marmaro and Constable Debono were despatched to the scene. They were prepared for the worst but hoped for the best, that all was well. But of course it wasn't.

After knocking on the door several times without success, they pushed the door open and entered the apartment. They found a woman's body in bed, apparently dead. A doctor from the nearby Floriana Polyclinic was called. When Doctor Grech arrived, he examined the body and said because of the advanced state of decomposition he couldn't exclude violence. At that stage the cause of death was unknown. The duty magistrate, Doctor Vella, was informed. He directed a magisterial enquiry was to be held *in loco*, in the apartment, the following day. He appointed Mr Aquilina, the police photographer, to assist and Doctor Grech to draw up the *Levée du Corps*, to make the arrangements for the transfer of the body.

The magisterial enquiry was held at 11.00 am on Saturday, 3 December in the apartment. Dr Dipasqual was assisted by Constable Aquilina, the scene of crime officer, and Constable Sammat as photographic expert. The magistrate ordered the removal of the corpse, which was conveyed to the mortuary of *Santa Lucia* hospital in nearby Pietà by Mr J. Borg and Mr J. Nojado. The body was formally identified by two local Floriana policemen, Constable Debono and Constable Barbaro, as Miss Mary Christina Ratcliffe. They had sometimes seen her safely home down *Triq San Frangisk* when it was dark and she was on her own. A post mortem examination was held at 1.00 pm on the same day by Professor Maria Theresa Camilleri and Doctor Ali Salfrag. The cause of death was established as natural causes, probably ischaemic heart disease. The magistrate then ordered the burial of the corpse and a death certificate was issued.

Christina had died alone and unnoticed in bed in her apartment high above Grand Harbour where a chill wind was now blowing through some broken windows. She had been dead for up to three months. She was 74-years-old and had lived alone in the same apartment for over forty years. It was now in a poor condition; even the enclosed balconies high above the surrounding streets and looking directly towards Valletta and across to the Three Cities had to be replaced.

There were lots of tins of cat food in the apartment; Christina must have been in the habit of feeding the many strays frequenting the gardens across the road from the large apartment block. There were always so many strays, living out their solitary existence, just like Miss Christina must have done in her final years. The cats would miss her kindness and understanding of their lives. Would anyone miss Christina?

Miss Mary Christina Ratcliffe, BEM, was buried at 10.00 am on Sunday, 4 December 1988. She was the second occupant in shared grave Number 161 in Section A of the East Division of the Government Section of *Santa Maria Addolorata* Cemetery in Paola. She didn't even have a grave to call her own. There were few to say farewell.

RAF Luqa, Malta, Wednesday, 27 August 1975

We first saw Malta through the small windows of a Royal Air Force (RAF) passenger aircraft. The tiny walled fields and the rocky, waterless landscape made an immediate impression. The sun's brightness and the heat hit Jackie and I like a wave as we exited the aircraft. It was a blisteringly hot day, such a change from the mild summer weather we had left behind at RAF Brize Norton near Oxford in England.

There was a lot to take in. RAF Luqa was nothing like the airfields with which I was familiar. Everything was light brown - even the airmen's uniforms - matching the stone colour of the buildings and walls surrounding the many tiny fields. The fields themselves were sun-baked, dry and dusty with no signs of greenery other than clumps of prickly pear. It was difficult to imagine Luqa as one of the most heavily-bombed airfields in the Second World War.

I was a 26-year-old flying officer, a pilot, about to join a photo-reconnaissance squadron. I had been in the Royal Air Force for four and a half years and had been married to Jackie for just over a year. The nearby squadron dispersals contained the unmistakeable shape of Canberras. Each was fitted with an array of cameras developed in the Second World War when the Royal Air Force gained a deserved reputation for photo-recce, a reputation it has never lost. To the north of my new headquarters, and across a disused runway, was the international terminal. The village to the left of the terminal gave the airfield its name, one of a number of surviving Arabic names on the island. Left of the village, the ground sloped downhill toward Grand Harbour. The whole area was dominated by a high hill to the north-west on the summit of which the town of Rabat adjoined the battlements of the ancient so-called silent city of Mdina.

We moved in with friends until we found a place of our own. They lived in Pietà on Guardamangia Hill in a fine looking villa with large rooms, a walled garden at the back with an old well attached to the rear of the house. The views were magnificent. Straight ahead was Marsamxett Harbour with Valletta on the right; there was a fort directly ahead called Fort Manoel on an island of the same name. We stayed in Pietà for about three weeks before moving to Birkirkara.

Our new home was on a street called Msida Heights overlooking Valley Road. Our balcony was a great vantage point to watch the regular and loud firework displays as nearby villages celebrated a *festa*, the feast of their patron saint. There was always a special *festa* in August, although it was some time before I learnt of its significance.

Over the next three years, I spent hours flying over Sicily and Italy photographing ports and harbours, all of them photographed many times before, but in far more testing circumstances. Italian military airfields were often practice targets and, like my predecessors, I always received a very warm welcome there, only in a very different sense. The *Regia Aeronautica's* successors were always hospitable, a spirited and professional lot, not unlike their predecessors, who in the Second World War often earned the respect of those posed by their politicians as Italy's enemy.

When returning to Malta at low level, our route usually took us to the island of Gozo. A left turn brought us to Valletta and Grand Harbour with Luqa soon in our sights. It took only a matter of minutes.

Our son Matthew was born in the Royal Navy (RN) hospital at Mtarfa, which is due north of Mdina on the other side of a valley which leads down to a dried-up lake, the location of the former RAF Ta' Qali. Long disused, it is home to small, flourishing craft industries operating from wartime Nissen huts. Nearby are the small, pretty towns of Attard and Balzan and only a short distance north is Mosta with its famed, some say miraculous, church visible from much of the island. On 9 April 1942 a bomb crashed through the dome in the middle of a service, rolling past the congregation without exploding; hence the church's reputation.

Mary, our Maltese babysitter, lived in Msida. Thirty-five years earlier in 1940, she was evacuated from the Three Cities to Birkirkara following heavy bombing around the dockyards. When she told us her story it seemed odd, given how close Birkirkara was to the main residential areas. Of course, these had become widespread over the years. The bombing was often localised around the docks and the airfields. Even so, on such a small island, nowhere was immune. The Three Cities - Vittoriosa, Senglea and Cospicua - are close-knit communities that grew around two fishing villages: Birgu, now Vittoriosa, and L-Isla, now Senglea. They prospered around the dockyards which ultimately led to their destruction under some of the most intensive bombing the world has ever known. Now rebuilt, they have become a rare and unexpected find: history, thriving communities and welcoming warmth, all hidden in the open and only visited by the more inquisitive of Malta's tourists.

Our second home was in Balzan. Our rear balcony overlooked San Anton Palace, the residence of Malta's President and the former residence of Malta's wartime governors. Our daughter Hannah was born in nearby Attard at St Catherine's nursing home in our final summer on the island. We were frequent visitors to a former barracks in Floriana, on the right just beyond *Porte des Bombes*. This was now the location of a British military medical centre and our nearest NAAFI shop.

My squadron was the very last RAF squadron based in Malta. It left on 4 October 1978, ending a tradition of RAF photo-reconnaissance from the island which had begun in 1940 with a few American-built aircraft built for the French, delivered to Britain and then brought to Malta by nine airmen led by an Australian. They created a legend.

On 1 April 1979 the destroyer HMS *London* became the last British warship to leave Grand Harbour, ending Britain's 179-year association with Malta which began when Malta asked Britain for help in expelling Napoleon's occupying French army. A previous warship of the same name, a cruiser belonging to the Mediterranean Fleet in the 1930s, proved to be yet another connection with this tale.

There is much that connects the two island nations of Britain and Malta and bears testament to the sacrifice of many in two world wars; testament that lasts regardless of politics and politicians who come and go. Some personal links and connections can never be broken and we now had two rather important ones that would draw us back to Malta twelve years later, each wishing to visit the country of their birth.

Malta International Airport, August 1990

We landed on the long main runway which was under construction the last time I'd seen it. It was built on top of what had been the longest wartime runway which had been disused in my day. The terminal seemed little changed and my old squadron's dispersals and buildings were still there, although there was no activity nearby.

Our former homes in Birkirkara and Balzan were now hotels, but San Anton Gardens was unchanged, its walls cutting out the noise and bustle of the nearby streets. Mdina, the old capital, with its narrow atmospheric streets is a magical place described as a hauntingly beautiful city dreaming quietly behind impenetrable walls. Whoever offered that image must only have visited as dusk approached when the tourists had gone. The former hospital high up on the hill at Mtarfa looked long-abandoned and quite forlorn. But St Catherine's in Attard was as we remembered it.

Matthew and Hannah were pleased to visit the places where their lives began. As we left Malta, just like in 1978, Jackie and I gave little thought to the possibility of returning, but we would be drawn back.

NATO Air Headquarters Ramstein Germany, April 2003

It had been a quiet morning. I was a group captain on my final tour before retiring after 34 years RAF service. I took a phone call and learnt the remains of a wartime RAF pilot had been found in the wreckage of his aircraft in Bavaria bringing to an end a 59-year-old mystery. The pilot's name was Adrian Warburton.

His funeral service, with full military honours, took place at *Pfarrkirche St Agidius*, Gmund-am-Tegernsee, on 14 May 2003. The interment was at the Commonwealth War Graves cemetery at Durnbach, south of Munich in Bavaria, with the service taken by Ramstein's RAF chaplain, Squadron Leader the Reverend Alan Coates. The Queen's Colour Squadron of the RAF Regiment was flown in from RAF Uxbridge in West London to act as pall-bearers.

My UK superior at Ramstein, Air Marshal Sir Roderick Goodall, represented the RAF's Chief of the Air Staff and the US military formed an Honour Guard. Warburton was clearly a man of some importance whose reputation extended even across 'the pond'.

The day of the funeral began sunny and remained so until the cortege arrived at the cemetery. The weather then turned bitterly cold, the heavens opened and it began

RAF Regiment pall-bearers carry Adrian Warburton into Durnbach cemetery.
(Heidi Burton, née Cox)

Former Malta airman Jack
Vowles lays a rose from Christina.
(Heidi Burton, née Cox)

to hail leaving the heads and shoulders of the pall-bearers covered with hailstones. In a particularly moving gesture, an elderly Yorkshireman stepped forward and placed a single rose on Warburton's coffin. His name was Jack Vowles, a former Malta-based airman. The rose was from a girl called Christina, he said. What was that all about?

Shortly after the coffin was lowered into the grave the *Last Post* was played. A lone piper then played *Lament*. As if on cue, the weather cleared and the sun came out. It was a fitting farewell to a long-lost pilot.

A year later, as Jackie and I were driving to Salzburg, we passed a signpost to Durnbach. I felt compelled to stop. Like similar cemeteries the world over, it is well looked after by the Commonwealth War Graves Commission. It was quiet and tranquil, quite beautiful despite the poignancy and air of sadness. The majority of the 2,934 graves are of British and Commonwealth airmen. The ages of those who lay there gave me pause. Warburton had just turned 26 years of age when he was killed. His senior rank at such a young age was not unusual given the circumstances of wartime service. But his decorations make him truly outstanding. He was awarded the Distinguished Service Order twice and the Distinguished Flying Cross four times, one of which was from the US President Franklyn D. Roosevelt. This made 'Warby', or 'Six Medal Warburton' as he was also known, the most highly decorated RAF photo-reconnaissance pilot of all time. He was also once described by Air Marshal Sir Arthur Tedder as 'the most valuable pilot in the RAF'.

'The most valuable pilot in the RAF'. *(Heidi Burton, née Cox)*

Five years later I read *Warburton's War*. I was struck by our mutual associations with photo-recce from Malta, albeit over thirty years apart. In Malta Warby became involved with an English singer and dancer. Her name was Christina - the 'Christina' referred to by Jack Vowles. She was a founder member of a troupe of entertainers on the besieged island and later became a civilian aircraft plotter working in the RAF headquarters known as Lascaris; she was one of a number of ladies of Lascaris.

The link between a Malta-based recce pilot and a civilian plotter reminded me of a post-war film called *Malta Story*. My interest was further aroused when I read *Carve Malta on my heart and other wartime stories*. Edited and published by the Maltese researcher Frederick Galea, the opening story is in Christina's own words. But it was far from finished and left me with many questions. What was her Malta story?

She was living in Floriana when Jackie and I lived in Malta in the 1970s. We often visited the NAAFI and the medical centre in the former St Francis Barracks which was overlooked by the house in which Christina roomed in 1937 and to which she returned in 1940. She was living there when the Italians declared war. Later she moved to an apartment, also in Floriana, one we drove past many times going to and from Valletta, or down to Malta's quayside. Christina was a talented writer and wrote extensively, yet she said little about her relationship with Warby and nothing about her feelings toward him until shortly before she died. It was as if she had deliberately drawn a veil of secrecy over their relationship for more than forty years. Why was that?

Was there something about Malta which allowed Christina and Warby to shine? Or was it simply the circumstances of life on an isolated island at war and the excitement of the times that brought these two people together, a shy loner who didn't fit in and an outgoing, vivacious dancer? And what was it about their story that drew me in, setting me off to find out the truth about a girl from Cheshire described as 'Christina of George Cross Island'?

Who was this lady of Lascaris?

Valletta, Malta, April 2016

Two days before the world premiere of Philip Glassborow's musical play *Star of Strait Street*, an article entitled *A Star for the Times* was published in the *Sunday Times of Malta*. It was written by Veronica Stivala and began: 'It's nostalgic, it's about love, and beautiful people, but it's also about strength and courage and serves as a window into life in Malta during the war.'

Mary Buhagiar was in the audience and said afterwards, 'the play was magical and the music lovely. The audience was so engrossed you could hear a pin drop.'

Edward Mercieca was also there too. He is one of Malta's leading actors and producers. Afterwards he posted a message on Facebook: 'Experienced first-class theatre yesterday when I went to watch the *Star of Strait Street*! A massive well done to Philip Glassborow for writing this wonderful piece of nostalgia and for his direction. Super well done to the stars Polly March and Larissa Bonaci ... and the superb pianist and musical director, Geoff Thomas! You kept me there, totally mesmerized the whole time, you made me laugh and you made me cry - a rollercoaster of emotions, the perfect ingredients of great theatre! I don't often feel patriotic these days, as the current atmosphere is so polarized and so filled with hatred that I forget our past and how, as a nation, we fought and were brave, together ... so I did shed a tear for us today! Thank you for the journey, thank you for your wonderful performances!'

Edward was with the actress Polly March for some time after the performance, and was still in tears. He said he had not felt proud or patriotic for many years, and the play helped him remember his identity. The performance received a standing ovation. Polly said she was very, very proud to be part of it. While many people who saw the show were also moved to tears by the memories it evoked, many younger ones seemed to have no idea what their grandparents and great-grandparents had endured. They were moved too, and wanted to know more.

And who was this star of Strait Street? Her name was Christina.

Christina Ratcliffe. *(Paul McDonald)*

Chapter 2

Dancing Shoes & Stepping Stones

1914 - 1939

Dukinfield is a small industrial town on the eastern outskirts of Manchester. It lies in central Tameside on the south bank of the River Tame opposite Ashton-under-Lyme. Historically part of Cheshire, the town was a product of the Industrial Revolution which saw its development accelerated by the growth of coal mining and the cotton industry. Inevitably this came at the expense of surrounding pasture and rolling meadowland. It was the cotton trade which shaped the town. At the beginning of the nineteenth century it had two cotton mills; by 1851 it boasted a population of 26,514 and by the end of the nineteenth century there were fourteen mills and the town served as a major rail junction. But the industries that sustained Dukinfield were dying as the twentieth century progressed and the cotton industry declined. In order to sustain its population the town increasingly relied on its location on the main road from Stockport to Ashton-under-Lyme and its easy commute to Manchester.

Christina Ratcliffe was born here on 1 July 1914. Christened Mary Christina, her birth was registered in September 1914 in the Ashton-under-Lyme district of Cheshire. She had two brothers. Her father Henry Marsland Ratcliffe originated from Glossop in Derbyshire and her mother Jeanie King Ratcliffe, née Downs, was Scottish. In 1914, Christina's father owned or managed one of the remaining mills in Dukinfield from the family home at 409 Cheetham Hill Road, Dukinfield. The landscape in which Christina grew up was therefore an industrial one.

The prospect of what she saw as a dreary, routine existence in the shadow of the Pennines in no way appealed. She yearned for something different. With an outgoing nature and a sense of adventure, she grew into a tall, slim, attractive girl with brown eyes and blonde hair. Intelligent and confident, her independent nature was apparent early on. Like many young girls, Christina began ballet lessons when she was 8-years-old. Few could have imagined just where her dancing shoes, her determination and search for excitement would take her.

'My ballet mistress shook her head and said to my mother: "I am afraid, Mrs Ratcliffe, that this little girl of yours will never get anywhere with her dancing. She's far too wooden." I was only ten when that devastating criticism fell upon me.

It came at the end of a charity matinee given by the pupils of a dancing academy I had been attending for the past couple of years. Lanky-legged, bent at the knees, I had just wobbled my way through an agonising ballet number and my ankles were throbbing with pain. But the pain in my ankles was nothing compared to the ache in my heart when I heard those shattering words.' The criticism simply acted as a spur for Christina to pursue her dreams.

The Ratcliffe family was well-placed in depression-hit Britain. Christina attended the private Ashton High School until she was 13-years-old then moved to Manchester High School for Girls, a leading independent fee-paying school established in 1874. The school on Grangethorpe Road, Manchester, was modern and progressive, although in its architecture there was no disguising its Victorian origins.

Known throughout her childhood by her first name Mary, her registration/report card records her father's occupation as cotton manufacturer. Christina was a day-pupil and travelled by train. She was awarded her school certificate in 1931 in seven subjects, gaining passes in English Composition and Art, and credits in History, Natural History, English Literature, Geography, and French. She was an active member of the school dramatic society, later joining the committee. She also took additional lessons in gymnastics and voice production which would prove important in her future career. The grounding Christina received academically, especially in English and French, also stood her in very good stead.

MANCHESTER HIGH SCHOOL FOR GIRLS.

Manchester High School for Girls in Victorian times. *(MHSG Archives)*

After leaving school having just turned seventeen, 'my father put me to work in his cotton factory. But I saw no future through the windows of our mill. I longed to go on the stage, to travel.' The factory didn't hold her for long. Her mother had hoped Christina might become a nurse. She kept up her dancing and appeared on the same billing as George Formby at the old Manchester Hippodrome. Then, having won some money in a crossword competition, Christina set off for the bright lights of London. Her prize of £40 could hardly have financed her for very long. The year was 1933; she was 19-years-old. She soon found work and danced in the film *Charing Cross Road,* starring John Mills and June Clyde, which was released in 1935.

Christina then joined an English dancing troupe, Miss Frances Mackenzie's Young Ladies and the lavish show, complete with nudes, was produced in Paris. It was called *Jusqu'aux Etoiles - To the Stars* - and toured France, Italy and Switzerland, as well as Algiers in North Africa.

Fascism was on the rise in the mid-1930s and there was growing concern about Hitler and Mussolini's territorial ambitions. In 1935, Italy invaded Abyssinia, modern day Ethiopia, and was soon victorious. Italy's actions were roundly condemned, particularly by Britain. Unfortunately, these events coincided with *Jusqu'aux Etoiles'* appearance in Genoa. 'To be British in that fair land of love and sunshine was to be unpopular. Italian theatre-goers have mastered the art of displaying their emotions to a high degree. I have been literally bombarded with flowers, showered with confetti, and over-enthusiastic admirers have even leapt on the stage to embrace me. But I had never been booed before that night in Genoa when the curtain went up on our toy soldier number. We girls were bewildered. Could it be our dancing? Surely not; it was a slick, cleverly performed number that usually brought the house down. Could it be our costumes? Surely not; they were smart, well-tailored outfits.

'Then we discovered the truth. The Italians were booing our backdrop - a specially designed curtain incorporating not only the Royal Coat of Arms, but also the Union Jack.' Miss Frances Mackenzie's Young Ladies were booed off the stage.

A six-month contract with the Rodney Hudson Girls was next at the Tivoli Theatre in Barcelona. 'The overland journey to Spain was uneventful until the train stopped at Moncada, twelve miles from Barcelona. We had been travelling all night and most of us were dead tired. Ten minutes passed; half-an-hour went by. It was high noon when the news came. The Civil War had started. Barcelona had been bombed. Three days later we were still in the train at Moncada. We lived on food and drink provided by villagers.'

The girls witnessed the opening round of what became a vicious, terrifying conflict. Eventually they were driven to Barcelona where they spent a wakeful first night listening to the sounds of bombs, shells, gunfire and rifle shots. 'We saw a wall riddled with bullets, which had passed through the bodies of executed rebels. We saw dead horses lying in gutters, wrecked cars, fallen lamp posts, shattered windows and street barricades behind which were tough-looking defenders armed with machine guns.' The three-year war was between the Republican government and the Nationalists, led by the fascist General Franco. It was he who emerged victorious. For Italy and Germany's military, Spain was a perfect proving ground.

Thankfully for Christina and the other stranded British nationals, the Royal Navy came to their rescue. They were taken on board the cruiser HMS *London,* the only rescue ship to berth inside Barcelona Harbour. The crew organised the warship as a reception centre accommodating 900 people in the first three days of the war. Their concerned charges were then sent in smaller groups to destroyers which took them to Marseilles. The Rodney Hudson Girls were a resilient bunch; while stranded two of them even found time to dye their hair. After a week in Spain, the destroyer HMS *Gallant* took the girls to Marseilles and safety.

Within a few days of returning from Spain, Christina was considering offers from Rodney Hudson for work in India and another from Francis A. Mangan Productions Ltd for a two-to-three month engagement in Stockholm. She opted for Stockholm. Coming so soon after such a traumatic experience in Spain, Christina's enthusiasm for her chosen career and for travel indicates something of the steel within her character and her thirst for further adventure. She had just turned 22 years of age, clearly a very resilient, determined and capable young lady.

The Swedish production came to an end after a month, Christina's only compensation being a day spent in Copenhagen on her way back to London. Still seeking work, she appeared as a guinea-a-day extra in *Dark Journey,* which starred Vivien Leigh and Conrad Veidt. Made at Denham Studious in Middlesex, it was released in 1937. Next Christina worked, again as an extra, on *The Mill on the Floss* with Geraldine Fitzgerald, which was released the same year. 'For getting soaked to the skin in the flood scenes the extras were paid half-a-crown over and above the daily guinea. I spent the difference on medicaments to ward off a severe chill.'

Christina's next film opportunity was in November 1936 as a dancer in the Hollywood-style musical crime film *Premiere,* made in Vienna by the Tobis Sascha Film Company. The work was hard with many rehearsals and constant retakes of the spectacular dances at the heart of the production. Christina was one of a group of twenty-four female and twenty-four male dancers. The star was the Swedish Zarah Leander who later became the leading female actress in Germany. The film's unlikely plot involved the wealthy backer of a Viennese musical revue, who wanted to replace the revue's stars for personal reasons, being murdered from the stage on the opening night. The suspects were the stars themselves. A police officer who just happened to be in the audience began his investigation backstage trying not to interrupt the show. Despite the weakness of the plot, some of the dance scenes, particularly the 'reflections' number, performed on black glass flooring, and the finale, were unique and spectacular. They were also less frantic and a little more relaxed than the usual Hollywood-style spectacular of the 1930s.

The hard work was more than balanced by a very active social life, dining in style in their hotel, the Heitzinger Hof, and waltzing to the music of Strauss. A highlight for Christina was listening to Richard Tauber in the opera *Tiefland* at the Vienna Opera House. *Premiere* was released in February 1937. Christina was eventually able to see it at the Regent Cinema in Valletta, Malta.

The beginning of 1937 saw Christina in London, out of work and living at the Theatre Girls' Club in Soho:

59 Greek Street, Soho
Lodgings for Young Women engaged in business, and students
Rent of bedroom, including use of sitting-room,
Three shillings to four shillings a week paid in advance
Breakfast or tea, tuppence-halfpenny
Dinner, sixpence

'January was not the best month for an out-of-work dancer to hit the town. The pantomimes and Christmas shows were only at the beginning of their long runs and no new productions were in the offing. As for film work the industry was not what might be called booming. "No Casting" was a familiar notice on the door of many an agent's office.' Every morning Christina joined other girls staying at the club trooping round agents' offices only to be fobbed off. 'If the pouring rain didn't exactly dampen our spirits, it most effectively rinsed out any traces of beauty or glamour we might have possessed. With our red noses, blue cheeks and waterlogged hair, it was not surprising that there was "nothing today".'

Seven weeks of a dreary, wet, cold English winter went by with time spent reading, knitting, sewing, or playing endless games of Ludo. Each Friday they hosted an 'at home' for friends and invariably a visiting parson was invited to give a talk. 'Hardly in keeping with a theatre girls' club, but we were never given the impression that he'd come to save our souls. Nor did he threaten us with hellfire.' Despite the pleasant company, Christina was bored and wanted to see the world, not sit around and watch her savings dwindle. And then someone mentioned Malta.

The idea came from Christina's closest friend, an attractive dancer with dark hair and blue eyes: 'Sheila, in a dripping wet mackintosh, burst into the clubroom. She was highly excited. "Work at last," she announced breathlessly. "I've got a contract." We of the fireside circle paused in our knitting and sewing to give heed to this astonishing piece of news.

"Where and what?"

"Malta. Cabaret."

"Malta? You need your head seeing to."

"There's one born every minute."

'Crestfallen, Sheila sat on the arm of a settee and listened with downcast eyes to the council of advisers.

"You'll be raped by drunken sailors."

"You'll never get back to London."

"Ever read *The Road to Buenos Aires*?"'

While the girls lacked any direct experience of working in Malta, they had all heard lurid stories about appearing in cabaret in the less salubrious establishments for which Valletta was renowned. Apparently it was a particular challenge for an attractive female entertainer when the fleet was in. As Valletta's Grand Harbour was home to the Royal Navy's Mediterranean Fleet, the fleet was in more often than not. Sheila hoped one or two of the others might join her but none seemed interested.

Christina listened to everyone's comments but kept her own counsel. A cousin of her mother had been married to a sailor once based in Malta and Christina recalled prints of 'a city of narrow, stepped streets and tall buildings with tier upon tier of romantic-looking balconies. I could remember his books about the island with their lovely old palaces and churches, horse-drawn cabs with curtains and little rowing boats with a hint of the gondola about them.' Christina's impressions, however, revolved around a Malta of long ago.

'Not so Sheila's counsellors. What they had heard in the Charing Cross cafés about the island would fill volumes. It was infested with low-down taverns and bawdy music halls, a date that only the dregs of the theatrical profession would think of working. It was certainly no place for a nice girl like Sheila'. Sheila left the room quite disconsolate.

"The silly bitch; that just shows you what happens when Miss Innocence goes out on her own round the agencies."

"She's certainly green."

"I bet they thought, 'Ah! Here comes a nice simple bit of stuff."

'It was then that Lillian spoke.' She was a little older and had worked in Malta. Working conditions were not perfect and cabaret in Valletta was not for the faint-hearted, she said. Any performer had to be capable of appearing in front of occasionally unruly crowds of servicemen, but there were advantages. The island itself was charming with wonderful weather and bathing and there was lots of sightseeing for those interested in exploring Malta's rich history. 'You needed guts to appear in front of a cabaret audience in Malta,' said Lillian, 'and above all, a sense of humour.'

Christina listened carefully: there was the prospect of work in the sun measured against no work while enduring a dreary English winter. While the pay could not be compared with that of the West End, neither could the cost of living. A well-furnished, comfortable flat could be rented for £2 a month and a daily maid to clean and do the laundry would cost a fraction of that. Food was very cheap and dressmakers could provide everything that would be required at next-to-nothing. While gown shops were few and far-between, there was an abundance of cheap good-quality material available in the many shops and Indian bazaars. As Christina looked outside at the rain-lashed windows during a downpour, with thunder growling in the background, her mind was made up.

A week later, Sheila and Christina were ready to leave. 'Despite all efforts to dissuade us from going we had decided that a three months spell of Mediterranean sunshine was infinitely preferable to an equal dose of London gloom.' They were contracted to perform a double act of song-and-dance numbers at a Valletta music hall called the Morning Star. Their last few days in London were spent in a flurry of cutting out and sewing costumes for their act.

Vera Willis, a friend of Christina's from her French revue days, and a girl called Rosa, saw them off from London Victoria on their long, mostly overland, route. Following an exhausting journey, passing through Paris and Rome, they arrived in Syracuse in Sicily on the morning of the fourth day. There they boarded the SS *Knight of Malta* for the final leg of their journey across the Mediterranean. On the short voyage they were accosted by the wife of a naval officer serving on HMS *Barham*, a battleship stationed in Grand Harbour. This lady regaled Christina with her tales of Malta, but her demeanour changed instantly and for the worse when she realised she was talking to a pair of cabaret artistes who would soon be working in one of Valletta's music halls. 'We might have been something the cat dragged in', said Christina. Such were the attitudes of some in those days of Empire and 'officers-only'. Those attitudes would soon count for little. Nor, sadly, would HMS *Barham*.

The SS *Knight of Malta* arrived in Malta after sunset. 'We had both heard that the view of Grand Harbour by night was something not to be missed but neither of us was prepared for the utter loveliness of the scene. Standing there on the deck of the slowly moving boat, it was as though we were passing through the portals of fairyland. The full moon illuminated the bastions and turrets of the ancient fortifications on either side of us and the entire harbour was aglow with thousands of twinkling lights. They were the lights, not of fairyland, but of a host of ships riding at anchor in their island base; ships of our Mediterranean Fleet, which in 1937 was in its heyday. It was an impressive, awe-inspiring sight. Indeed, although I did not realise it at the time, I was looking out on a display of British naval power and glory such as the Grand Harbour of Malta was never to witness again.'

With its headquarters at Fort St Angelo, the Mediterranean Fleet was a showpiece of Britain's naval power and the pride of the Royal Navy. It was a prestigious command and postings to such an exotic and lively island were highly sought after, not least because of its idyllic anchorage. With thousands of sailors, there was a constant stream on shore leave in Valletta for 'rest and recuperation'.

Little wonder the bars and dance halls for which the city was renowned were often full to overflowing and there was a constant cry for entertainment of every kind. The large, totally male service population resulted in the island being a desirable trawling ground for females looking for a husband. Little wonder many of the young and not-so-young women from Britain who were in Malta's social arena were referred to as 'the fishing fleet' with the ladies' lounge of the Union Club in Valletta's Kingsway as the 'snake pit'. The Union Club, the former *Auberge de Provence*, was a favourite drinking haunt for officers on 'a run ashore'.

With several dances each week aboard the many battleships or cruisers there were many women in Malta who thought ships were there merely for the dancing. No doubt there was a dance the very evening Christina and Sheila arrived. With ships bedecked with pennants and flags, and their crews' 'whites' reflecting the lights, guests danced to music played by the Royal Marines. These were the good times. Two of the ships on display, unrecognised by Christina, were HMS *London* and HMS *Gallant*, her rescuers from the Spanish Civil War. As the girls stepped off the *Knight of Malta* on that idyllic spring evening they looked back in wonder at the many magnificent well-lit warships lying serenely at anchor. If they had any idea what was soon to befall those very same ships and their crews, they would have wept.

The presence of the Mediterranean Fleet had a huge impact not only on Malta's social scene but also on the economy. It provided employment and prosperity for many, from the little *dghaisas,* one of the picturesque brightly coloured boats

Lascaris Bastion topped by Upper Barracca Gardens with the Barracca Lift on the left overlooks Valetta's Customs House and the SS *Knight of Malta.*

rowed by a man standing at the prow, which provided a water-taxi service, through to the many laundries, shops and bars and food retailers. Some of the *dghaisas* were even paid a retainer by individual ships.

Christina and Sheila were taken by *dghaisa* to the landing-stage in front of the Customs House steps. There they were met by Gianni Fiteni, owner of the Morning Star music hall, who politely enquired if they were Miss Sheila and Miss Christina from London. In his mid-thirties, Gianni's charm and opulence were as impressive as his large Daimler and uniformed chauffer. 'Rolling back in the cushions, purring smoothly along in super-luxurious style, life seemed exceedingly good. There was moonlight. There were twinkling stars and a silvery sea. Yes, on a warm scented Mediterranean evening such as this, life was exceedingly good. Sheila and I had done well to take the plunge. The poor girls back at the club would be huddled around the fire still knitting, still sewing or playing Ludo and the rain would still be beating ceaselessly on the window panes. "The first thing we should do," said Sheila, "is to write to the girls and tell them what they are missing". We both felt very smug, very pleased with ourselves as we sympathised with the left-behinds in a highly elated manner.' Christina was still only 22-years-old.

Near Valletta's main entrance gate - *Porta Reale* - the island's capital boasted the magnificent Royal Opera House, very much a showpiece on the *Strada Reale.* But this showpiece was most definitely not for Jolly Jack. Italian theatre companies

Kingsway, Valletta. The Royal Opera House is on the right, and Wembley Store is on the corner on the left.

performed there regularly and with its pomp, glitter and splendour, it would rarely see a matelot pass through its grand entrance.

For Jolly Jack, apart from one small uncomfortable cinema which showed old fifth-rate films, there was little else except the bars and music halls and it was to these that sailors turned in their thousands. The most popular haunts were on a street called Strait, known to many a matelot who sampled its pleasures as 'The Gut'.

As Christina later recalled: 'The Gut, a long, narrow avenue of honky-tonks, bars and eating houses, is the name given to the lower part of what was once *Strada Stretta* and is now named Strait Street. Known to sailors the world over, it has an inconspicuous beginning in a turning off Ordnance Street and continues in a die-straight course to the lower regions of Valletta. Although still very much in existence, the halcyon days of the Gut belonged to the years preceding the Second World War.

'To capture its mood, to see the place as it really was, it had to be visited by night. During the hours of daylight it put up its shutters and slept off the hangover in an atmosphere of peace and sobriety, a drab, dusty and sunless alley where, curiously enough, Dirty Dick's bar had the cleanest look of the lot. In the evenings the Gut leaped to life and opened its doors and its heart to teeming masses of servicemen on the lookout for an hour or so of vice and pleasure. Noise was the overriding feature of this alleyway and the later in the evening, the louder the racket, as the wine went in and the worst came out - raucous singing, yells, foul language, brawls in plenty. And above it all the din of the scores of jazz bands beating and sawing out their melodies on the rostrums of pocket-sized dance halls. At almost every door sat small groups of heavily made-up women, some young and pretty, others distinctly passé but all adorned with gold earrings and bangles and all cajoling the passers-by to sample the delights of their particular establishment.'

There were respectable establishments on *Strada Stretta*, such as the Rexford, the Moulin Rouge and Auntie's but these were very strictly 'for officers and civilians only'. Sheila and Christina's destination, the Morning Star, shared with the Lancaster Ear, the John Bull and Charlie Palmer's, the distinction of not actually being on the infamous Gut. The Morning Star escaped by a matter of yards being at 105 *Strada San Nicola*, an adjacent street running across the lower end of the Gut at the bottom of the slope leading down to Fort St Elmo.

As the Daimler, with its very smug passengers, wound its way into downtown Valletta, the girls had little idea of their final destination. Having left the twinkling lights of Grand Harbour behind, they came to a narrow, dingy and ill-lit street which seemed grim even in the moonlight. 'The car caught up with a horse-drawn vehicle, the upper part of which closely resembled a sedan chair. Overtaking it, we had a glimpse through its half-drawn khaki curtains of a lone sailor. With his head slumped on his chest and cap tipped over his eyes, he appeared to be sound asleep.

'A short distance ahead a brightly-lit building illuminated a large patch of the gloomy street. As the car drew near we could hear the sound of loudly played jazz music and roar after roar of laughter. A feeling of apprehension came over me. This couldn't be the end of our four days' journey. But instinctively I knew that it was and my instinct rarely plays me false. "Here we are girls," Gianni confirmed with an unmistakeable note of pride in his voice. "This is the Morning Star."

'The chauffer switched of the engine and jumped out of the car to open our door. He stood stiffly to attention as the pair of us alighted with aristocratic grace and dignity.

'So far so good: We had been given the full VIP treatment. We had driven up in style in a shiny limousine. But there was no red carpet and only a one-man reception committee was waiting. A massive creature that towered above us on the entrance steps, his rolled-up shirt sleeves revealing muscles mightier than those on the celebrated village blacksmith and they were tattooed into the bargain. A broken nose and a black-eye-patch put me in mind of a boxer at the end of his career - a career that on the whole had not been too successful.'

This was Manwel, the finest chucker-out on the island, whose ferocious expression soon relaxed into a grin and he turned out to have a very high-pitched voice. 'But Manwel's mission in life was not dedicated solely to chucking out customers from the Morning Star. He had first to inveigle them in. Even as he spoke, the *gharry* we had passed further down the street arrived on the scene and the sailor, hiccupping loudly, stumbled out. Catching sight of his hat-band, Manwel mounted a step higher, flexed his muscles and bellowed in a voice decidedly more in keeping with his Goliath-like physique: "Come right inside now *Queen Elizabeth,* all your ship's company inside." With killing wit he added: "All drunk".'

Once inside, the girls realised the term 'music hall' was somewhat misleading, but it was as good a term as any. 'After all there was music and there was a hall. The music was loud and lively, the hall long and narrow with mirrored walls and a tiled floor packed with dancing couples. The dancers were mainly sailors partnered by dark-haired, heavily made-up girls and sailors partnered by sailors. Those of the clientele who were not dancing were seated on benches and stools around old-fashioned, marble-topped tables, smoking and drinking.

'Through the haze of blue smoke, I could see at the far end of the hall a set of orange and purple curtains, covering what was presumably the stage. Immediately beneath in the orchestra pit, sat the band - a pianist and a drummer. "Nice place, eh, girls?" Gianni said, fairly bristling with pride. Before either of us could reply a great burst of cheering broke out and a chorus of wolf-whistles went up from a group of sailors at one of the tables. They were all looking in our direction.

"Whoa, smidget," one of the sailors yelled.

"Hi there, blondie," another called out.

"Come over here, blondie."

21

'I felt the blood mounting to my cheeks. Sheila caught hold of my hand and dug her fingernails into the palm. The wolf-whistles and yells grew louder. Soon the whole place was in uproar and Sheila and I found ourselves surrounded by a seething, ogling mob.

'Not without difficulty, Gianni managed to extricate us and get us into his restaurant next door. "Don't worry girls," he said cheerfully. "You'll soon grow used to it." His face wreathed in smiles, it was evident that he was highly pleased with the reception we had just been given, which was perhaps understandable considering he had paid the fares from England for a couple of "blind dates". It could have been that we both had faces like the backs of cabs, or figures like sacks of potatoes. "You are going to be very popular, if you ask me," said Gianni and flashed his mischievous smile.'

He later gave them the unexpected news they were to be joined three days later by their friends Vera and Rosa who had seen them off from Victoria Station. This was all the more surprising given the views they had expressed on cabaret in Malta. Maybe the work situation in London had worsened. Nevertheless it was good news, especially when they saw the standard of performance as well as audience reaction.

'Slowly the gaudy set of orange and purple curtains parted and a fat, rather elderly lady, attired in a costume of white feathers and pink ballet shoes, lumbered on the stage. "Budapest Bessie," Gianni whispered, "she goes back to Hungary next week." I detected a hint of relief in his voice.' Her 'ballet' to the music of *The Dying Swan* was rewarded by catcalls, whistles and shouts.

'The second act was a song and dance routine by two attractive English girls, Marie and Eileen, who were first-class cabaret artistes. Disappointingly, their very polished performance got no better reaction to that afforded to Budapest Bessie.

'I tried to picture myself on that little stage. My imagination, elastic though it could be at times, did not stretch that far. I began to wish I hadn't come and that I'd taken the advice of the girls at the club. I could not vouch for Sheila but I was pretty sure she was thinking on similar lines. Desperately I wanted to turn tail and make for home, running all the way. Suddenly I remembered Lillian's words: "You need guts to appear in front of a cabaret audience in Malta and above all a sense of humour." Well, never let it be said I was lacking in that respect. I hauled my drooping spirits back into place and laughed until the tears came.'

Soon there were six talented English girls working together - Christina, Sheila, Marie, Eileen, Vera and Rosa. Gianni had been, 'fed up with the goulash that old Budapest Bessie and others of her like had been serving in his music hall, he had been only to eager to change the bill of fare. He was now offering a feast of venison, roast beef of old England and Lancashire hot-pot dishes, which he was in no hurry to scratch off the menu. Gianni, it could be said, knew his onions. So did we. The customers did not want tripe. With this in mind and with individual and combined effort, the six of us raised the entertainment value of the Morning Star to an unprecedented level.

'We took our stage career seriously and we were determined that our audiences should do likewise. Carefree and rollicking sailors, though they might be, catcalls must go! They went. Shouts of derision were out. They made a speedy exit. Whistles - we could do nothing about those. Long, low whistles from packs of wolves in ship's clothing could not be silenced. We did not particularly want to silence them. It was the boys' way of registering their appreciation of the show we were giving them free of charge for their beer.' Soon the Morning Star was a byword throughout the Mediterranean Fleet with the well-dressed, well-presented girls putting on a popular revue. With British sailors rolling up in their hundreds, Manwel no longer had to persuade a passing sailor to enter the establishment. The dancehall enjoyed such popularity the British authorities opened the Vernon United Services Club in an attempt to break the monopoly of the Morning Star.

'There was always keen competition to dance with us after our turns were over. Emerging from our microscopic dressing room beneath the stage, we would be whisked away into a waltz or foxtrot before we had time to say, "No". We would never get far with the same partner, every dance seeming to be a "Gentlemen's Excuse Me". Wigi at the piano kept the ball rolling and the girls in a state of near exhaustion with a non-stop medley of lively tunes. Of the six of us, only Rosa refused to enter into the spirit of the thing. She remained steadfastly aloof and spent most of the time sitting in the dressing room between her appearances on the stage. Cooly disdainful, she insisted there was nothing in her contract that required her to shake a leg with the rank and file of HM Forces. But her performance on the stage was in itself a great attraction and she was so utterly lovely that Gianni would forgive her anything.'

Gianni employed local dance hostesses, or 'sherry queens', as the sailors called them. The word 'sherry' covered a multitude of innocuous, watered-down drinks bought by the clientele at sixpence a tot for their dance partner. The 'sherry queens' received a token called *landi*, worth threepence, for each drink purchased and they exchanged these for cash at the end of the evening. They also shared profits on a fifty-fifty basis, so were anxious to maximise their low income.

The cabaret artistes worked from 6.00 pm until 11.00 pm when the Morning Star closed, but the hostesses worked longer hours. By comparison, Christina and her colleagues were well off; well paid, with free accommodation, light work and if they wanted to make more money they could also earn *landi* by dancing with clients after their performance. As the hostesses relied entirely on their tokens for their income, a number would move on to Cinderella's, a dancehall on *Strada Stretta* which stayed open until one in the morning. The Morning Star hostesses wore jumpers and skirts, whereas the girls in the up-market 'For Officers and Civilians Only' establishments wore full evening dress. The trade was the same, but the 'sherries' were now 'cocktails'. 'And "civilian" meant just that. Indeed, it was a punishable offence for any "other ranker" to masquerade as a civilianised human being. In "civvies" he could get through the door, he could stand at the bar or sit down at a table, but the risk of being recognised by one of his superiors was too great to take.'

For Christina and her friends, with only five hours work each evening, life was good. They lived in a large, well-furnished house in Floriana, owned by Gianni, in which Christina shared a room with Sheila. From the roof they could see Grand Harbour and at the front it looked toward St Francis' Barracks in Floriana. The house was near Queen's Store, owned by Felix Mallia, on *Strada San Tomaso* where they obtained their groceries. These were delivered by the Mallias' niece, Connie, who enjoyed her daily visits to the house of the *Inglizi*.

'The price of food was fantastically low. Eggs were sixpence a dozen, potatoes and tomatoes one penny a pound, a loaf of bread threepence. For one shilling one could buy a rabbit or a chicken. It was a boozer's paradise, whisky, gin and brandy costing but sixpence a tot and beer four pence a bottle. For those who preferred soft drinks these could be had for a penny per bottle. As for milk, well, the price depended on the size of the jug. There were no cows on the island but there was an abundance of fresh goats' milk. This was provided by herdsmen who drove their flocks through the streets of the towns and villages and sold the produce direct from the animal's udder!' Shopping at the many Indian bazaars was an adventure and also inexpensive, although no self-respecting customer would ever dream of paying the price originally asked for an article.

The Gould Family

Marion Gould was born in Devonport Military hospital on 1 April 1926. Her father Charles was a Royal Artillery bombardier; Millicent, her mother, was a local girl; her maiden name was Martin. The family lived in Bovisands, a remote station on Plymouth Sound visible from the Hoe, before moving into married quarters on the Hoe itself, the Citadel. By then Charles Gould had already seen service in Turkey after the First World War and had also served in Gibraltar for five years. He was a professional soldier having joined the army as a 14-year-old bugle boy in 1916.

Marion maintained an attachment to Plymouth through her mother's family and has fond memories of walks with her grandfather on the Hoe, and to the Barbican to see the fishing smacks come in at the Mayflower Steps. Marion was joined by two sisters, both also born in the Devonport Military hospital: Doris in 1928 and Betty in 1930.

In 1932 the Goulds moved to Woolwich Arsenal and in 1935 they left for Singapore. By then Dennis had been added to the family, born in the families' military hospital in Woolwich. Marion was 9-years-old when her great adventure began, starting with the boat train from Waterloo to Southampton where they were fitted out with topis, a pith helmet popular in the 1930s as protection against the sun. They set sail on the P&O liner *California* to the sound of bands playing with ship-to-shore streamers and hundreds of well-wishers on the quayside. Marion vividly recalls going through the Suez Canal and seeing groups of Sudanese warriors with curly black hair, wearing simple loin cloths and carrying spears. They were 'Fuzzy Wuzzys', Marion was told, a term later made famous by Corporal Jones in the acclaimed BBC comedy series *Dad's Army*. One of their stops on route was at Aden, their first sight of which was the clock tower on Steamer Point.

They arrived in Malaya at the island of Blakang Mati, now Sentosa, after a journey of almost six weeks. Singapore became the Gould home for four years, during which another brother Raymond was added to the family, born in 1939. Marion visited Kuala Lumpur and Jahore and saw many places through which an unstoppable Japanese army would soon advance. King George VI's coronation was a time of great celebration which Marion spent in the grounds of Raffles Hotel. The Changi tree which towered above the clock tower in the barracks also looms large in Marion's memory. It first appeared on maps in 1888 and, at a height of 250ft, was a major landmark. According to folklore, the fall of the tree would result in the fall of Singapore. Marion and her sisters, all members of the Brownies, were among thousands who paraded before Lord Baden-Powell and Lieutenant General Sir William Dobbie in the grounds of Government House for the World Scout and Guide Jamboree; it was the last before war broke out. General Dobbie was the Deputy General Officer Commanding Singapore at the time and later became Governor of Malta. The Gould family left Singapore in May 1939 on route to Malta. 'It was a case of out of the frying pan into the fire,' said Marion.

The P&O liner *Chitral* took the Goulds to Egypt; they then travelled overland to Alexandria on a train reminiscent of General Gordon's era. They stayed in Alexandria for a week before the troopship *Dilwara* brought them to Valletta. With Charles Gould based at Mtarfa the family lived in a bungalow known as the Engineer's Quarters near the hospital. Marion's first impressions were of the great bastions surrounding Grand Harbour and the almost constant sound of church bells.

The Longyear Family

For many British residents, especially those on colonial postings in pre-war Malta, life was comfortable, with the population largely pro-British. Family life often involved swimming, beach picnics, lunches and sight-seeing. Michael Longyear has fond memories of those years. His father Victor was a regimental sergeant

The Longyears in Malta, 1937. Left to right: Pauline, Victor Longyear, Pamela, Cyril, Michael sitting atop the table, Doreen, Mary Longyear, Peter. *(Michael Longyear)*

major with the Royal Engineers. A regular soldier, Victor was posted to Malta in 1937 with his wife Mary and five of their six children: three daughters and two of their sons. Their eldest son Cyril was already serving with the King's Shropshire Light Infantry in India.

Victor's post was in Floriana Barracks with the family living in married quarters at Msida Bastion overlooking Marsamxett Harbour and Manoel Island. On arrival, Victor was hospitalized with peritonitis. Visiting him at Mtarfa gave Michael his first taste of, 'a military hospital with the regimental line up of beds and blankets and the fearsome autocratic matron at the time. I believe the blankets were coloured either red or blue and the floor shone with polish. The uniform of the walking wounded and sick was the standard "Hospital Blues": blue trousers and jacket, white shirt and red tie.' Michael would see that uniform again when he was eventually evacuated to England: both of his brothers would be wearing it.

Lunch at the Savoy Hotel in Queen Street, Valletta, was to be savoured, said Michael: 'A luxury was to have an ice cream called "Eskimo Pie" which was in the shape of an igloo but embedded with glace cherries, angelica and nuts; all for sixpence, which I suppose, was a lot of money then. We also enjoyed the Maltese workers' lunch which was a pennyworth of bread (*hobz*) and a ha'porth of tomato paste. The chunk of bread, about half a loaf, had the middle scooped out and filled with the tomato paste, which tasted of basil and rich tomato, and a drizzle of oil: quite a little feast.' Maybe Michael's fond early memories of such food were heightened given what he would soon experience. Michael attended the army primary school not far from the parade ground below Floriana Gardens and overlooked by the Phoenicia Hotel.

Pre-war social events such as balls were popular and well attended. Victor and Mary attended many at the Vernon United Services Club in Valletta, with its large terrace overlooking Floriana and Grand Harbour. The ladies wore long dresses with their men in Mess kit or 'Blues'.

On 23 June 1938 the Vernon held a ball in honour of visiting ships of the *Regio Marina Italiano*. Michael still has his sisters' dance cards from the ball. Music was provided by the dance orchestra of HMS *Malaya*. Within a few months those very same sailors, hosts and their guests, would be ranged against one another.

But Britain was re-arming. It was from Malta that the Longyear's middle son Peter joined the Suffolk Regiment; he was 14-years-old. The regiment shipped back to England soon afterwards, Peter's photograph appearing in the *Times of Malta*. 'He looked such a small soldier in his big shorts and military topi', said Michael.

Life in Malta was a far cry from the grey, industrial landscapes in depression-hit Britain that many, like Christina, had left behind. Despite concerns expressed in Britain about Germany and Italy's military ambitions, few in Malta anticipated the tiny island would soon be on the front line of a world war. With the Mediterranean Fleet based there surely the island was impregnable, especially with its fortress defences? Maybe the constant movement of warships and RAF aircraft painted a false picture as to the vulnerability of Malta. Much of this traffic was simply because Malta was a staging post. Few civilians realised just how inadequately the island was defended, how ill-prepared it was to meet the onslaught of modern warfare. The powers that be knew. They did nothing, judging Malta indefensible.

Christina and her friends, like most in Malta at the time, were probably oblivious to the looming political issues that would soon threaten. And anyway, their contracts in Malta were relatively short and they would soon move on. They never became infatuated with the Morning Star but they lived well. So did Gianni, who invoked an option to engage them for a further three months until September 1937. While they all enjoyed the summer Christina, Sheila and Vera were focusing their minds on their futures. They didn't opt for the free journey back to England to which they were entitled, but looked for further adventure. They teamed up as *Three Smart Girls,* named after the 1936 Hollywood musical of the same name, and obtained a contract through the Maltese theatrical agency Short and Loscoe to dance for fifteen days at the Tabarin Tunis. Once there they were assured they would be engaged by the French theatrical agents, Marly Brothers, who had offices in Oran and Casablanca.

'Gianni had tears in his eyes as I took leave of him. "But you will come back," he prophesised, "and work for me again. I am going to build a beautiful nightclub, the finest in Malta. You will return. I know you will. You mark my words."'

Christina initially spent September 1937 to May 1938, in French North Africa visiting places she may only have seen before in a school atlas. After her contract in Tunis, she headed west to what was then French Morocco where she travelled widely: Casablanca, Fez, Moulay Bouchta, Sidi Harazem, Marrakech, Immouzer, Oulmes, Rabat, Taza, and Tangier. At some stage she stayed in a villa in Marrakech; she may also have stayed at the *Hotel de Thermes* in Oulmes. But the focus of Christina's life in Morocco seems to have been Fez where she lived in an apartment on the top floor of *Immeuble de L'Urbaine*. At the time it was a modern, eight-storey block, very much the pride of French colonial architecture and the first building in Fes to be equipped with lifts.

Christina took dozens of photographs during her stay. Some are of friends she worked with, but most are of the places she visited and the local people she met; including many children. Members of the French Foreign Legion also feature in a number of images. There are a few of one officer in particular, Jacques Bellon. Some show him in uniform, while in others he is in civilian clothes. He and Christina were close and they were together in Marrakech and Oulmes. They may have become engaged. There are three photographs taken on the same day, 14 May 1938, the day of Christina's departure from Morocco. Two show them arm in arm with Jacques in uniform. The third, perhaps prophetically, is of Christina on her own. Written on the back of all three, in pencil, in Christina's distinctive handwriting, are the words, '*Jour départ, 14 Mai 1938 → Dakar → Ksar es Souk.*' Christina was heading for Dakar in Senegal, while Jacques was heading into Morocco's interior, to Ksar es-Souk, a French Foreign Legion base.

Christina sailed to Dakar, probably on the SS *Medie II*. In its heyday Dakar was a major city within the French colonial empire. She had another cabaret contract but again, as she travelled, she took many photographs of people and places. She and Jacques were in touch by letter. How long Christina remained in Dakar is unclear but she later returned to Morocco.

In July 1939 Christina's father helped her arrange a passage home, probably via Gibraltar, maybe to meet a ship bound for England. She certainly spent long enough in Gibraltar to invest in a pair of jodhpurs and take horse-riding lessons. But what of her relationship with Jacques?

Christina was 23-years-old when she had left Malta in 1937. 'Sailing away that September evening to Tunis, I watched the island of Malta slowly disappear out of sight. Little did I realise then that Gianni's words were to ring so very true, for I was to return to Malta two and a half years later.' By then Great Britain and the Commonwealth would have been at war with Nazi Germany for six months.

Rabat, Morocco, 1937. (*Miriam Farrugia*)

Taza, Morocco, 1937/38. *(Miriam Farrugia)*

Casablanca, 1938. (*Miriam Farrugia*)

Dakar, 1938. (*Miriam Farrugia*)

Fez, Morocco, 1939. (*Miriam Farrugia*)

Chapter 3

War

Friday 1 September 1939

Marion Gould's first three months in Malta were very pleasant with weekend excursions to the golden beaches and shallow waters of Sandy Bay and Armier Bay. Schooling was at the English Curtain School in Valletta. All service children travelled there daily by bus. But life changed dramatically on Friday, 1 September 1939, when everyone became news-minded. That was the day Hitler unleashed his vastly superior forces on Poland, his next-door neighbour. With Britain and France tied by treaty to Poland what was likely to happen next seemed inevitable.

Good radio reception in Malta from Britain was virtually impossible without a first-class radio because of atmospherics. It was much worse in daytime. As a result most people used the island's unique radio network, Rediffusion. Based in Valletta, radios and amplifiers transmitted programmes through thousands of loudspeakers in towns and villages, bars and barracks. It had two channels: Channel 'A' relayed a BBC programme and Channel 'B' broadcast in Malti, relaying concerts as well as talks and announcements. This was how most people received the news.

At 11.15 am British Summer Time the Rediffusion announced Britain and France were at war with Germany. Demand for loudspeakers went through the roof. Priority was given to villages as the Rediffusion, often the only means of sending information rapidly, was to be used to broadcast air raid warnings.

The Longyear family were anticipating the announcement. They were all at home sitting round the living room table listening to the Rediffusion when it came. Michael rushed out of the house to tell everyone; he was full of excitement. He had quite different ideas about the reality of war, having grown up on a feast of books about bravery, Biggles and the like. How all that would change. As if to highlight the change, the family was issued with gas masks and a mobile gas chamber came to the married quarters to test the masks.

The Longyears had a tradition of military service and a keen sense of duty. They had two sons in the army and their middle daughter Pamela was engaged to a soldier. Barely two weeks after war was declared, their eldest daughter Doreen married Royal Marine Corporal Bert Leaman, serving at HMS *St Angelo*, the Royal

Doreen Longyear marries Royal Marine Bert Leaman in September 1939. Mary is on the left and Victor on the extreme right. Michael is to the right of Doreen; Pauline is next to her father, with Pam in-between. *(Michael Longyear)*

Navy's headquarters in Malta. Doreen and Bert had their reception in the ballroom of the Vernon and their honeymoon in the Riviera Hotel near Ghajn Tuffieha. Later, the Longyear's eldest son Cyril moved back from India to Britain and soon found himself, along with Pam's fiancé, in France as part of the British Expeditionary Force.

In Malta and in London there were major concerns about the likely impact of war with Italy, which many thought inevitable. While these were long-standing concerns virtually nothing had been done to address them. Malta is only sixty nautical miles from Sicily, which can be seen on a clear day as a faint line on the northern horizon. Malta's lifeblood was the supplies delivered by sea, lifeblood that could easily be interrupted. With Britain allied to France, there was some security of passage through the Western Mediterranean, but if Britain found herself alone, many in London thought nothing could be done for Malta. It could not be defended.

There were concerns, though rarely expressed, about how the Maltese might react to war with Italy, a Catholic neighbour which had long been friendly toward Malta. Also, how would the Maltese react to bombing? Visions of the bombing of Guernica in the Spanish Civil War loomed large in the minds of military planners. A few heavy raids on Malta could reduce the island to rubble, they said. How would the Maltese react then? And what would it cost to defend the island? It was probably this which held sway in an unprepared and parsimonious London.

The Admiralty advocated strengthening Malta's defences but the Air Ministry said the proximity of Italian airfields rendered the island unsafe. This view prevailed. The Mediterranean Fleet relocated to Egypt at the outbreak of war. At the political level, Neville Chamberlain and his French counterpart tried all they could to keep Italy out of the war. But it was only a matter of time.

Malta's garrison was wholly inadequate, totalling less than 6,500 British and Maltese troops. The one thing the island had in its favour was radio direction finding, or radar; in fact, the island was the first location outside Britain to have such equipment. Even so, and despite it being located on Dingli Cliffs, one of the highest places on the island, aircraft flying at 2,000 feet could only be picked up thirty miles from the island. This would give Malta's defenders less than ten minutes' notice of an attack. But what use was radar when there were no fighter aircraft? The lack of any front-line defensive aircraft left the population of 220,000 terribly vulnerable. The entire island had twenty-four heavy anti-aircraft guns; Coventry had forty-four.

Christina was probably back in England when war was declared. One source has suggested Christina decided to return to Morocco, via Malta, to make final arrangements for her marriage to Jacques. Travel to or through France was still possible as Britain and France were as yet largely untouched, experiencing the so-called 'phoney war'. While all eyes were on the Franco/German border, the Mediterranean was something of a backwater. Perhaps overtures from London and Paris to Mussolini were bearing fruit?

Christina arrived back in Malta at the beginning of March 1940 on another three-month contract with Gianni Fiteni at the Morning Star. Gianni had been right after all. But something happened to change Christina's mind about traveling further.

She moved into the same house in Floriana overlooking *Porte des Bombes*. But the circumstances were now very different. Gone was the Mediterranean Fleet on which many of Valletta's nightspots relied and Christina no longer had the stimulating friends from earlier to live and work with. Perhaps the reality of war was also beginning to set in. 'The first few weeks went by at a funereal pace. I spent a lot of time wishing I had stayed at home and a good deal more longing for the expiry of the contract whereby I had bound myself to work for three months in Gianni's gin palace. The situation was vastly different from that of 1937 when, with the other girls, I had stood at the beginning of a road to adventure - when there had been a purpose to our performance in what, after all, was nothing more than a low dive. Now with Morocco definitely off, my work seemed aimless and I was conscious, as I had not been before, of the almost sordid atmosphere of my surroundings.

'Mercifully, the wild unruly crowds I had met with during my previous visit had departed from the scene and walking home unescorted at night was not the ordeal it used to be. The "Hi Blondie's" were not as loud and frequent as of yore, the wolf-whistles scarcely audible. Although it would never have done to let Gianni know I was heartily glad that of all the ships of His Majesty's navy only three were now in harbour. These were the monitor *Terror* and the gunboats *Aphis* and *Ladybird*.'

Earlier, work had been fun, now Christina just wanted to go home. Gianni's sentiments and those of other Valletta businessmen could not have been more different. 'Fill the port with ships, cram his cabarets with rollicking sailors and everything was fine, fine. But weigh the anchors, set the ships a-sailing and Gianni was like a man who had lost his all. To him empty harbours could mean only one thing - ruin. There were the soldiers and airmen of course, but since these were comparatively few in number, there was no making up on the roundabouts for what was lost on the swings. As for the local gentry, it was considered not quite the done thing for any decent Maltese citizen to spend his evening down the Gut and there were not enough indecent ones about to keep Gianni's place running at a profit. It just had to be admitted that it was Jolly Jack who sent the big money rolling into the cash registers. But these days Jolly Jack, the playboy, was now very much the earnest warrior, with a mission important enough to keep him away from the bars and cabarets of Malta. Hence poor Gianni was often very glum indeed.'

The only other occupants of the rambling three-storey house beyond *Strada Capuccini* were Cecil and 'Babs' Roche, a young English couple who performed in another of Gianni's cabarets. With them often working or sightseeing, Christina found the Rediffusion a godsend. The announcements in Malti, usually followed by an English translation, were a great way for her to learn the language. The late evenings often found all three on their roof high above Grand Harbour, or on Christina's balcony at the front of the house looking inland. As the weeks dragged by, their discussions turned to worrying events all too close to home. The phoney war came to a brutal end when Hitler unleashed his armies on Denmark and Norway.

With Britain assuming unimpeded access to Malta, little was done to bolster defences or increase provisioning. Some contingency planning took place, but many at a senior level thought it a matter of when, not if, Italy entered the war. One early decision was when the RAF borrowed four obsolescent Sea Gladiator biplanes from the Royal Navy. They had been in crates on Kalafrana's slipway. Training began with an ad hoc bunch of pilots all untrained in the art of air-to-air combat.

News soon reached Malta of Hitler's *Blitzkrieg* on 10 May and the German rapid advance into the Low Countries. The RAF then suffered catastrophic losses in France while holding back the *Luftwaffe* from Dunkirk. The evacuation was portrayed as a miracle, and it was, but the bulk of the British Army's equipment was a total loss.

Although Malta was still untouched, many families on the island were affected by what occurred in France. Pam Longyear's fiancé was killed. Victor and Mary Longyear then received the telegram they dreaded: their son Cyril was posted missing presumed killed at Dunkirk, his unit having formed part of the rear guard. A few days later, good news: Cyril was brought out on 4 June, the very last day of the evacuation. His unit had defended a bridge over the Merville canal against armoured vehicles for three days, with Cyril armed only with an anti-tank rifle. He personally wiped out a German machine-gun post before being critically wounded. In England he spent many months in hospital. He was later invested with the Military Medal by King George VI before being honourably discharged in 1942.

Malta had a new governor: Sir William Dobbie, who had been listed for retirement. He immediately saw the island's vulnerability and urgently requested reinforcements. He received an additional battalion of soldiers. The Admiralty expressed concern about the lack of fighters. The Air Ministry's response was Malta would have to make do as all modern fighters were needed for home defence: Malta was on her own.

Little wonder Christina, Cecil and Babs wanted to be back in England. Christina declined Gianni's requests to extend her stay. Meanwhile, she and the Roches were, 'frittering away their days on the golden sands of Ghajn Tuffieha, bathing in the cobalt blue Mediterranean, fattening ourselves with foodstuffs long listed on the ration cards in Britain - all that was nice work if you could get it, but having it we were quite prepared to trade it for a ticket back to England.' Christina was due to return home on 17 June.

The enormity of the calamity that had taken place in France wasn't widely known in Malta; even in Britain there was censorship. But as far as they could the Maltese followed events, and they hoped and prayed. Life remained quiet for most civilians, but there was intense military activity as the authorities did what they could to prepare for the inevitable: war against Italy. By the end of May, Sir William Dobbie was again warning London of serious and extensive deficiencies. Anti-aircraft guns were far short of the requirement and the infantry was stretched. He highlighted the absence of fighters as the real danger. He was advised his requests could not be met.

The authorities in Malta did what they could: Practice blackouts were held, anti-aircraft units reorganised and air raid exercises carried out. In the event of an air attack against Valletta or Grand Harbour, a red flag (*bandiri hamra*) would be hoisted on the roof of the *Auberge de Castille* as a last minute warning to take cover. A volunteer Special Constabulary was formed to ensure people reacted to warnings and to enforce the blackout and curfew. A Passive Defence Corps was established to deal with the feared use of gas, along with centres with first-aid posts, decontamination chambers and medical staff. The Malta Volunteer Defence Force, a forerunner of the Home Guard, was also formed, as were demolition and clearance squads who would hurry to the scene of destruction to recover anyone trapped beneath debris.

Accompanied postings overseas for married service personnel had ended once war was declared. Repatriation of families began if the head of the family was posted home, although this was not a priority. Malta's governing council planned to move families away from military targets with three evacuation centres having been selected, one for each of the services. Entirely on a voluntary basis, the families of Army and Royal Navy personnel were to be evacuated to the barracks at St George's and St Andrew's, near Sliema, with RAF dependents going to the Parisio Palace in Naxxar. Owned by the wealthy Scicluna family, the palace had enormous rock-hewn cellars, ideal air raid shelters in the eyes of the planners. The plans were tested with RAF wives and children from Kalafrana moved there.

'Le Ménage de Marks'

Yugoslavian-born Tamara Marks, married to Kalafrana-based Squadron Leader Ronnie Marks, was required to pack personal belongings and they were taken to what might become her new home in the Parisio Palace. Most untypical of a palace, the sleeping accommodation was split between rooms for twenty and smaller ones for six. The beds were simply-constructed three-tiered wooden bunks. Knowing this was an exercise, and hoping war would never come, few paid much attention to the 'rules'. Those new to barrack room life were introduced to 'biscuits' - the service name for coarse canvas bags used as mattresses. Although Tamara stayed only one night, she realised if they were required to live there, it would be very different from life at Birzebbugia, which was a happy community in a beautifully situated village with comfortable houses and well-stocked shops nearby. They could bathe from their own doorsteps, Tamara said, and play tennis at the well-kept and popular courts at Kalafrana and Hal Far while, 'the tongue wagging was not any more venomous than it usually is in circumstances where everyone knows everyone's business.'

Monday, 10 June 1940

The scheduled *Ala Littoria* flight took off from Malta as normal to head for Rome. Before setting course it leisurely circled Kalafrana Bay and the RAF airfields at Hal Far and Ta' Qali. Everyone knew what it was doing, filling its camera magazines with the most recent images possible. Later that evening, having determined the war was all but won, Mussolini declared war on Britain and France. So began the second siege of Malta, described by many Maltese as its greater siege. On that Monday, Christina had seven days of her contract left to run. Despite the continuing bad business, Gianni had implored Christina to renew for another three months, but she refused; she was definitely returning to England, or so she thought.

'I was at work when the blow fell. It was one of those nights when there were more waiters and hostesses about the place than customers; in fact, what business there was could be counted by the glasses on three tables. At one sat a lone sailor who appeared more interested in a crossword than his beer. Up near the bandstand, four young soldiers were celebrating a birthday and, with belts off, tunics unbuttoned, they had settled down to enjoy themselves. The third table was occupied by Charlie Farrugia and myself. Charlie was a highly respectable young man of good family whose main purpose in being at Gianni's was to help me along with the Maltese language. Or so he said. Since my arrival he had been dropping in almost every evening to teach me a few words and thus I had been able to make good use of what might have been some very boring hours.

'As we sat talking quietly, a radio in one of the bars across the street was turned on full blast and a torrent of Italian came hurtling through the open doors of the gin palace. It was the voice of Mussolini.

'Immediately there was a hubbub and the waiters and bandsmen led by Gianni came charging down the room to the doorway, where they stood listening with cocked ears. Our table being near the entrance there was no need for Charlie or me to move. The ranting was perfectly clear to Charlie, if not so much to me. My knowledge of the *dolce idioma* was such that I could not keep pace with the fast and furious speech, but I got the gist of it all right. Had I not, Charlie's white face, as he took in every word, would have warned me that something disastrous had happened. So too, would have the muttered oaths, the *Maria santissimas* of Gianni and his employees.

"Charlie, have I understood correctly?" I asked. "Is it really war - for Malta?"

"I'm afraid so," he replied. "Italy's come into it now, against Britain and her allies. And that means us as well."

'As from midnight, Mussolini had said. There were only a few hours to go. Charlie was visibly upset. He finished the remainder of his beer and took his hat from the chair at his side. "I'm off, Christina. My father and mother will be worrying. See you tomorrow." He added another new word: *"Forsi."* (Perhaps). He left and suddenly I felt very, very lonely.

'The news spread like wildfire throughout the towns and villages of the island. Rediffusion programmes were interrupted by "special announcements". Notices ordering all service personnel to report immediately for duty were flashed on cinema screens. Military police visited bars, restaurants and other public places clearing them of those members of the Forces who were still blissfully ignorant of what had been said in Rome. Two of the Red Caps came into Gianni's. The quiet boy with the crossword puzzle had already gone. The merry-making soldiers were taking their time. A few words of command from the policemen and they downed drinks and left at the run fastening belts and tunics as they went.'

That Monday evening Ronnie and Tamara Marks were at the 8.00 pm film at the Capitol Cinema in Kingsway, Valletta. 'Halfway through, the film was cut and the following notice appeared on the screen:

ALL MILITARY PERSONNEL ARE TO REPORT TO THEIR RESPECTIVE STATIONS IMMEDIATELY

'At the exit, one of the picture house's officials was there to initial our tickets which, it seems, we could use some other time. I am afraid we never availed ourselves of the opportunity and I have to this day kept that ticket as a souvenir. The street was full of people but uncommonly quiet. The meaning of the words on the screen was clear to everyone and the three red danger bulbs were glowing very red indeed on the Castille mast. We had to wait for a bus which was to take us to Birzebbugia, a small village a mile away from RAF Station Kalafrana, where my husband was stationed at the time. We travelled the eight miles or so in silence, there was just nothing to say, the worst had happened. It is true that we had been expecting it for some time but for all that, it was a blow. How inadequately we were protected, no one knew better than we, the wives of the men in the services. Although everyone laughed at the Eyeties and their bombastic threats when there still was a faint hope that they would see sense and we would only have the Germans to fight a good many miles away, it was no joking matter now that war was on our doorstep.

'We got home. The first thing to do was to have a nice hot cup of tea to restore us a little and then find out when my husband had to report to Kalafrana. I was still praying with all my heart that it was only a false alarm. The man next door popped in for a minute. "Well, folks, we are in for it this time. Got your gas-mask ready, Missus?"'

Back at the Morning Star, with the 'initial excitement over, a pall of gloom settled over those of us left in the cabaret. For a while I sat among the deserted tables, discussing the situation with a couple of the dance hostesses. My opinions were eagerly sought but they were worth no more than those of anybody else. I had not the faintest idea of what was likely to happen. At length I got up and went out into the narrow street where I found Gianni, his face ashen, surrounded by his bandsmen and the remainder of the staff. Worried and anxious, they pressed him for information about the future of their jobs now that Italy had entered the war. Would he close down? Or would it be business as usual? Gianni, hands in pockets, eyes on the ground, moving his weight from one foot to the other, mumbled something about having to wait and see. I added my quota of questions but before Gianni could reply, a wild commotion broke out a little further down the street. An angry crowd had assembled outside the shop of an Italian barber.

'As I watched the demonstration I could not help but feel sorry for the poor Italian. At one time the cries of the enraged mob reached such a pitch that I feared for his safety. Fortunately, the police were not long in arriving and the barber was taken into custody, presumably to be interned. At that moment my thoughts went back to the Spanish Civil War, to Moncada where I had seen the same sort of thing happen. Where in the course of a single day erstwhile loving neighbours had been transformed into deadly enemies; where respectable, law-abiding citizens had been dragged from their homes or places of business, to be reviled, humiliated and put away, for no better reason than that they were on the other side. It all seemed so senseless, so futile.

'The incident over, we all trooped back into the empty cabaret. Gianni and I sat at one of the tables at the top end of the room. The bandsmen took their places on the rostrum and in an effort to be cheerful struck up a lively tune. But Gianni was in no mood for such levity. He scowled at the bandsmen and signalled them to stop. They went on playing - louder, if anything. "*Bizzejjed*", Gianni roared, his face flushed with anger. The music stopped abruptly. Gianni buried his face in his hands and, taking the hint from the bandleader, I left him well alone.

'The gloom in the place deepened. Faces grew longer. The conversation took on a melancholy tone. It was a long time since I felt so depressed. Why, for Heaven's sake, didn't somebody laugh or crack a few jokes? We were all behaving as if we'd lost the war and as yet it hadn't even started. When Gianni came back to earth, it was to tell us that we could all go home, which was very sensible. There was little prospect of any more business that evening and he was not the only one whose nerves were getting frayed. We thanked him and got ready to leave. "Tomorrow, Gianni? Are we to come tomorrow?" Gianni shrugged his shoulders. Tomorrow was another day.'

Christina's comment about the war not having yet started shows how little impact the ten-month long war had had on Malta. Most on the island felt remote and untouched by events in France. Now there was the sudden realisation the curtain on Malta was about to go up. The impact of Mussolini's speech on the Maltese was dramatic and shocking: Italy was Malta's next door neighbour, Roman Catholic too, and until a few years earlier the Italian language was the language of the 'educated' in Malta. Many of the capital's streets were in Italian; that would soon change.

As Christina walked home that evening, she was deep in thought. 'At the centre of the patch of open ground between the gates of Valletta and the little suburb, the war memorial pointed to a cloudless, indigo sky, a sky interwoven with the beams of searchlights. It was a celestial scene that in recent weeks had become part and parcel of the Maltese night. By now we had all grown accustomed to searchlight practice, just as we had grown accustomed to having Rediffusion programmes interrupted by the seemingly far-fetched statement that the island was about to be attacked from the air. When the novelty had worn off, few of us paid much attention to the practice announcements broadcast in English and Maltese:

Air Raid Warning - *Sinjal ta l-Attakki mill-Ajru*

'I, for one, and there were many others, never seriously believed that the day would come when the somewhat bored, matter-of-fact tone of the announcer's voice would take on a ring of compelling urgency - the day when the mock air raids would be substituted for the real thing.

'Arriving at the residential area, I made my way along *Strada Capuccini* - a short steeply-rising street at the top of which is a huge wooden cross mounted on a ten-foot plinth stood silhouetted against the sky. It was a beautiful evening but very warm and people in no immediate hurry to retire into the heat of their homes were sitting about the doorways - some on the steps, others in chairs placed out on the pavement. From the snatches of conversation I overheard, in which the name of "Mussolini" cropped up repeatedly, it was evident that the main topic was Italy's entry into the war. Every now and then came the low murmur of prayer as the members of some family circle, united for the evenings' devotions, recited litanies and counted their rosary beads. I saw no signs of panic anywhere along the route yet an unmistakable atmosphere of foreboding hung heavily in the air of that June night.'

The Roche's had invited one of their friends, Billie, a pretty blonde dancer, to stay the night. They spent some time on the roof of the house discussing the situation. With war on their doorstep would they be able to leave the island? What would happen to them if they couldn't leave? Would there be any work for them to do? Question followed question but none could be answered and with their problems unresolved they retired for the night. They would simply have to wait and see.

At their home in Birzebbugia, Tamara helped Ronnie pack and he soon left to report for duty. When would Tamara see him again? 'I felt very small and lonely. It was a beautiful night, as June nights usually are in Malta, so I thought I would walk as far as St. George's Bay. Little clusters of people were on their doorsteps discussing animatedly. No one thought it would be serious. The island was too small, they said, for any bomb to fall on it. It was one chance in a million that this could happen. Look at the map. A mere pinpoint, surely nothing could hit it, especially if it was dropped from any height. This view was held by a great number of people and curiously enough testified to by the pilots. No, there was nothing to worry about.'

Yes, Malta is small, smaller than the Isle of Wight but, as all the pilots knew, it couldn't very well be missed. The four RAF stations were all close to one another, their proximity dictated by Malta's rocky terrain. The *Regia Aeronautica* knew exactly where they were having been given the intelligence gathered by their national airline, updated that very day.

How could bombers possibly miss Grand Harbour? Many Italian aircrew had learnt their trade in Spain. With Malta's very obvious targets closely surrounded by towns and villages 'collateral damage' was inevitable. Every civilian was now on the front line. Yes, the RAF pilots knew what could befall Malta; their words were worthy but the reassurance offered was misplaced. It would have been better had they talked about precautions and being prepared. The only hope in the coming days was that Italian bomber crews did not share their leader's enthusiasm for war against their small Roman Catholic neighbour. They had the skill and the courage for the task, but would they be willing to press home their very obvious advantage?

It was nearing 10.00 pm as Tamara walked slowly home. 'The blackout had to be rigidly observed. I did not dare put the light on in the landing as with all Maltese houses it was the devil's own job trying to black them out completely. There would always be a small unexpected crack somewhere, so we had concentrated on the drawing room and the two bedrooms. I groped my way upstairs, so I went straight to my bedroom. I did not feel hungry. A little light reading would do me a lot of good. I had been recommended *Scarlet Runners* by John Glider and as it turned out, it could not have been a better choice. I laughed so much that all my fears and apprehensions were allayed. It was not a bad world after all. Of course nothing could happen while there still were people with such a lovely sense of humour. I could not rest till I had finished the book. By one o'clock I put the bedside lamp out and went off to sleep.

'I woke up with a start. Was that someone knocking at the door? Surely not, why, it was only seven o'clock. No one would dream of knocking at my door at this unearthly hour and the maid always let herself in quietly; and then another crash. It sounded like guns going off. I jumped out of bed to the tune of all bedlam let loose, put my corduroy trousers on and a pullover. I had to find out what the commotion was about. Were they testing the guns? I hoped it could not possibly be anything else. There was a disquieting roar of aircraft but it seemed unlikely that it could be the Italians. They were too well-known for their *dolce far niente*; they could not possibly start a war so early in the morning when they had the whole day to do it in. I looked out of the window. Flashes of fire and great sheets of smoke were coming from the direction of Kalafrana. The noise was terrific; the doors and windows were rattling as if they would jump off their hinges. I ran in the street. There was no one to be seen, not a soul. I wondered where everyone had got too. If only the guns would stop a minute, I could collect my wits and do something. Another sickening thud, that was near. I had heard that under the table was the safest place. Yes, I must hide under a table. I shut the door and climbed the stairs four at a time. No the door was rattling too much. I had better leave it open.

'Down I rushed, opened it, dashed upstairs again and slipped under the dining-room table, which was of thick mahogany. After a minute in a very cramped

44

position, the ridiculous sight I must have been struck me forcibly. I could not possibly cower like a rabbit, it was too silly. Besides it would have been better for me to do some packing. Another salvo; the aircraft were coming nearer and nearer. If only I had someone with me. Anyone, I had to get away. Then, just as I ventured out of the door, the guns would go off; the door nearly slammed in my face and I did not have the key. Then, for five minutes nothing could be heard. The police station - that was it. Why had I not thought of it before? There was bound to be someone there. I ran for sheer life, little metallic sounds clicking off all round me.' The metallic sound was shrapnel; the Second World War had finally come to Malta.

In Floriana, Christina had an advantage over Tamara that morning as she was not alone in the house when the air raid siren sounded. 'It must have been about seven o'clock in the morning when I was awakened by a series of bangs on my locked door. It was the Roches, making frantic efforts to rouse me from a peaceful slumber.

"Christina, for goodness sake, wake up. The Air Raid Warning's gone."
More bangs and then a kick.
"Christina dear, do hurry. We are going down to the basement."
'Grunting an acknowledgement, I lay back in the pillows and listened to the clip clop of Bab's heels on the stone steps as she and her husband hurried below. For a while I stared vacantly at the ceiling, not quite certain what all the fuss was about. Then, slowly, I got up and still half-asleep groped for my slippers and dressing gown. Nothing was happening. There was no apparent need to go rushing down to the cellar like that. Ten to one this was just another practice raid. And anyway, I had not heard the siren - maybe Babs and Cecil had been imagining things. Perhaps I ought to go down, I thought. I sat at the dressing table and began to undo my curlers. I didn't like being seen in curling pins.

'Then it happened. Without further warning there was a deafening crash and the building rocked and shook as if was about to collapse; another crash, the roar of aircraft, the drawn out whine of a bomb followed by an ear-splitting explosion, a loud salvo of gunfire. For a few seconds I sat where I was, terrified. Then I got up and made a mad rush for the door. On reaching the stairs I grabbed hold of the banister and raced down them. One of my slippers fell off. Cinderella-style - but I didn't let that bother me - I got rid of the other and continued the descent barefooted. More crashes and roars. I never realised before that it was such a long way down to the cellar and I began to feel that I would never get there alive. But I made it. I ran in like an Olympic champion and, the great race over, tried to recover my breath. "Billie, where's Billie?" demanded the Roches when they saw I was alone.

'Before I could reply she came bounding down the last flight of stairs at breakneck speed; a vision of loveliness clad in a flimsy pair of chiffon camiknickers, which left nothing at all to the imagination. Like me she had been caught napping. But at that particular moment none of us had a mind for the niceties of dress. The main thing was to save our skins with or without the covering.

'The cellar was full of junk, including some pieces of old furniture. In one corner there was a sold-looking marble-topped table festooned with cobwebs. I suddenly got the bright idea that we would be a good deal safer crouching beneath it than standing where we were. Another loud crash and I was certain beyond doubt. Under I dived, quickly followed by Babs and Billie. Cecil was left to brave it alone. The din of battle grew louder and more terrifying as we sat huddled together beneath the old table. I was firmly convinced that our last moment on earth had come. There had been nothing like this in the practices! In our ignorance we did not realise that most of the noise was coming from the anti-aircraft guns and the ships in the harbour. There was indeed far more bark than bite to the whole affair, as we would find out.

'At long last, after what seemed like a day trip to the infernal regions, the racket subsided and only the faint drone of aircraft could be heard. At the okay from Cecil we crawled cautiously out of our hideaway, trailing yards of dirty cobwebs behind us.

"Is it over?"

"Have they gone?"

"Better wait a bit. They're probably still around".

'I was thankful for Cecil's presence and his steadying influence. And I'm sure Billie was doubly grateful. Few men in similar circumstances would have done what Cecil did. He gathered up several sheets of dusty brown packing paper that were lying around the floor and before Billie knew what was happening she had been wrapped up into a neat parcel of respectability - and warmth. For it was decidedly cool in the sun-starved cellar, despite the red-hot atmosphere of the world above.

'A few minutes later the anti-aircraft batteries opened up again, but this time we girls remained where we were; Cecil reassuring us that there was really nothing to worry about because you never heard the bomb that hit you. And as the gunfire grew to a crescendo he attempted to dispel our fears still further by providing a running commentary. There was a series of thunderous roars:

"That's the *Terror*".

Another series not quite so deep in tone: "That's the ack-ack".

Then suddenly: "Quick - under the table - this is a bomb".

But before we could get back under our marble roof, the bomb exploded, proving to Cecil's great satisfaction that his theory was correct.

"What did I tell you?" he grinned, a trifle sheepishly, I thought.

'Although that first alert of the war lasted only twenty minutes it seemed as if we had been down in the cellar for many hours when finally there came the long steady drone of the All Clear. A few moments of silence followed; the sort of profound almost eerie silence that follows the sounding of the *Last Post*. Then came the *Reveille*. The silence was broken by a chorus of high-pitched voices and a terrific clattering from the iron grating in the pavement above as our next-door neighbours rushed out of their house. We were not exactly slow in getting mobile ourselves and up the cellar steps we went, almost as fast as we had come down. Arriving in the hallway, I was sorely tempted to dash out into the street with the fully clothed Roches, but remembering my slippers I continued the upward climb with the be-papered Billie.

'On reaching my room, I ran on to the balcony to find out what had happened while we had been cowering in the lowermost regions of the house. From the noise of battle and the cruel buffeting we had just received I expected to be confronted with a scene of large-scale destruction and havoc, with at least half the buildings of the district reduced to ruins. But life is full of surprises. Dust there was in plenty, the roadway was strewn with the glass of shattered windows and a strong smell of cordite hung about, yet from where I stood I could see nothing to detract from the familiar pattern of the surrounds.

'I studied the people milling about in the street, curious to see how they had taken this sudden attack on their homeland by their former friends. From their actions as well as their words it was manifest that their anger and indignation bordered on the flash point. The usual decorum of my neighbours was thrown to the winds as they shook their fists at the now deserted sky and rained down curses on the whole Italian race. The air grew blue with blasphemy as a hunchbacked old grandmother expressed in no uncertain terms her personal opinion of the love-child Mussolini.

'From the people below, my roving eye wandered to the top of the front wall of St Francis Barracks, just across the way where a young soldier stood surveying the roofs with a pair of binoculars. In due course his sights were set on my balcony. A few seconds later I heard a loud chuckle. When I thought about it afterwards, I realised that the soldier had every reason to chuckle. Not only was I dusty, dishevelled and covered in cobwebs, but half my head was still in curlers. No pin-up by any means. But I hadn't got round to caring.

"Any casualties?" I called across, eager for information.

"Don't know," the soldier replied.

He lowered the binoculars and jerked a thumb over his shoulder.

"That was a near do, miss, right on our doorstep."

'It was too.'

Christina learnt later the bomb she heard whistling down as she sat unwinding her curlers was one of two which hit a Water and Electricity department building at *Porte des Bombes* of all places. It claimed the first two victims of the war from a group of Maltese workmen.

Porte des Bombes looking inland from Floriana. St Francis Barracks is to the left.

Life changed for everyone that morning. Michael Longyear recalled, 'there was a fairly large air raid that appeared to be directly over us. My mother had been designated as an air raid warden and was given a large hand bell to ring around the married quarters as an air raid warning. She continued ringing long after the first bombs were dropping until she was unceremoniously bundled into the makeshift shelter. These were dug in the grassed area between the road of the quarters and the bastion. The shelter was really a slit trench covered with corrugated iron and further covered with earth. Seating was on an army bench on either side of the trench so that we all faced each other. On that first day a soldier was detailed to sit outside the open entrance with no protection, other than his tin hat, because it was thought that we civilians might panic. When the sound of shrapnel dropping from our AA guns was heard hitting the ground near us it was suggested that he should come inside with us. He agreed to the suggestion only when assured that we would not panic, but he still sat at the bottom of the steps in case we did.'

The old monitor HMS *Terror*, anchored in Marsamxett Harbour, seemed to Michael to fire every gun it had, the black smoke quickly drifting across the creek bringing with it the acrid smell of cordite and powder.

Tamara safely made it to Birzebbugia's police station where she met up with other wives. When the All Clear sounded, they returned home and her husband Ronnie arrived soon afterwards. By then she had heard the RAF families were to be evacuated immediately to the Parisio Palace in Naxxar. 'I remembered the place with a sick feeling in the pit of my stomach. That was where we were going to stay for goodness knew how long. Not a bright prospect!

'At that moment the maid arrived. Kitty had been with me for a long time and was very sorry to hear that I was being evacuated and that I would not take her with me as only women with children were allowed to have maids. Although another raid started, Kitty and I carried on with my packing.

"Now let's see. Have we got everything? My summer frocks and undies in this suitcase. Sheets, pillowcases, towels in the brown one. My shoes in the hat box, my toilet implements in the leather handbag and the lunch stuff in the shopping bag. That seems to be all."

'Kitty was genuinely upset.

"Cheer up, it won't be for long. I will be back in a fortnight or so. Keep the key. Get some mothballs from the chemist and please pack up my winter frocks carefully in the trunk. Make a neat bundle of the carpets with newspapers and plenty of mothballs; sweep and dust the flat won't you? We don't want to leave it in a mess, war or no war. You can send me the key by post. Here is my address. And by the way, do we owe the grocer anything?"

"There is a bob to the greengrocer; you remember, Misses, the artichokes we had yesterday."

"Well, alright then, here we are and there goes the All Clear. See if you can find a boy to carry my bags to the police station."

"I will do it for you Misses."

'I called to my husband who was still on the balcony. "Let us go. We will be late or some other raid will materialise."'

Tamara took a last look at her compact but very convenient flat with a lovely view of Kalafrana Bay: 'The sun streaming through the French windows and glistening on a sea of burnished cobalt made this sample of Italian "morning hate" seems so very imbecile.' The early morning 'hate' was the first of the day's eight air raids. Inevitably bombs fell on Valletta. The RAF Gladiator fighters all attacked but without apparent result, then their pilots had to watch helplessly as the Italian bombers simply accelerated away. The Gladiators were too slow.

No bombs fell on Floriana during the second or third raids and the Roche's friend Billie bravely returned home. 'By now we were all feeling considerably bolder. Cecil even suggested a stroll up to Valletta for a meal and to find out from Gianni what the form was! So much for our intentions! We had scarcely reached the gates of the city when the sirens sounded once again and our leisurely pace broke into a gentle trot as we followed a fast-moving stream of people heading towards the Opera House. Eventually we found ourselves in a long tunnel, a relic of the one-time railway from Valletta to Rabat. This raid was particularly heavy. So much so that the many hundreds of people herded together in the shelter bowed their heads in prayer and called fervently upon the Holy Virgin to deliver them from harm.'

Later, while walking down Kingsway after the raid, Christina saw that every shop was still closed, leaving them to predict that Gianni's place too would not be open. It was firmly bolted and barred. 'The street called Strait was as silent as a pathway to the grave.' They returned to Floriana.

When Tamara got to Birzebbugia police station, it was crammed with luggage. 'Women and children were everywhere talking excitedly of the morning's happenings.

"My dear, you never saw such flashes. The house was shaking to its foundations. I did not know what to do with myself. And Albert away!"

"A nice cup of tea, that's what I always say. Let me get a nice cup of tea in me and no Eyeties with their monkey business are going to frighten me."'

The RAF evacuation from Birzebbugia was well organized with three buses to take wives and children to Naxxar. Halfway there the buses stopped dead. 'The drivers got out looking shaken. "Air raid, air raid," they shouted.

'Panic seized us. An air raid in the middle of the road with no shelter for miles; we did not know what to do. We got out of the buses carrying the children and the luggage. We scanned the sky. The sun was at its highest and it was a strain to look into the intense blue. Some sat down on stones; some lay flat and advised others to do so. It was the safest thing to do, they said. Some stood up and then lay flat as soon as aircraft were audible. I had found a flat stone and made myself comfortable in the ditch. Another woman, a Mrs Smith and her two children were there too. We could see the aircraft like small dots very high up.

"These must be ours," I said. "It is really silly to be crouching here like this, we ought to go on."

"How many aircraft can you see?"

"About five."

"I make it six. Follow my finger, that's another one."

"Those are certainly ours, there is no ack-ack."

"Don't you believe it, they are eyeties all right."

"But surely we must have our aircraft up too."

"Yes, but we could not have so many."

"So MANY? What do you mean, there are only six."

"Well, that's three too many."

'I made frantic calculations. Six minus three; that left three. Ridiculous! I said so. "Don't tell me we have only got three aeroplanes. I can't believe it."

"That's it though. Three aircraft: *Faith, Hope* and *Charity,* our three gallant Gladiators."

"At least they have fitting names," said I. "I do hope it is not common knowledge. Three planes, we would better give ourselves up this very minute as it really is madness to carry on with Sicily only sixty miles away".'

But that was the reality of the RAF's fighter defence of Malta in June 1940. Tamara and Mrs Smith were soon joined in their ditch by some others: 'We had no other concern but the immediate future and it was quite pleasant sitting there in the sun chit-chatting to the muffled sound of the anti-aircraft guns in the harbour. The aircraft had disappeared over the sea and the white puffs caused by the shell bursts were slowly flattening out and looking like innocent cloudlets. The drivers came to fetch us. They had found a hole to hide in. The All Clear had sounded but we had not heard it. We resumed our seats and drove hell for leather to Parisio Palace.'

Tamara was not surprised to find life in the Parisio Palace was to be 'ordered'. 'We all trooped in with our luggage. The wives of the men stationed at Headquarters had preceded us. The long hall we entered had some fine murals and sculptured pillars. White wood benches and white unpolished tables were placed here and there. Busy looking officers' wives (they were to be the ruling class) with little bits of fluttering paper in their hands, were running importantly among bewildered looking women and wailing children.

'Three calls to order failed to produce any result whatsoever. A wooden mallet was handed to the group captain's wife who looked very natty in a grey travelling suit. She was to be commander-in-chief. Some sort of order was obtained. The roll was called. We were all present. It had been arranged that each group of ten or so would be under the charge of an officer's wife. Many a woman wore her husband's stripes that day - and subsequently.'

Officers' wives and other ranks' wives had separate dining rooms. Only women with children were allocated rooms; those without, like Tamara, slept on landings. Buckets served as lavatories placed at the corners of balconies. There was one just outside the window on Tamara's landing. There were three air raids the first night which saw everyone without exception scurrying to the shelters in the old cellars. Most people felt like wrecks the next morning.

On this first day of Malta's war, eleven civilians were killed and 130 injured. Six members of the Royal Malta Artillery were killed at Fort St Elmo and six Maltese sailors at Xghajra. While damage to military property was relatively slight, many civilian buildings around the dockyard were hit. No Italian aircraft were shot down. But the old Gladiators had been seen by a fearful civilian population to be opposing the Italians and this had a profound impact on morale. The RAF biplanes, together with the guns of the Royal Malta Artillery and the Royal Artillery, helped break up the Italian formations and disrupt their aim. Many bombs fell harmlessly into the sea. The Italians had been challenged and they knew it.

While the first air raids awakened the islanders to the reality of modern war, it was the very last air raid that day which demonstrated its totality when the primarily residential areas of Gzira, Zabbar and Cospicua were heavily bombed. This particular raid had a dramatic impact on the civilian population.

Earlier, after the All Clear and when it was still daylight, Christina and the Roches collected bedding and went back to the tunnel. 'The road to Valletta was crammed with hundreds of people with the same idea - to get out and get under good, solid rock. It was a slow-moving procession that we joined - a stream of human beings of all ages and from all walks of life that had seemingly been transformed into beasts of burden. Old folks and youngsters alike staggered along with weighty loads of blankets and pillows; many people carried cushions and little folding seats. Some of the more stalwart of the men and women balanced rolled-up mattresses on their heads. More than one load of bedding went to the shelter by wheelbarrow and many a pram was put to a purpose far removed from that of its primary function. A man trundling an iron bedstead along on its castors had all my admiration.

'The tunnel was now one vast communal dormitory with rows of mattresses and deckchairs stretching the whole length of the floor. All along the walls were pictures of the Holy Virgin and the Sacred Heart of Jesus. Here and there was a white card bearing in bold black print the words *Ikun Imbierek Alla* (Blessed Be God). Oil lamps and candles provided lighting - something the Roches and I had overlooked in our flight from Floriana. As darkness fell, so the tunnel became more crowded, for it was generally believed that having visited us no less than eight times during the hours of daylight, the *Regia Aeronautica* would surely strike again by night. But the raiders did not come and the shelterers made themselves as comfortable as possible in the cramped surroundings and tried to get some sleep. When the time came for me to lay down my own weary head I found that the floor space claimed earlier on at the side of the Roches had been reduced to an almost invisible strip. Cecil was very gallant but, under the circumstances, I felt I could not accept the kind offer of his place next to Babs. I should have stayed put instead of going off on a fact-finding tour. Collecting my rolled-up blanket and pillow I went further along the tunnel in search of new lodgings.

'In the dim light of the oil lamps and candles I steered a way in and out of the groups of shelterers, tripping occasionally in the darker patches over the legs of some prone body and now and again barging into the end of a camp-bed. It was an almost hopeless quest, this search for a vacant spot, but I kept doggedly on until eventually I came across a few feet of bare ground right up near the entrance. While not the safest of places, there was a certain amount of solace in the fact that the crowd up here was not quite so thick, the air not nearly so foul as further down. Unrolling my blanket I folded it into four thicknesses and with a sheet I had also brought along I made up my bed on the rough, stony floor. Then I slipped off my sandals and putting them under my pillow, as if it were the most natural thing in the world to do, I sat down very tired yet in no mood for sleep.

'I looked around at my bedside companions. On my right a family of four, husband and wife and two little girls, lay huddled together on a mattress, all of them sound asleep. Beyond them, a young mother sat propped up against the wall, feeding a tiny infant at her breast. Down by my feet two boys, about ten and twelve years old, were curled up on a blanket and a woman who looked as if she might be their mother sat dozing above them in a deck-chair. On my other side a wizened old man was making a fuss of getting himself ready for bed. I watched, fascinated, as he struggled slowly out of his shirt and trousers, folding them neatly and placing them at the side of my pillow. Standing in underpants and singlet he scratched his head thoughtfully for a few moments, then he picked up the sheet covering his folded blanket and wrapped it round his shrunken body. After making the sign of the cross he sank to his knees, shook up his pillow and firmly settled down at my side.

'Sandwiched in among total strangers, I lay awake for a long time trying hard to imagine what the future held in store for all of us in Malta. My thoughts became morbid, as not unnaturally I wondered if I would live to see my mother and father and brothers again. Whether I would be killed outright or horribly maimed. I tried to cheer myself up by thinking how the girls at the Theatre Girls' Club would have laughed if they could have seen me tucked up for the night next to this wizened old man. At length, to a lullaby of subdued conversations and loud snores, I fell asleep.

'It must have been about two hours later when I was awakened, not by the sound of the air raid warning, exploding bombs, gunfire, or the All Clear, but to the mischievous giggling of the two lads at the bottom of my makeshift bed, one of whom was in the act of tickling my bare toes!'

The following morning, Christina and her friends took their bedding back to their home in Floriana before setting out once more to see if they could find Gianni, their employer. War or no war, they would soon need to earn a living. When they reached the main Valletta-Floriana thoroughfare they were confronted by a scene similar to the previous evening, except this time the crowds were moving in the opposite direction. While there hadn't yet been any raids that morning, people were doing their very best to get as far away from Grand Harbour as possible. In scenes similar to those seen in Belgium and France, Malta now faced the shocking and pitiful sight of refugees streaming away from where they felt threatened. Women carried babies, while their other children held onto their skirts or pushed overloaded prams. Most people were on foot; some were on wheels, as hundreds of civilians streamed away to what they considered safer towns like Hamrun, Birkirkara, Naxxar, Rabat and St Paul's Bay. They took with them all their worldly goods; lorries and horse-drawn carts all stacked high with furniture, bedding, carpets and cooking utensils, all heading out of the city in a continuous stream, desperate to put as much distance as possible between them and their former homes before the next bombs fell.

About 100,000 people, nearly half of the island's entire population, left their homes in the first chaotic few days. Thankfully, unlike refugees in Belgium and France, they were not strafed from the air to cause panic. It took days for the authorities to impose some form of order. Schools and churches were opened to house refugees; in fact any suitable buildings were brought into service. With so many people having fled the areas where they felt most threatened, how would they react if the bombing intensified? Could the people be inspired to take the air attacks in their stride?

The Cuell Family

One family who sought safety were the Cuells. Walter Cuell was British and served in Malta in the Royal Navy in the First World War, reaching the rank of Chief Petty Officer. He met and fell in love with a Maltese girl, Carmella Zammit. After they married they made their home at 24 Sacred Heart Street, Casalpaola. Walter found himself 'on the beach', retired in 1922, but with a small pension. He continued to work for the navy as a civilian. They had eight children, five girls and three boys, at approximately two yearly intervals.

Left to right: Wallace, Elizabeth (known as Betty), Carmella (sitting), Joseph, Monica (known as Mona), Joan, Agnes (sitting), Helen, Eddie. *(Eddie Cuell)*

When war began, Walter was recalled in his old rank. Before being sent to Egypt, he suggested to Carmella they have a family photograph taken, maybe the last opportunity for the family to be together. Carmella was well aware that appointments were needed for such things, often well in advance. When she approached a photographer who specialised in family portraits, she expressed concern her sons didn't have suitable smart clothes to wear. The photographer said if she could get hold of a couple of army blankets, he could arrange for them to be made-up into something appropriate. By then Walter was on his way to Port Said in Egypt; he served there until 1945. The family photograph, less Walter, was duly taken, a striking image of a proud mother and her eight fine children.

When the bombing began Carmella, like many others, judged it best to move away from the vicinity of the dockyards. Thankfully the elder Cuell girls, Agnes, Elizabeth (Betty), and Helen, were well capable of helping their mother with a move to Birkirkara, to Carmella's cousin who was headmaster of the government school there.

Back in Valletta, Christina and the Roches found all the shops and offices, the market, the bars and restaurants still closed. At Gianni's home, the only information was from a woman on the balcony of the house next door. With up-turned eyes and upturned hands she simply said: '*Mhux hawn.*' Gianni had hopped it.

They returned home worried, jobless and stranded; they were also hungry and their cupboards were bare. How long the shops would remain closed was anyone's guess. 'It was then that a miracle happened. We were sitting in the Roche's room, ruing our fate, when there was a knock at the door. Opening it we found standing there our old and faithful friends, Mr and Mrs Mallia. When they could have been excused for worrying about their own affairs and neglecting the needs of customers, they had found time to pack a box with tins of meat, a loaf, eggs, milk, tea and sugar and bring it round to the house. It was a gesture of kindness that left us deeply moved.

'We spent the next few nights in that tunnel, lying on blankets on the floor, packed in like sardines. Rich man, poor man, beggar man, thief - they were all there. But by the end of the week, many took to sleeping once more in their own homes. Rock shelters were increasingly made available and the efficient air raid warning system usually allowed time to take cover.' Despite the personal danger, Christina very much preferred the comfort of her top floor room to that offered by the former Malta Railway Company.

The respite from bombing on 12 June was a godsend, but the Italians returned the next day with a series of raids; they suffered no losses. The following day they were back and lost a bomber and its crew of six, not to the island's defences, but to airframe icing causing loss of control.

Sir William Dobbie visited six villages on Sunday, 16 June, a day when attacks intensified. He arrived in Zetjun in the middle of a raid and finished in Mosta soon after bombs landed nearby. His visits were a much-needed morale boost, but he harboured doubts about how long morale would hold up under intense, indiscriminate bombing. He always exuded an inner calm others found hard to explain. His calmness was needed now.

During that first week two thirds of the 150 civilian casualties were women and children. Things were then quiet for a couple of days before bombing resumed, focused on Grand Harbour. The RAF had its first success on the evening of 22 June when an Italian reconnaissance aircraft was shot down. Witnessed by many on the ground in Sliema and Valletta, it caused quite a stir. Further success followed in the days ahead. Although the Italian bombing was often inaccurate, Malta's gunners were not. The Maltese were rightly jubilant over shooting down an Italian aircraft and the ad hoc group of RAF pilots in their antiquated biplanes felt they had justified the confidence everyone had shown in them.

In London French capitulation was expected and the Admiralty considered abandoning the Eastern Mediterranean altogether and concentrating the fleet at Gibraltar. Churchill strongly opposed this as it would spell doom for Malta. On 24 June, France duly surrendered and the balance of power in the Mediterranean changed significantly.

Two days later Italian bombers hit Luqa, Hal Far and the dockyards. The so-called accurate bombing resulted in a bus being hit by an incendiary bomb at the Marsa crossroads; thirty civilians died.

At Naxxar, Tamara found trying to catch up on lost sleep during the day on her landing proved impossible, in fact sleep became the most elusive thing and she learnt to snatch at it at any odd moment. The air raids lasted anything from one to three hours and the anti-aircraft guns boomed continuously. 'Still we settled in. I was amazed and agreeably surprised at the friendliness and adaptability of English women. My three years' experience in England had not been very successful and at Birzebbugia, contacts had been superficial. Seeing them at close-quarters, I liked them. They were clever at makeshifts, polite and kind to each other. It was like being back at boarding school again. We played pranks, made apple-pie beds, sewed pyjama sleeve ends and leg ends together and had mock-battles with flit-guns.

'We were sorely tried by the lack of bathrooms. Two wash-sheds had been rigged up in the back garden and two others were on the first floor, but only three bathrooms were available for about seventy women and an equal number of children. Old pruderies had to go by the board. Two or three women had to use the same bath at the same time and they did. Children washed *en masse*. There was no other way out of it.'

When six bathrooms were built out of sacking and corrugated iron, three were labelled 'Other Ranks' and three 'Officers' wives only.' Duties were assigned and came round by rotation. These included washing up, bathroom cleaning, potato peeling and blacking-out the many windows, doors and cracks. They got used to the order of the air raids. There was usually one at midday, lasting an hour or so, and one at 11.00 pm in the evening usually of two hours duration. Sometimes there would be one or two in between for good measure. After the first week, the RAF wives became expert at carrying on in the shelters the same activities that they had been engaged in upstairs. One of the ladies, Mrs Cox, was taken to hospital to have a baby, her fourth. Her other three children - all boys - were looked after by other residents. Tamara was asked to look after 5-year-old Harold. 'I had doubts as to my qualifications as a mother, but I liked the idea immensely and accepted the charge.

'I went over to where Harold was and sat beside him. He was very shy that first day. He would not eat; no amount of coaxing would make him. I was worried. He did not cry, he mutely refused every advance. I put him to bed early that night. I bought some biscuits from the NAAFI and mixed a flask-full of powdered milk ready for the ten to eleven o'clock air raid, which was sure to materialise. I knew poor Harold would be too ravenously hungry to hold out any longer.

'As I carried him downstairs and sat him down on my lap well wrapped in a blanket, he looked up at me and put his little arms around my neck. The sweet darling, he looked lovely all flushed with sleep. "Now Harold pet, we will have a picnic just you and I. Shall we? It will be great fun. Here you are; six biscuits for you, six biscuits for me. Would you like something to drink? Of course you would, my angel. Here… lovely cold milk to wash the biscuits down."

'We got on famously after that. He was the most loving and obedient child I had come across. Although it was hard work negotiating the stairs, when he was asleep he seemed to weigh a ton and I always had to be back for his bedtime. I loved every minute of it and was selfishly sorry when Mrs Cox came back with the new edition to her family…another boy.'

Life went on. There were no restrictions on husbands coming to see their wives at any time of day but they were only allowed in the garden. They were not permitted to enter the dining room and most certainly not the sleeping quarters. No one infringed this rule. To begin with the curfew was at 6.00 pm, but this was extended after a month to 8.00 pm. None of the residents stirred from the Parisio Palace for the first week; their imaginations far too active even though no bombs had fallen within a mile. They all expected to be killed and worried constantly. It was worry that produced their only casualty, a warrant officer's wife who went completely out of her mind and died at Mtarfa hospital a month after Italy's declaration of war.

Tamara and the others realised that they needed to venture out from the confines of the palace. They found their first reappearance into the world after a week's seclusion something of a revelation and from then on got bolder. Not a day went by without a party of the RAF wives going down town to eat or shop, or to go to the cinema during the afternoons. However, it was absolutely imperative they return to the Parisio Palace by 8.00 pm, or they would be locked out. Their home was dubbed by some of the 'inmates' as 'the concentration camp' which Tamara thought rather unjust as the Entertainments' Committee was very active. Concerts were organised, there were whist drives every other night and tombola twice a week, although the latter was often interrupted by an air raid. Everyone would grab their tickets and rush the children to the cellars hoping the raid would not last long so they could finish their game before going to bed. They seldom did.

'One night we had a carnival party. Everyone was to dress up but was to use only material to hand; nothing was to be brought from outside. Two prizes were to be awarded for the most ingenious costumes. I decided to go as Eve and for two days, had three carefully picked fig leaves in a vase by my bedside. They were to be sewn, one on a pair of pink panties and two on a pink brassiere. I thought the idea simple and effective but was dissuaded from putting it into execution as Sgt Baker had been invited too.

'So at the last moment I had to change my mind from being Eve and turn up as a naughty child wearing a play suit, a big red bow in my hair, short white socks, flat heeled shoes with a strap buttoning at the side and a toffee apple borrowed from one of the children. I was as naughty as I could be and pulled everyone's hair but was outdone in my crying, bad tempered moments by the baby in the pram and the baby twins. A "caught in an air raid" which consisted of two towels wrapped around hips and breasts, was a big success. But the prizes (boxes of chocolates) went to Mrs Barnes and Mrs Wickham who impersonated Gert and Daisy.'

By the end of June some confidence had been restored and life began to return to normal with shops re-opening and people beginning to go about their day-to-day business. When the sirens sounded, the shutters came down but they were lifted just as quickly when the all-clear sounded. A great fillip to morale was the arrival of a handful of Hurricanes. At the beginning of hostilities everyone had gone to their shelters as quickly as possible after they heard the siren; now they stood on their flat roofs and other vantage-points to witness the thrilling aerial battles.

Despite improving morale on the island, Britain's situation in the Mediterranean was extremely serious. The Royal Navy held both ends with strong forces at Gibraltar and Alexandria. Italy held the centre with strong naval, land and air forces on either side of the narrow gap separating Sicily from North Africa. The Italians significantly outnumbered the British in terms of warships and had over 100 submarines to the Royal Navy's eight. In the crucial area of aircraft, Italy could call upon 2,000, whereas Britain had about 200, precious few of which were based in Malta. The ninety-mile wide Sicilian Straits would also have to be negotiated by any merchant ship attempting to re-supply Malta from the west. Would Britain risk its capital ships as convoy escorts in such a narrow channel?

Another Italian air group moved to Sicily. Things were about to get tougher. Bombing raids continued with Italian aircrew describing defensive fire over Grand Harbour as 'infernal'. Malta's gunners had been waiting their chance to show their worth and they took it in both hands. In fact they fired at such an intensity there were concerns ammunition would only last thirty days. The Italians thankfully lost their enthusiasm and the situation improved. But casualties, including many civilians, continued to mount. Anti-Italian feelings ran very high.

Chapter 4

The Whizz-Bangs

July - December 1940

Malta's music halls and cabarets all remained closed. With servicemen at their posts and a curfew in place at 8.00 pm, there was little prospect of employment for the many artistes and comedians, dancers and hostesses. Yet even if they were out of work, Christina, Cecil and Babs were not the ones to admit it. 'In conformity with the best traditions of the theatre, we were merely "resting".

'Cecil did not remain in this inactive stage for any longer than necessary. One afternoon I looked over my balcony to see him walking towards the house dressed in a khaki drill uniform and blue forage cap.

"What's all this?" I called down.

"I've joined the RAF," he replied.

'He came up to the room to tell me about it! His eyes sparkled as he described how he had gone a few days previously to see Major Shephard, the Provost Marshal. Major Shephard had made arrangements for him to join the Royal Air Force and now here he was, all dressed up to kill as AC2 Roche, Cecil, of No 8 Malta Sector. He had been posted for duties in the underground Fighter Control Headquarters at Lascaris, Valletta; the nerve centre of our aerial defences.' Cecil was an Aircraftman 2nd Class; he held the RAF's lowest rank.

There were many other stranded entertainers who had the same idea as Cecil. Two were male comedians, Chris Shaw and 'Vicki' Ford. They also went to see Major Shephard, a Royal Marine officer, to offer their services. He suggested they form a concert party in the style of ENSA (Entertaining National Service Association) formed the previous year in Britain. 'He knew that there were other English performers on the island who, due to the closing of the music halls, were all but stranded. We were in for a long war and these boys and girls could best serve their country and the island of Malta by helping to keep up the morale of the troops already here and the thousands yet to come.'

Chris and Vicki got in touch with others and a group of eleven turned up for a meeting at their flat in Floriana. Christina was one of them. The four men and seven girls were a mixture of comedians, singers and dancers and all agreed to form a concert party. The appropriately named Whizz-Bangs was born. 'I knew only one or two of the party by sight, the others were complete strangers, but we soon introduced ourselves and exchanged details of our own particular line of entertainment. Mary Miles, a tall strikingly handsome girl with jet-black hair and big brown eyes, told me she was a singer. Eve Ascot, petite and ginger-headed, specialised in red-hot momma songs and naughty monologues. Rita Moya was a soubrette who had appeared in many musical comedies in England. Julie Hart was the other half of a sister-act performed with Eve Ascot, but she also had her own repertoire of songs and dances. Dorothea Sendea, tall, willowy, with mid-brown hair and an amazing length of leg, claimed to be a champion high-kicker and skipping-rope dancer. The remaining girl, Marigold Fletcher, better known as "Pickles", was a ballet dancer and contortionist who also had a very sweet singing voice.' Christina was an extremely talented dancer.

The first two weeks of July were hectic. Having assembled such a group of talented and keen entertainers, one of their priorities was to find a rehearsal venue. What they came up with was in Valletta and it was certainly 'convenient': 'The Victoria, as a rehearsal room, was perhaps not quite to everyone's taste, situated as

Christina practices the flamenco on her apartment roof. (UK MOD)

The Old Vic on Strait Street is the green-painted building beyond the public convenience. *(Paul McDonald).*

it was next door to a public convenience mid-way down the Gut. But beggars could not be choosers and it was ideal for our purpose. A good stage, a fine set of plush curtains, a piano - what more could one ask for nothing?'

The next priority was to form a band. Two out-of-work musicians from yet another closed cabaret were found. Micky Saliba was a brilliant pianist and Joe Fiteni was a well-known violinist, and they were joined by Sonny Foster. Sonny's mother was famous throughout the Mediterranean Fleet as 'Auntie'; apparently the itinerary of any upper-deck run ashore in Malta before the war was almost certain to include a visit to Auntie's cabaret in *Strada Stretta.*

Life for the newly-formed Whizz-Bangs became frantic. 'For two weeks we slogged away at rehearsals, toiling and boiling in a temperature topping the eighties. During this period Major Shephard was a regular visitor to the Victoria, sparing a few minutes of each busy day to spur us on with words of encouragement. His wife was also very kind, coming along as she did to give a helping hand with costumes, which we cut out and sewed up during the breaks in rehearsals. While we had been fortunate in obtaining the Victoria free-of-charge, we could not expect the show to be dressed for nothing. It was therefore with an element of personal risk that Chris and "Vicki" advanced funds for the purchase of materials. We each had our own costumes for individual turns but for ensembles and sketches many more had to be made. A dressmaker was engaged to ease the situation and she ploughed her way admirably through yards of cheap silks and satins bought from the Indian shops, producing some splendid results. But scores of props, including a stuffed snake for "Vicki" to charm in the eastern scene, had to be manufactured. The task of turning out the reptile fell upon me and I can say with pride that not even the Garden of Eden could have boasted so fine a specimen!' For the Whizz-Bangs, and all those who supported them, there was a lot riding on this first show and everyone was very keen for it to be successful.

At the end of rehearsals Major Shephard announced he had persuaded the owner of the newly-built Regent Cinema to re-open for one afternoon performance of the very first show. While the cinema was small it had a large stage and perfect acoustics. 'And as the Provost Marshal had invited several service "brass-hats" to our first performance, to assess the show's suitability as "stuff to give to the troops", we were delighted with the opportunity of displaying our efforts to the best advantage.' As theatres and cinemas might not open for some time, the cast did everything possible to advertise their show. A large order for handbills was placed with a Hamrun printer and a small boy was hired to distribute them in the streets and shelters. On 13 July 1940 there was an important entry in the official *Diary of the War on the Malta Front*:

> The first entertainment to be given in wartime Malta was presented
> by the Whizz-Bangs concert party

'The show was a riot. The house was packed to capacity, something we had not dreamed possible with the threat of air raids ever present. But the war seemed far, far away as songs and dances, sketches and ensembles brought forth cheers and applause such as had not been heard in Malta since the last Carnival. Long before the interval we guessed what the verdict of the service chiefs would be. At the end of two hours' run we were left in no doubt. Overjoyed, we were convinced that we were well on the road to success, that our concert party was no longer the gamble that it had seemed a couple of weeks ago.'

Major Shephard was delighted with the Whizz-Bangs triumphant debut and from then on he agreed to act as booking agent. Even before he drew up a list of potential venues, the troupe was asked to give a show the next afternoon at Fort St Elmo. 'We performed on a miniature stage before an audience of Maltese troops, many of whom could not understand a word of English. Nevertheless they roared with laughter at the comedy scenes and were almost over-anxious to applaud the songs and dances. They thoroughly enjoyed themselves and so did we. At the end of the show, after a prolonged bout of cheering, one of the soldiers went round the audience with a steel helmet collecting a substantial sum of money which he proudly presented to us as a token of appreciation.

'Until then no serious thought had been given to remuneration for our services, but it was obvious that some sort of charge would have to be levied if the show was to prosper. For well over a month none of us had been in paid employment. We had to eat, rents had to be paid, war or no war. Major Shephard agreed that going round with the hat, although traditional, was at the same time a precarious way of earning a living.' He stipulated a charge of sixpence per head for performances.

This then was the beginning of the Whizz-Bangs concert party, true stars of Strait Street, which was destined to go on strongly throughout the most difficult period in Malta's wartime history. They toured all the barracks, gun-sites, searchlight batteries and airfields on the island not once, but many times entertaining the troops, their repertoire consisting of burlesque singing, Arab dances, ballet, impersonations and speciality acts. One critic in 1942 wrote:

> Their new show is perhaps the best and it is a tribute to the versatility
> of the artistes concerned that after two years' constant performances
> the Whizz-Bangs are as popular and entertaining as ever.

Al fresco entertainment 1941, courtesy of the Whizz-Bangs. Christina is on the far left. Note the officer on the front row using binoculars while two men on the back row seem more interested in getting their picture taken. (*UK MOD*)

Later taken over by the NAAFI, the entertainers no longer had to rely on the troops to pay for the shows. With everyone on a fixed salary they toured the island putting on performances wherever they could mount their makeshift stage.

Over south-east England in that summer of 1940, the Battle of Britain began. If it was lost, with an army shattered after Dunkirk, Britain would be occupied. If the *Luftwaffe's* march against England was successful, Europe would be a very different place. With Britain secure, firmly anchored off the coast of France, the possibility of liberation remained. That was the period in which the fate of the western world was shaped by a few young men. Those same summer days of 1940 saw another handful of young men in Malta, though far less numerous, fighting just as desperately. Fewer still were trained fighter pilots. While events in Britain determined the outcome of the war, events in Malta determined its outcome in North Africa.

Robert Carter Jonas, known as 'Jonah', arrived on the island in July. He came from Egypt where he had commanded 80 Squadron operating Gladiators for two years. Now he was a newly-promoted wing commander and became Luqa's first formally appointed station commander.

It wasn't until the middle of July that the valiant Gladiators operating from Luqa were actually named by their pilots *Faith*, *Hope* and *Charity*, but there is no doubt about the positive effect of the names on the population. *Charity* was soon lost. Only *Faith* and *Hope* remained; a perfect reflection of the situation on the island. By the end of July, the RAF was in a desperate situation with no spares or ground crew trained on the aircraft in use. It took hard work and improvisation to keep them in the air. With so few pilots trained in air combat, everyone - pilots and airmen - had to acquire new skills 'on the job', tools of a demanding and deadly trade in the face of an experienced and skilful enemy.

Malta's reliance on convoys was total; single ships making fast runs could only supply bare essentials. With the fate of Malta resting on a band of courageous defenders and the seamen who provided their lifeblood, Sir William Dobbie made strong recommendations to London. His major concern was civilian morale. He judged it could only be maintained with a minimum of fifty fighter aircraft and more anti-aircraft guns. Without action there would be a disaster, he said.

Few in London thought much of Malta's chances, yet against all expectations the very poorly defended island was doing rather well. Churchill demanded action. Twelve Hurricanes were flown in on 2 August from the aircraft carrier HMS *Argus*. How long could such a thin blue line last? Despite Churchill's demands the situation was made more complicated when the Italian army began a slow advance against considerably smaller British forces in Egypt.

The first convoy to attempt the run to Malta left Alexandria on 29 August. Three battleships, one aircraft carrier, four cruisers, and seventeen destroyers were required to protect four merchantmen. The convoy was successful with only one merchantman damaged. The word 'damaged' disguises the reality of what many merchant ships suffered. In this case, the ship couldn't sail again for six months. This first supply run delivered 40,000 tons to the besieged island. To fulfil Malta's needs, two 40,000 ton convoys were needed *each month*. When would the next arrive?

There was a lone and unexpected reinforcement in the shape of a French *Latécoère* torpedo bomber, a floatplane. It was crewed by *Premiere-Maître* (Warrant Officer) René Duvauchelle and *Quartier-Maître* (Sergeant) Jacques Méhauas of the French Navy. They had escaped from the Vichy French base at Bizerta in Tunisia to join an increasing number of Free French who rallied to the Allied cause.

With the authorities having coped with the first weeks of the crisis, thoughts were turned to a more distant evacuation of service families. Popular opinion among service personnel was against compulsory evacuation. For many the removal of wives and children even though they were all now on the front line, hung threateningly above their heads. Sometimes it rose to a climax of rumoured urgency before fading away into the limbo of almost forgotten things. For the authorities, a key factor was the effect such an undertaking might have on the Maltese. Would the islanders become demoralised by the sight of British families being forcibly made to leave? Or would they take it in their stride?

Voluntary evacuation of dependents began with women with children offered assisted passages to South Africa, although any sea passage was not without risk. Tamara Marks initially put her name down as she felt she was of no use in Malta and yet, only an hour before she was due to leave, she changed her mind. This created a major fuss which only served to strengthen her resolve to stay. Her decision proved fortuitous: a few weeks later, the billet where her husband Ronnie would have been sleeping had she left, received a direct hit and four of its occupants died.

One evening in September 1940 the Whizz-Bangs entertained RAF Luqa's officers and airmen with a concert in the canteen. Jonah Jonas, the station commander, sat at the back of the room, and found the experience particularly reflective: 'For stretching out below me I could just discern the dark silhouettes of hundreds of heads, with grey clouds of smoke rising above them from their pipes and cigarettes, and the sounds of creaking and scraping as the men shifted their bodies on the hard wooden benches. At the far end of the long narrow hall was the improvised stage, with its makeshift curtain, the homemade scenery, and the crude lighting. It wasn't a West End production and the players would not have got a job in Shaftesbury Avenue. Yet the atmosphere was there; men down below in the gloom were obviously enjoying the show, but I felt their thoughts were thousands of miles away. The hardworking actors and actresses this evening were bringing to their audience vivid thoughts and perhaps painful memories of happy and forgotten days, of a world at peace.

'Now the troops joined in the chorus of *It's a Lovely Day Tomorrow*, led by a dark-eyed brunette, in a long satin dress, whose rich and lovely voice carried her audience far beyond the boundaries of our little world. Sitting there in the gloom at the back of the room, I quietly wondered to myself whether it really was going to be a lovely day tomorrow, or whether we were going to be bombed to hell?' The dark-eyed beauty was Christina's friend Mary Miles.

By the beginning of October the Maltese, always an adaptable people, were learning to take things in their stride; they did not rate the efforts of the *Regia Aeronautica*. If Italy's intent was to overwhelm their defences, or frighten the islanders into submission, then their plans were foiled by a handful of fighters and the sterling work of the British and Maltese gunners.

Agnes Cuell, the oldest of the Cuell children, was 19-years-old; she was already engaged to Bill Cooper, a British sailor. He arranged for Agnes to move to the Cooper family home in Newhall in England where they married later that year. The rest of the Cuell family stayed put, having returned from Birkirkara to their home in Casalpaola after about six weeks. Malta was the Cuell home; they would not be driven out. By then Betty, who had just celebrated her eighteenth birthday, had decided to contribute to the war effort and began working at the RAF headquarters in Valletta.

With the increasing number of defence installations on the island there was plenty of work for the Whizz-Bangs. By October they had already given well over fifty performances and their second revue had gone into production. As Christina recalled: 'Wherever we went we were entertained with boundless hospitality and were thoroughly spoiled by the scores of parties in our honour.

'At Fort Ricasoli we were invited to a dinner presided over by Major and Mrs George Fleetwood, a popular English couple and staunch supporters of the concert party. Whenever we performed at the Fort we could always count on a helping hand being given by the tall, monocled major who delighted in pottering about behind the scenes, assisting us with the lighting effects and "noises off".

'A unit of the King's Own Malta Regiment was stationed at Mellieha and here the after-the-show entertainment reached a boisterous level when cabaret turns were given by members of the regiment, followed by forfeit games and rip-roaring community singing.

'The mess at the Hal Far aerodrome, in existence since long before the war, was probably one of the most elegant on the island. After a buffet supper, the beautiful blue carpets were rolled back and we danced to the music of a radiogram. Our host, the commanding officer of the Fleet Air Arm squadron stationed there, was himself a performer of no mean ability and he danced a Russian gopak, cobblers an' all, with an ease and grace that drew tumultuous applause from his admiring audience.

'Tigné, Imtarfa and St Andrew's were among the larger army stations visited by the Whizz-Bangs and very often families from married quarters outnumbered the uniformed members of the audience.

'The show was given a scrupulous combing when it was known that women were to be in the audience. This upset "Vicki" who was not averse to introducing the odd bit of smut into his act: "Don't like women up front," he would growl, "cramps my style". Yet he was as pleased as Punch when he read a critic's report of one show which stated that the beautiful dresses worn by Chris and "Vicki" in the marriage bureau sketch were the envy of all the ladies present! "Vicki's" most popular turn was in the eastern scene where he burlesqued a slave dance performed by Marigold Fletcher at the behest of the Sultan of Birkirkara - born Bobby Vernon. Bobby was the perfect oriental potentate until he opened his mouth and betrayed his Scottish ancestry. We, "Les Girls", draped ourselves round his throne, all dolled-up in the traditional garb of the harem-dweller, which incidentally bore no resemblance whatever to that of the *purdah* women I had visited in Morocco. Chris, as the Sultan's daughter, was superbly arrayed in gold satin pantaloons and a tiara, a perfect bosom provided by a pair of "falsies" in a sequin-encrusted brassiere. His clever disguise earned him much well deserved applause.

The Whizz-Bangs 1940/41. Christina is in the front row, second from the left. Marigold 'Pickles' Fletcher is next to her sitting in the centre.

'Many an old chestnut was cracked in this scene but no matter how stale a joke happened to be we could always count on quite a few people "out front" not having heard it before. One such joke occurred in the pattern preceding "Vicki's" spectacular entrance. Chris, to the sound of many gongs, entered and bowed low to the Sultan:

"Oh, father, there is a woman without."

"Without what?"

"Without food or clothing."

"Give her food and bring her in."

'That always guaranteed a laugh, but when the "woman without" came in, something near to hysteria broke out among the audience. "Vicki's" bulging muscles fooled no one into believing that he was anything else but a full-blooded male. And as for his costume, Mohammed the Prophet would have rubbed his eyes in bewilderment if he could have seen it. "Vicki" wore a pair of blue lace-trimmed bathing trunks beneath voluminous red trousers, caught in at the ankles with bicycle clips. He had tailored the trousers himself out of home-made mosquito netting. His midriff was bare and for a brassiere he wore two aluminium saucepan lids held together over his chest with a piece of elastic. A diamond tiara encircled his dark wig, holding in place a strip of moth-eaten butter muslin doing service as a *yashmak*. He carried a little fibre attaché case on which was scrawled in white chalk the initials "BF".

'After many salaams to the sultan in which the blue bathing trunks were very much in evidence, "Vicki" turned round to face the audience and sat down cross-legged on the stage. Uttering appropriate magical words, he opened his little attaché-case and to the vast amusement of the onlookers "charmed" - by means of a length of sewing cotton attached to its head - the realistic looking serpent I had made.

'The hilarity reached its climax toward the end of "Vicki's" dance, when grasping the pan lids by their handles he drew them away from his chest and clapped them together like a pair of cymbals. That always raised the roof, but when at a later date the uplifted pans revealed two enormous eyes painted over his nipples, we thought the building would collapse. It might have been coarse and corny stuff but it made the lads laugh and that was the purpose of our mission.'

Tamara said later that although she thought some of the sketches rather crude, 'they never failed to make the spectators roar with laughter. These men had been in the "blue" for months on end and although Malta is no more than seventeen miles by eight, the restriction on transport and the curfew hours made it impossible for most of them to go to Valletta. Besides, even there, there was nothing else in the way of entertainment but going to the pictures.'

While some dependents left Malta, others chose to stay, including the Longyears, who were relocated to St Andrew's Barracks inland from St George's Bay on the north-east coast. While Victor Longyear remained in barracks in Floriana, Mary and her three remaining children, Pam (first name Jean), Pauline and Michael, lived in one of the large barrack rooms with twenty families to a room. A blanket and piece of rope was all they had for privacy. It did have good bathing nearby and grand views across Dragonara Palace and northwards along the coast to Comino and Gozo. Some families took comfort in the communal lifestyle as a fair imitation of the pleasant homes and domestic atmosphere they had relinquished on account of the war. While Michael Longyear loved the excitement of the new location and its surrounds with the opportunities to swim and explore nearby caves, many parents, including his, were not at all happy. Soon the Longyears rented a large house in Pietà, sharing it with another service family, the Kings, who had two daughters.

There were a few new civilian arrivals. One was Sybil Dobbie, the daughter of Sir William Dobbie. She travelled from Singapore to work as her father's secretary, the last part of her journey from Egypt on board an armed merchant ship, the SS *Lanarkshire*. It arrived on 11 October 1940. 'I was told we were going into the Grand Harbour of Valletta, and presently through the drizzle and mist I could begin to trace towers and bastions, rising steeply up from the waterside, looking in the uncertain light almost like a cloud city. Then I became aware, as we reached the narrow entrance, that the sea walls and moles and quays were black with people who waved and cheered as we came in.

'It was my first contact with the Maltese and I like to think of them as I first saw them, standing patiently in the rain, regardless of possible raids, cheering the British ships that had broken the blockade to bring them food, petrol and ammunition. When they saw three women on board our ship they gave us an extra cheer. So many English women had left the island and so few had been able to come in, that they gave us a most heartening welcome, and as I stood waving and kissing my hand to the crowds I felt my heart warm to the island and its people.'

Wing Commander Jonah Jonas spent an anxious few hours waiting for the *Lanarkshire* to dock. One of its few passengers was his wife Gina whom he had left in Egypt three months earlier. 'What the hell are they waiting for?' he repeatedly asked himself as he caught occasional glimpses between the rain storms and low clouds of the apparently stationary ships about two miles beyond the breakwater. But at least the poor weather kept the bombers away. 'And then, almost unexpectedly after the hours of waiting, the tall bow of the *Lanarkshire* loomed out of the gloom - towering high above the little sodden group clustered on the wharf; then I saw Gina, aloof and laughing, and I waved a damp hand self-consciously in her direction.'

For the Parisio Palace residents now enjoying a greater degree of freedom 'the great events of the season were the concert parties given by the Whizz-Bangs who had an unlimited supply of *joie de vivre* and the knack of putting it over.'

On one occasion Tamara and about a dozen of the other RAF wives headed off to RAF Kalafrana to attend one of the Whizz-Bangs shows being performed at the Sergeants' Mess. They all enjoyed the performance even though there were 'scenes and jokes at which no lady should have laughed and yet, although there is not a more prim and proper person than the serviceman's wife, we all laughed uproariously and slyly remembered some of them for future airing.'

With the Sergeants' Mess well known for its hospitality, they had all been looking forward to a lavish tea afterwards. On this occasion Tamara had a particular reason for wanting the show to end as she had learnt of the arrival of the two Free French airmen from Bizerta and she was dying to meet them. She spotted them as soon as she entered the Mess. Despite their RAF uniforms, Tamara thought they would have been unmistakably French anywhere.

'Both spoke only French. I was in my element. I studied them covertly while sipping my tea. Jacques was busy with Gallic gesticulations explaining something to Christina Ratcliffe, the star of the Whizz-Bangs show, a striking blonde. He was of medium height and looked very young. How could he help it? He celebrated his twentieth birthday in Malta. I looked at him intently. I could not understand how such a youth could take the terrible decision which meant complete severance from family, traditions, beloved surroundings and could come to a completely foreign land where they spoke a language he did not know. The moral courage of such youths was only surpassed by their physical courage.

'René was older, about twenty-eight, I guessed. He came and sat next to me. He had startling green eyes set wide apart, curly black hair, an aristocratic high-bridge nose, a beautifully modelled mouth and largish chin, lovely artistic hands with long tapering fingers. Time went by with lightening rapidity.' The two Frenchmen, and especially René, had made quite an impression on Tamara.

They impacted similarly on Christina. She too commented on René's great green eyes and brilliant smile. 'Jacques was much younger, a lightly built youth with light brown hair and grey eyes. His pale face was drawn and wore a most solemn expression. After we had exchanged a few words in French, Jacques sat down beside me, apparently pleased with the opportunity to converse in his own language. A few minutes later, René joined us with an RAF officer and a very attractive girl whom I had noticed in the audience during the show. The couple were *le ménage de Marks* - Ronnie Marks, a squadron leader and his Yugoslavian-born wife, Tamara. Tamara spoke perfect English and French and I learned later that she knew four other languages almost as well.'

The girls listened avidly to the Frenchmen's story. Despite the establishment of the puppet Vichy government, not all Frenchmen accepted defeat. Some chose to fight as members of the French Underground while others escaped from France and her former colonies and joined the growing ranks of the Free French. René and Jacques were typical of the latter.

René was a pilot and Jacques a wireless operator/air gunner. When France collapsed, they were stationed in Tunisia where René's single-engine floatplane had been lying without fuel in Bizerta Bay. The signing of the Franco/German Armistice came as a blow as René was in favour of continuing the fight. Very few officers supported the idea, preferring to lay down their arms and wait, no one knew for what. This lack of action with hangars full of aircraft, but with little fuel, was more than many could bear, but the majority, married and accompanied by wives and children, feared reprisals on their families. Isolated escapes had a chance but mass escapes without a leader and good plan risked bloodshed. Very few were prepared to take the risk.

Getting sufficient fuel for his aircraft was far from easy, but René succeeded in gaining the support of a few trustworthy and enthusiastic friends. Eventually they were able to half-fill the tanks of the small seaplane. The nearest British territory was Malta but René was none too sure of their likely reception. He elected to take Jacques with him as he was the only member of their group who was unmarried. Under the cover of darkness, they climbed into the cockpit and took off at 8.00 pm one evening. The guns immediately opened fire and a stream of tracer lit up the night sky. René believed they were purposely aimed wide. They had been lucky but would their luck hold? With no one in Malta aware they were on their way, and no way of contacting Malta's defences, would the British open fire?

At 10.00 pm they sighted Malta. They were tired and anxious, having heard the island's anti-aircraft guns were second to none. Jacques signalled the word F-R-A-N-C-E. They were quickly caught in the searchlights but the guns remained silent. After landing they clambered out of their aircraft covered with oil as a pipe had burst. They were wearing shorts and shirts and no flying gear as they had had to walk nonchalantly to their aircraft so as not to arouse suspicion.

In Malta they were welcomed with open arms. Following a trade test, René was given the rank of sergeant in the RAF, although he had been a warrant officer in France. He was soon promoted to flight sergeant. René and Jacques were stationed at Kalafrana flying their aircraft on reconnaissance missions but they hoped the RAF would soon give them a better aircraft as the *Latécoère's* performance was inferior to that of all the Italian fighters. He later told Tamara: 'It is a good little ship but I do not like being the rabbit every time.'

After the Whizz-Bangs performance at Hal Far, as the Parisio Palace ladies made their way back to Naxxar, they were forced to stop in Lija, arriving in the middle of an open-air church service: 'The villagers, men, women and children were all kneeling on their doorsteps, while a black-robed priest read the litanies in the middle of the street. Ever since the entry of Italy into the war, it was a common sight for villagers to assemble in the evening and have half an hour or so of communal praying. They did not go to the church as the exits usually were small; if a raid started (and they all wanted to get out in a hurry) jams occurred and people were hurt. So, they stayed on their doorsteps, grabbed blankets, stools and children and plunged into the nearest shelter where the litanies were continued, the lead often being given by a layman, the padre having been mislaid in the rush.'

Soon afterwards Tamara was admitted to Mtarfa hospital for a pre-planned minor operation. She had asked René at their first meeting to visit her in ten days' time when she was convalescing. 'He interested me very much. I wanted to know how one could take such a tremendous resolution and carry it out to its successful conclusion. He promised to come and see me.'

René visited three times, the second visit being unexpected a day earlier than arranged, for which he apologised. 'But he said that he was going with Jacques on a secret mission that night. He might not return and asked me as a favour, when the war was over, to return his diary to his mother and tell her that his last thoughts had been for her. He handed me twenty pounds to meet the expense of the journey. I promised to do what he asked, tried to laugh him out of his pessimistic mood and made him promise to come and see me when he returned safely.' The following afternoon, he returned and presented Tamara with an enormous bunch of flowers, as a thanksgiving he said. 'After that René and I became firm friends. We had so very much in common. Our education had been the same; we both had the same propensity for talking our heads off and about nothing and everything. After we finished chattering, the world was a better place to live in, in theory. Besides, there were few people in Malta who spoke fluent French.'

After her stay at Mtarfa, Tamara stayed with her husband for a week at the Riviera Hotel, Ghajn Tuffieha. They never felt threatened even though enemy aircraft frequently passed nearby. With an army rest camp half a mile away, the hotel bar was lively and most evenings, raid or no raid, Tamara and Ronnie danced in the moonlight on the open air terrace.

So far, damage to property was slight and there were relatively few casualties. Also air raid shelters were being built everywhere; eventually there would be one on every street corner. With her husband now posted to Luqa, Tamara decided not to return to Naxxar. She moved into the Metropole Hotel in Sliema while looking for a flat to share with Ronnie in Floriana or Valletta.

'The food at the Metropole was amazingly good. After three months of war, no rationing of any kind had been introduced yet. The room we were shown was large and sunny, the sea about fifty yards away. One bathed off the rocks. Undressing was easy; one just slipped one's frock off and appeared in a bathing suit. Dressing was a bit trickier; one had to look as unconcerned as possible and hope that no one was looking. I lazed in the sun all-day reading, writing and getting as red as a boiled prawn. I could never acquire that lovely tan I admired so much in others; wrong pigmentation or something. It was never too uncomfortably hot,

Malta being blessed with a wonderful breeze which keeps the temperature even and prevents sultriness.

'Finding an apartment in Valletta was well-nigh impossible. After exhaustive enquiries, I was lucky in securing a third floor furnished apartment at the corner of *Pietro Floriani* Street and *Piazza Miratore* (Gunlayer Square). It had two bedrooms, dining-room, entrance hall, kitchen and bathroom, a covered veranda running all round the house and a beautiful view of Grand Harbour with Senglea and St Angelo in the background. There were three shelters only a few yards away. One, under the Salvation Army building, was mostly used by the servicemen on leave in the hostel and later, when enlarged, by a limited number of families. It was a private shelter, the cost of its excavation having been borne by Salvation Army funds. At the next corner there was a public shelter, but very often with standing room only. The third one was the cellar of Vincenti Buildings.' It was the latter that Ronnie and Tamara most often used.

Near neighbours were Jonah and Gina Jonas. They too used the same air raid shelter. Jonah described their home as 'being in a lovely position. For only a narrow strip of public gardens separated the building from the blue waters of the Grand Harbour itself; while from many of the numerous windows and balconies which it possessed, a delectable view was obtained of the whole harbour, with its entrance through the breakwaters to the open sea. Immediately opposite the flat, on the far side of the harbour, lay the dockyard with its sheltering creeks, its cranes and its busy bustling tugs and picket boats. And beyond the steep cliffs, which rose precipitously at the back of the dockyard, were the fairy-like jumble of houses and roofs and domes belonging to the three cities of Vittoriosa, Senglea and Cospicua. By leaning far out over the stone balustrades toward the narrow head of the harbour away to the right, one was even able to catch a glimpse of Luqa aerodrome.'

Tamara was very pleased with her apartment, which had a telephone, hot water in the bathroom, and the kitchen had a brand new gas stove. 'This was an enormous improvement, as in Birzebbugia I had to do all my cooking on a Primus stove and a three-burner kerosene stove which was one of the most temperamental ever made. Baking was carried out in the most primitive fashion. The oven, in the shape of a beehive with a hinged door, was made of thin sheet iron. It had one shelf inside and a round hole in the bottom. The contraption rested on a four-legged iron trestle. The primus was used for quick roasting and the stove for finishing off. The stoves, one at a time, were placed under the trestle and fitted in the hole. Many housewives used their apology for an oven very successfully; I was an utter failure. The second time I tried it, the stove, for some reason or other, decided to smoke. I went out shopping and left it unattended as it was the maid's day out. I returned to find the apartment full of black greasy soot, which hung in lumps from curtain rods, the curtains and the picture frames. I never used it again. I knew when I was beaten. My husband found a maid, the sister of one of the Maltese who worked at his station, very thorough and spotlessly clean, like most Maltese and with their partiality for padding barefoot around the house.

'By then rationing of such things as sugar, tea, milk, butter, lard and soap had come into force. Service people could get their supplies of either at the NAAFI. There were such extra things as rice, spaghetti, tomato paste and salad oil. The staple food of the great majority of the Maltese, besides macaroni, was bread spread with oil and tomato paste. At 4.00 pm, after school hours, it was usual to see children with great big chunks of this mixture in their hands fairly smacking their lips over it. It made one's mouth water.'

Christina had also decided to move home. During the autumn she relocated to a top floor apartment in Vincenti Buildings at the other end of Floriana. This put her just around the corner from Tamara's new home. 'Overlooking Grand Harbour, and the approaches to Valletta, the flat commanded what was possibly the finest view in Malta. The panorama took in at the left the still uncompleted Phoenicia Hotel and across the way the statue of Christ the King towering majestically at the top of a palm-lined avenue. The imposing pile of St John's Cavalier rising above Hastings Gardens, the old, narrow gateway to Valletta, with niches on either side, holding statues of L'Isle Adam, the first Grand Master of the Knights of St John to land in Malta and Jean de la Valette, founder of the city; St James' Cavalier, its ancient walls embracing a modern NAAFI shop and at its side the Vernon Club, a Services' hostel for other ranks. The War Memorial to the dead of the First World War and to its right St James' Counterguard with its picturesque turret and battlements. In the immediate foreground was King George V Merchant Seaman's Memorial Hospital, better known as the KGV and beyond were the Barracca Gardens and the Lift, its dizzy heights an irresistible lure to many a would-be-suicide. The bastions of Lascaris and the Customs House were also in the picture.

'On view to the right were Fort Ricasoli, the Rinella Wireless Station, the naval Bighi Hospital, Fort St Angelo and seemingly only a stone's through away from my balcony the Three Cities - Vittoriosa, Cospicua and Senglea.

'At the top centre and dominating the whole scene was the *Castille*, former *Auberge* of the Knights of *Castille* and Portugal, the roof of which was being used by a signals unit. It was by the flags hoisted high above the *Castille* that we knew what to expect when the air raid sirens sounded, a red flag indicating the approach of enemy bombers, a red and white chequered one, fighter aircraft only.'

One of Christina's two balconies overlooked, in part, George V Gardens facing the Three Cities. The only disadvantage of her idyllic location was the climb of eighty-eight stairs. It was also a very long way down, especially in a hurry. Like Tamara's apartment, it was also very close to Grand Harbour, a key military target. Nearby was the Engine Room Artificers Club, known as the ERA Club, also on Vilhena Terrace. Before the war, club membership was strictly limited, but now it was open to all service personnel, irrespective of rank, as well as their guests. It served meals and was very popular, the Wednesday and Sunday dances being particularly well attended. Tamara and Ronnie were also regulars: 'I don't know where so many girls came from. At any other dances the percentage of men to women was about five to one but at ERA's everyone seemed to have a partner to himself. We had all the latest tunes and dances from England, although no convoy had come in for a long time. But then trust the navy, the nimblest men on their feet. Such dances as the *Lambeth Walk*, *Boomps-a-Daisy* and *Knees up, Mother Brown* were in great favour and I have never seen *Under the Spreading Chestnut Tree* danced more correctly than in Malta.

'It is true that it would get rather stuffy dancing with all the windows shut and the curtains drawn because of the blackout, but we were happy though perspiring. If an air raid started in the middle of a dance, we used to go to the Vincenti shelter, which was the nearest one and wait until it was over. Bolder spirits however ordered three drinks at a go as the bar shut and stayed where they were. The drummer and pianist always remained behind playing for all they were worth.' It was at the club one Wednesday in October, that Ronnie and Tamara met René and Jacques again. They were with Christina.

Jacques took a keen interest in the Whizz-Bangs, often accompanying them to help out back-stage. He and Christina became great friends. Even though Christina was six years older and initially described Jacques as a youth, friends were firmly of the view they fell in love. Perhaps falling in love in a siege was all too easy. Sadly for many, it was also short-lived.

Christina said: 'And so life continued. Everything considered it was not such a bad war after all. We still had plenty to eat. There were entrances to air raid shelters in almost every street. Our defences dealt effectively with the enemy bombers and no great havoc resulted. There seemed very little to worry about. Morale and spirits were very high in that autumn of 1940.'

Life for Christina and Tamara and their friends must have verged on the surreal. They were all stranded on an island at war and under siege. Bombing was regular but, so far, could hardly be described as intense. Targeting, as far as it went, was focused on the airfields and the docks, although inevitably the built-up areas of the Three Cities suffered given their proximity to the dockyards. While the air raids were frequent, Malta was full of young men in the prime of their lives, all eager for whatever relaxation and entertainment they could find in whatever off duty hours they could snatch. The Whizz-Bangs provided a perfect boost for morale and the former cabaret performers worked tirelessly doing essentially what they loved, staging five or six shows each week with rehearsals in between. They had guaranteed and appreciative audiences and were well-hosted after their shows. Despite the harsh reality of war, maybe put on hold for a few hours now and again, the boys and girls of the Whizz-Bangs led active social lives that were usually full of fun. Who could blame them for living life as best they could, while they could?

Victor and Mary Longyear, daughters Pam and Pauline, and their youngest son Michael, were by then well-established in their shared home at 75 Guardamangia Hill in Pietà. It was at the top of the hill close to St Luke's Hospital overlooking Manoel Island, with a clear view of Valletta, which was within easy walking distance. A green-painted veranda ran the length of the house which overlooked their walled garden, with Marsamxett Harbour beyond, then Tigné Point and the sea. The garden included a large almond tree, orange, lemon and vine trees and a grape vine. Despite the exotic plants, Michael and his friends preferred to 'scrump' spring onions from the next door garden which boasted its own well in the garden.

Schooling for Michael and Pauline was arranged in a convent school in Valletta, but they spent a lot of time in a deep shelter carved out of the limestone rock. School lunches were in the restaurant on the first floor of the Wembley Store opposite the Opera House. Michael and Pauline often spent their lunch breaks in the Upper Barracca Gardens, next to the Barracca Lift. If an air raid warning occurred when having lunch they never went straight to the shelter - they always finished their food first.

The air raids hadn't bothered Michael at all and he and his friends continued to enjoy the same activities they had taken part in previously. They went into Valletta with few worries: 'There was a blackout imposed almost immediately. I remember well, going into Valletta with my sister in the evening, she carrying a torch which was suddenly painted with a deep blue lacquer by somebody who came out of the dark as we entered the *Porta Reale*. It was some chap who was either employed or took it upon himself to carry this out. The torch shed so little light that it was virtually useless. He put his life at risk by leaping in front of cars and bicycles to paint their headlights, with a similar result.' Michael had seen at first hand the work of one of the locally recruited Special Constables.

The Battle of Britain officially ended in October and the prospect of invasion of Britain receded. Now was the time for Malta's tiny fighter force to be strengthened, perhaps with Spitfires, but no. Hitler later cancelled plans to invade Britain. He turned his eyes east. One consequence of his change of focus was soon apparent in the Mediterranean. The *Luftwaffe* no longer needed a very well-equipped *Fliegerkorps* X in Norway and Denmark. Where else could this highly experienced air group be used to best effect? In North Africa, outnumbered British and Commonwealth troops slowly withdrew ahead of an advancing immense Italian army. But then the Royal Navy struck out, the Fleet Air Arm enjoying a spectacular success on the night of 11 November 1940, devastating the powerful Italian battle fleet at Taranto in Italy.

In November, René and Jacques were posted to No 431 (General Reconnaissance) Flight at Luqa. This small flight operated American-built Glenn Martin Maryland aircraft, originally destined for France, but taken over by the RAF and led out to Malta by an Australian nicknamed 'Tich' - Tich Whiteley. The *Latécoère* was taken out of service and René and Jacques found themselves flying the Maryland.

THE WHIZZ-BANGS

During the last few months of 1940, air raids continued spasmodically. There were two or three every fortnight, with slight casualties and damage, and then none for a week. Tamara and a friend attended a two-month First Aid and Home Nursing course, becoming qualified as Voluntary Aid Detachment nurses. 'To celebrate the successful end of the course, Mrs Ray, the Commandant, gave a tea party in the garden of her home in St Julian's Bay. In the middle of it, an air raid started; the Spinola anti-aircraft guns opened up with a terrific din making conversation impossible. The garden was enclosed by high rock walls, which were honeycombed with large holes. Shrapnel having started to fall like rain, we each took shelter in one of those niches. It looked like a new version of the statue game.'

After a couple of weeks Tamara was appointed to the Floriana Medical Inspection Room. 'The first day we wore our VAD uniforms, beautifully starched, the head-dress correctly pinned in butterfly fashion and the black St John's Cross prominently displayed, we were oozing keenness and pride. Our patients were mostly Maltese labourers working on the camp as cooks, stone masons, or shelter excavators, but we had soldiers in as well. Most of them suffered from big ugly boils, which it was our duty to prepare for lancing. Later we were allowed to lance and drain them ourselves. We dispensed medicine, syringed ears and bandaged limbs with great enthusiasm. After closing hours we were given long lectures by the orderlies on how to treat the patients. "Treat 'em rough, see, not the way you go about it," and then, mimicking us:

"Sit down here. Is the poultice too hot? Does it hurt? You poor man."

"Blimey, we'll have the whole blooming lot of 'em here every day, treating them the way you do."'

Tamara stopped going to the shelter in daylight and only rarely went at night. She and her husband and friends held the Italian prowess as fighters and bombing experts in utter contempt: 'They very seldom gave fight; three quarters of the time their bombers failed to cross the coast, or their bombs fell in the sea. Greatly appreciated was the joke of the Italian bomber pilot, who returned to his base in Italy with his bombs still in their racks because, as he said himself: "I could not very well drop them, the raid was over - the All Clear had gone." It was a good war.'

The *Regia Aeronautica* was held in contempt by many civilians. Their attitude may have been encouraged by the authorities. But RAF pilots knew better; and so did many within the Royal Navy and the Merchant Marine. Italian pilots were skilled and able and they demonstrated their courage often when in combat against their RAF counterparts who held them in high regard. Italian bomber crews were equally skilled and when targeting Allied shipping they pressed home their attacks with great courage and accuracy. Yet against targets on Malta itself, their attacks seemed less precise. Why was that? Did they not share their leader's willingness to bomb their former friends and Catholic neighbours?

René and Jacques now had an English observer, George Taylor, and they enjoyed their work flying the Maryland. But reconnaissance is a highly dangerous game and Tamara greatly feared for the safety of their young French airmen knowing they 'depended upon René's skill of manoeuvrability to get them out of many a tough spot. Jacques only laughed at our concern, apparently enjoying the excitement and risk involved in the operations. He never spoke to me of his own gallant deeds over enemy territory, but he was full of the dare-devil exploits of his companions in the flight, one of whom he held in particularly high esteem. *"Il est absolument magnifique. Formidable,"* he would say, his eyes shining.

'One day he told me how this pilot, in order to get really clear pictures of an Italian battleship in Taranto harbour, had dived down to within fifty feet of the decks, taken his photographs amid the flak of anti-aircraft gunfire and then made off for home chased by a heavy formation of fighters. On another occasion he was again flying over Taranto harbour when an engine cut out, however, he completed his mission and managed to get back to Malta; his photographs proving to be of the utmost value.

'Another time Jacques laughed *"comme il est bête"*, and I was given an account of how one night this devil-may-care comrade of his, an old blue raincoat covering his officer's uniform, had made a bar-to-bar reconnaissance of the Gut, finishing up *trop saoul* to get back to camp. Jacques's friend appeared to be intrepid and death defying, fearless in the face of the enemy, mad as a hatter.' Tamara thought René was in his element flying the Maryland. 'He was as pleased as a dog with two tails because, as he explained to me: "A plane is like a horse, it must answer to your smallest whim and this one is a thoroughbred and a thoroughbred will never let you down"'.

Tamara asked others about the Maryland as she thought René's enthusiasm made him biased. Most thought it a good aircraft, although there was room for improvement. René made light of their views. After he came back with an engine on fire, Tamara was never again happy when he was flying. She had become very fond of the Frenchman; perhaps she even allowed herself to fall a little in love with him.

'He was known as a reckless pilot; he deemed it a disgrace ever to turn back without bringing the information he had gone out for. "It is like a glorious game of hide and seek," he would say. "I have to fly very steady and low over the target to take good photographs. I can see the gunners below waiting for me, cocking their guns, firing. The flaming onions, revolving on themselves, come up slowly, slowly. One almost feels like putting one's hand out and pushing them out of the way. They take their time. They know where they are going to hit. Nothing can stop or deflect their course now. They explode at the spot where I was only a few seconds ago. More come up. But they are always too high or too low, too much forward or too far behind me. It is a battle of wits. I put myself in the gunner's place and fool him every time. Besides, these Eyeties are too temperamental. They would much rather fire first and calculate afterwards."

'He had a different tale to tell when the Germans took over. Their tactics, then new, of the "wall of fire" had nothing temperamental or happy-go-lucky about it. René explained it to me. This is how I understood it worked: at a calculated area a certain number of guns would fire at the same time, each one at its respective point, making thus a square of solid fire.' Jonah Jonas described René and Jacques as 'a grand pair' who carried out innumerable reconnaissance missions to Sicily and North Africa.

In mid-November three merchant ships delivered troops and cargo. Following victory at Taranto there was growing confidence, although Malta's anti-aircraft guns and fighter strength were still inadequate. There was also reassuring news from the Western Desert where the Italians were expelled from Egypt with 30,000 of their number taken prisoner. By then, Mussolini had prodded his unprepared army to move against Greece. Britain offered support to Greece and inevitably that came from Egypt. Reinforcements earmarked for Malta were also diverted. A second operation to deliver Hurricanes took place in November. By then only four serviceable Hurricanes and one Gladiator were left on the island. The operation was a disaster with only five making it, nine others being lost having run out of fuel. Only one pilot out of the nine was rescued.

There were some privations on the island, but food and drink was available, even alcohol if one knew where to get it. Rationing was not severe and the shops were still full of good things to eat and there was still a large range of attractive items on sale at low prices. Transport was scarce but there were dances, concert parties and even a flourishing amateur dramatic society. Ladies were sometimes seen wearing evening dresses escorted by officers dressed in Mess kit.

The Parisio Palace finally shut its doors with the inhabitants having either been evacuated or, like Tamara, moved elsewhere. As for the many children on the island, they didn't worry about the war at all, doing much as they had done previously and still attending school. The blackout was something of a limitation, but it was almost as if the 211 air raids between June and the end of December were something of an irritation that could be lived with.

With the curfew lifted by December, the cinemas re-opened, but the highly successful Whizz-Bangs remained the only live entertainment on the island and as popular as ever. They hit on the idea of putting together an English pantomime and the manager of the Manoel Theatre in Valletta agreed to host the production. 'This was to be our third production and we intended to take the pantomime on the road afterwards. When Chris announced that *Cinderella* had been chosen as the pantomime, my thoughts went back to the little backyard affair in Dukinfield many years ago. But this time I was not to be an Ugly Sister. "With your long blonde hair," Chris had said, "you shall be *Cinderella*." The obvious choice for the Ugly Sisters was of course Chris and "Vicki" themselves.

'The Manoel was an ideal theatre for our show. Although at the time it was being used as a cinema, it was originally an opera house and reputed to be one of the oldest still in existence in Europe. It was built in 1731 at the command of the Portuguese Grand Master, Antonio Manoel de Vilhena, famed also for his town planning of Floriana. The stage was large, the acoustics perfect and the seating accommodation for over seven hundred provided by stalls, tier upon tier of ornate boxes and a sky-high balcony.

'The number of dressing rooms allowed us to spread ourselves out in comfort. Quite a luxury compared with some of the places we had visited. At many of the smaller units dressing rooms were non-existent and we had to manage as best we could at the back of our portable stage. At a camp in Boschetto Gardens, described as "a paradise of greenery beyond Rabat", we gave *al fresco* entertainment in true concert party style. Here we made up and changed into our costumes among the tangerine and lemon trees, hidden from our public by army blankets suspended from the branches. On one gun-site, cramped conditions compelled us to cast respectability aside and the entire company dressed and undressed in the Whizz-Bang's bus. But as Bobby Vernon said as he struggled into the frilly underskirts of his Can-Can costume: "Och, why worry, we're all girls together."

The Manoel Theatre, Valletta. *(Paul McDonald)*

'Cinderella went down very well with the Maltese people, few of whom having seen an English pantomime before. Scenery was scant but we managed to construct a woodland glade with plants and ornamental shrubs hired from a Hamrun nurseryman, helped out with what tree branches we could purloin from public places when nobody was looking. The least of our worries was the pumpkin, hundreds of which could be seen out in the country ripening on the flat-roofs of farmhouses. An out-of-service *karozzin* lent to us by its philanthropic owner provided an excellent fairy coach.'

'Chris and "Vicki", as the Ugly Sisters, kept the audience in stitches. Terry Blair was Buttons and Rita Moya made an admirable Prince Charming with her shapely legs and the ability to sing as well as dance. The ballroom crowd was made up of youngsters from the dancing school, one of whom was little Shephard, daughter of the Provost Marshal, very thrilled at making her stage debut in pantomime.

'Marigold held the audience spellbound as she transformed from an ugly old crone into a beautiful fairy and her ballet dance was given a great ovation. The applause was ringing out as "Vicki", the Phantom of Delight, drifted onto the stage wearing a replica of Marigold's lovely dress of white satin and tulle, his magic wand - a converted fishing rod - topped by an enormous silver star, He was perfect except for his feet, which were encased in the largest pair of football boots I have ever seen.

'When the screams of laughter had subsided, "Vicki" sang a verse and chorus of his celebrated *No One Loves a Fairy When She's Fo*rty (a specially laundered version for the Manoel) and went into his dance. And how that boy could dance! In those boots it was nothing short of miraculous. Yet he leapt airily and fairily from one end of the stage to the other, finishing the number with a series of *fouettes* worthy of Pavlova at the height of her career.'

Cinderella ran until May 1941.

Chapter 5

Heartbreak

Christmas 1940 - January 1941

Many in Malta enjoyed a happy Christmas in 1940. Tamara had been looking forward to it a great deal: 'Wembley's, one of the largest grocery stores in Valletta, was full of lovely sun-ripened, fat, glossy raisins and currants, flour gleaming white, luscious mincemeat that almost tempted one to eat it straight out of the jars; nuts and oranges for the baking. We had saved as much of our sugar ration as we could. I voted for a duck, two chickens and a three-pound piece of pork with pink flesh and nice firm fat. Maltese pork compares - to its advantage - with any I have eaten elsewhere. Chemists displayed a great variety of English and French made potpourri jars, which is one of my favourite presents for people. It looked as if it was going to be a very successful Christmas. My husband took the drink problem in hand and solved it excellently too.

'On Christmas day, friends started to arrive by 11.00 am. It was an old established custom to always have the "unattached men" - or men whose wives were in England, to call in for a drink at every house and as there were still a few families left in Malta, it was best to start early. The apartment looked very festive with paper decorations and holly and a big bunch of mistletoe hanging in the hall. The drawing-room had a large, white marble fireplace and a cheerful fire burned in it. We had a few friends in to lunch. The duck and the pork were found excellent and justice was done to the wine. For coffee we retired to the drawing-room. Mellow conversation flowed easily. Belts were let out a few notches, limbs relaxed. Two air raids passed as unnoticed as if they had never started. No one did them the honour of so much as mentioning them. Tea was mostly drinks. A special dance was featured at ERA's, so towards nine o'clock we all trooped there. The dance was in full swing when we arrived and everyone was in high spirits; Christmas 1940, goodwill towards all men! We had dined well, wined well and it looked as if we were going to have great fun. Most of the pilots and aircrews who had become such dear friends were there. It was almost like peacetime again.'

Christina was one of Ronnie and Tamara's many guests. 'They were splendid hosts and spared no effort to make things go with a swing. There was an abundance of food and drink and their flat lacked nothing in the way of decorations, an illuminated tree, balloons and streamers, holly and mistletoe combining with the great red poinsettias of the season to make a truly festive scene. René and Jacques were among the guests and they were deeply grateful for the hospitality showered upon them by *le ménage de Marks*. Away from their loved ones, alone in a strange land, they shrugged off their homesickness with a philosophical *c'est la guerre* and enthusiastically joined the rest of us in the fun and games.' Life was almost normal - apart that is from almost daily air raids. Tamara gave Christina a potpourri jar for Christmas and its undying fragrance would provide her with 'a poignant reminder of the Christmas spent in the company of those two brave French boys.' But the war was never far away.

A number of other Free Frenchmen escaped from Tunisia and made their way to Malta. Some brought their own aircraft; some were lost in the attempt. The French colony on Malta grew significantly with the arrival of the Free French submarine *Narval* with its crew of forty. Between Christmas and New Year, the submarine failed to return from patrol. 'René and I, who knew most of the crew, especially Jean Bouet and Fred Larocque, used to go and sit for hours on the rocks facing the submarine pens. We would see it gliding softly in, looking shiny and black like a sea-lion. For a whole week we hoped in vain.'

René was something of an artist, sensitive too, and he rented a small flat in Valletta to which, Tamara said, he could escape from the boisterous surrounds of the Sergeants' Mess. He had begun a drawing of Tamara. 'When the news of the "presumed lost" *Narval* was given by the BBC, two tears fell on my hands. It was the first time I had seen a man cry. It wrung my heart because I could not help. I tried to comfort him with the "maybe's" used in such circumstances but unfortunately neither of us believed them.'

Wing Commander Jonah Jonas recalled the grand ball held at the Union Club on New Year's Eve: 'What a lovely dance that was, the war forgotten for an evening, among friends, an exquisite panorama of colour and movement beneath the priceless painted ceiling of the *Auberge de Provence*.

'A few minutes before midnight we linked hands singing the familiar words of *Auld Lang Syne*. Slowly, the hands moved across the clock face. Soon the old year would be gone. Standing there singing that old, old sentimental song, I thought of the past few months, of how war had come to Malta. And of the sorrow and the tragedy that had come, too. Of the bravery and the courage; and of all those who had died for the cause in which we believed.

'Now only thirty seconds remained. I asked myself what the New Year would bring. Who could answer such a question? Perhaps there would be more sorrow, more courage and more death? Perhaps it would bring peace?

Then the twelve strokes of midnight struck out. The lights were dimmed for a moment, and someone kissed me on the lips. A new year had begun.'

Not long after the New Year festivities, a pale and agitated Jacques arrived unexpectedly at Christina's flat. He had only a few minutes before returning to Luqa to prepare for another mission. 'He warned me that from now onwards I must take cover immediately the air raid warning sounded. He could not tell me why. The information he had was Top Secret, not even to be shared with me. He looked into my eyes. "Promise, Cherie", he pleaded. His own eyes were tired and strained. To please him I promised.'

By the end of 1940, the RAF fighter strength in Malta was still pitifully small. With ground defences inadequate, a more resolute opponent could have invaded with the gravest of consequences. Instead Mussolini sought to satisfy his territorial ambitions by focusing on Greece. Nevertheless, Malta had defended herself against superior forces with great determination. Following constant prodding by an ever-aggressive Churchill, the RAF was directed to provide Malta with sufficient air power to maintain its defence and also take every opportunity to use the island as a base for attack. By then, Hitler's gaze had fallen on the island and he sent *Fliegerkorps X* to Sicily and Southern Italy in the final weeks of the year. It was the arrival of this formidable force which worried Jacques.

The RAF's reconnaissance Marylands had first spotted the build-up of *Junkers* 88 bombers and *Junkers* 52 troop carriers on Catania and Comiso airfields in Sicily. As Jonah Jonas recalled: 'The following day there were more, and by the end of the first week in January a young, fair-haired Maryland pilot announced to a wide-eyed collection of officers in the mess, "that every aerodrome in Sicily seemed to be stiff with the bloody things". And after further questioning I learnt later that the word "things" included, besides *Junkers* 88s and 52s, *Dornier* and *Heinkel* bombers, *Junkers* 87 dive bombers and *Messerschmitt* fighters. And the final conclusion reached in the mess by that time appeared to be - "that we are in for a party all right this time, chaps"; while the remainder of the civilian population, both English and Maltese, informed one another in confidential undertones, with much nodding of heads and knowing looks, that - "the Germans were in Sicily".'

The first Malta-bound convoy of 1941 delivered cargo, twelve crated Hurricanes and a number of anti-aircraft guns, but it came at a cost: one cruiser sunk, another cruiser and a destroyer damaged. Most serious of all, the aircraft carrier HMS *Illustrious* was terribly mauled. Although she made Grand Harbour, the crew suffered one hundred and twenty-six killed and ninety-one wounded. All night long the injured were carried off the stricken vessel. There was considerable doubt as to whether she could be made seaworthy to attempt the long run to Alexandria. More importantly, would the *Luftwaffe* give the Royal Navy and the shipyard workers sufficient time to try?

Earlier that evening, Jonah and Gina Jonas, like many others including Christina, watched *Illustrious* being slowly brought into Grand Harbour to cheering and the strains of *Roll out the Barrel*. The carrier, down by the stern and listing badly, was berthed only yards from their respective flats. Christina saw that in the wake of *Illustrious*, being towed by another ship, 'came the very destroyer that had carried me away from the horrors of the Spanish Civil War, HMS *Gallant*. Her bow blown away by a mine at sea, she was now little more than a pitiful wreck but living up to her name she struggled gallantly on and succeeded like the carrier in reaching port.' HMS *Gallant* lost sixty killed and a further twenty-five wounded. She had sailed her last voyage.

The day after HMS *Illustrious* entered Grand Harbour, 11 January 1941, Tamara went as planned for a sitting at René's flat at 4.00 pm, but he did not arrive at the appointed time. Tamara waited until about 6.00 pm. 'I had no misgivings. I thought he had left Luqa late on his flight and was not back yet, although I knew that he had been scheduled to take off in the morning, but then their instructions often changed at the very last minute. Or maybe he was standing by. Anyway it was not the first time that I had waited in vain. In those cases he would always turn up the next time with a present. "My concrete way of showing how sorry I really am," he would say.'

'I strolled back to Floriana, which is about twenty minutes' walk from Valletta, promising myself to go and see him the next day, which was a Sunday. He would certainly be there then. They only flew every other day.' The next day, Sunday, Tamara waited another three hours without result; even René's landlady asked if she knew where he was. 'I went home feeling rather disappointed. I was having late tea on the veranda when my husband came in. I was in two minds whether to ask him news of René or not. Wouldn't asking put my fears into words and so prove there was something to dread? I did not even want to imagine that there could be anything wrong. My husband broached the subject himself.

"I suppose you have heard the news," he said.

"What news do you mean?"

"About René and Jacques; they are missing."

'Oh! But that was absurd. René simply had to come back; he had left everything behind. No one I had known so well had disappeared just like that before. I could not believe it.' A message had been received from their aircraft about shipping at Brindisi, then nothing. On Monday, there was an announcement on the Rediffusion, picked up from Italian radio:

> On the 11 January, an enemy aircraft of the bomber type was shot
> down in flames over Catania. The three occupants were dead.

'The announcer went on to talk about the weather and the crops. No fuss, no military honours, no big cortege, nothing. Three young men had died in the flower of their manhood. Their hopes and aspirations and their joy of living had been to no avail. Their contribution to a better, saner world ended. I felt stunned. Was such a thing possible? For three mothers and sweethearts the war was ended too … in defeat. Which side won or lost was immaterial now.

'Next morning I went to the studio to inform the landlady and pack up René's things. The French Consul was already there. He had also heard the tragic news. As he had everything in hand I left him to it. I still had the twenty pounds and the diary René had given me in hospital. I arranged with the consul to go and see him to hand them over to him for transmission to René's mother. I only asked for the red leather travelling clock and a life-size doll in peasant costume, which René had given me as a New Year present.

'René's death affected me more than I dared tell or show. We had believed so firmly in his lucky star. "Experience and a little luck, that is all one needs," he would say. "I have always been lucky. I started out as a matelot. Here I am a pilot, in the aircraft I have longed for and more than 900 hours flying to my credit. Do not worry. I shall come back every time."

'Remembering those words, hope started anew. Maybe they had landed somewhere and it was some other aircraft that had been shot down. Such coincidence was possible.'

By then Christina had heard the news; she was heartbroken. 'For the first time in my life I knew what it was like to grieve.' As she was the only other person in Malta who had known René and Jacques well, Tamara decided to go and see her. 'It is true that we had not been introduced properly, but I thought that under the circumstances such a small breach of convention was warranted, I rang her up and she asked me to call on her. Two of her girlfriends were already there. At the mention of my errand she burst into tears. She had been very fond of Jacques; there had even been talk of their becoming engaged. It was heartbreaking to see the racking sobs shaking her whole body. She was so slim and fair; it seemed impossible that such unutterable pain could be contained in so small a being without shattering it. With tears running down our cheeks we did our best to comfort her. Stories of men missing for months and then turning up were retold. One of the girls knew for a fact of one such case. Hope eternal hope. There it was shining again through her swollen, tear-dimmed eyes. They were alive; she knew it. Jacques had promised her he would come back always. He was too much in love with her to go away like that, without saying goodbye. He was alive, she was sure. No matter what some silly Italian announcer had said. They were forever boasting of shooting our aircraft down. And, as another instance of their lies, had they not said that they had wrecked our railway lines and completely destroyed Malta's coal mines, or was it gold mines? That was a good one.

'As everyone knew, there were neither coal mines, nor gold mines; as for the railways, the last one had stopped functioning more than ten years ago. The intelligence officer at Luqa was dismissed with a wave of the hand. She had better go and wash her face and powder her nose. What if they turned up this very moment and found her in that shocking state? Her high spirits were infectious. We started planning the rousing party we would have to celebrate their return. Christina and I decided to see lots of each other. We found a little solace in telling each other for the nth time all the little traits that had so endeared the two boys to us. She talked herself into believing that they would come back some day. The other alternative was too horrible to contemplate. She firmly refused to entertain it.'

The entry in RAF Luqa's operational readiness book for the 11 January 1941 made the situation clear: '1 Maryland (F/Sgt Duvauchelle) recce TARANTO. A/C brought down by fighter (?) near Catania - all crew killed.'

Jonah Jonas said the loss of two such brave and popular figures was regretted throughout the RAF in Malta, and particularly in the Sergeants' Mess at Luqa where they had made many friends and were admired by all.

Christina continued with the Whizz-Bangs. Earlier Jacques had urged her to stop but now she was glad she hadn't. Her work made her mix with others and forced her to look happy and cheerful and engage with others. This helped assuage her pain. Tamara had nothing for hers, which she felt deeply, but kept hidden. She sought work, which proved very hard to find. Many officers' wives were employed by the RAF as cypherines, but there were no vacancies when Tamara applied. She sought similar work with the Royal Navy at Fort St Angelo.

Meanwhile, she and Christina became firm friends; they were already close neighbours. With Ronnie, whom Christina called 'Marko', away all day at Luqa, Tamara accompanied the concert party on its travels. The Whizz-Bangs now had their own tour bus. Because of restrictions on transport, many servicemen had no prospect of ever visiting Valletta so the concert party was their only entertainment and they always made the entertainers welcome. Tamara saw for herself how hard they all worked. 'They toured the island playing at all the out of the way little posts dotted everywhere. No detachment was too small to be overlooked. Very often the audience did not amount to more than seventy or eighty people. The welcome, however, was no less wholehearted or the performance less high spirited. It is true that dressing room accommodation was of the sketchiest and proper lighting almost non-existent.

'Frequently the men and women of the party undressed and dressed in the same room, the only privacy being afforded by a moth eaten curtain hung up on a string, thus dividing the small space into two cubicles. Often it was so cold, that the make-up would not run out of the tubes. Once when there had been no dressing room provided at all, the artists undressed and made-up in the bus and waded through ankle-deep mud before getting on the stage. As they were usually scantily clad, it must have been a terrible ordeal. And yet they never broke an engagement. The show went on raid or no raid. Sometimes, if playing for an anti-aircraft battery detachment, they went to the slit trenches, the crews being recalled to their guns.

'The Whizz-Bangs worked hard but it was a good life. One could not harbour sad thoughts and pessimistic moods in such company. My husband being on duty every other night and sometimes more often, I usually had Pickles, the acrobatic dancer of the Whizz-Bangs, come and stay with me. She was unruffled in air raids and had an inexhaustible supply of interesting adventures which, with her lovely and unusual sense of humour, made most entertaining listening to. She was American by birth but had lived in England for a long time, doing all sorts of odd jobs.'

The war began in earnest for the islanders on 16 January 1941. The only surprise was the *Luftwaffe* waited so long after *Illustrious* docked. Tamara went to see Christina immediately after the sirens sounded during the late morning. Like many others, Tamara had got out of the habit of running to the shelter each time the sirens wailed, and had come to accept *Sinjal ta-l-Attakki mill-Ajru* as part of daily life. Much of her confidence, and that of others, was based on their assailants being Italian. Often their attacks never materialised and when they did, the bombers were very high and the bombing scattered, a large proportion falling into the sea. Also by then the gun defences were increasingly effective. For some reason Tamara was scared on this occasion, although she did not want to admit it. She found Christina on her landing, her sixth sense having alerted her.

Christina had heard the Germans would try and finish *Illustrious* no matter what the cost. 'On this occasion there was something sinister in the wail of the siren, a deep note of foreboding that reminded me instantly of my promise to Jacques. With HMS *Illustrious* now berthed in Grand Harbour the names of many of us might well be written on the bombs that were almost certainly to be showered on and around that sitting target. Tamara and I went below.'

When they arrived in the cellar they found Gina Jonas was already there. She confirmed what Christina had said, that the target was most likely *Illustrious*. 'More officers' wives arrived. This was not a day to stay in one's flat, they hinted darkly … and then it started.'

'The din above Grand Harbour as the battle of *Illustrious* broke out will never fade from my memory. It was the noise of an aerial Armageddon that beggar's description. As I stood there with Tamara, saying nothing, only clutching her arm just a little tighter each time a bomb exploded, I realised the significance of Jacques' warning. These were none of your Italians flying at 15,000 feet, dropping their lethal loads into the sea and making off for home before our fighters could get at them. The German *Luftwaffe* was here on business and had brought along a very fine range of samples. But Malta was a little too quick with the orders and the Germans got far more than they expected when the harbour box barrage opened up with a terrific roar. The intensity of the assault was such that when Tamara and

I emerged from the shelter we expected to find Floriana and Valletta wiped out of existence. It seemed incredible that anything could be left standing after the attack. Yet around us nothing had changed. The *Castille* was still in place, the Barracca Lift seemingly intact, the war memorial solid and straight as ever. And, by all that was wonderful, *Illustrious* stood unmoved at her berth.

'Then suddenly the streets were alive with people. Everyone started running wildly towards the ramparts of the harbour. Tamara and I joined them. It was only when we reached the bastion walls that we realised how devastating the attack had been; from where we stood we could see the terrible havoc that had been wrought upon the Three Cities. Dust was still rising in clouds from buildings that were no more and we knew that there must be hundreds of people lying beneath those piles of rubble, dead or critically injured.

'For a while we stood on the towering height, looking helplessly at the stricken scene beyond the water, each of us slowly realising that this was but a forerunner to the many perils that were to beset the island in the months ahead.'

This first raid on *Illustrious* lasted an hour, but it seemed longer. That evening in the shelter, an army officer who acted as a raid watcher described how the gunners put up a barrage through which the *Luftwaffe* had to dive. He watched as one aircraft after another peeled off, diving straight into the flak; they never came up again. Six enemy aircraft headed for Luqa, perhaps hoping the defences were focused on protecting Grand Harbour. Not one made it back to Sicily, he said.

The following day was crisp and cold, but free from air raids with the Germans scouring the Sicilian Channel in search of missing airmen. Christina and Tamara ventured out, taking the ferry from Customs House steps across to Senglea. Tamara described the heartbreaking sight: 'The destruction that greeted our eyes was appalling, boulders everywhere blocking our path, half-hanging balconies at dangerous angles. It was a problem how to get from one street to another. Mountains of rock slabs had to be climbed with danger to life and limb. One street of about fifty houses had been razed to the ground. Pitiful remnants of frocks, shoes, hats and other oddments were mixed with the rubble. A string of washing flapped dismally against the only remaining wall of a three-storied house. Dead goats seemed to be everywhere. The order forbidding itinerant goats' milk vendors had not come into force in Senglea, it seemed. Goats had been swept of the streets of Valletta and Floriana a few months previously. Before that order had been promulgated, it was nothing unusual to see herds of about twenty goats under the charge of a herdsman stopping at front doors in the busiest streets, the herdsman milking the goat straight into the purchaser's receptacle. We came away from Senglea feeling that the war had started in earnest.

'On the nineteenth, there was another raid on *Illustrious*. More than 135 aircraft came over and although they dive-bombed her, the untiring dockyard workers made her seaworthy enough to go to Alexandria under her own steam. This time the parish church of Our Lady of Victories - which had taken more than 400 years to build and decorate and was hit on the previous raid on *Illustrious*, was left a mass of ruins.' The clock had stopped at 2.20 pm in a silent reminder of the first raid; now the church was gone forever. The three ancient and picturesque cities of Vittoriosa, Senglea and Cospicua were now cities of the dead, inhabited by ghosts and memories.

The *Luftwaffe* came back the following day, and the carrier was again badly damaged. Repair work intensified. The Axis aircraft did not have everything their own way with a total of seventeen aircraft shot down, one of which was brought down by a Gladiator.

Despite the bombing, the dockyard workers and sailors laboured desperately to get *Illustrious* sufficiently seaworthy to make her escape. Their efforts paid off. She slipped her moorings as soon as it was dark on 23 January and by the following morning was well on her way to Egypt. A very battered and operationally useless ship arrived in Alexandria on 25 January. It took eleven months and the work of two dockyards in two continents before she was fit for manoeuvers once more.

In their attempts to destroy the carrier, the *Luftwaffe* mounted eight large-scale raids in eight days. They used over 500 aircraft of which they lost 61, about half each falling to the fighters and the gunners. *Illustrious* was hit twice and suffered many near misses but the area around the dockyard was reduced to a wasteland of stone and rubble with not a single building left standing.

The attacks were witnessed by Eddie Cuell whose home was less than half a mile from the action. The Cuell home was severely damaged when a bomb exploded only three houses away. They were allocated another house off Cospicua Lane, also in Casalpaola. It was even closer to the dockyard.

The Longyears experienced the raids on *Illustrious* from their home in Pietà. Even though they were a mile and a half from the barrage and bombing, it was so intense the ground was shaking. 'The vibrations were so great and lasted for so long that my father ushered us all into a narrow passage in the house for safety should the house collapse.'

From dawn on 17 January, the Three Cities were utterly deserted. After the first attack many were now wiser and no longer watched the raids from the rooftops but headed for cover in the limestone shelters. There were many casualties. While many Maltese had lost their homes, and some historic buildings were shattered beyond repair, to many the survival of the *Illustrious* and its escape to Egypt was inextricably linked to Malta's spirit. Over 3000 houses were destroyed by 220 tons of bombs dropped within an area of only a few hundred square yards. Neither Coventry nor Stalingrad saw such a weight of bombs visited upon them in so short a time. On the morning of 24 January everyone on the island heaved a collective sigh of relief, although it looked as if the Germans had come to stay. Maybe what had fallen on the Three Cities was a sign of things to come. However, two days before *Illustrious* made her escape, Commonwealth troops advanced westward through Libya and captured Tobruk. Perhaps this was a good sign.

With not a single pane of glass remaining in their apartment, Jonah and Gina Jonas decided to move to St Julians with, 'only a handful of shrapnel and the nose cap of a German bomb that we found on the roof, to remind us that we had ever resided in a "target area".'

On the evening of 24 January the ERA Club was unusually crowded. During the previous week of intense air raids many had stayed away. On that evening there was no dancing and people were content to laze in the easy chairs and chat. Christina had gone there with Ronnie and Tamara. 'Suddenly the peaceful atmosphere was shattered by an outburst of raucous singing and yells. A group of unruly young officers stampeded down the entrance steps and crashed into the room. They appeared to have been celebrating on a somewhat grandiose scale, for among the trophies collected on the way to the club was an air raid shelter signpost.

'As they stood laughing and joking at the door I noticed that all the officers, apart from one, wore naval uniform. The exception was a blond RAF flying officer, good-looking and of medium build. The next thing I knew the RAF officer was coming towards us - towards me. After a quick word with the Marks he introduced himself and then said in a quiet voice: "I'm terribly sorry, Christina, about poor old Jacques and René. They were such wonderful fellows." I was puzzled. He had called me "Christina".

"But how do you know me? And that I knew them?"

"Because Jacques was always talking about Christina of the Whizz-Bangs, and I've seen you in a show or two myself you know."

'Then the penny dropped. Here in front of me was Jacques' hero: "*Magnifique. Formidable*". As we talked I noticed that he was wearing the ribbon of the DFC, beneath his pilot's wings. It seemed brand new. I noticed too how incredibly blue were his eyes. His mouth was full and sensitive. When he smiled a deep crease came into his left cheek and tiny lines crinkled about the corners of his eyes. His hair was golden and rather long, waving slightly above the ears. He's like a Greek god, I thought.'

Chapter 6

'A Greek God'

February - June 1941

The pilot Jacques described as *absolument magnifique, formidable* was Adrian Warburton.

He had made quite an impression on Christina. He also seemed to know a lot about her. All she knew was Jacques' description of this 'hero' and what she could see standing before her: a very young Royal Air Force pilot, a flying officer, wearing the distinctive, but still rare in Malta, mauve and white diagonally striped ribbon of the Distinguished Flying Cross. This was the 'young, fair-haired Maryland pilot' Jonah Jonas had listened to earlier. While everyone seemed to know the young pilot, not many knew a great deal about him, although he was widely popular. Whenever Christina saw him he was in a crowd, but none of them talked 'shop'.

Warby standing on the wing of a Glen Martin Maryland recce aircraft, 1940/41.
(*Miriam Farrugia*)

Christina set out to learn much more over the next few weeks, more about the man everyone called Warby. He was 22-years-old, a photo-recce pilot decorated for gallantry for his work over Taranto. He had also shot down a number of Italian aircraft, which was most unusual for a recce pilot. He arrived in Malta in September 1940 with 431 Flight, the unit René and Jacques later joined. It was re-designated 69 Squadron the day after they were killed.

A New Year football match took place to raise money for the RAF Benevolent Fund. It was such a success other methods of fundraising were considered. Encouraged by the popularity of the Whizz-Bangs created seven months earlier, the Raffians was formed. Cecil Roche, now a corporal, was the producer for the new group of musicians, all officers and men in the RAF HQ, working in their spare time. Other former entertainers joined them, including Cecil's wife Babs. They weren't in competition with the Whizz-Bangs as there were more than enough potential venues to go round. They toured airfields and out-stations often using the bomb disposal lorry when transport was short. Both troupes brought relief and amusement to many, sometimes appearing together as the RAF Fly Gang.

Tamara continually sought work. Her application to be a cypherine with the Royal Navy was put on hold when it was realised she could speak seven languages fluently, amongst them Italian and French. The authorities recognised her linguistic skills could be put to better use. She was asked to go and see the Information Officer whose offices were in the museum in *Strada Mercanti*, Valletta. 'I was shown into Captain Gerard's office. I had already heard of him and read most of his books. They were of the high-class thriller type. He was a most distinguished looking man in his late thirties, tall, slim, and with a knack of making one feel at ease at once.

'His first question was, "How would you like to broadcast?" I was taken aback for a moment. Pictures of my mother, whom I had not seen in four years, listening to me in America, flashed through my mind…Broadcast? It was too good to be true. I accepted enthusiastically. Nothing was yet definitely fixed but they needed a broadcaster. He was in favour of a female for the job, although his immediate boss would not hear of it. Anyway, if the test of my voice went well, if it was pleasant enough to listen to, he promised to see that I got the job. My duties would consist of translating English news into French, reading it over the air as well as reading the same news in Italian. The translation of English news into Italian was already done for me. I said the work would suit me perfectly.

'An audition was arranged for a fortnight hence at the Rediffusion studios in Valletta. I was never as nervous as on that first day. After the test I waited for the result in one of the ante-rooms. Captain Gerard came in beaming, offered me a cigarette, which I needed badly and told me that everything was quite satisfactory. I could start work immediately if I wanted to. I did.

'A week later Captain Gerard, who in the meantime had been promoted to major, fell ill with acute appendicitis. I worked all that time he was in hospital. A week after he resumed his duties, I was called into his office and told that plans were held up. Until things had been straightened out, there was no point in my continuing work. I was terribly disappointed at being stood off. My only meagre consolation was that I had not sent any cable to my people asking them to listen in.'

February saw heavy bombing with many aircraft destroyed on the ground. The *Luftwaffe* knew its business. From then on, day after day, it attacked with careful deliberation, pressing home its attacks against fierce anti-aircraft fire. British and Maltese ingenuity saw damaged Hurricanes quickly repaired to struggle into the air against odds of up to twenty-to-one. The skies were rarely empty of the enemy. With few defending fighters, German fighters often flew low, machine-gunning anything they wished. And all the time, the relentless bombing of dockyards continued.

A new cinema, the Coliseum, opened in February. Construction started before Italy declared war, but the owners decided to press on with it, war or no war. It was the largest cinema in Valletta and, from the moment it opened, the public flocked to the three performances each day often playing to a full-house. Tamara watched a newsreel of the Battle of Britain while an air raid raged above. The sound of guns and explosions on screen, matched by the sound of guns and explosions outside were perhaps a trifle too realistic. Yet very few spectators left their seats for shelter. This was foolhardy but demonstrated the spirit prevailing in Malta.

London was continually pressed for reinforcements. Sir William Dobbie expressed concern about how the Maltese might react if faced with invasion and hinted the army might have to be used to control the population. His pessimism had some effect and two battalions of infantry were despatched from Egypt. Meanwhile, a relatively little-known German general arrived in Tripoli. His name was Erwin Rommel; his unit was the *Afrika Korps*.

The SS *Knight of Malta,* which had brought Christina and her friend Sheila to Malta in 1937, had been involved in convoy duties since hostilities began. She ran aground east of Tobruk. Attempts to salvage her were abandoned under bombing; so ended another valiant vessel. HMS *Terror,* which had helped defend Malta during the very first air raids, was also sunk off Tobruk.

Axis sorties continued to increase and the RAF's Hurricanes struggled against the latest cannon-armed *Luftwaffe* fighters which they met from mid-February. In the next three months, one battle-hardened *gruppe* of nine aircraft claimed forty-two British aircraft destroyed. It proved impossible to base bombers on the island on a permanent basis and they were withdrawn. One German raid against Hal Far left only one Gladiator fit for use; it was *Faith*. The obsolescent biplanes had served the island well. Sometimes faith is enough.

To cope with the increased air activity, the RAF began improving its system of fighter control. The original operations room, which contained a small plotting table, was in St John's Cavalier, near Hastings Gardens in Valletta. As the system of fighter control expanded a filter room with a new plotting table was built in a small cellar at 3 Scots Street Valletta, a corner house overlooking South Street. It opened in March 1941 and was linked to various visual observation points such as the rooftop of the *Auberge de Castille*. The work in this residential location in the middle of the capital was top secret and RAF policemen carefully vetted all personnel who worked there.

Tunnels at Lascaris, beneath Upper Barracca Gardens overlooking Grand Harbour, were being excavated and equipped. These opened as summer approached, with the filter room and the St John's Cavalier operations room closed and staff transferred to the new facility. This was No 8 Sector Operations Room, often simply referred to as Lascaris. However, manpower was a major problem and the RAF soon began to look outside its ranks for more personnel.

Christina and Warby began going out with one another within a few weeks of having met. At the time, Christina shared her apartment with Pickles, who lived there until mid-March. Pickles sometimes stayed overnight with Tamara. As well as being Christina's friend, maybe Pickles was also discreet.

With increased calls for photography, Warby flew often, but he is unlikely to have said a great deal to Christina about his work. He was known not to brag. Expressions such as 'walls have ears' reminded everyone to guard their tongues. Shop-talk tended to be limited more in social gatherings by service personnel themselves. As Tamara explained, 'We seldom heard at first hand of their exploits. The phrase "shooting a line" having already been coined, there was nothing any one of them hated so much as being accused of doing so. Another phrase aircrews were fond of using as soon as shop was talked or when they did not want to answer an awkward question was "Close the hangar doors". Usually they brought their hands together and said "Clang".'

There were many among the 'air boys' who knew of the unconventional, near suicidal, tactics Warby adopted to ensure he always returned with the all-important images. Even if he tended to be reticent, others were not and when it came to his exploits, Christina would have been 'all ears'. It didn't take her long to realise the risks he took. He was often at greater risk trying to get back to Luqa. While it was possible to evade enemy fighters over Sicily and Southern Italy, the enemy knew where RAF aircraft would eventually have to go on completion of their tasks: a very small and totally isolated island in the middle of the Mediterranean.

Christina gradually discovered many facets to Warby's character. What struck her most was his love of adventure, his devil-may-care attitude and what she described as his cool cheek. These were all ideal attributes for a successful recce pilot. On the evening of 6 March he told Christina he would be flying the next morning but if she heard later he was missing she was not to worry. He asked her not to tell a soul. Warby's favourite drink was a 'Horse's Neck' - brandy and ginger ale - and he was embarrassed at having drunk all of Christina's limited stock. As his trip the following day would take him close to Athens, he intended to develop engine trouble and land to pick up a few bottles of Greek brandy before returning to Malta the next day. He also intended to replenish his squadron's stock of alcohol.

The next day, Ronnie Marks telephoned Tamara saying he had bad news: Warby was missing. 'My heart sank. Were we to lose all our friends? I wondered how Christina, who was Warburton's best girlfriend, would take the news. I went over to her flat to try and help her, if she had heard the news and was taking the blow too badly. I found Christina at home and although she looked quite perturbed I somehow felt that she was not as heart-broken as I had expected her to be. Pickles, who was sharing Christina's flat at the time, was also in and, as my husband was on duty that night, we decided to have a hen-party. A very successful bubble and squeak was cooked by Christina and was helped down by countless cups of tea. I went and fetched my knitting, so we sat around sewing and talking and passed a very agreeable evening.' Apparently there were some very glum faces at the ERA Club that evening.

The following morning Christina had to work hard not to show any grief. 'I was having such a good laugh to myself when one of the air boys said news had just been received that Warby's plane had been shot down in flames. I was horrified, heartbroken.' The confusion arose because on the same day, 7 March, another 69 Squadron Maryland was intercepted and shot down in flames just as it crossed the Maltese coast. Only the navigator survived.

The following day Luqa's intelligence officer heard from Warby: he had been chased by enemy fighters and had run short of fuel. He had therefore landed at Menidi in Greece to refuel. Tamara heard Warby would be back in a couple of days. 'The news of Warby being safe spread like wildfire. All his friends seemed to hear about it at the same time and decided to celebrate it fittingly at the Monico bar. Malta lacked many things but to the end of my stay there was no lack of liquor. The party seemed to want to go on forever. I had to get up early in the morning as we had to clock in at eight and no excuses for being late were valid. So, toward ten o'clock I said goodbye to those who were still sober enough to notice whether I was there or not and made my way home. At eleven o'clock, the air raid siren went. As my husband was not back yet, I could not be bothered to carry by myself all the necessary to make a minimum of two hours stay' in the shelter bearable. I just pulled the blanket over my head and assured myself that the attack was directed against the aerodromes as there was no shipping in the harbour. Somehow or other I managed to get to sleep. The next day I learnt from my husband that a five hundred-pound bomb had fallen on the sergeants' mess next door to the Monico. "We felt the blast," my husband said, "but that was all".

'Two days later Warburton came back looking none the worse for his misadventure. Having found some cheap priced Greek champagne, he had purchased a dozen bottles, which came in very handy for his birthday a few days later. He had also brought back cosmetics, reels of cotton and press studs and so I was able to have my latest summer frock finished at last. I had had to wear it and keep my hand on my hip doing a "Mae West" so as to hide the safety pin that was holding the side opening together. Zip-fasteners or press-studs could not be had in Malta for love nor money.' It wasn't often Warby could provide the essentials of dressmaking. He also restocked 69 Squadron's cellar and contributed several bottles of brandy to Christina, as well as Greek gramophone records and an ashtray he had 'swiped' from some hotel. He also gave Christina a brooch in the shape of an Evzone's shoe.

When sewing cotton became unobtainable, Christina demonstrated how much she cared about how Warby looked by extracting threads from the seam of his uniform trousers and repairing his threadbare, somewhat battered Service dress hat. From then on Warby was never without it, often wearing it in the air on top of his flying helmet. Sometimes he wore a pair of baggy casual grey flannel trousers, or long sheepskin trousers, depending on whether he was flying on low or high level missions. Yet by contrast, for any of the rare formal functions he was required to attend, he would often arrive immaculately turned out in his No 1 Dress uniform.

Soon it became almost impossible to obtain replacement items of uniform and Warby's attire became much more of an expression of his individuality. He often wore an army battledress blouse with his RAF rank on slides on the shoulder tabs. Sometimes he wore a cravat rather than a tie, and rarely wore uniform shoes, preferring something more comfortable. Cravats and scarves soon became a normal part of RAF flying kit, so important was it to swivel one's head looking for 'the hun in the sun'. With flights often lasting many hours, who can blame him for his relaxed dress? Yet this was very much against the RAF 'norm' even in those testing days.

Warby and Christina probably became recognised as a couple, and a very glamorous one at that, from late spring. This was a relatively quiet time for both of them. They worked hard, Christina with up to five Whizz-Bangs performances a week plus rehearsals and Warby flying at least every other day. But they still had time to spend together, especially as air raids began to reduce as June approached. He didn't drink a great deal and smoked little. In fact some of his colleagues never saw him drink alcohol at all. Although they both openly enjoyed parties they were probably conscious they should live up to the glamorous image with which they were labelled. They were certainly not constant party-goers, often preferring their own company and a quiet life in Christina's apartment overlooking Grand Harbour. Indeed, an early photograph of Warby shows him in the apartment winding wool. There was a shy side to Warby's character, often masked by his 'front', and he was easily embarrassed. He was also a poor dancer, but knew Christina loved to be taken to dances; sometimes Warby brought one of his friends along to dance with her.

As well as being an excellent swimmer, Warby was a fine horseman, often borrowing a horse from the army stables in Valletta to ride down to the Marsa racecourse. Christina was happy to accompany him having taken riding lessons in Gibraltar. She was able to wear the jodhpurs she bought in Gibraltar for the first time in Malta. 'As we rode to the Marsa racecourse I grew very nervous. The horse Warby had chosen for me was anything but a slow-mover - it appeared to have all the makings of a Grand National winner. What it would be like when we reached the track heaven only knew. "Don't worry. I'll keep alongside all the time," Warby said when we arrived. "But first of all let me have one good gallop round the course by myself."

'With that he shot off like an arrow, leaving me alone with my steed. The horse broke into a slow trot and we followed, all very calmly and peacefully. Then it happened. I let go of the reins to fasten my hairslide, which had come undone and before I knew where I was the horse was carrying me at breakneck speed after Warby. How I remained on that animal I don't know, I dug in my knees, gripped the front edge of the saddle and hung on like grim death. It could have been only a few minutes but it seemed like hours before Warby came to the rescue. Once alongside he swooped down, grabbed the dangling reins and somehow managed to bring the horse to a halt.' From then on, whenever Warby was out with Christina and ordering drinks he was discreet enough to refer to his favourite drink as 'brandy dry', rather than its more usual name in those days of 'horse's neck'.

The Gould family had by then moved to Tigné Barracks in Sliema where the catacombs were used as air raid shelters, a much safer option than Mtarfa's slit trenches. For Marion and her brothers and sisters, schooling came to an end as bombing intensified and more and more time was spent in the shelters. Marion thought some raids seemed to last for twenty-four hours. Nevertheless, British padres continued religious education and Marion was confirmed by the Bishop of Gibraltar in 1941 in St Mark's Church, Tigné. Social life also continued despite the risks and the shortages, and Marion often saw ladies still sometimes dressed in their evening gowns. Everyone tried to make the best of things. By then her father's anti-aircraft unit was deployed at Marsa racecourse. He might well have witnessed an out-of-control Christina out riding with Warby.

In March, four merchant ships successfully made Grand Harbour; four out of six. When it came to enemy ships, although Warby deserved his reputation for always coming back with the goods, there was a growing suspicion among recce crews there was more to some of their tasking than met the eye. Were the locations of some ships already known? Could another intelligence source be at work?

Senior officers were content with the rumour there was a British spy in an Italian naval HQ, which nicely protected the real source of intelligence which was of course Ultra at Bletchley Park. This was why recce aircraft were sometimes sent to specific locations where enemy vessels were known to be. If a slightly secretive pilot was used, what better way was there to protect the existence of Ultra? That was why Warby, unaware of the intelligence source, was specifically selected and briefed for certain missions. Everyone else put his results down to 'Warby's luck'. A similar subterfuge was used in Britain where the highly successful night-fighter ace, 'Cat's Eyes' Cunningham, was said to have phenomenal eyesight because of his love of carrots. His success was of course due to early airborne radar fitted to his aircraft.

Warby was not always taken at his word. When he reported an Italian ship by name and the harbour in which it was berthed, the Royal Navy did not accept his report. A few days later, he presented the senior service with a photograph of the ship in question. It was taken so low and at such close range its name could clearly be read. Word of this became widespread.

For many living in or near Valletta the evenings during the spring of 1941 often developed into something of a routine. First they took in a film at the cinema before finding somewhere for dinner and a few drinks, perhaps at the Monico bar in South Street opposite the Opera House. These were the days before severe shortages. It was on one such evening at the Monico that Tamara heard her first bomb whistle. 'I instinctively ducked under the bar, comforting myself with the saying that, "You never hear the whistle of the bomb that kills you". Of course, once you are dead you can hardly say whether you heard the bomb whistle or not, but that is beside the point. Walking back from Valletta to Floriana in an air raid was an arduous and lengthy job. In normal times, the walking distance does not take more than twenty minutes. In an air raid it took usually twice as much, sprinting from one slit trench to another, waiting until the guns in each area boomed a little less loudly and looking skywards to see if any more shrapnel was likely to fall.' While many preferred to be in the open during a raid, Tamara always felt much safer under some sort of cover.

At least the alerts were only for air raids. 'Rumours of invasion were rife. Every day and every night we expected to hear the air raid siren give one long unending wail. This was to be the signal for everyone to rush to his combat post as soon as possible. The Home Guard had been issued with rifles and we had all the rabbit shooters turned into para-shooters. They looked proud with their brand new rifles under their arms and they scanned the sky in a business-like manner.

'One night in early April, my husband and I, after the usual indecision on my part about going or not going to the shelter, decided to go as the barrage was pretty heavy. Carrying rugs, stools, pillows, fur coats, and a small leather bag in which I kept my most valued possessions - a few letters, some photographs, odd pieces of jewellery, a book and a flask of coffee, we left the flat. Vincenti's shelter was already packed. Bodies stretched in all directions, on benches and stools. We stepped gingerly trying to find enough empty space to spread our ground sheet. My husband sat on the stool, propped his back against the wall and was asleep in no time. I envied him. The air was stifling and heavy with mingled sounds. I turned and tossed trying to make myself comfortable on the concrete floor.

'Suddenly after what seemed to be the heaviest bomb ever dropped right in the backyard, the siren went off. One long piercing unending wail. The whole cellar woke up with a start. One thought was uppermost in everyone's mind. INVASION. It could not be anything else. It was the signal which was to be given in such an emergency. So it had come at last. We were all prepared to give a good account of ourselves. Mothers clutched children tightly to their bosoms; men grabbed tin hats, gas-masks and made for the exit although the barrage was terrific. The bombing went on. Bombs whistled continuously. Some of the men were undecided as to whether their duty did not rather lie in staying where they were to protect the women and children. At this moment a most un-martial looking Royal Artillery sergeant burst into the cellar. Although his face was begrimed, a big smile was spread over it. We all looked up at him resenting his cheerfulness in such serious circumstances. "Relax, relax," he said. "False alarm; a bomb has short-circuited the dockyard siren and it won't stop. They'll repair it as soon as the air raid is over."' On that occasion the siren blew for two hours and few within its hearing slept. This was a serious scare and living under such conditions was gradually taking its toll on people physically and mentally.

On 8 April, Tamara witnessed the terrible demise of the Admiralty buoy-tender, *Moor*: 'I was at home idly watching the traffic of tugs, ferries and smaller craft in Grand Harbour. The sight never ceased to fascinate me. It was a lovely evening just after sunset. A moment of respite before the night raids, a leisurely high tea on the balcony and a little light reading. Suddenly the whole house was shaken as by a terrible earthquake. A swirl of water, the aft end of the ship showing for a minute and then it was gone. One survivor was picked up.' *Moor* had hit a mine; twenty-eight people lost their lives.

As each week went by, the raids grew in violence as both Grand Harbour and Marsamxett Harbour were regularly targeted. With Floriana situated between the two, bombs inevitably landed in this densely populated, residential area. A girl Tamara knew had a particularly haunting experience. 'She and her boyfriend had just come downstairs when the bombs began to fall. They were on the doorstep still debating whether to go to the shelter or not. She was in favour of going; he could not make up his mind. Just as the noise of the enemy aircraft grew louder and louder, she instinctively rushed down the road. When the raid was over, she came back to find her house a mass of ruins, her boyfriend killed and her sole possessions the clothes she was wearing - a jumper, a pair of trousers, an old overcoat and a pair of slippers. This horrible tragedy played on her mind. After a couple of months of continual rushing to the shelters, she lost her reason and had to be taken to hospital where she still was when I left the island.'

If the Longyear children were ever outside when the air raid sirens sounded, they always tried to get home rather than find a shelter. The school in Valletta was eventually bombed out and Michael moved to Frere's School in Sliema, quite a walk to and from home with the route winding round the various creeks and inlets. As the weather became warmer and, with no buses, Michael found the walk increasingly wearing, especially as reduced food began to have a telling impact.

He became friendly with the gunners manning a Bofors anti-aircraft position on top of Guardamangia Hill next to the hospital. It afforded a good view toward RAF Ta' Qali and Michael and his friends often watched attacks on the airfield. Between raids, the gunners allowed them to rotate the gun and vary its elevation. Once an alert was sounded, the children stood nearby and watched the gun in action. The gunners' living quarters were in part of the hospital mortuary. It was here Michael first saw a dead person. The gun crew were soon posted to another emplacement near the airfields. They were all killed when their position suffered a direct hit.

Toward the end of April, everyone noticed a reduction in the number of raids and a slackening in their intensity. Rumour had it the Germans needed their aircraft on other fronts. This was true; Axis offensives opened in the Balkans and in Libya. Whatever the reason, there was a sense of relief. This was the very moment when concentrated raids by the *Luftwaffe* might have had a telling impact. Instead, Malta's hard-pressed defenders were given a breathing space. But bad news soon followed for Britain with another costly retreat and evacuation from Greece followed by the German airborne assault on Crete. Another Allied defeat followed. In May, Sir William Dobbie again reported on the inadequacy of Malta's air defences which was causing him considerable concern.

Tamara joined a more advanced First Aid and Nursing class in order to gain her bronze medallion as a VAD. Lady Dobbie and her daughter Sybil attended the same course. Tamara also joined an amateur dramatic society started at the ERA club with rehearsals often continuing by candlelight. 'On my birthday in May, my husband and some friends decided to celebrate the occasion in rousing fashion. Actually anything was an excuse for a party. Someone I knew celebrated the Siege of Gibraltar. If anyone asked him why, he would look serious and explain that as it lasted a year, he did not need to think up new excuses. If one insisted and wanted to know why an excuse was necessary at all, he would look hurt and say: "But one must be celebrating something, otherwise one is only a common drunkard."

'We all met at the Monico bar by 6.00 pm. We were a party of twenty originally, but as the evening wore on, the place was absolutely packed with people. They all had to have a glass of champagne. By 10.00 pm, closing time, a lot of it had been drunk and a lot more spilt on the floor. Everyone agreed it had been a grand birthday party. The commanding officer of Hal Far sent me an enormous bouquet of flowers the next day. The flowers were a little withered and dusty, some bombs having fallen on the officers' mess garden a few days previously. I appreciated the gift much more for that. When I swore, the day after my birthday party, that there had been no raids that night, I was informed that there had been three very heavy ones, a few incendiaries dropping in Floriana itself. The only other time I remember not waking up for an air raid was when Cilia's bar in South Street, Valletta, received a consignment of Bass beer. My husband rang up asking me to meet him at Cilia's. It was about 2.00 pm. Four bottles of the stuff were all I could drink. Without saying goodbye to anyone, I solemnly saw myself to a *karozzin*, which is a horse-drawn vehicle, went straight home and to bed. I never woke up until 8.00 am the next morning, feeling beautifully refreshed and very hungry.'

Desperate for work Tamara, who was a former teacher, placed an advertisement in the *Times of Malta* offering French lessons, but the continual air raids played havoc with her teaching schedule. However, not all who replied to Tamara's advertisement wanted to learn a new language. 'The strangest was the major, who wrote a very polite letter asking for 'French' lessons. At the interview, in his best Oxford accent, he opened up with the astonishing words:

"I do not really want any French lessons."

"You don't? Yet that is what your letter said."

"Yes, I know but did you notice that I wrote 'French' in inverted commas?"

I could not see the connection. Stammering slightly, he explained:

"Well, you see, I have a nice villa and a lot of money I do not know what to do with, so I thought ..."

Suddenly it dawned on me. I was flabbergasted. Containing myself as best I could, I asked him calmly whether he had ever been to France.

"Yes, many times, I even lived there for a while."

"So you know France and all you can remember of that wonderful country are the yellow pictures or blue pictures or whatever they are called. You are so stupid, I won't even be angry with you, now get out of here."'

Tamara kept looking for meaningful work.

In early June, German attacks stopped. For over a week, there were no raids. Then the spotters reported something not seen for months: bandits approaching the island at 20,000 feet; they were identified as Italian. They were back, along with their slightly lackadaisical, intentional or otherwise, medium-level bombing. Hitler was now gazing toward the Russian steppes, allured by thoughts of Caucasian oil. Everyone in Malta rejoiced. The population made the most of it, for a while at least. The bars filled up once again, especially popular venues like Monico's and Cilia's. In daylight, the Maltese emerged from their shelters to watch the air battles from their rooftops once again. Some even returned to what was left of their damaged homes.

Warby developed a special relationship with the ground crew who looked after his aircraft. While his squadron commander, the Australian Tich Whiteley, encouraged his crews to help service their aircraft, Warby went further, befriending many of the airmen. He was often found sitting on the floor in a hangar or storeroom playing cards, but he also shared his cigarette ration and was first to help any airman in trouble. Warby treated the airmen as equals and many became devoted to him.

But he was now living on his nerves. Already an acclaimed recce pilot, he had proven his worth as an aggressive fighter pilot, with a number of 'kills' to his credit, and had shown aptitude as a bomber pilot. Having been at the forefront of action for the best part of nine months, the strain was showing. He was already thin and, like everyone else, living under regular bombing in demoralising conditions. The Officers' Mess and the airmen's barracks at Luqa were long gone and tents were often the best that could be found. Warby spent ever more time with Christina. There was no avoiding the casualties his squadron was suffering and the deaths of colleagues affected him more and more. He was not immune and he knew it, despite the blasé front he put on. Against such a background, the escape and comfort he found with Christina was hugely important, even if it only lasted for a few short hours. He had found great solace and love in Christina and there can be no doubt she provided a firm foundation from which he could express his individuality in the air. She also offered Warby a safe retreat, where he could unwind whenever he was off-duty. Nevertheless, Warby needed a rest.

They knew the risks for both of them; tragedy was always close at hand. For the moment, and neither of them knew for how long, they spent whatever time they could together. With their vibrant personalities, love of life and determination, they soon became symbols of Malta's spirit. Chris, as Warby called her, filled a vital part of Warby's life. She, like everyone else, called him Warby. She provided an escape for him from the Mess life he had never felt part of and didn't enjoy. She offered him stability and unconditional love. He was not a show-off, but Christina certainly provided him with a sense of self-worth and as a result his flying achievements developed further. Those achievements were a great boost to everyone, servicemen and Maltese alike. There were jealousies of course: few knew him well and he was seen as a loner. He also monopolised one of the most attractive girls on the island, although it was clear to anyone who looked that Warby and Christina were genuinely fond of one another.

Many talked of his so-called luck; others simply considered him irresponsible, a reckless pilot who took too many risks. But his reputation grew, and those close to him on 69 Squadron, those who flew with him, knew those risks were calculated. He planned his missions carefully and although he might alter a plan in the air, this showed flexibility, not necessarily any lack of responsibility. His devil-may-care attitude did not, however, lie far beneath the surface. Although he always maintained an air of bravado, he had a sensitive side to his nature, especially with regard to the losses happening all around him. Those that occurred on his own squadron affected him a great deal and, unusually, he recorded in his log book the names of friends and colleagues killed or listed as missing. It was a long list.

A new senior airman arrived on the scene in June, Air Vice-Marshal Hugh Pughe Lloyd. When he arrived he saw at once the damage to residential areas. He was particularly concerned some RAF headquarters facilities were above ground although the main operational headquarters was underground at Lascaris. What he saw at Lascaris was supposedly a considerable improvement on what had gone before but he still described it as an underground stable. It had a long, winding, underground passage with a cavern at the end of it which was without ventilation and smelt abominably, he said. Lloyd watched the controller handle an air raid with the plots shown on a single table with all the other staff using the same table to coordinate their tasks. He described it as bedlam. Anyone from an equivalent operations room in Britain would have fainted on the spot.

A tour of RAF facilities elsewhere left Hugh Lloyd depressed. The airfields were small, the airmen's shelters woefully inadequate. Underground facilities existed in name only with the equipment needed by a modern air force stored above ground. Transport was inadequate and there were no underground fuel lines. In fact there wasn't a single petrol pump on the whole island. Petrol was distributed in five-gallon tins from dumps open to the elements and the enemy. As Lloyd completed his tour he drove past a *gharry* - one of the one-horse carriages much in evidence. How long would they last, he wondered? He knew the well-looked after animals were the reserve meat ration. In Lloyd's view, it would not take many concentrated attacks to make his airfields untenable.

Lloyd's most pressing problem was manpower. Even with the highly skilled Maltese workforce, Lloyd simply didn't have enough to run the island's disparate air force even had it not been subject to daily attack. He set about finding more people, leaving no stone unturned in his search. He recruited civilians, including wives and daughters of servicemen, as well as stranded civilians. He hijacked personnel and aircraft en route to Egypt and sought support from the other services. He also tapped deeply into Malta's greatest asset: its people.

There was a major reinforcement of Hurricanes in June and they had an immediate impact on the situation. These were heady days for the pilots who enjoyed success in the air and adulation on the ground. Men would raise their hats as they passed, and elderly ladies would curtsy or even step off the pavement to make room for an approaching airman. To many, the aircrew were modern Knights of St John. Of course, the Hurricane's success was principally against the *Regia Aeronautica*.

Tamara was finally offered a job within the RAF headquarters in the strange-sounding Standing Committee of Adjustment. She accepted gratefully not knowing what was entailed. 'When I found out that my job consisted in taking down and typing out condolence letters, inventories of casualties' kit and the general work connected with missing or dead personnel, my first impulse was to leave. But I resisted. After all it was a job of work that had to be done and that is all there was to it. In the beginning I could not open a new file without tears springing to my eyes, or write to a mother or wife without feeling miserable all day, but I got used to it.

With the permission of the casualty's family, items were sold with the proceeds going to the RAF Benevolent Fund. Any letters were read before forwarding to ensure next-of-kin didn't receive a tainted picture of their loved one. 'The letter of a twenty-one year old acting squadron leader to his parent was a monument of courage in one so young. How proud parents of such youths must be. Very often we received letters of praise for the work we were doing.'

This work was hugely important for families trying to come to terms with the loss of a loved one far from home and Tamara was desperately keen to make a contribution. But was she strong enough emotionally to deal with such a task day after day?

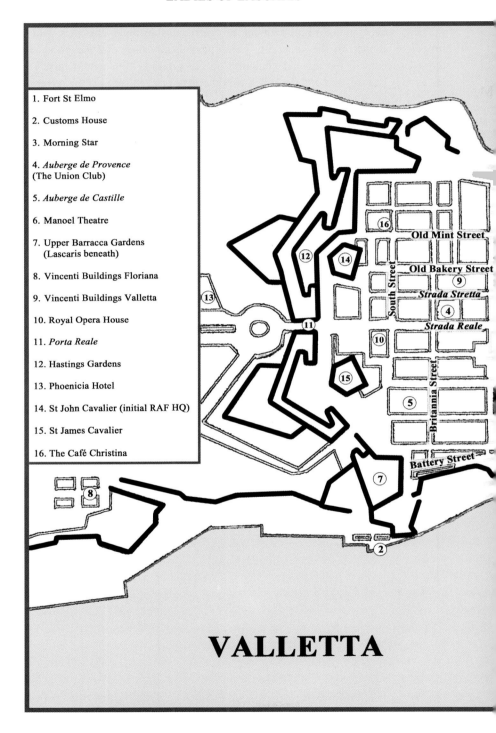

1. Fort St Elmo

2. Customs House

3. Morning Star

4. *Auberge de Provence* (The Union Club)

5. *Auberge de Castille*

6. Manoel Theatre

7. Upper Barracca Gardens (Lascaris beneath)

8. Vincenti Buildings Floriana

9. Vincenti Buildings Valletta

10. Royal Opera House

11. *Porta Reale*

12. Hastings Gardens

13. Phoenicia Hotel

14. St John Cavalier (initial RAF HQ)

15. St James Cavalier

16. The Café Christina

VALLETTA

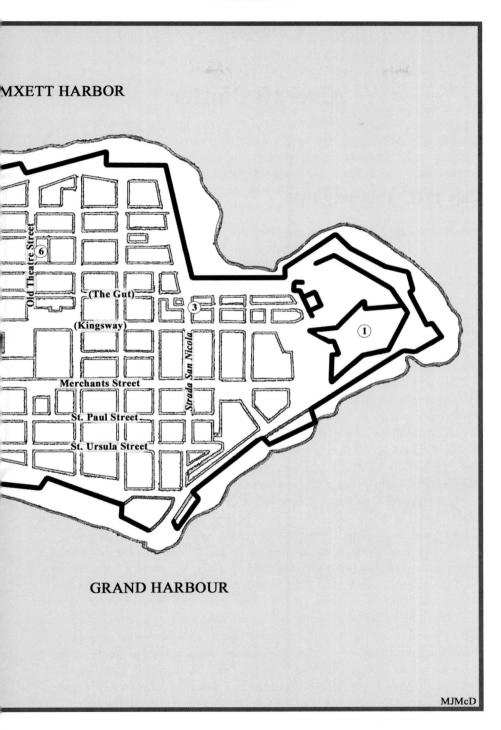

MXETT HARBOR

Old Theatre Street

⑥

(The Gut)

③

(Kingsway)

Strada San Nicola

Merchants Street

St. Paul Street

St. Ursula Street

①

GRAND HARBOUR

MJMcD

Chapter 7

Aircraft Plotter

July 1941 - February 1942

Petrol rationing affected everyone, including the Whizz-Bangs. Despite their valuable work, restrictions reduced their shows to three each week, leaving the performers with time on their hands. Christina was contacted by Cecil Roche, who had been in the RAF since Italy's declaration of war. Twenty British girls were needed for training by the RAF, he said. Christina applied and was accepted. She had little idea what she would be doing other than her duties would be similar to those carried out by the Women's Auxiliary Air Force (WAAF) in Britain.

Her first days were spent as a telephonist, but she soon trained as an aircraft plotter employed in the top secret No 8 Sector Operations Room at Lascaris.

The unit had its own badge with a Latin motto, *Supera Assequi* - Reach the Heights. Christina soon realised controllers at Lascaris often talked and listened to Warby's aircraft on its way to and from his targets. Pilot's voices were often broadcast from the loudspeakers. She sometimes moved the block representing Warby's aircraft across the plotting table, 'the plot' as everyone called it. She had been desperately keen to contribute. Now she could. She just hoped she could handle it. Apparently some of the calls from the 'air boys' could be quite distressing.

From then on, Christina combined plotting with concert party performances, often changing duties with her opposite number on another watch to make an engagement. It was tough going but immensely satisfying.

The Ops room was in the old communication tunnel built by the Knights of St John which had so unimpressed Air Vice-Marshal Lloyd when he arrived; it had indeed been used as a stable. It was located 400ft beneath Upper Barracca Gardens, at the south-eastern end of the ditch crossing the Scuerras peninsula separating Valletta's inner and outer walls. What took place there was one of the best kept secrets of the Second World War in Malta. The secure but dark and sunless rooms became the nerve centre of Malta's defence, the whole complex ventilated with metal piping and ducting retrieved from ships sunk in Grand Harbour. Christina said: 'Some people have likened the RAF's underground operational headquarters in Valletta to a maze of rabbit warrens. I think the name best suited is the one by which it was known to us all: The Hole.'

AIRCRAFT PLOTTER

Christina at the
plotting table.
(UK MOD)

The plotting table in the RAF operations room Lascaris. (*Miriam Farrugia*)

The plotting table measured eighteen feet by twelve, and showed a map of Malta and the surrounding area, including part of Sicily and its main airfields, as well as the islands of Linosa and Pantelleria. The map was divided into lettered squares each sub-divided into numbered grids. Malta was within '*N*' for *Nuts* and '*H*' for *Harry* covered the area toward Sicily. '*M*' for *Monkey* was west of Malta and became the scene of hectic activity whenever a convoy approached from Gibraltar.

Aircraft tracks, labelled in the filter room, were passed by telephone to a plotter. A typical message was 'Hostile 15, '*H'* for *Harry* 4628, twenty-five plus at 15,000 feet, heading south-west.' The plotter placed a coloured pointed counter on the table at the appropriate reference. A small arrow-shaped plot was pushed out to the marked position using a wooden rod, 'like a billiards cue,' said Christina. A wooden block, or marker, was then assembled and placed alongside the track. It gave details of the number of aircraft involved, whether friendly or hostile, and the aircraft height. The blocks were continually updated as the aircraft positions moved. The senior controller, sitting above 'the plot' in the centre of the dais, directed the fighters. Alongside him were his deputy, known as Ops B, and the guns and searchlight liaison officers.

The Ops room was divided into four watches: A, B, C and D, each comprising on average of fourteen girls. The long overnight shift was of nine hours from 11.00 pm until 8.00 am the next morning. The two day shifts ran from 8.00 am until 1.00 pm and 1.00 pm until 6.15 pm. The evening shift was from 6.15 pm until 11.00 pm. All the girls were sworn to secrecy, which extended even to admitting in which room they worked. Three listening stations picked up bearings from aircraft and passed them to the radio direction room, located under the dais. The resultant plots were marked on a blackboard to the right of the main table. Any 'mayday' call picked up by the direction finders resulted in the distressed aircraft's position being plotted. An air-sea rescue launch could then be despatched from Kalafrana.

Although it took many months for all the RAF's operational and administrative staffs to come together at Lascaris, the new facility was already a huge improvement, bringing together the anti-aircraft artillery control room only feet from the senior controller and the plotting table. Malta now had a very capable nerve centre.

With Hitler having unleashed his armies on the Soviet Union toward the end of June, Malta's defenders were afforded a breathing space, time to reorganize and better prepare for the assaults that would surely come. There was more emphasis on disrupting supplies to North Africa. Blenheims were flown in for short periods, but they were very vulnerable, all too easy a target for any ship with effective flak weapons. Surprise on those beautifully clear days of a Mediterranean summer was rarely possible. Nevertheless, the crews persisted with great courage and determination, despite mounting losses. Two consecutive Blenheim detachments lost thirty-one of their aircrew in three months, including both squadron commanders; another lost twenty-nine in a few weeks. The loss rate was unsustainable. With crews lost at the rate of six each week, it didn't take them long to realise they had little chance of surviving a six-week detachment. Theirs was a conscious courage.

The girls at Lascaris were well aware of the numbers sent out and how few returned. Casualties among other crews were also heavy, but they never reached the scale of loss experienced by the Blenheims. At one stage, Lloyd refused to send his Blenheims against strongly escorted vessels saying it was 'sheer murder'. He was subsequently rebuked for this remark by a more senior officer from another service.

The Marylands of 69 Squadron were often at the forefront of these anti-shipping attacks and Christina knew when Warby was on the plot, even if he said little to her about what he actually got up to. It was rarely Warby speaking; more often than not it was his wireless operator, but his call-sign was unmistakeable. His aircraft often returned damaged, a fact well known in the Ops room. On one mission, having lost an engine over Taranto, even he admitted the return flight was a 'shaky do'. These hair-raising episodes kept occurring but Warby simply carried on. But they were taking their toll on him.

For the Maltese, the summer of 1941 was quiet. There were anti-Italian slogans here and there though these were more of an expression of annoyance at their near neighbour for making war on their small island than anything else. Most, simply did not take the Italians seriously. Allied airmen and sailors did. In June there was the timely arrival of a convoy which replenished stocks; artillery ammunition and aviation fuel in particular were being used at a colossal rate. Some rationing was introduced to limit hoarding and black market activities although food rationing was not yet stringently applied.

Aida Kelly also worked in the RAF headquarters. She became Tamara's best girlfriend. 'She was tall, dark, lovely and so unalterably cheerful that she did me a lot of moral good as I am rather inclined to have the "blues". She was a good swimmer, a good tennis player, an indefatigable dancer and absolutely unafraid of raids. The only woman I have ever known who could get anything she wanted. Aida and I had silk stockings when all the other women on the island had to wear lisle or none at all and we did not pay black market prices for them either. She unearthed an inconspicuous little shop in an inconspicuous little street, the owner of which sold us at pre-war prices. We wondered whether he had heard that there was a war on and that such things fetched astronomical prices. We bought enough to last us for the duration.

'In those days, my husband never came home for lunch and Aida lived too far from town to be able to have lunch at home. So we decided to eat out. Her pay being rather small, it was imperative to find an inexpensive restaurant to feed at. The only reasonable priced ones were those with Maltese cooking. Having travelled since early childhood, I was not very faddy about food. The British Hotel in St Ursula Street, Valletta, which despite its name was run on

Maltese lines, suited us perfectly. The cooking was wholesome even though the dishes were unusual. Besides macaroni and baked rice, which were available every day, there were such things as octopus in onion sauce. The dish I was very partial to was *calamari* fried in rings or made with a special caper sauce. A full meal, that is baked spaghetti or rice, stuffed aubergines, jelly bread (no butter - I did not eat butter for three months) and a glass of local wine cost only 1s 6d [about 7½ pence]. The place was patronised by very mixed company, labourers, porters, small shop owners, low-paid clerks and so on. We often met Christina there.

'The British Hotel was situated on Grand Harbour and, as Aida had exceptional eyesight and loved nothing better than to watch raids, we had a grandstand view of any attack on Grand Harbour. Usually I was rather uneasy but stayed with her. We had the experience of watching a shoot-up of Fort St Angelo by the Italians. It was thrilling to see the glint of the planes in the sun, then the bombs leave the aircraft, the long, long whistle growing to a crescendo and finally an outsize splash as they fell in the sea. There were some quite good near misses. We always hoped there would be a raid at lunch time for, as everyone scattered to the nearest shelter, we would be served quicker, with bigger portions and we would manage to get the table in the corner by the window.'

Daylight bombing had reduced to a couple of raids each day by the summer, although the island experienced more at night. Aida often spent the night at Tamara's flat. 'As she never wanted to go to the shelter, we usually stayed awake and talked far into the night. Sleep was out of the question with our pet Bofors gun about fifty yards from the bedroom windows. This life of continual raids started to tell on me. I lost two stones in eight months and although my health was not impaired, I looked very much a scarecrow.

'Our only relaxation in those summer months was swimming. Tennis was impossible for all open spaces not used for cultivation or aerodromes, had been cluttered with disused cars, empty oil drums, coils of barbed wire and such like, as a measure against paratroopers.

'I was in Kingsway on 25 July, the principal street of Valletta, when the only enemy aircraft to crash into the town was destroyed. We could see the plane out of control, careering madly all over the sky. Then, it went into a steep dive and, each one thought, made straight for him or her. The panic was terrific. It was 11 am and the street was filled with people who had been watching the raid. Everyone rushed madly for the nearest shelter. Some flung themselves on to the pavement. I followed suit. After what seemed an age, the machine dived into a crater made in an earlier raid so that no one was injured. The crater was at the back of La Valette Band Club where, in peacetime, enjoyable dances had been held. At the outbreak of the war, Rosetti, the Maltese bandleader with Italian sympathies, had left for Italy. We got up and dusted ourselves, the light-hearted

Maltese laughing at the fright they had had. As one wit said: "Rosetti had come back to conduct his orchestra for the last time."

'That same night, four air raids were sounded. My husband and I got up for every one of them, although at that time most of the night raids were only of "nuisance" value. That is, one aircraft would go round and round the Island for an hour or so, drop a bomb here and there and be relieved by another one which would do the same and so on all through night.

'Toward 5.00 am on the twenty-sixth, the All Clear having sounded, we heaved a huge sigh of relief, gathered our shelter paraphernalia together and made for home and bed. Just as I was trying to snatch an hour's sleep before getting up for work, heavy gunfire was heard again. I put my head under the blanket and swore that if this were to be the end, I would die in bed. I was too tired to worry. I could not help noticing however, that the guns had somehow a different note, more rumbly than usual. My husband came into my room and asked me whether I had seen the thrilling sight out to sea.

"What is going on?" I asked.

"I think it is an attack by E-boats."

'I jumped out of bed and rushed to the veranda. The spectacle was worthwhile getting out of bed. The enemy craft could be seen plainly in the searchlights, which were all focused out to sea. The E-boats could not be farther than a mile from the mouth of the harbour. Tracer bullets made a fine firework display. Most of the missiles struck their targets effectively. I heard that the operation, which failed dismally, was intended to destroy the vessels in harbour. Eight of the nine explosive boats were sunk, most of their crews being killed. Only about half a dozen prisoners were taken.'

This was an attempt by the Italian navy to destroy recently arrived ships and also attack the submarine base at Manoel Island. Bletchley Park gave warning of the attack and the Maltese-manned harbour defences were ready. As soon as the enemy boats came within range, the guns of St Elmo and Ricasoli went into action. The Italians planned to use a human torpedo to blow a hole in the torpedo net protecting the harbour entrance but it arrived late, so its crew exploded it as soon as it reached the net, sacrificing themselves for their mission. The explosion destroyed the net, but also the outer span of the breakwater viaduct, which collapsed, closing the gap almost as completely as the net had done. Six single-man explosive motorboats then found their way blocked and were engaged by the coastal batteries. The Italians displayed great courage in what was a forlorn hope.

The Longyears watched the engagement from their vantage point in Pietà. Michael said it was like a very noisy and deadly firework display with gun flashes from defenders and attackers, searchlights, tracer shells and exploding boats. 'It is surprising that the thought of invasion did not enter our heads. It was just another episode in the daily bombardment.'

Many on the island were lulled into a false sense of security that summer of 1941. The *Luftwaffe's* expertise had been felt, now thankfully it was busy elsewhere. Cargo was getting through although the tenuous nature of the supply chain was only recognised at the top. The authorities knew it wouldn't take much to break the chain and the consequences would be immediate. In this time of relative plenty, now was the time to conserve, even to enforce stricter rationing, and certainly the Maltese people, as much on the front-line as the troops, should have been made more aware of the situation.

There was a wide gulf in ranks between Warby, still a flying officer, and Air Vice-Marshal Hugh Lloyd, who was six ranks senior, but their relationship was crucial. To get the best out of Warby he needed to be given a free hand. That's what he got, with Lloyd turning a blind-eye to Warby's involvement with Christina, a relationship of which he must have been well aware. As far as Lloyd was concerned, Warby was a single man involved with a single lady who happened to be a member of his staff. Their work was in no way affected and there appeared to be nothing improper in the relationship. This was just as well, as service attitudes toward 'social misconduct' by officers were extremely strict; it was simply not tolerated, war or no war.

It was obvious to others Warby had Hugh Lloyd's ear; even if some had misgivings about Warby they had little choice but to leave him well alone. Some saw Warby as an eccentric loner who rarely socialised with officer colleagues. There was some truth in this. Also many frowned on Warby's attitude toward the airmen seeing it as inappropriate rather than enlightened leadership. For their part, the airmen worshipped Warby, not just for his exploits but for the interest he displayed in them. They would have done anything for him, followed him anywhere.

Warby kept Christina under wraps, away from many and this provoked further jealousy. She was of course incredibly busy as a plotter and with the Whizz-Bangs, but the haven she provided Warby was vital and there can be no doubt what she brought to their relationship ensured his survival from mounting physical and mental strain. Every pilot who arrived at the same time as Warby had been rested having flown their operational quota. So too had many others who arrived after him and had flown far less. By the summer, Warby had flown three times as many sorties as any other 69 Squadron pilot, yet he soldiered on. Hugh Lloyd worked Warby very hard indeed.

Warby's position was secure, although his frequent visits to Lloyd's office in the Ditch did nothing to suppress the jealousy felt by some. In fairness to Warby, Lloyd often dealt directly with some of his pilots. He later described how Warby would often 'breeze' into his office in the ditch and give him the benefit of his views on how to deal with Italian merchant ships and their use of ports such as Palermo and Tripoli. Warby of course was a consummate planner but so was Lloyd and one can well imagine the benign smile on Lloyds' face as he allowed his young subordinate to hold forth.

Lloyd later recalled Warby's fair-haired good looks reminded him of Lawrence of Arabia; like Lawrence he was absolutely unorthodox and a complete individualist who had to be allowed to do things his own way. Lloyd said Warby simply went on and on: tireless, controversial, cynical and aloof, but in value absolutely beyond price. He would 'reprimand' Warby for shooting down the 'poor Italians' as Lloyd referred to them. 'And he would answer a little shamefacedly:

"Well, sir, it was too easy."

'Then later on he would come into my office and say rather sheepishly:

"I've shot down another one."

"You mustn't do that Warby," I told him.'

This reveals something of the unique relationship between Lloyd and Warby.

Lloyd liked Warby and was impressed by his character. Perhaps he recognised in Warby's unorthodoxy some of his own qualities as a young pilot. Warby was very thin and Lloyd never thought he had enough to eat. But what Warby did have was a magic all of his own as well as courage and flair. Whatever his task, Warby was never deflected from it invariably returning with first class photography and detailed descriptions of his targets. If Warby was late in returning from a mission, even by ten minutes, Hugh Lloyd, a man with far reaching responsibilities over thousands of personnel, often left Lascaris to drive to Luqa to await the young pilot's return. This was not simply because Lloyd was eager for the information Warby brought, nor was he a soft touch overly concerned for one man. Lloyd simply couldn't afford to lose the man he described as the absolute king of photographic reconnaissance, the pearl of the Mediterranean. Little wonder this remarkable young man was Lloyd's recce pilot of choice in the battle of supply, the key to the contest in the Mediterranean. On its outcome, victory in North Africa for either Allies or Axis depended.

As long as Warby delivered the goods, Lloyd closed his eyes to the length of his hair and his dress or his very battered, but beloved, service dress cap. But Warby was far from having an easy time under Lloyd's patronage, working desperately hard. Warby was awarded a Bar to his Distinguished Flying Cross at the beginning of August 1941. The citation was published in the *London Gazette* on 9 September 1941:

> This officer is a most determined and skilful pilot and has carried out 125 operational missions. Flying Officer Warburton has never failed to complete the missions he has undertaken, and in the actions fought, he has destroyed at least three hostile aircraft in combat and another three on the ground.

Christina was very proud, 'to accompany him to Griscti's military uniform outfitters in Valletta, for a small silver rosette to sew on the blue and white striped ribbon he was now wearing. Warby was good at most things, but not so with his needle. It was left for me to sew the increasing number of rings and decorations on his tunic.'

Upon awarding this second DFC, Hugh Lloyd was quoted in the *Times of Malta* as saying Warby and his crew of Sergeants Paddy Moren and Frank Bastard had a price on their heads having shot down a total of eight Italian aircraft. Warby's two DFCs and each of his sergeant's DFMs made them unique. Lloyd's comment was widely reported. Maybe now was the time to rest this very able crew.

The ditch had by then been adapted for an additional purpose: The solid limestone walls on either side now contained rows of little holes, each containing a Maltese family or two. Lloyd's Maltese driver, Sergeant Aquilina, always made a point of sounding the car's distinctive horn resulting in scores of small children lining the ditch as he drove past. Lloyd described the salutes from these young children as straight from the Guards Depot. For a time, Lloyd offered a bottle of champagne for each aircraft shot down. The Lascaris staff then demanded a bottle for every ten aircraft shot down. Inevitably in the heady days of summer and autumn, the supply of champagne ran out; it was good while it lasted. But everyone understood there would be an inevitable German response.

A young Halifax-born airman met Warby in August. Jack Vowles described Warby as nearly six-foot tall, with blue eyes and a shock of light brown almost blonde hair far longer than the regulation length. Jack thought him strikingly handsome. From their first meeting Jack was required to look after Warby's aircraft. They developed a comfortable, easy-going relationship. Jack said Warby had a mild manner and was a man of few words, without a temper. But he had a look that could rivet people to the spot. Jack never heard him swear, apart from the occasional word 'bloody'. 'He sometimes wore no rank, as well as some unusual clothes and clobber. He would turn up in any odd thing - old battle dress, Oxford bags and there was nothing exceptional about seeing him in carpet slippers. He wore flying boots, but he also had some sheepskin chaps, like cowboys used to wear.

'He wasn't boastful or overpowering - but overall, he was a most exceptional man.'

Whenever Warby flew to Egypt he always asked Jack and the other airmen what they wanted him to bring back. They invariably replied it didn't matter, as long as it was something to eat. Sometimes he also brought cigarettes, but food was always far more important.

On one visit to Valletta, Jack ventured down the Gut where a certain 'Yorkie' gave Jack a tattoo on his right arm. It read 'The Fighting 69' mounted over an RAF eagle crest. Seventy years later the tattoo was still there, if a little faded, an unusual unofficial motto for a recce squadron, but one that recognised 69's Marylands could shoot back. Only three people had the same tattoo: Jack, Warby and one other.

After many changes of accommodation, Jack Vowles found himself in the former Poor House next to the old lunatic asylum near Luqa. It was here Jack saw

Warby meeting visiting Soviet officers.

Christina for the first time during a Whizz-Bangs performance. The airmen had long recognized Warby and Christina as an 'item', but it caused no comment; they said much more about Warby's dress. Military uniforms suffered greatly under the harsh working conditions and, without an adequate supply system, it was a case of having to 'make do and mend'. Little wonder Warby was often seen in unusual, often bizarre dress, although maybe he did take it to extremes.

Jack described Christina as a lovely person, good looking and pleasant, and Jack and his friends often saw them together in Valletta. They walked arm in arm, the tall handsome pilot and the very attractive, and always smartly dressed, blonde. They smiled at everyone, and despite the hardships, everyone smiled back. Jack said people sometimes applauded as Warby and Christina passed and he described their attraction for one another as magnetic. 'She looked after him. By the time he arrived at the airfield each morning, he was ready for anything.'

September saw a successful convoy arrive from Gibraltar. It was greeted by spontaneous and moving applause. Seamen paraded on deck and Royal Marine bands played as if they were returning from a peacetime cruise. Malta now had sufficient supplies for four or five months and was in a very different position to a year earlier with her garrison now numbering almost 25,000. But how long would these latest supplies have to be made to last?

Warby often reassured Christina he was safer in the air than on the ground. This was partially true as Allied aircraft often had a better chance of survival if airborne when daylight raids took place. More aircraft were destroyed or put out of action by damage on the ground than were ever shot down. In fact, it was losses on the ground that brought the RAF and the whole defence of Malta to crisis point.

Despite Warby's reassurances, Christina knew the risks. She didn't have to use her imagination; she witnessed them every time she was on duty. No doubt Christina would have asked about the bullet Warby wore on his wristband as a lucky charm. Toward the end of 1940, while attacking an Italian seaplane, Warby's Maryland was hit by defensive fire. The aircraft's canopy was shot away and a bullet hit the instrument panel before penetrating Warby's harness and then his chest. His aircraft also caught fire. Flying on only one engine, Warby successfully got the aircraft back to Luqa having extracted the bullet from his chest on the way. Hence the lucky charm. He may not have explained the details to Christina, but others would.

Some of Warby's exploits were witnessed; others took place while Christina was on duty and what occurred was there for her to hear. Often the most dangerous part of their missions was taking-off or landing when they were 'bounced' by fighters. And not just by enemy fighters.

Once, Warby was fired at by Malta's own anti-aircraft guns and his aircraft damaged. His response was to telephone the battery commander to congratulate him on his shooting, before pointing out the error of his ways. He then invited the officer concerned for a drink. On another occasion, his Maryland was shot at by a Hurricane soon after Warby had taken-off. Despite firing the colours of the day, and orbiting the prescribed 'safe' rocky islet of Filfla, the Hurricane pilot persisted. After his aircraft was hit repeatedly, Warby ordered his gunner to return fire. Only when the Hurricane had also been hit, and its pilot wounded, did the Hurricane break off. The Hurricane only just made it back to Hal Far while Warby had to abort his mission because of damage. After landing, he and his crew counted thirty-six bullet holes in their aircraft. They were lucky; too often, friendly fire ended in tragedy.

Much was made of Warby's luck. He was fortunate many times, especially when his aircraft was damaged, although many of the risks he took were calculated, based on thorough planning and preparation. He spent hours with intelligence staff learning about 'his enemy' and would use whatever tactic was appropriate to give him best advantage. Sometimes he flew at high level, other times at extremely low level. He also had the advantage that a number of his later missions were based on information from Ultra, although this was known to very few. Having found a particular ship, in order to protect Ultra, he was required to radio back to Malta confirming the ship's location, immediately giving his own position away. A number of 69 Squadron pilots questioned the rationale behind this. The response that an anti-shipping strike awaited the recce report only went so far. That Warby always came back with excellent photography, regardless of weather, or enemy action, was certainly not simply down to luck.

Warby's self-confidence increased with his continuing success. Maybe he became overconfident trying to accomplish something extra, something more than simply bringing back images of his targets. Sometimes he attacked an airfield; sometimes he actively engaged enemy aircraft rather than avoiding them, but he would only 'mix-it' with the enemy if he judged the circumstances favourable. His score of downed enemy aircraft was very unusual for a recce pilot. Of course most recce aircraft didn't have guns but the Maryland, designed and equipped as a light bomber, was unusual in that it had forward-firing guns as well as a gunner in the rear turret. For a while Warby was the top scoring pilot in Malta, although his 'kills' usually also involved his gunner, often the extremely able Paddy Moren.

Christina continued with her arduous shifts at Lascaris and regular rehearsals and performances with the Whizz-Bangs. She too was under immense pressure, spending as much time with Warby as she could when they were both off duty. Something had to give. She was desperate for Warby to be posted somewhere safer, and for a rest.

Living within walking distance of Lascaris had advantages, but it could also be extremely dangerous. At the end of one night shift when Christina was tired to the point of exhaustion, she walked home despite an air raid warning still being in force. As she made her way back to Floriana, fighter bombers swooped low dropping anti-personnel bombs indiscriminately. With masterly understatement, she later said she was far from amused by this incident. Christina's was also a very conscious courage.

Warby had ten days local leave in September, which was one of the quietest months of his first tour of duty on the island. Even so, he still shot down two Italian aircraft. He was expecting a posting back to Britain at any time. What did Christina think about that? She more than anyone realised Warby must be given a rest from operations, even if this meant separation. If he went back to Britain the chances were she would never see him again. Would that have been it, the end of a very intense relationship probably typical of many in wartime? There was little doubt Christina had completely fallen for Warby but what were his feelings toward her? Like her, he had enjoyed relationships in the past. Would he now simply move on?

Autumn in Malta is often a pleasant season once the harsh, dry winds from the south abate. Rationing was resulting in belt tightening but it was Malta Dog, similar to dysentery, which laid low those un-acclimatised to conditions. Swimming and sunbathing were favourite pastimes but sailing had obvious limitations. Dancing in the evenings was also well liked, as was the cinema, and the concert parties remained extremely well attended. The volunteer 'artistes' from Lascaris continued to do a magnificent job.

Michael Longyear still went swimming sometimes from the rocks at St George's Bay. 'There was little chance of being bombed there as there were no targets worth the effort, although there were instances of enemy planes firing machine guns at people.' With young boys renowned for having 'hollow legs', food shortages had an increasing impact which increased the fatigue Michael often felt: 'School dinners did not exist then and there was little chance of taking sandwiches when there was no bread, no butter and little to put between the bread if it was available.' At such a low level of subsistence, disease became more prevalent and there were incidences of typhoid, scurvy and amoebic dysentery.

Michael contracted sand-fly fever: 'The fever was quite nasty with a very high temperature and hallucinations for some days and physical weakness that lasted some time. I had little treatment other than the appearance of the doctor once and a lot of care from my mother. One night during this illness there was a particularly heavy raid close to us and my father asked if I would like to go to the shelter. On saying "yes" he slung me, wrapped in a blanket, over his shoulder and took me across the road to the shelter. I looked up and could see the searchlights and the tracer shells from the Bofors gun by the hospital arcing gracefully through the sky and then the flashes of bombs exploding. We sat for some hours in the shelter with me shivering, whether from cold - for the shelter was quite damp and cold - or fear I don't know: probably a bit of both.'

Michael's dad travelled to and from Floriana barracks on a motorbike. One day a stick of bombs fell close to him. One landed behind him throwing him forward and one landed in front throwing him backwards. Bruised and battered, he staggered into the First and Last Bar on Floriana's main street *Strada Sant' Anna* and helped himself to a brandy before heading to barracks. There it was pointed out that his tunic was burnt on the back and on further investigation, he was found to have a piece of shrapnel embedded in his shoulder. He was totally unaware of his injury.

George King, the head of the King family who shared the Pietà house with the Longyears, was also a Royal Engineer, a lance-sergeant. He was a stalwart of the regiment's bomb disposal squad. Some of the bombs he made safe became household items at Pietà. Two 250kg bombs, painted red, were in the hall along with a couple of aluminium bombs about a foot high with black fins, probably anti-personnel bombs. The Longyears also had an incendiary canister that they used as a wastepaper basket. Maybe Michael became a little blasé about bombs. However, they had an effect on the King family: A combination of the bombing and her husband's daily exposure to dealing with unexploded bombs turning George's wife Phyllis into a nervous wreck. She and daughters Isabel and Susan were soon evacuated.

The Royal Engineers extended the air raid shelter from the cellar diagonally opposite the Longyear home in Pietà, across the road, to an exit just outside their kitchen window. It was lit by candles which burned in niches cut into the rock; they flickered when bombs dropped close by. The shelter was only about eight feet long, the width of the road and it was cramped, damp and cold, often with condensation on the walls. There was no heating but it was safe. 'Once the exits were partially blocked and the shelter filled with choking dust when a bomb exploded very close to us. No harm befell anybody other than the initial concern of the possibility of being buried; above all there was no panic.'

Christina got her wish: Warby was posted. Not back to Britain, but to Egypt as an instructor. Hugh Lloyd would have had a hand in that, knowing a return to Malta for Warby was unlikely if he went beyond Lloyd's sphere of influence. Christina was delighted and hoped beyond hope that somehow she would get to see her beloved Warby again. He and his crew left for Egypt on 1 October 1941.

Late October and early November became known as the 'Great Deluge'. Torrential rain then returned in December which lasted into the New Year. Gone were the days when coal could be obtained even on the black market. Tamara remarked: 'The only way to keep warm was to go dancing and that is what we did.'

Shipping strikes were cancelled as aircraft became bogged down. With no tractors, muscle-power was needed to move aircraft and repair damaged runways. It was a miserable time for the hard-pressed, ill-equipped airmen working in very difficult, wet and muddy conditions. Desperately needed aircraft repairs were postponed for the needs of manual labour. The only shelter was often under the wings of aircraft with rain pouring down for hours on end. Afterwards, there was nowhere to dry clothing. Jaundice and sickness rates soared; maintenance rates fell. The many aircraft transiting through Luqa on their way to Egypt added to the problems. With refuelling carried out using five-gallon cans, the situation bordered on the chaotic. Ta' Qali's grass surface resembled its origin, a lake. There was no choice but to park many fighters in rows at Luqa where they were terribly vulnerable. Hal Far was also unusable for days at a time.

The Allied offensive in the desert began in mid-November, its success largely due to Malta's attacks on Rommel's supply chain. But it followed, as night follows day, that the island's growing ability to staunch the flow of supplies to North Africa would draw down retribution. With the onset of winter on the Russian Steppes came stalemate for the previously victorious Germans. Denied the quick victory he anticipated, Hitler turned his attention back to the tiny rock in the Mediterranean that stood in his way. He tasked *Generalfeldmarscall* 'Smiling Albert' Kesselring with obliterating the island. Malta was to be 'Coventrated', the term devised by Goebbels to describe the scale of destruction the *Luftwaffe* achieved in one night in Coventry.

A second *fliegerkorps* of battle-hardened veterans was withdrawn from airfields facing Moscow and Stalingrad and moved to Sicily and Southern Italy. They were joined by others from Belgium and France until Kesselring had about 900 aircraft to unleash against tiny Malta. Preparations were also in hand for an aerial assault. As a number of personnel on the island had forecast, Malta was about to 'cop it' with the RAF relying on outdated and clapped-out Hurricanes kept in the air by a band of intrepid pilots and hard-pressed engineers. Elsewhere in the Mediterranean, there was bad news: the aircraft carrier HMS *Ark Royal* and the battleship HMS *Barham* were both sunk by U-boats, the latter with very heavy loss of life.

The lull in bombing of Malta was over by the first week of December with bombing increasing in intensity. Tamara said: 'The authorities had been aware the Germans were moving aircraft back to Italy from the Russian Front but the news was kept secret and no official announcement was made. Yet for well over a month shelter suits (we called them "siren" suits), were being made right and left. Warm, strong material was run up into being two-piece trousers and battle dress top affairs. Some used lightweight blankets, others their husband's discarded civilian suits. Ingenuity had full scope.'

Heavy bombing intensified as Christmas approached. To the civilians the bombing appeared indiscriminate with incendiary as well as high explosive bombs used, many of which fell in residential areas. As the year drew to a close, the raids went on increasing. More and more people began to use the shelters by day as well as night. Unless one actually lived in a shelter it was often difficult to find sufficient space as Tamara and Ronnie found out. 'My husband and I failed to stake a claim in any of the shelters, chiefly through my fault of course, so that very often we had to stand up through a raid. One night, being more tired than usual, I simply had to have somewhere to lie down. Necessity being the mother of invention, my husband made me a bed out of a ladder, one end of which rested on the steps leading to the bottom part of the Salvation Army shelter and the other on an empty box of tinned bully beef cans. We spread our blanket on the ladder and I eased my hip in between two rungs and my shoulder in the space between two others. It sounds most uncomfortable but actually it was not and I slept like a log.'

By the end of December Warby's former squadron, 69 Squadron, had lost ten aircraft in the air and many more on the ground. Twenty-one of its aircrew had been killed. The Hurricanes were also struggling desperately, always outnumbered and increasingly outperformed. The only answer was Spitfires but none had been allowed out of Britain.

Then there was good news from North Africa. The siege of Tobruk was lifted and, by the end of December, Benghazi was in Allied hands for a second time.

AIRCRAFT PLOTTER

Everyone thought Rommel and his *Afrika Korps* was doomed. But bad news came from the Far East: Japan struck Pearl Harbour, Hong Kong and Malaya. The impact of the Japanese onslaught was soon felt in North Africa where, once again, and as had happened with Greece, when Allied forces were on the verge of victory in the desert they were denuded in order to reinforce failure, and an abject failure at that. Nevertheless, the surprise attacks in the Far East resulted in the United States entering the war.

The impact of the Japanese attacks was felt on the Longyears. Mary Longyear's brother-in-law, Alec Howard, worked for the Colonial Office in Hong Kong. He was also a member of the colony's Volunteer Defence Force. He was captured by the Japanese on Christmas Eve 1941. Initially incarcerated in North Camp he was eventually shipped to mainland Japan to work as slave labour. Luckily, Alec's wife, Mary's sister, escaped in time to Australia via the Philippines.

In stark contrast to Christmas the previous year, for most people Christmas 1941 was a cheerless affair with little food and nothing to protect them from a cold wind howling through broken and pane-less windows. When the sirens sounded everyone was affected, even those living in relatively remote villages. Only Gozo and the tiny island of Comino were raid-free as neither island had any targets of military significance. November and December were also torrid months for the RAF with thirty bombers shot down, a rate of attrition that simply could not be sustained. Malta's fighters also suffered heavily. By the end of 1941, there had been 1,169 alerts. Many wondered what 1942 would bring. For Christina, it brought Warby.

While Christina knew Warby was fearless, she also knew all about the mischievous side of his nature. Sometimes it was pointed in her direction. She quite enjoyed that; he made her laugh easily. And she had never been happier than when she saw him laugh or smile. Heaven knows he had been under such strain before he went to Egypt given what he had been doing every day and with so many of his friends having 'bought it or 'gone in'. Many were her friends too. They hid the horrid reality of what happened behind such terms. But through her work as a plotter she knew how they died and it was often a horrible and lonely death. In the few quiet moments they shared, Christina knew the losses affected him. She also knew there was likely to be no escape for either of them until this terrible war was over. If she was his sanctuary when he was in Malta, even a temporary one, then she was happy. She had missed him terribly when he was in Egypt, but inside she had been pleased for his sake.

It was quiet on the bus that late December morning. The Whizz-Bangs were going to Ghajn Tuffieha in the north. Some of the boys and girls were asleep, or maybe they just had their eyes closed. Perhaps they had been partying until the early hours and were catching up on their beauty sleep. Today's show was in front of the 8th Manchester Regiment. She was tired too, very tired, but she hadn't been partying, she had been on duty. There were only three raids but they were quite enough to keep D Watch busy with little chance of any shut-eye on the Ops room floor.

She had today and tonight free, before reporting back tomorrow morning, free except for today's show, her very last regular performance. Christina had known for months she couldn't continue; she had to give up either the Whizz-Bangs or her work in Fighter Control. Even though she had loved her eighteen months with the troupe, and often thought her performances were the most important of her career, she never had a moment's doubt about what she must do. Her work had never been so important, so needed, as when she was on shift at Lascaris. More and more dependants had been evacuated and they had lost many from the Ops room. Thank goodness for the Maltese girls who volunteered. They were very good and had surprised many despite some of them being terribly young. There was no way she could bring herself to leave, especially now she was about to take over as Captain of D Watch.

In many ways, she wished Warby had been posted away permanently. But now he was back, typically with no advance warning and to everyone's surprise, especially hers. There was just a small parcel waiting for her in the Ops room, neatly wrapped and tied with string. It was a 'blitzed' parachute which she could easily make into a nightdress. Warby was such a thoughtful man and so caring. Few knew what he was really like.

As their ancient bus made its way slowly through the open countryside with the tiny fields on either side, some of her friends simply stared out of the broken windows. Unbroken windows were a rarity in Malta these days. They were as rare as hens' teeth! Hens! What a joke! Suddenly there was a squeal of brakes as the Maltese driver brought the bus to a shuddering halt: 'Air raid!' he yelled. That woke everyone up!

'Making a hasty exit, he stood for a few seconds pointing excitedly at the plane he had seen then made off like a madman down the road. The rest of us got out and stayed behind the bus. We were out in the deserted open country; there was one solitary plane in the sky. No need for alarm.

'The aircraft came closer and lower. It seemed to be making straight for where we stood. I recognised a Beaufighter. Then it dawned. "Don't worry." I told the others. "It's only Warby. He told me last night that he was going to do a reconnaissance flight over our bus today."

'Fascinated, we watched the aircraft coming closer and closer. Some of us waved the gaudy, frilly costumes we were carrying. Then suddenly when it was almost overhead, the plane went into a vertical dive. "Look out - he's crashing," someone screamed and several of the party threw themselves to the ground.

'With an ear-splitting roar the plane skimmed over the bus by what seemed inches. Poor Warby. Sick at heart I closed my eyes and waited for the crash. It never came. When I had recovered my senses the Beaufighter was climbing away to the sky, the roar of its engines coming back to us like a loud mocking laugh.' Sometimes, Christina wished Warby wasn't quite so mischievous.

Warby had arrived back from Egypt the day before his impromptu, yet typical, call on Christina. In Egypt he hadn't taken to instructing and fixed a posting to No 2 Photo Reconnaissance Unit (PRU) based at Heliopolis. The unit's two Beaufighters operated with a crew of two: pilot and photographer. On his so-called rest tour, Warby was flying operationally within seven weeks of leaving Malta. It was with a recce Beaufighter that he returned to Malta on 29 December 1941.

During this second stint on the island, Warby flew all his sorties except one in the dark blue Beaufighter that so startled many of the Whizz-Bangs. The Beaufighters were fitted with three 20in cameras, and operated alongside 69 Squadron. Warby found himself once again under the direct control of Hugh Lloyd.

The various concert parties still did what they could to maintain morale. For Christmas 1941 it was the Raffians turn to stage a pantomime, this time *Babes in the Wood* in a theatre in Sliema. Cecil and Babs Roche were key members of the cast and production team as they had been throughout the year. This time Babs played Robin Hood and Cecil played a robber, appropriately named 'Grab um'. The previous year *Cinderella,* staged by the Whizz-Bangs, ran until May. This year, in sharp contrast, the final performance of the season for the Raffians' production, which was also attended by Sir William Dobbie and Air Vice-Marshal Lloyd, was 10 January. This had nothing to do with any lack of popularity but a clear indication the authorities anticipated troubled days ahead.

January was a cruel month for 69 Squadron. Wing Commander John Dowland, the squadron commander, and a George Cross holder, was attacked over Malta when returning from an early morning flight. Only his navigator was able to bale out. The Wireless Operator/Air Gunner, Pilot Officer Bob Gridley, who had accompanied Warby to Malta in September 1940, was probably already wounded. Many watched Dowland successfully ditch his aircraft only forty feet from Tigné Point east of Sliema. Despite the efforts of Gunner Izett, a Maltese gunner, who swam out to the aircraft, it sank, taking with it John Dowland and 20-year-old Bob Gridley. The following day, Bob's Maltese wife Doris gave birth to their son. Two days later, one of 69 Squadron's most experienced pilots Flight Lieutenant 'Willie' Williams, DFC, was killed along with two airmen when his taxiing aircraft detonated a nearby bomb trolley loaded with bombs. Warby would have felt the loss of Bob and Willie a great deal. But his famed luck continued.

Three days later, he was fired at by allied ships approaching Malta. Minutes after that a Hurricane patrol, led by Sandy Rabagliati, Ta' Qali's wing leader, attacked the lone Beaufighter five times before breaking off. Warby was reported as saying to Rabagliati afterwards he thought it rather a poor show as he only found one bullet hole in his aircraft's left aileron. Soon afterwards Rabagliati was posted to the Lascaris Ops room as a controller.

Warby stayed regularly with Christina, driving to and from Luqa in a battered old car although few knew exactly where Warby lived. Once when he arrived at dispersal one morning after a night raid he told Corporal Cyril Wood that some bastards had blown them out of bed. He later told Luqa's adjutant the same thing.

Christina loved to dance, so Warby asked Johnnie Walker, the other Beaufighter pilot, to go along with him and dance with Christina. This indicates something of the strength of Warby and Christina's relationship. Interestingly, Johnnie never saw Warby touch alcohol.

While some said Warby was boastful and a show-off, these views rarely came from those who worked closely with him. He was often disconcerted by the respect shown him and the fame and adulation surrounding him. At the Union Club, Johnnie Walker introduced Warby to Lieutenant Commander Wanklyn, captain of HMS *Upholder*. Wanklyn had just been awarded the Victoria Cross. He already held the Distinguished Service Order and the Distinguished Service Cross; he was now the most successful RN submarine commander of the Second World War. When Wanklyn referred to Warby as 'the great Warburton', Warby was highly embarrassed.

Despite widespread changes implemented by Hugh Lloyd to improve Lascaris, much more needed to be done. The Ops room itself was often overcrowded with spectators distracting duty staff. Many spectators were off-duty personnel anxious to see what was going on, what was on 'the plot'. No doubt a number were also interested in the ladies of Lascaris. Their presence contributed to the ventilation system being taxed beyond capacity with the air quickly becoming fouled which affected everyone's efficiency. The control room was therefore placed out of bounds to all except those on duty.

It was finally recognised Malta, in addition to the existing radars, needed some form of ground interception radar. Because of the Hurricanes' poor performance, they had to climb away from the approaching enemy to gain height. Without ground control interception radar, very good judgement - which few had - was demanded of the controller; some also lacked experience and knowledge of controlling fighters and were untrained in operations room procedures. The arrival of Group Captain 'Woody' Woodall changed that. He was a man already well known in the fighter control world, a man whose distinctive voice and controlling ability in the Battle of Britain was renowned. He took charge of fighter operations just as the *Luftwaffe's* new onslaught began. This brought into sharp focus Malta's most pressing need: Spitfires. How much longer would the beleaguered defenders have to wait?

The increase in the *Luftwaffe's* missions was dramatic, extremely well-planned and closely coordinated. It was the beginning of a long and bitter battle, ferocious in its intensity and of unparalleled duration. Although many Hurricanes were lost in combat, it was the scale of losses on the ground which demanded constant reinforcements. Over fifty were destroyed in January, which ended with only twenty-eight airworthy. With damage to hangars and repair facilities, it was more and more difficult to keep aircraft airworthy. The Hurricanes did their best but their top speed was only slightly faster than the bombers they were trying to intercept. These were heavily armoured and bullets had relatively little effect. In the same period that so many were lost, only twenty-three Axis aircraft were shot down.

The airfields were subjected to an avalanche of bombs, with night intruders flown in relays which often caught aircraft on the ground. Fires formed beacons for further raiders. Delayed action and anti-personnel bombs made runway repair extremely hazardous and many personnel were killed and injured. There were also regular night-time nuisance raids, all of which followed a similar pattern. Two enemy aircraft patrolled a few miles off Malta before returning to base, immediately being replaced by two more which repeated the performance. This continued throughout the night resulting in wearying work for the Lascaris staff as any one of these nuisance raids could easily turn into an actual bombing raid. This was the pattern for January which brought 250 separate bombing raids involving 1,500 bombers.

Shortages were now very severe and Sir William Dobbie was becoming increasingly concerned. Aviation fuel was lacking, as well as ammunition for the guns, which were often in constant action. There was also an increasing scarcity of food despite many attempts to re-supply the island by ships making the hazardous journey on their own. Rationing was increased but this came a little late. Communal feeding was introduced in January 1942. Further reductions in the ration were necessary and the Maltese people were probably not sufficiently informed of the true situation early enough. Maybe this was another case of misplaced concern about how the Maltese would react or cope with the reality of what they faced. The authorities should have had more faith.

Josephine Valetta was 15-years-old at the time. She had grown up in the family home in Floriana where music seemed to be played all the time. She had fond memories of idyllic family picnics and get-togethers. That had all come to an end in June 1940. From then on she had become used to witnessing many of the distressing aspects of a small island under siege.

From her home in Floriana, the family had a good view over Grand Harbour and they witnessed the frightening attacks on the *Illustrious*. From Josephine's perspective, this was when the real damage was done, when the real war began. She was often frightened and, as the siege intensified, she worried constantly about where her next meal was coming from. Some people actually ate rats, something she couldn't ever contemplate. Josephine's mother had doubled her monthly food order from the moment Italy declared war, stockpiling food that would keep. She later gave food to children who didn't have any. One lady who migrated to Australia after the war sent Josephine's mother a Christmas card every year in thanksgiving, saying she could never repay her for saving her babies. For Josephine, kindness to others transcended the boundaries of war. She felt sorry for a young German boy, a prisoner-of-war at the barracks at Luqa. He was starving so Josephine gave him some sandwiches. She had two brothers serving in the RAF and hoped others would show them some kindness if they found themselves in a similar position.

There were many large houses in Floriana occupied by soldiers whom Josephine said didn't stand a chance with the local women. She had often been frightened of them and usually ran past the army barracks. But the soldiers were hungry too, and a long way from home.

But Malta's problems paled into insignificance when news emerged from North Africa where the situation swung in favour of Rommel. Benghazi fell at the end of the month and Rommel's *Afrika Korps* kept going until stopped only thirty miles short of Tobruk. He had advanced 250 miles in less than ten days. The impact of this on everyone on Malta was devastating, particularly for the bomber crews whose colleagues had been slaughtered trying to stop supplies reaching Tripoli. The *Luftwaffe* was now far better placed to challenge convoys trying to reach Malta from Egypt. It soon stopped a three-ship convoy from Alexandria. What had occurred in North Africa was a catastrophe for Malta.

The pattern of attacks set in January continued into February, by which time some of the RAF's most experienced fighter pilots were lost. Tamara remembered the afternoon of 15 February well: the packed Regent cinema in Valletta received a direct hit. 'Twenty-five servicemen and twenty-six civilians were killed and a few had miraculous escapes. A sailor, who was at the bar of the picture house at the time, was rescued after three days gloriously drunk. He was very surprised when they told him what had happened. I had already seen the film, and in that Aida and I were lucky. I remember it was *North West Mounted Police*, for Aida was in favour of going. Two very good friends of ours were killed by flying rocks from the building. That particular raid did a lot of damage to Valletta and roused the Maltese to a frenzy of hatred against the Germans, for it was carried out in broad daylight and was another instance of wilful destruction of civilian property.'

Michael Longyear's elder sister Pam, who worked at the dockyard, had also gone to the Regent and arrived only moments after the cinema was hit. She witnessed the awful aftermath. She saw, 'a woman with virtually no face, it having been nearly sliced off, stagger a few paces towards her and drop dead.' Pam returned home in deep shock. Seventy-five years later Michael could still recall that day: 'She was quite traumatised as I can see her sitting in the dining room recounting it over and over to our parents; nobody noticed that I was listening intently.' Pauline Longyear also listened to the account of her older sister's ordeal. Maybe it increased her resolve to do something. But what could a 14-year-old girl do to contribute to Malta's defence?

That morning, the RAF had twenty-six Hurricanes; by the day's end there were eleven. The raids were so frequent it proved impossible to land, refuel and re-arm before the next one. The Hurricanes had had their day, yet their pilots continued to try and come to terms with their enemy. And Hugh Lloyd had no choice but to send them up, knowing he was sending some to their deaths. He knew better than anyone when the Hurricanes were out of the battle, the RAF had nothing left. Command can be a lonely place, but perhaps not as lonely as the cockpit of an outclassed fighter well past its best.

Poor weather resulted in a slackening off in raids. Even so, with on average two aircraft destroyed on the ground each day it wouldn't take long before the island was defenceless. Each airfield was then allocated two army regiments. From that moment on, there were never less than 1,500 soldiers working on the airfields and sometimes as many as 3,000. Lloyd said later he would have been out of business but for the soldiers. They were supported by civilians, officers, clerks, storemen and aircrew, by anyone who had a few hours to offer, regardless of the enemy or the weather. Gradually the work came together, the soldiers, sailors and airmen well supported by Maltese civilians and the Maltese police.

Woody Woodhall considered Hugh Lloyd a born leader who more than anyone else saved Malta in her darkest days. While he worked his subordinates hard, very hard, he worked himself harder still. Wherever trouble was worst, Lloyd would be found encouraging, helping and directing. His piercing eyes seemed to take in everything, but there was always a twinkle lurking behind them. Always supportive of subordinates if they did their jobs, he was ruthless with those who did not. He led by personal example and was so quickly on the spot when one of his airfields was being bombed, many expected a raid as soon as he arrived.

With sirens warning of enemy aircraft within thirty-five miles of the island, Lloyd established a system of flag warnings for the airfields similar to those in the dockyard. A red flag hoisted at Luqa or Ta' Qali showed the enemy was making for that particular target. This was augmented by an officer with a radio on top of San Anton Palace which afforded a view over much of the island. He warned Lascaris and the defending fighters of the location of enemy aircraft, often remaining at his post until he saw bombs leaving the aircraft. Later, an organization similar to the Observer Corps was established, manned in the main by Maltese university students locally enlisted in the RAF.

In February, Tamara and her friend Aida 'escaped' to tranquil Gozo for three days leave. They stayed at the Duke of Edinburgh Hotel in Rabat. 'The room was comfortable, the food excellent. There were no tiresome regulations. We could have our meals whenever we wanted them. The fare was simple but plentiful. The hotel baked its own bread - the most wonderful bread I have ever eaten, with a lovely crust to it and an exclusive nuttiness. We consumed an enormous amount of it. The cheese too was grand. It is called "Gozo cheese" and is made with goat's milk in small round cakes about four inches in diameter. It is an acquired taste, but once acquired, it is difficult to forget. This cheese is creamy and white and absolutely melts in one's mouth. Our favourite supper was the old English time honoured one of bread, cheese, pickles and beer. We would have it in the bar where years had put a comfortable smoky colour on the wainscoting. There was congenial company, mostly small farmers. After supper we would play rummy. Bedtime was at half past ten.

'On the second day, the veterinary surgeon who was a friend of Aida's, called on us in his car and offered to take us round the island after he had finished his calls. We said we would like to go with him to see his patients. He agreed. At the first house we stopped, we were greeted warmly by the farmer's wife. Any friend of the vet's was a friend of theirs. The vet made a tour of the island twice a day and was greatly welcomed everywhere. The Maltese prize their animals enormously and look after them wonderfully well. Goats and pigs are to be found in every farm. However, one rarely comes across bullocks or cows. The car drive proved most enjoyable. We stopped at every beauty spot and there were many. At five o'clock we went back to the small flat the vet rented for the summer months and, wonder of wonders, he had a vegetable garden with things growing in it. To make a cup of tea was a matter of minutes. Fresh turnips eaten raw, some cheese and warm new bread made a lovely meal. Our days were over too soon. We went back to Malta feeling rested and ready to take another six months of raids without flinching.

'By what we heard and saw, in the three days that we had been away, Malta had had an awful time. Damage was widespread, casualties high. We went back to the usual routine. Raids, work, drinking parties to well past midnight. I don't know how we stood the pace, especially as rations were getting smaller and smaller every day. I am sure I could not do it now. Bread rationing had been introduced and it was pretty strict. Three slices of black bread per person. Rice and spaghetti were impossible to get. Eggs went up to a shilling each, that is if one was lucky enough to find any to buy.'

For the plotters, the night shift was often wearying work because of the constant nuisance raids, made much worse by interrupted sleep during the day because of the regular raid warnings. Christina recalled one incident: 'Arriving home, I got ready for bed. Sleep for all of us had become a rationed luxury, but on that particular morning I was determined to get a double issue. I undressed and put on my favourite nightgown, one I had made out of a blitzed parachute Warby had given to me. Long and flowing, trimmed with Malta lace, it was quite a glamorous model.

'And so to bed. It was good to get between the sheets and blankets and lay my weary head on a soft pillow. Snug and warm, I couldn't care less about air raids. Let the entire German *Luftwaffe* come that morning - I would stay where I was. I was soon asleep.

'But I had tempted the devil. I awoke with a terrific start to the roar of aircraft gunfire and the sound of crashing masonry. Then came one tremendous explosion which burst open my bedroom door and sent the window splintering into fragments. The whole building rocked as if it were going to collapse. My only thought was to run for it, to get out of the place before it caved in and crushed me to death.

'Not stopping to get a coat or even a pair of slippers, I rushed out of the flat and flew down those eighty eight steps. When at last I reached the hall I paused for a few minutes. The firing had ceased; perhaps the raid was over. Then with a terrific roar the harbour anti-aircraft guns opened up - the battle was on again. The shelter, I must make for the ERA shelter. I ran out into the street and stood there absolutely dazed, shrapnel dropping all round. Should I run on or go back? "Quick, miss, come in here," a voice called out.

'It belonged to a soldier who was sheltering in the hall of the next-door flat. I dashed in and stood beside him, shivering with cold (I refused to call it fear), blissfully unaware that all I had on was my nightie. Long and flowing, trimmed with Malta lace, it was chic but transparent. But the soldier was very gallant. He took off his greatcoat and army boots and made me get into them. Then he offered me a cigarette and we saw the rest of the raid out together. When the All Clear sounded we viewed the damage around us. The corner flat, two doors away from mine, had been hit and the coping stone lay in pieces on the pavement. Later that afternoon Warby arrived breathlessly at my flat. "Was I worried," he said. "They told me when I landed it was your flat that had been hit."

'Still suffering from the effects of shock, I sobbed out my story. But Warby never had time for tears. Seeing that my emotions were getting the better of me, he said sharply: "You mean to tell me that you 'ran' all the way down those stairs in your nightie?" I nodded. "That was a very silly thing to do, wasn't it? You should have baled out of the window. You had your parachute on."'

Chapter 8

Ladies of Lascaris

It had been quiet since D Watch took over. They were all at their places, waiting. It was the waiting that got to them, the gradual build-up of tension. But the girls knew what to expect. The first messages would burst into their headphones and the plots would appear. Everyone would spring into action. But not yet, all was still quiet.

The early morning 'hate' delivered by the Eyeties from on high was widely scattered as usual. Any hits were called 'lucky' hits as the bombs seemed to land almost anywhere. It was hardly 'lucky' if the hit happened to be near you. There were too many 'lucky' hits on someone's home, or on a packed shelter. The hit near her front door a few days earlier must have been one of the 'lucky' ones.

The pride of the *Regia Aeronautica* had 'legged' it a lot earlier, off home for coffee and Chianti, long before Christina left her flat in Floriana, their flat. He had been up early, well before she was awake. He always tried not to disturb her. Sometimes he didn't even fully dress before leaving; he was so considerate when she was tired, as she often was these days. He would have been quite a sight sometimes when he got to Luqa. She smiled at the thought.

It was the siren that awakened her. It always did, but she didn't run down those eighty-eight stairs to the shelter like a mad thing as she had in the past. That would probably happen again she realised, but not today. Had it really been a year and a half since she ran helter-skelter downstairs for the very first time in the house she had shared with the Roches overlooking St Francis Barracks? How quickly time had passed. And not just time but Jacques, poor dear Jacques, and René, and so many more. And how much had happened since that very first raid - the Whizz-Bangs, Warby, then the RAF and fighter control at Lascaris. And now Captain of D Watch. What next, she wondered.

She had no doubt about the identity of the early morning attackers; the Italians had a set routine, you could almost set your clock by the timing of their raids. Her actions at home that morning would have been different if they were Germans. Was she getting just a little blasé? She knew they were back en masse.

As she looked at the plot she knew Warby was airborne. She felt very close to him when she moved his counter across the table until Malta's radars could no longer see him. She had then removed him from the plot. She always hated doing that; it seemed terribly final. She feared she would do that once more, and that would be it, he wouldn't reappear. They had lost so many friends, and the recce aircraft had suffered terribly. They took such risks to get their photos, he took such risks. He laughed at her worries and said he was immune. 'Don't you know about Warby's luck?' he said. But she still worried and hoped and prayed.

Why had they brought him back? Couldn't he have stayed away a bit longer until the heat died down? Couldn't they post him away again, even though that would mean separation? Would he forget her and move on? She didn't care, she loved him too much. She wanted him to live and she doubted he would if he kept doing this job. He said there were greater risks where she was. She couldn't argue with that, but she couldn't help but worry.

Everyone said he was too valuable; that's why he'd been brought back, that he was the one who always came back with the goods. And he did. Air Vice-Marshal Lloyd always seemed to be around when Warby was due back, hovering, taking everything in while holding his long cigarette holder to one side. Did he actually smoke, she wondered? She hadn't actually seen him. She wondered if the cigarette holder was just something to make him stand out, the Air Officer Commanding (AOC), the man in charge, the man who held lives in the palm of his hand, the man who held Warby's life in the palm of his hand.

Did Hugh Pughe, as they called him behind his back, know about them, know he often stayed with her? Once, when she glanced at him, it was as if he sensed her looking and he turned to look directly at her. He simply nodded. No smile, just a nod to one of his team. He must know, she thought, how could he not? There were so few secrets down here in the Hole. He can't have minded, he could easily have put a stop to it and order Warby to live on base at Luqa with the rest of the air boys. Warby would have hated that. Maybe Hugh Pughe actually approved, sensing he needed an escape. He certainly gave Warby a lot of rope. Some of the clothes Warby now wore when he went flying were quite outrageous. He just laughed but he could look so smart in his service dress uniform. But, please, please, sir, please send him away again, this time somewhere far away from Malta.

Things were happening. Something was beginning to build, messages were coming in and the girls were assembling the aircraft blocks. Christina was standing at one side of the plotting table wearing her headphones. Soon she too began to receive messages from the filter room. Aircraft - hostile aircraft - were forming up over Sicily. Things were different now the Germans were back.

She was always amazed by the calm voices in her headphones. Surely the girls in the filter room must be as apprehensive as she was, but they sounded so relaxed. Maybe she sounded calm too, but often it was a mask; inside she sometimes felt like a jelly. Now the plots were moving south, approaching the island. She used her long stick, pushing out the small arrow-shaped blocks to grid positions, first in *H* for *Harry* and then in *N* for *Nuts*. She tracked the course of each of the raids

Chaps-in-the-gods prior to action. (*Miriam Farrugia*)

updating the information on the block as necessary. They did this for friendly as well as hostile aircraft; those she was moving now were hostile and there were lots of them, bombers and fighters.

Things were happening up on the shelf. The 'chaps-in-the-gods', as they called the senior controller and his team, were getting ready for action. They sat high above the plotting table in the gallery, looking down as the picture below began to take shape. Then they would make their decisions. D Watch's senior controller was talking rapidly to his right-hand man, Ops B. That was Flight Lieutenant Guy Westray. How on earth could Guy listen in one ear and talk to Luqa or Ta' Qali or Hal Far on the phone at the same time? Had he already relayed that all-important word 'scramble' to one of the squadrons? They would all know soon.

Guy was always a flurry of activity, either on the 'blower' or writing frantically in his log. When it was all over he would then go through the operations log making sure it was accurate and inserting clarification here and there. She had seen the log often, all written in pencil in a hardback book. It reminded her of the exercise books she used at her old school, Manchester High School for Girls, a world and a lifetime away. What would her teachers think of her now? But here, such books recorded in fine detail the facts of a war, a minute-by-minute account of the air battle of Malta. She had often looked at the log.

Each squadron had its own call sign. *Stallion* was used for recce aircraft, that's how Christina was able to immediately identify Warby. *Pinto* was 249 Squadron.

134

Each squadron was divided into sections: White, Blue, Red, and Yellow etc. Each individual aircraft could be immediately identified by its call-sign, such as *Pinto Red Two*. Within Ops B's log, announcements on the tannoy and other vital information were written in capitals. One entry read:

0911: Scramble *Pinto* Squadron
0913: *Pinto* Squadron airborne
0917: AIR RAID WARNING
0919: *Pinto Red* Section TALLY HO
0923: *Pinto Red Two* going down, no parachute
0927: *Pinto* Squadron pancake
0929: RAIDERS PASSED

Six or seven lines to describe a bombing raid with heaven knows how many people killed or injured. And another Hurricane pilot lost.

Other girls were now moving friendly plots as our fighters scrambled. That was always reassuring. Sometimes there had not been a single fighter to meet the hordes from the north. She noticed the AOC was up on the gallery now, his cigarette holder at the ready, standing quietly behind the senior controller. He wouldn't interfere, that wasn't his style. He was just there, supporting, reassuring. It almost looked as if he was holding a conductor's baton, looking at his orchestra as they tuned up, getting ready to direct the opening movement. In a way, he was. Do all senior RAF officers have some sort of affectation like the cigarette holder? Come on girl; concentrate on the plot and the voice in your ear. Christina began to repeat the words she heard in her headset, through her microphone to the senior controller.

'Guns' - the gunnery liaison officer - was now also busy on the shelf. He was new, an army captain as usual. She hadn't seen him before, although he seemed to know his business. The air raid warning had sounded long ago and the signal flags she knew so well would be flying above the *Auberge de Castille*. The shelters would be full and the guns would be busy high above their secret world. Bombs would be falling now, but not too close to cause any white dust to descend on them from the roof of the cave. They only rarely wore their tin hats. At least hers would protect her hair. It was underneath the plotting table, along with the bag containing her gas-mask, and her make-up. Make-up! That was another laugh these days, but she always tried to look her best. 'Guns' was becoming quite animated now, talking to the artillery. They needed to know where our fighters were; we couldn't afford to lose any of our precious boys to our own guns. But someone on the airfields was catching it. That's where the bombers were focused these days.

The plots from the north began to converge with the plots from the south, soon they would merge. Then it was up to the fighter boys. Some senior controllers were

Hurricane pilots having a 'rest'. It was their job to interpret the plot, make the decision about when to scramble the handful of fighters and where to position them, and at what height, to give them the very best chance of a successful interception. Unlike some controllers who used first names, D Watch's senior controller stuck to the correct R/T procedure when he spoke to the fighter leader. Not that it mattered a great deal as they all seemed to recognise one another's voices. There was a familiarity that came across the radio - respect.

There was never a dull moment in the control room when things were like this, but she and the other girls had to pay careful attention to what was going on and to listen carefully to the instructions in their headphones from the filter room. They all relaxed slightly when they heard the words, 'Tally-Ho', then it was up to the fighter boys. That's when the girls looked at one another and crossed their fingers and hoped; they prayed a little too. They were such brave boys and they were always against such awful odds. Yes, there were thrills when an interception worked like clockwork, but there were also some terrible shocks when you heard on the radio one of ours had 'bought it', or so and so was 'going in.' He had been 'bumped' they would later say. Were those words and phrases some sort of disguise to hide the horrible truth of what had actually happened? All the fighter boys realised their chances of surviving a tour in Malta were very remote; that was the awful truth.

The plots moved north again and our fighters headed for home, some of them damaged no doubt, some of the pilots hurt. It was over. Perhaps Warby was right, the safest place for him when all hell was breaking loose over Malta and its airfields was far away in sunny Italy taking snaps. But she knew what he did was no sinecure, 69 Squadron's losses demonstrated that.

She took the call on her headphones from the filter room and then pushed a new plot onto the table, a single aircraft. It was a friendly, heading south into *H* for *Harry*. She sensed it was him, she just knew it. Soon the aircraft called up on the radio: *Stallion Two-Seven*. That confirmed it. It was Warby.

The controller answered in his normal calm manner. But there was another plot, only a few miles behind and it was a hostile. They were fighters. She hoped beyond hope they were Eyeties. In his blue Beaufighter he could outrun the best old Benito had, provided his faithful steed wasn't damaged. But his aircraft was often damaged. And they weren't Eyeties were they, they were Germans, almost certainly Me109s and they were getting closer, ever closer. She felt the blood drain from her face but she had to stay calm, be professional, regardless; others counted on her and looked up to her too.

It was only a few minutes flying time from the Sicilian coast to safety but it seemed to take forever. There was little they could do or say. He was descending, trying to gain more speed; he must have known he was being chased. Then the controller spoke once more: 'Look out, *Stallion Two-Seven*, two 109s on your tail.'

Warby didn't acknowledge; he would have his hands full, wringing every knot out of his aircraft; twisting his head to check if either of his assailants was within range for that killing shot. As he closed the island, Christina continued to plot his course trying not to think too much, just getting on with her job. He was now in *N* for *Nuts*. She also plotted the course of the two *Messerschmitts*. They were dangerously close. Then all went silent in the Ops Room; a deadly hush as all eyes were focused on the table. It was as if they were up there with him. The plots merged.

Then Christina heard the words from the filter room she hoped never to hear in her headphones:

'Plot on *Stallion Two-Seven* faded.'

Her heart thumped. But she was determined not to show the tension she felt inside.

'Plot on *Stallion Two-Seven* faded,' she repeated.

The senior controller's face was grim, fearing the worst. Christina was having the utmost difficulty carrying on. But she had to. Personal feelings didn't count in this game. There were no further plots on *Stallion Two-Seven*, only on the Me109s. She knew what that meant. Her Warby had been 'bumped'. It was the end.

Five minutes later a message came from Luqa:

'*Stallion Two-Seven* landed safely.'

Christina allowed herself to breathe again. He had flown in so low the radar stations were unable to detect his aircraft. That was all he could do to stop the pursuing 109s from getting into a killing position. I bet he'll laugh about the worry he caused, Christina thought. And he did. 'Didn't they know about Warby's luck?' he said.

The RAF headquarters at Lascaris had been under development from the moment war had been declared. Significant expansion began in June 1941 with the arrival of Hugh Lloyd as AOC and it was he who turned to the women and girls of Malta, to the wives and daughters, sisters and nieces of civilians and servicemen, Maltese and British, to alleviate his very serious manpower crisis.

When Christina applied for a job at Lascaris she did so with her close friend Marigold 'Pickles' Fletcher, another member of the Whizz-Bangs. They were two of fifty-nine applicants, such was the level of interest among women who wanted to contribute to Malta's war effort. Christina and Pickles began training on the same day, 15 June 1941, and their careers as aircraft plotters followed similar paths, both becoming captains of their respective watches. Pickles became Captain of B Watch and Christina Captain of D Watch. Christina went on to become Assistant Controller of D Watch. Pickles gained a reputation for never being late for duty, despite the hazards getting to and from work. She was noted for the high standard of her work and for her courage and steadfastness. While on duty she was told her home had been destroyed in an air raid; she continued as though nothing had happened. American-born Pickles, 'ballet dancer and contortionist who also had a very sweet singing voice', was an inspiration to everyone who worked with her. It wasn't until Christina and Pickles got right into the heart of their new jobs that they realised to what extent the lives of everyone in Malta depended on radio-location, radar. But they weren't the first ladies of Lascaris.

Mrs Phyllis Frederick arrived in Malta in February 1940. She was one of the early female civilian recruits employed in the Hole from the moment Italy declared war in June 1940. She liked living in Malta despite the bombing and found her new work interesting. As her section expanded she was became responsible for training the newcomers. She said the work became particularly onerous from December 1941 when the heavy German air offensive began. She considered any air raid consisting of less than fifty enemy aircraft a small attack. Phyllis was renowned for her courage, cheerfulness and devotion to duty. She lived in Sliema and crossed Marsamxett Harbour by ferry to get to and from work. When the ferry was cancelled because of raids, she used a rowing boat despite shell fragments falling around. Like many others, her example was inspirational.

Like Phyllis, most of the girls lived a long way from Lascaris and were at great risk travelling to and from work. When air raids were in progress, transport services were often closed down but the Ops room still needed to be fully manned. Somehow the girls still found their way to work, which resulted in Lascaris gaining a reputation for efficiency with Malta's military authorities. Until early June 1942, only the cypherines were normally brought to and from work by RAF transport. The plotters and others had to make their own way there. They were then included on the transport schedule along with other key female civilian personnel, some of who came from as far afield as St Paul's Bay, St Georges and St Julians. But the girls were not immune on or off duty and faced the same risks as everyone else and made the same sacrifices too.

There was at least one mother and daughter combination and five pairs of sisters who worked within No 8 Sector Operations Room at the same time. Irene and Patricia Cameron were sisters. Irene was the elder of the two and began work on the same day as Christina and Pickles in June 1941. Often known as Rene, Irene was an accomplished dancer and joined the Raffians concert party. She also appeared in *Babes in the Wood* playing Maid Marion opposite Babs Roche's Robin Hood. Irene was another who never failed in her duty even during the heaviest of attacks. When the flat in which she lived with her family was destroyed in an air raid she and her mother were injured. Sadly, her sister Patricia, only 18-years-old, was killed on her way to Lascaris in the same raid. Nevertheless, Irene was determined to get back to work and was back on duty after only two weeks in hospital. Always cheerful, she had no regard for her personal safety. The Cameron family had a strong service connection. Irene's father was in the RAF in Malta, she had a brother in the RAF, and another was a sergeant in the Royal Artillery. Irene later married a South African pilot, Major William Clark, who was later awarded the Distinguished Flying Cross when serving under Warby on 69 Squadron.

Irene Arnold was another girl with family service connections, her father being a gunner with the Royal Artillery on Malta. She began training three months after Christina, on 7 October 1941. She was another who showed marked devotion to duty, especially during the heavy attacks on the island, and was always one of the first to volunteer if there was ever an absentee.

There was another issue for the RAF hierarchy to consider and it needed prompt but sensitive handling. Many ladies of Lascaris were young and unattached. Others were married but separated from their husbands. Many more were daughters of British and Maltese parents, some of whom were children under the age of sixteen. They were working closely in a highly-charged atmosphere with young airmen in their prime often fighting for their lives on an island under siege. While senior staff could hardly influence what occurred between unattached adults when they were off duty, nor should they have done, they did have responsibility for the younger girls and also for wives separated from their husbands because of the war. The RAF didn't shirk that responsibility. Social misconduct in the form of extra-marital affairs, between military personnel and married ladies was simply not tolerated. An early example had been made for all to see.

One of the original and decorated members of Fighter Flight, credited with a number of aircraft destroyed, became involved with the wife of a naval officer serving away from the island. When word of this reached Sir William Dobbie, the individual concerned was history. Despite Malta's desperate shortage of experienced fighter pilots in the summer of 1940 the pilot was posted away from Malta within twenty-four hours. A few weeks later he was shot down and killed in Greece.

Hugh Lloyd had the same attitude as Dobbie. A few days before he took over in Malta, a highly decorated senior officer and veteran of both the Battle of France and the Battle of Britain arrived as a controller at Lascaris. Hugh Lloyd was desperate for such men. But the individual concerned also arrived with something of a 'reputation' of which Lloyd was aware. Lloyd became aware the senior officer concerned was becoming inappropriately involved with his subordinate female staff. He too was posted away within twenty-four hours. The military hierarchy made it very clear they would not tolerate any behaviour, especially amongst officers, that might impact adversely on morale. At the same time, many of the older girls at Lascaris, including Christina and

Pickles, acted as 'big sisters' to the very young charges they had within their respective watches.

All the girls in the various operations rooms had one thing in common: they were sworn to secrecy. While there was no hiding the nature of their employer - or even the broad location of where they worked - that was as much as they could share. They couldn't ever say anything about their work. Many took this responsibility so seriously they never spoke of what they did even after the Second World War was long over. Some took the secret they had sworn to their grave.

One was Pauline Longyear, still only 14-years-old. She had volunteered to work for the RAF and was now a fully trained aircraft plotter and a member of B Watch under the watchful eye of Christina's friend Marigold 'Pickles' Fletcher. Pauline was so tiny she was given the nickname 'Tuppence' by the other girls. On her way to and from work Pauline passed Upper Barracca Gardens where, only a few weeks before, she shared school lunches with her younger brother Michael. She never talked about her work with the RAF. Her older sister Pam was going out with Hugh Nettleton, a corporal radio operator in the RAF. Hugh was one of the RAF chaps billeted opposite the Longyears in Pietà; he also worked at Lascaris. So maybe Pam became aware of what her little sister was up to.

By late 1941, with the full-scale evacuation of British civilians well underway, there was an inevitable impact on the girls working at Lascaris. By then the Ops room was operating a four-watch system with on average fourteen girls in each watch. It was at that point Pickles and Christina became captains of their respective watches. With their additional responsibilities, it was no longer possible to swop duties to fit in with concert party performances, which was why they both gave up the Whizz-Bangs at the end of the year to concentrate on their expanded RAF duties. The concert party was an important and hugely enjoyable part of their lives for eighteen months, but now they were involved in something far greater. There were others waiting in the wings to join the entertainers, but fully trained plotters capable of leading a team were very rare.

When Group Captain Woody Woodhall arrived in February 1942 he was surprised when he realised all the plotters were civilians, wives and daughters of service personnel together with Maltese girls. He described this unusual mix as extremely good. This was praise indeed from a man who knew better than anyone how a fighter operations room at war should operate. But the strain on the Lascaris staff during the first half of 1942 was intense. They had to maintain a continuous watch for twenty-four hours a day, with very little rest possible when off duty. There had been some initial reluctance to recruit Maltese girls. Some thought they might be temperamentally unsuited to the work and unable to cope with the pressure. They were quite wrong. Their numbers swelled in the months ahead as more and more Maltese girls came forward to swell the ranks left empty as British women were repatriated. By the end of 1942 the majority of female plotters were Maltese.

Hugh Lloyd recognised he was well served by a very efficient team of ladies, the equal of any similar team in Britain. He said they did superb jobs as telephonists, typists, plotters, cipher clerks, secretaries and also supported a host of other operational and clerical duties. Tamara Marks and her friend, Aida Kelly, were two of the latter. Tamara lived in Floriana, Aida in Marsa. The majority of girls lived in Sliema and the area around Grand Harbour. They got to and from work regardless of air raids. Lloyd was fulsome in his praise for the civilians he often saw making their way through a devastated Floriana to report for duty on time: 'We would not give pride of place to any equivalent team in Britain in efficiency.'

The Cuells were another remarkable family even in a country which was home to some very remarkable people. Over time, three of their daughters - Betty, Helen and Joan - became ladies of Lascaris. Later, one of their younger brothers, Eddie, found himself on duty in the same Ops room, a gentleman of Lascaris.

Betty was the first of the Cuell girls recruited by the RAF in 1940. In the same year her sister Helen, younger by eighteen months, 'had completed my schooling and had found a job as a salesgirl with Grech and Hicks, shoe dealers in their Valletta branch opposite St. John's Co-Cathedral. One fine morning, on going to work as usual, I was shocked to discover that the shop and the buildings around it were reduced to mounds of rubble. I was therefore told to report for duty at the firm's other branch at Rabat and subsequently at the Hamrun outlet, but when the supply of leather dried up, the firm started closing down their shops and discharged their employees.'

Helen's sister, Betty, was now well established at Lascaris and suggested Helen put in an application for a similar job. 'I was called up for interview and employed. That was in June or July of 1942. There were sixty Maltese girls employed as plotters at the time, as well as a few British girls who had worked as artistes before the war and had decided to stay in Malta when the war began. Among the latter I remember two by name: Christina Ratcliffe and Melita Rustidge, who, as Auntie Melita, subsequently took part in Father's Born's children's programmes on the Rediffusion.' Helen joined B Watch working alongside Betty and young Pauline Longyear under the watchful eye of Pickles Fletcher. For two pairs of sisters, the Camerons and the Cuells, to be doing such work was highly unusual, although sadly, by the time Helen began work in the Ops room, Patricia Cameron had been killed.

As the bombing intensified and no transport was available, 'by walk' often became the only way to get to and from Lascaris. Helen and Betty usually

'B' Watch, No 8 Sector Operations Room, Lascaris, 1942: Left to right: Back row: Marjorie Hedley, Helen Cuell, Maria Warren née Falzon, Anne Button, Gladys Aitken, Betty Cuell, Helen Cauchi, Priscilla Tomlin, Phyllis Hoyle, Jessie Barber. Middle row: Cpl Oliver Trenholme, Sarah Darmanin Demajo, Carmel Smith, Rosemary Tomlin, Pauline 'Tuppence' Longyear, Jane ?, Lillian Griffiths, Doreen Lardeaux, Cpl George Arnold. Front Row: Cpl Gibson, Doris Hersey, Sgt Jock Craighee, Marigold 'Pickles' Fletcher, Cpl Max Surman, Margaret Hersey, Not known. Front Centre: AC Vassalo.

walked via Marsa and then by way of the harbour road. 'Curfew was in force and we had special passes to show if stopped by military patrols. We were often overtaken by air raids on the way and we knew the location of every shelter by heart. At night roads used to be in pitch darkness and even the striking of a match was forbidden: besides that, the road lay through an area which was often under attack. Sometimes we used to hire a *karozzin* to take us to Valletta; the fare was five shillings (25 cents), a hefty sum when one remembers that our weekly wages were thirty shillings. I do not think we were doing that job for the money but because we felt that our country needed us. Our job was a very sensitive one and before we were employed we had to declare under oath that we would under no circumstances divulge any information seen or heard in the course of our duty.'

Nearly seventy-five years later, their younger brother Eddie, living in Queensland, Australia, can still vividly recall his sisters setting off and returning from shift at all hours of the day and night, often during bombing.

Two sisters, both ladies of Lascaris: Helen & Joan Cuell. *(Eddie Cuell)*

Helen later wrote: 'In spite of the war social life for us girls was quite hectic, with lots of dances organised for every imaginable reason. The dances were usually held in the afternoon, as a rule between 3.00 and 6.00 pm and the venue was generally the Vernon Club, now occupied by the Central Bank. Malta was literally packed with servicemen. If the walls of the Vernon Club could speak they would tell stories without number of the nice time we had there, in spite of the rigours of war. There was an abundance of nice boys. Air raid warnings used to send us scurrying down to the shelter in the old railway tunnel and as soon as the all clear sounded we would be back on the dance floor. When the war began to recede from our shores, I began to frequent the Catholic club of the Knights of St Columba at Pietà, where we also enjoyed every moment'.

Betty was courted by Captain 'Mac' MacTavish of the Royal Signals. When he was posted to North Africa, he sought permission to marry Betty by borrowing a motor-bike and riding to Port Said in Egypt to see Betty's father, Walter. The round trip took two days. Betty and Mac were married in Casalpaola on 27 July 1943 with their reception in the family home.

At the reception, Eddie and his younger brother Wallace were told by their mother to make themselves scarce. They happily did so, and stumbled across some bottles containing gin and soda, all made up. A twelve-year old and a ten-year old enjoyed a fine party together.

Betty Cuell's wedding 1943; from left to right: Walter, Helen, Betty, 'Mac', Carmella, Bill Edwards (best man). *(Jane Passmore)*

Following her marriage, Betty was discharged from the RAF. She received a reference from Wing Commander C.H. Compton, senior controller on her Watch:

> The above named person was employed by this section in the capacity of a Civilian Clerk Special Duties from 23rd April 1942 to 27th July 1943, leaving on the occasion of her marriage.
>
> During this period she became fully conversant with all types of Fighter Operations Room work and Observer and Control Room duties.
>
> At all times her work gave every satisfaction even under extremely difficult conditions during heavy air attacks upon the island.
>
> It is understood that this lady proposes making application to join the Women's Auxiliary Air Force in England and she is highly recommended for the trade of Clerk Special Duties (O).

Betty left for England in September 1943. By then Helen had been joined at Lascaris by her younger sister Joan, which kept up the family tradition. This must have made the Cuell girls unique in their contribution to the RAF operational headquarters. They were unique in another way too; all three were courted unsuccessfully, at different times of course, by a young soldier called Ted Baker.

Carmela Galea, known as Nelly, was another Maltese girl who worked in the RAF headquarters. She also had a brother serving in the RAF in India. Nelly was employed as a private secretary before the war and her skills served the RAF particularly well. On 31 July 1941, at the age of eighteen, she became Air Vice-Marshal Lloyd's personal assistant.

Tony Spooner and his Wellington crew had particular cause to be thankful to Nelly. On one long-range night mission they were unable to find their way back to Malta. Out of radio contact, with no sign of land, they were down to their last few gallons of fuel. In a last throw of the dice, Tony instructed his radio operator to transmit and keep repeating an SOS in plain language. Nelly just happened to be in Hugh Lloyd's outer office in the ditch and heard the distress call on the loudspeaker. With great presence of mind, she telephoned her boyfriend, Flying Officer Bob Povey, who was officer-in-charge of the radar station near Kalafrana Bay. Bob ordered the radar aerials swung to the south-east, the most likely direction for the Wellington to appear. The powerful set picked up an unknown blip at a range of eighty miles. Bob took a chance and ordered a bearing to be sent. It worked. Tony landed his Wellington at Luqa on the 'fumes' after a mission lasting thirteen hours, probably the longest ever in a Wellington. He and his crew owed their lives to Nelly and Bob.

Nelly's 'day job' was working directly for Hugh Lloyd at the very centre of RAF activity at Malta's most critical time. Her office was in the Ditch immediately outside the tunnel entrance leading into the Lascaris Ops room. Often she walked the six miles to work yet even under the most severe bombing she never failed to get there. Twice she was blown over by bomb blasts and injured. On both occasions, after receiving medical treatment, she made her way to work. Lloyd worked exceptionally long hours; so did Nelly, often in the most trying and hazardous of circumstances. This cheerful young lady was noted for her courage and determination to do her duty, another fine example to everyone who worked at Lascaris.

In April 1942, Josephine Valetta's elder sister married George Ellis, an airman stationed at Luqa. Josephine was the bridesmaid. On their way to the ceremony, the vehicle she was travelling in was strafed by a German fighter. Once the car stopped, Josephine threw herself to the ground and lay flat, but shook her fist at their attacker. Later, her sister shouted at her for getting her dress dirty before the wedding photographs.

Very few houses in Floriana could hide from the bombs during the worst part of the siege in 1942. Josephine's home was one of them. She was in Sliema when she heard the news her home had been hit and ran five miles to get there. She could have beaten Roger Bannister that day, she said. The home she loved had been cut as if it was a piece of cheese. Her parents were very lucky, having been in the shelter beneath the house when it was hit. Even so, with all the water pipes burst, they were up to their knees in water when they were rescued. Josephine and her mother were most distressed about the loss of their beautiful home and their precious china which meant a great deal, but their father quickly put things in context by saying people were dying all over the world in the war; they were very lucky to be alive. The house could be rebuilt, he said, and they could buy new china. For a while, Josephine stayed in a bombed-out house used by British soldiers; they gave her an army blanket for privacy.

Josephine was 17-years-old when she was recruited to work for the RAF as a civilian plotter, another lady of Lascaris. She felt very safe in the Ops room. Only if bombs fell in the harbour near Lascaris Bastion could they feel the vibrations.

It was a Welshman serving with the Manchester Regiment, who eventually swept Josephine off her feet. They met on a bus when Josephine was going to a wedding. His name was Ted Roberts and he said he fell for Josephine straight away, knowing immediately she was the girl he wanted to marry. Josephine wouldn't normally have chosen to sit next to a soldier because she would have got into trouble with her parents if they had found out. But with the bus full, she had no choice. Fearing the consequences, Josephine kept their relationship a secret from her Catholic family for a long time, fearing they wouldn't have accepted it. Once Ted proposed, he had no choice but to ask Josephine's father for permission. Her father couldn't understand why Josephine didn't want to marry someone Maltese, but he gave them their blessing despite Ted being a British Protestant.

Marion Gould was also swept of her feet by a soldier. In 1942, she met Eric Childs, a sergeant medic in the Royal Army Medical Corps based at the aid post at Tigné. For Marion, just 16-years-old, it was love at first sight; Eric was five years older. They spent time swimming off the rocks in Sliema Creek and visiting Sliema's two cinemas, the Majestic and the Carlton. Marion was then recruited by the RAF as a civilian aircraft plotter, a very young lady of Lascaris. Travelling to and from work became increasingly hazardous. For evening and night duty, she was collected by bus but for the day shift she had to make her own way using the ferry across Marsamxett Harbour, often under attack. She was accompanied by her friend Peggy Christie on the hazardous journey. When the ferry was cancelled because of raids, rowing boats were used and she too experienced shell fragments falling around the open boat. In Valletta they scrambled over the rubble up to *Strada Reale*. Near the ruined Royal Opera House, covered steps took them down to the ditch and on to the Lascaris Ops room. Marion later said scenes in the film *Malta Story* offered a very true picture of their journeys to and from work.

Marion joined D Watch with Christina as her Watch Captain. She later transferred to B Watch under Pickles Fletcher. Marion said both ladies were very good to the younger girls.

Personnel from 'B' Watch, late 1942. Marion Gould is on the front row on the left.
(Marion Childs)

The Whizz-Bangs 1942. Front row, left to right: Julie Hart, Rita Moya, Marigold 'Pickles' Fletcher, Eve Ascot Hayes, Christina Ratcliffe, Mary Miles, Marion Gould. Back row, Terry Blair, 'Vicki' Ford, Chris Shaw, Bobby Vernon. *(via Frederick Galea)*

A number of girls and airmen were recruited for the Whizz-Bangs. Marion was a very good singer having sung to the troops at Tigné Barracks. Now she was taught to dance by Christina and fitted out with costumes as a fully-fledged member of the troupe; they put on a week's performance at the Manoel Theatre in Valletta.

Marion, as well as everyone else at Lascaris, was aware Adrian 'Warby' Warburton was Christina's boyfriend; they all thought them a very glamorous couple.

Zoe Meade was one of the kindest girls Marion ever knew; she also thought Melita Rustage, older than most and a former professional actress, was a truly brave lady doing exactly the same job as the younger girls. A number of young aircrew and Lascaris girls, including Marion's best friends Peggy, Carmel Smith and Mary Raynor, would sometimes gather at Doris Grimstead's flat in Sliema. Among them was Rene (Irene) Cameron who married South African Bill Clark. Marion has fond memories of Rene's sister, Patricia, a beautiful girl with violet eyes, killed in the entrance to an air raid shelter where she was sheltering on her way to Lascaris.

With raids almost continuous, many people were exhausted. Food was desperately short. By then, the Goulds had moved to Hughes Hallet Street in Sliema.

A near neighbour, a Maltese postman and his wife with five small children, showed extreme generosity by sharing equally any food they obtained from relatives' farms. Personnel from Marion's father's regiment, the 7th Heavy Anti-Aircraft Regiment, also helped with offerings; by then, the Goulds were the only family in the regiment still resident on the island, all the others having been evacuated via South Africa. Marion recalled years later: 'We did not have the heart to leave our Dad.' Despite the ever-present danger and the privations, Eric and Marion took every opportunity to swim, or to dance at the Vernon Club, Rockyvale and the Café Royal.

Another pair of sisters who worked at Lascaris were Gladys and Mary Aitken. Gladys was born in Pietá on 7 September 1925 and Mary in May 1927. They had a younger brother. Their mother Mary was Maltese, from the Cassar family, and their father Alexander was Scottish. At the war's outbreak the family was living in Valletta and Alexander was recalled to the Royal Navy to command one of the crucial boom defence vessels operating in Grand Harbour. Once bombing intensified, the family was evacuated to St George's Barracks. It was from there that Gladys was recruited by the RAF in January 1942 for work at Lascaris. She was sixteen-years old.

Gladys became a civilian aircraft plotter on 'B' Watch, under Marigold 'Pickles' Fletcher, and she is pictured with her Watch toward the end of that year. With long shifts, and far from her family home, Gladys was issued with a travel permit but buses were often cancelled at night or because of air raids. She was therefore also issued with a permit if she was unable to make it home giving her permission to sleep in Pembroke Fort Tunnel or Battery.

Later Gladys joined 'D' Watch and she is pictured with five other plotters, including Christina, dancing on the roof of Christina's Strait Street apartment.

For many of the girls at Lascaris their limited social life revolved around dances and Gladys was no exception. She kept some of her invitations for the rest of her life. One was to The Vernon Club on Saturday 12 December 1942 and another was to the Annual Boxing Day Dance at the Knights of St Columba Club in Pietá. Despite the limitations of living under siege conditions, evening dress was stipulated for ladies. A third invitation was from the Mess Committee and Members of the Sergeants' Mess Air Headquarters Valletta on 1 April 1944. By then Gladys had been joined at Lascaris by her younger sister Mary.

Gladys Aitken, 1942; age sixteen.
(*Sarah Patterson*)

On 1 June 1942, there were at least fifty-three female civilian plotters employed in the operations room at Lascaris. There were also a number of cypherines and clerks (see Appendix A). There was at least one WAAF officer who spent some time on detachment in the RAF headquarters. Section Officer Aileen Morris, MBE, was an accomplished linguist and a specialist in radio interception. She worked in Y Service, housed within the Lascaris complex, intercepting enemy radio communications and receiving similar intercepted communications forwarded from Alexandria in Egypt.

On regular visits to the airfields, Hugh Lloyd was distressed at how quickly some personnel took to their shelters. This resulted in a loss of man hours and delays in rectifying Malta's precious aircraft. Lloyd asked Aileen if she was afraid of bombing and she quite naturally said yes. Lloyd then asked her to accompany him on his next visit to Luqa. Soon after they arrived the sirens sounded and it became obvious Luqa was the target.

Woody Woodhall recalled: 'Throughout this raid those two, AOC and Section Officer, walked calmly up and down the tarmac, smoking cigarettes. Stout-hearted little Aileen told me afterwards that she had never been so frightened in her life! Foolhardy? Perhaps, but it worked!' Their example was not lost on others. Aileen's courage epitomised that of the ladies of Lascaris.

Personnel from 'B' Watch 1944: Left to right; Back Row: Not known, Carmen Borg, Kate Xuereb, Win Turk, Sarah Ellul. Middle Row: Stella Vella, Julie Xuereb, Mary Aitken, Not known, Not known. Front Row: Not known. (*Sarah Patterson*)

Chapter 9

Breaking Point

February - May 1942

On 28 February 1942, Christina's wish was granted. Soon after the incident when he was chased back to Luqa by two German fighters 'Warby was posted on temporary special duties to Egypt. I was sorry to see him go, but on the other hand I was relieved. The conflict here was reaching its most savage stage. Without Warby to worry about, both on and off duty, I felt I could get on with the war in peace.'

Warby had spent about nine weeks during this second tour on the island and had accomplished some of his most important work. Three weeks later, following the award of the Distinguished Service Order (DSO) to Warby, Christina would have been thrilled to read the following from the *London Gazette*:

> This officer has carried out many missions each of which has demanded the highest degree of courage and skill: On one occasion whilst carrying out a reconnaissance of Taranto, Flight Lieutenant Warburton made 2 attempts to penetrate the harbour, although as there was much low cloud this entailed flying at a height of 50 feet over an enemy battleship. In spite of the failure of his port engine and repeated attacks from enemy aircraft he completed his mission and made a safe return. On another occasion he obtained photographs of Tripoli in spite of enemy fighter patrols over the harbour. In March 1942 Flight Lieutenant Warburton carried out a reconnaissance of Palermo and obtained photographs revealing the damage caused by our attacks. This officer has never failed to obtain photographs from a very low altitude, regardless of enemy opposition. His work has been most valuable and he has displayed great skill and tenacity.

The description of how Warby entered Taranto harbour gives an indication of how he coped with challenges. Most entries in squadron operations record books cover two or three lines of abbreviated notes. The entry for Warby's flight on that particular day covers nine. He photographed two battleships, nine submarines, two destroyers, one torpedo boat, a hospital ship and a merchant ship. He also reported visually on four battleships, four cruisers, six to eight destroyers and nine merchant ships. His Beaufighter was subjected to intense ground fire from Taranto and he had to shut down the port engine because of oil failure. They were then chased by four Italian fighters which he evaded. Warby proceeded to Messina on one engine and reported the presence of three cruisers, four destroyers and five merchant vessels. At Messina they were fired at by heavy guns. On the way home he also spotted another hospital ship ten miles south of Reggio di Calabria.

But even this doesn't tell the full story. For that we need Corporal Ron Hadden's account; he was the photographic technician on the sortie. His description of what occurred offers a fascinating insight into Warby's world: It took two attempts to penetrate Taranto harbour on a day of particularly low cloud. Once inside, Warby flew three runs at fifty feet despite intense flak which damaged the aircraft and caused it to bounce around. The armour-plated doors separating Warby and Ron were blown open. Warby was sitting calmly with a cigarette in the corner of his mouth. His elbows were propped up on the sides of the cockpit and he had his beloved hat pulled over his flying helmet. By this stage one engine had already been damaged and the other was running hot. Nevertheless, Warby pressed on. Little wonder he was Hugh Lloyd's recce pilot of choice.

The award of a DSO to a junior officer not in command of a unit was very rare. It often indicated the individual had been very close to being awarded the Victoria Cross. This was Warby's third gallantry award. With Warby already back in Egypt, Christina's needle stayed in her darning basket this time.

Sir William Dobbie submitted a gloomy telegram to London reporting deteriorating morale. A critical point had been reached, he said. Without further re-supply, military operations from Malta were expected to cease at the end of June. Elsewhere for Britain there was more bad news. In Singapore, the Changi tree, that noted symbol of another island's survival, was felled in February 1942 to prevent the advancing Japanese army using it as a ranging point. Singapore fell a few days later with the surrender of its 75,000 strong garrison. Churchill was extremely anxious; he did not wish to contemplate the possible loss of Malta.

The first attempt to deliver Spitfires in February was an abject failure, cancelled before it began after a fault was discovered in untested overload fuel tanks. Anticipating their arrival, a few battle-hardened pilots had been flown in. As they walked from the jetty at Kalafrana, the air raid siren sounded. Within minutes they saw four antiquated Hurricanes desperately trying to climb through the early morning haze. That was the sum total of Malta's fighter defence that morning. Circling high above the lumbering machines were a dozen or more cannon-armed German fighters. Soon they swept down from their lofty perch, their characteristic 'blue note' an ominous precursor of what was to follow. It was a chilling spectacle for the new arrivals.

Early March saw fifteen Spitfires delivered. Armed with cannons, they were a match for the Germans. But it was impossible to keep their arrival secret and the *Luftwaffe* attacked soon after they landed. The pounding of the airfields then went on and on, day and night, making aircraft maintenance a nightmare. One comment that did the rounds was, 'yesterday's all clear lasted all of ten minutes'.

Two weeks later, nine more Spitfires arrived and a few days after that, another seven. But a single squadron of Spitfires did not make a Maltese summer, or even a spring. By the end of March only a handful were able to take to the air and they were not enough to make the slightest difference. Those not destroyed by bombing were soon grounded through lack of spares. Spitfires in far greater numbers were needed, but so was a far slicker organisation on the ground. Aircraft delivered in dribs and drabs were not the answer. They needed to be delivered in strength to have an impact. Lloyd was left with no alternative but to ask his courageous Hurricane pilots in their worn-out aircraft to hold the line.

Kesselring sent over dozens of fighters in advance of the bombers to lure the Hurricanes into the air. After the main bombing raid, he then sent more fighters to catch the Hurricanes at their most vulnerable, coming into land, short of fuel and with little ammunition. In one week, eight Hurricanes were destroyed in this way. Others had to be written-off after crash-landing out of fuel. The RAF could do little to stop the *Luftwaffe* and it was obvious the bombing was moving toward a climax, the RAF nearing breaking point. On 21 March, the *Luftwaffe* hit the Point de Vue Hotel in Rabat, which was in use as an RAF Officers' Mess. Five pilots and an intelligence officer were killed.

Then, at the moment of the RAF's most serious weakness, Kesselring switched tactics. He ordered the *Luftwaffe* to target Grand Harbour where prizes recently arrived from Egypt awaited. These were the *Pampas* and *Talabot,* all that remained of a convoy of four.

Both ships were moored close to Ronnie and Tamara's apartment. Tamara vividly recalled *Pampas'* ammunition exploding all night after it had been hit, and a sheet of burning oil spreading into the harbour. She and Ronnie watched *Pampas* burn until morning before the ship settled on the bottom. *Talabot* was anchored practically under the windows of their apartment and when she was hit she began to burn fiercely. Thick, black smoke from burning oil enveloped their home. She was scuttled because of ammunition on board, although her upper-deck remained above water belching fire and dense smoke which became a nightmare for the people of Floriana. Many were evacuated. *Talabot* burned for two days; Tamara was allowed back home after three. There were many individual acts of great courage by Maltese workers, some of whom lost their lives. One naval officer was awarded the George Cross and two Maltese policemen the British Empire Medal.

SS *Talabot* burning in Grand Harbour. (*via Frederick Galea*)

The warning flags on the *Auberge de Castille* in Valletta were visible from the Longyear's home in Pietà. Michael duplicated the system in front of their house. On the day of the *Pampas* attack Michael, 'sat on an unfinished tombstone in a spare piece of ground at the bottom of the garden waiting for the flag to go down. Suddenly the ground shook violently for some time and a great column of smoke and debris rose up from Grand Harbour reaching thousands of feet and then the noise of a vast explosion arrived. It was the biggest explosion that I have ever witnessed.'

At dusk on 26 March, made even darker by the smoke over Grand Harbour, the total RAF fighter strength on the island was eight. The only positive outcome was in the mind of Kesselring. He had thrown everything at the ships and airfields and paid dearly. Yet as far as he was concerned two cargo ships successfully made harbour and it took his air force three days to sink them.

Attempts at salvage continued until the end of April and Sybil Dobbie witnessed officers and men of the Cheshire Regiment retrieving what they could from *Pampas*. 'Many of her holds were flooded with oil and water, in the midst of which barrels of oil fuel and other things were floating about. Men were swimming in this filthy mixture and guiding the barrels to the sides, where others roped them together and attached them to the cranes. When we saw the work it was a warm day and the sun was shining brightly, and there was no raid at the moment, but, as the colonel, who had been swimming about with the rest of them, told me, we were seeing things at their best. Most of the unloading had been going on at night, when it was dark and very cold. At intervals the cranes would not work, or else the power was cut off so that everything had to be man-handled. Severe raids kept coming on by day and night, but so urgent was the need to get the cargoes away that no raid, however bad, was allowed to stop the work. Those Cheshire lads went grimly on, no matter what happened.' Just over half of *Pampas*'s cargo was salvaged, but only about a tenth from *Talabot*. Despite what was saved, it was nevertheless a severe setback for everyone on the island.

Earlier in March, Tamara and Ronnie had a narrow escape when a bomb exploded within fifty yards of their home. 'I shall never forget the blinding flash of fire, the blast that picked me up and threw me against the far end wall of the drawing room. My husband and one of our friends were at home with me. The men rushed out before the raid was over to see if they could be of any assistance. After an hour or so they came back with their shirts blood-stained. They did not talk much all that day. The saddest tragedy in that raid was the death of a 19-year-old girl engaged to an army boy. They had been standing on her doorstep enjoying the sun and chatting when they heard the screams of the aircraft diving. She rushed down the incline towards the shelter. At that moment the bomb hit one of the buildings which collapsed, burying her. By some strange fluke the boy, however, escaped all injury and started his hopeless task of clearing the stones away in an endeavour to find her. After three days, during which he would neither eat nor sleep, he succeeded in discovering the body quite unharmed. The stones had fallen in such a way as to form a sort of niche. She had died of suffocation.

'There were not many buildings around us which did not bear some trace of indiscriminate destruction. Some were minus a balcony, others lacked a roof, not one of them had a pane of glass left yet people insisted on inhabiting them. Short of having them razed to the ground, people refused to abandon their homes. Pickles, who was renting a flat opposite the Floriana granaries, had to move into her kitchen as it was the only place in the house where she could keep comparatively dry when it rained.'

Tamara experienced further near misses that month: 'Once when a bomb fell on top of the shelter I was in and the second one when a bomb destroyed part of the palace in Valletta on 24 March. Aida and I had only just left the heavy doorway in which we had been sheltering behind, when the blast blew the iron doors down, killing ten people who had been taking cover there with us.'

A few days later, Tamara accompanied a friend to the Customs House as he was leaving Malta for good. They sheltered on the Customs House steps waiting for the all clear. Later, as she tried to retrace her route, Tamara found the few bombs had completely changed the topography. 'I stumbled along trying to find the steps we had used to come down to the quayside. They had vanished. Big puddles of water and enormous boulders were everywhere. I could hardly see. I felt hopelessly lost. Suddenly a light flashed somewhere in the distance. I made for it. It turned out to be a small ambulance slowly edging its way back to town. I signalled to the driver and he stopped. I asked him whether he would not mind taking me back to Valletta. He agreed and opened the door for me to climb in. The sight that met my eyes nearly made me faint. On the four bunks of the ambulance, four dead bodies stretched out partially covered with blood-stained sheets. I thanked the driver but said that I'd much rather walk. I was quietly sick over the side of the wharf into the water. I don't know how I ever reached home that night.'

One evening Tamara received the call she dreaded: Ronnie had been injured in a raid. After a frantic few hours trying to establish contact with Mtarfa hospital she was given the reassuring news he had only suffered shock and a fractured shoulder blade. It could have been very much worse. Nevertheless he needed a three-week stay in hospital. Three days later, Saturday afternoon working was introduced in Tamara's office. On the first such afternoon she received another call, one she had been expecting for a long time: her home had been hit. But for the new working regime, and Ronnie's injury, they would both have been at home.

Tamara was given time off from work to see what she could do and Aida agreed to come and help. When they got to the apartment block they found a bomb had exploded about five yards in front of the house sucking one of the walls outwards. The block was surrounded by policemen who wouldn't allow anyone into the building as it was considered unsafe. After much wrangling Tamara got permission to enter to see what of her possessions she could rescue.

'Climbing the first lot of stairs was easy. The flight leading to my flat, however, was in a bad state. The banister had come away from the steps; there were large cracks on the walls and the landing had most of its flags missing. The door leading to my flat had burst open and one side of it was out of its hinges. The whole place was an awful shambles. Very carefully, trying to make ourselves as light as possible on our feet, we edged our way round the overturned furniture. The wardrobe had fallen, trapping some of my frocks beneath it; the rest were scattered about the rooms. The bed was one heap of twisted metal. Aida and I slowly carried the heavy trunks from the small recess in the bathroom and systematically started to fill them, trying not to pull too hard on anything in case the whole building came tumbling over us.

'Wearing apparel was the most important item as materials were frightfully scarce; I knew that anything I lost would be irreplaceable. We worked like Trojans. Most of my frocks had shrapnel burns in them. My best dressing-gown, the scarlet silk velvet one which my mother had sent me from America as a birthday present, had long tears on the sleeves and down the front just as if someone had purposely slashed it. Two air raid warnings were sounded but we were too busy to heed them. I dare not think what would have happened if the attacks had been made on Floriana. Aida was truly magnificent and unsparing. Thanks to her we finished clearing the bedroom in record time.

'The drawing-room, which was on the same side of the house as my bedroom, was in a pitiful state too. The thing I valued most in that room was the doll René had given me. Although the floor was unsafe with large gaps in it, I insisted on getting my doll. She had been propped on the settee against some cushions. One of the big square stones of the ceiling had fallen on her and only one of her legs was visible. Trying to dislodge the stone, I must have put too much weight on one of my feet. Suddenly there was a horrible crashing sound and there I was, clinging to the settee for sheer life, with my leg, up to the thigh, dangling in empty space. I let out a shriek. Aida, who was busy in another room, rushed in and very cautiously edged her way towards me and at last succeeded in pulling me up. The shock had been great. My leg was badly cut and bruised. I don't know how I managed not to faint. The doll had to be abandoned.' Before leaving, the floor again collapsed; this time Aida was lucky not to fall through. They left the apartment with what they could.

For the next three nights Tamara stayed with Aida while looking for somewhere else to live. Many landlords were asking high prices for barely habitable flats without gas or water. Early one evening, as Tamara and Aida made their way to Valletta after another futile attempt to find accommodation, they found Queensway, near the Vernon Club, strewn with rubble.

'We noticed three new big craters and then we saw people running towards *Porta Reale* - Kingsgate. We increased our pace to see what the commotion was all about. On reaching Kingsgate, tears sprang to our eyes. The Opera House, dear to every Maltese heart, had received a direct hit during the evening raid of 7 April. The woodwork was burning fiercely, charred or still-burning bits of material from the stage curtains were falling in the street. People were paralysed with grief and just stood there with bewildered faces.'

The raid which destroyed the Opera House set an awful pattern for April, the cruellest month for many, as the blitz reached its climax. Many of Floriana's houses became ruins and many historic buildings and monuments were destroyed. Two days later, Sir William Dobbie was watching an air raid from the roof of San Anton Palace when he saw a bomb strike the dome of nearby Mosta church. Knowing how attached the people were to the church, he went to see for himself. He expected a scene of great desolation, but to his great relief saw the church apparently intact with a bomb lying on the marble floor. Looking up, he saw a neat hole bored through the nine-foot thick dome with the bomb having fallen onto the hard marble floor 200 feet below. A congregation of 300 was at worship at the time. That the bomb failed to explode was celebrated as a miracle.

The Maltese regarded Sir William with a mixture of admiration and awe. He was often seen in towns and villages, threading his way through the debris of ruined houses and streets encouraging everyone. His daughter Sybil said this period was a horrible time that it was like, 'pain that recurs at regular intervals.

The Royal Opera House after the evening raid of 7 April 1942. *(via Frederick Galea)*

In between whiles the sufferer forgets about it; then, with a cold sickening dread, feels the first warning pangs and knows that another paroxysm is coming on.' The paroxysm was yet another raid. Tamara probably felt much the same; she eventually found a room in the top floor of a private house in Valletta that had been turned into a hostel. The bathroom was on the top floor, the water tap a hundred yards down the street.

Schooling had ceased totally by then and Michael Longyear spent more and more time with his father at the barracks. His education was now based on harsh experience. 'If there was an air raid whilst I was in the barracks I would accompany my father to his post on the top of the higher Msida bastion where he manned a twin Lewis gun mounted on a revolving stand. I would sit in the sandbagged covered part of the post until all was over: as safe as anywhere I suppose.' On one occasion Michael was sent home from the barracks on the back of a despatch rider's bike without explanation. He found out later that his middle sister Pam had been buried under rubble at the dockyard where she worked. Michael's father and some of his men from the Royal Engineers went to help in the recovery of her and her colleagues. Luckily she was found after a few hours, uninjured but shaken up.

As Michael recalled, 'During this period the bombing was getting more intense and prolonged. We lost all of the glass from the windows to the rear of the house when a bomb dropped in the well of the next door garden. Although the well was right beside the veranda the explosion caused no damage to the house but opened a great crater in the next door garden which exposed a brick-lined tunnel where the water passed each house. I often wondered where the water came from as we were at the top of the hill. The lounge and dining room were covered with a layer of damp soil and some dead birds that were blown out of the nests in the ventilation bricks in the outer wall. The glass was replaced with some material like cellophane with a very loose weave of little squares of cotton running through it for reinforcement. It was translucent rather than transparent. The house opposite had the rear of the house sliced off by an unexploded bomb at breakfast time. Our front windows went then. Luckily the RAF chaps who were billeted there had gone to the shelter that morning even though they were in the middle of breakfast. They went back and finished breakfast in the half of the kitchen that was left which was now open to the garden. All of their neighbours, including us, wandered through to see the damage with the unexploded bomb still there. The airmen took little notice of the crowd or the bomb and carried on with breakfast *al fresco*.'

Michael had his share of good fortune: 'A bomb hit a hotel at the bottom of the hill by Pietà Creek but did not explode. We children all rushed to see the damage. Of far more interest was the bomb nose, found some distance from where the bomb landed. The nose still full of deep yellow/orange TNT, had fractured at the weld on the main body and presented an opportunity that we could not miss. We chiselled out some of the TNT and went back to a friend's house and up to the flat roof. There we placed the TNT onto a sheet of newspaper, lighted the edge and retired behind a dustbin to watch the explosion. All that happened was that it burned furiously without any explosion. Little did we realise that we had been in far more danger chiselling the explosive out.'

From home Michael had a perfect view of Manoel Island, the Royal Navy's submarine base. He found *Luftwaffe* attacks on the base disconcerting as their tactic was to fly in low over the sea from the north, before climbing over Tigné Point and releasing their weapons. Some were the much dreaded land mines which caused so much damage and loss of life. The aircraft then had to pull up sharply directly above Michael's house. 'At times it seemed as though they would come into the living room.' He and his family witnessed a submarine being hit and a fleet of *dghaises* crossed from the Valletta side to pick up survivors despite the raid still going on. Enemy aircraft also seemed to use the hospital next door as a landmark when targeting Grand Harbour. The aircraft were so close Michael could often see the pilots and was able to track the bombs for some seconds after they had been released. By then Michael, like so many boys, could recognise and differentiate between the noise of the Merlin-engined Hurricanes and Spitfires from the very different sound of the *Luftwaffe* fighters and bombers. The bombers' engines made a throbbing sound, very different from the higher frequency fighter engines. He could even detect the subtle difference between the Me109 and the Me110. The Ju87 *Stuka* made a different sound altogether. All in all, Michael was having quite an education.

Michael's eldest sister Doreen Leaman had her house bombed; this was not long after the birth of her second child. She and her two babies survived because they sheltered under the stairs. They re-joined the family in Pietà until they were evacuated to England via South Africa. Her husband then joined a commando unit.

The tonnage of bombs dropped in March and April amounted to twice that dropped on London in the worst year of the Blitz. *Fliegerkorps II* flew nearly 10,000 sorties in April, twice as many as in March, killing 339 civilians and 209 servicemen. Many judged the attacks as a murderous assault to break the spirit of the people. Little wonder life was coloured by whether the attackers were German or Italian. Sybil Dobbie heard of an old lady, crouching in a shelter during a particularly bad German raid, praying fervently 'O Holy Mother, send over the Italians'.

The Maltese dug themselves in wherever they could, into cliffs, or ridges, expanding cellars or even burrowing into Malta's many fortifications. New homes with stone floors and roofs and walls were carved out. Whole families lived like

Life goes on in Valletta. (*via Frederick Galea*)

this, terribly cramped and on meagre rations, only venturing out to salvage what they could from their destroyed homes. Many preferred not to come up in daylight in these months of heavy bombardment. And all the time they hoped and prayed for relief from Britain. Meanwhile their hatred for the Italians increased as their fear of the Germans deepened and spread.

The strain was once again beginning to tell on Tamara. 'I was starting to lose my nerve. Not so much in the daytime but at night lying in bed. I would feel cold trickles of sweat running down my back as I listened to the whistles of the bombs and the sickening thud that followed them and yet I could not make up my mind to go and sleep in any of the public shelters. For one thing they were frightfully crowded. Some people had moved into them ever since 1940.

'In the old railway shelter, people had given birth and others died in them. For another, sanitary facilities were inadequate. After a couple of hours the air became stifling. Then, of course, as there were no empty bunks, it meant sleeping in deckchairs. I don't know what I would have done without Aida. She was imperturbable. Whilst I cowered in a shelter, she would more often than not be in Hastings Gardens watching the raid. When I remonstrated with her: "Don't worry," she would say, "only the very good die young and I am not very good, so it is all right." Her absolute fearlessness was contagious. Two or three times I went into the gardens with her but I must confess I did not seem to take the same delight in watching raids as she did.'

'By that time, a shelter was taken over by the RAF and allocated for the sole use of officers and their families. This shelter, in the shape of a long corridor, was divided in two by a small open-air garden. One graduated from the first part of the shelter, which was shallower, to the second part, which was deeper and therefore safer. I went to see the adjutant who was officer in charge of the shelter and asked him whether I could sleep there. He said there was enough room in the first part of the shelter and that I was welcome to it. Aida was allowed to come and sleep there too.

'At night we would undress in the room I rented, which was not far from the shelter, put our pyjamas and our overcoats on and go to the shelter. There was no privacy whatever. We never knew who would occupy the bed next to ours out of dozens of officers working night shifts in the Operations Room. In the morning we would go back to the room and have a wash, air raids permitting. However, a very ingenious system of flags was devised. From my balcony we could see the Palace Tower where the flag was hoisted. Red meant "bombers"- take cover, red and white "fighters only". We took it in turns to watch the colour of the flag, thereby having a chance to get on with our ablutions. Often we rushed out in our petticoats, the danger signal having been given too late. Good job we thought it was funny. Once, just as we were going out the door, a piece of red-hot shrapnel whizzed past me, missing me by a few inches.

'Our usual routine those days was as follows: We would finish work at five o-clock, clean the room, have a wash or attempt a bath, dress and be at the Monico bar at seven. My husband and our friends would be there by then. Cocktails until nine followed by dinner at the club - breadless very often, as we would have eaten our ration for the day. At ten, we would adjourn to Maxim's, the latest nightclub where drinks were served until past midnight, then a supper of sorts at the Mayfair Hotel.

'One evening at the Union Club (*Auberge de Provence*) in Kingsway, Valletta, I suddenly could not stand it any longer. I told Aida that I had an awful headache and would like to go to bed but she was not to accompany me. I would be quite all right. She insisted on coming with me but I firmly refused. I walked home in a daze. Sleep, everlasting sleep, was the only thing I craved.

'On one of my trips to Egypt, I had been able, after a lot of wheedling, to buy a tube of Veronal. I don't know what made me buy the stuff but I always carried it with me. Curiously enough, it gave me an enormous amount of courage in air raids. I knew that I could then kill myself painlessly if ever I was badly injured. I seemed to be acting in a trance. I quietly dissolved the contents of the small tube in a tumbler-full of water, undressed, opened the bed, swallowed the mixture, which tasted something like crushed aspirin and stretched myself comfortably on the downy bed. In about ten minutes my legs started to feel like cotton. I would move them about but it was as if they did not belong to me at all. Slowly the numbness reached my arms and it could not have been more than a quarter of an hour, before I was sound asleep.

'The next thing I remember is waking up in a strange bed. I was at the King George V hospital in Floriana. I had been unconscious for three days. Even then, I still had an overpowering desire to sleep. For another three days I slept most of the time.

'My husband came round to see me. He was looking wan and hurt. I apologised for all the trouble I had given him and tried to explain what had made me do such a silly thing, but words failed me. I could not explain it to myself. Nothing more terrible than usual happened and yet my resistance had snapped. For a few days after I left hospital I felt that my husband and Aida were watching me closely but my temporary madness was well over.

'An amusing incident occurred one evening at the Union Club, when someone asked me what I had done to my nose. Whilst unconscious, I had slipped off the bed, it seems, so that I had badly bruised my nose and cut my cheek. Obviously I could not tell my enquirer the truth. I was too ashamed of the whole business to publicise it. I wracked my brain for a plausible answer. Try as I might, however, the only thing I could think of was to say brightly that I had been fighting.

"Well, he has fixed you up badly, hasn't he?"

"Fixed me badly? That is nothing, you should see what I did to him."

'As coincidence would have it, one of the captains who had been injured in a raid walked in at that moment with his head bandaged and his arm in a sling. Pointing him out to the crowd of RAF officers who were sitting with Aida and myself:

"There you are," I said, "that's him."

'Everyone burst out laughing: they did not believe me, but to my great relief that matter was closed.'

Ronnie was by now making desperate attempts to have Tamara evacuated. Everyone has their own limits; Tamara had gone beyond hers and then had simply snapped. Her descriptions of life under incessant bombing are fluent and moving and she paints a shocking picture of someone struggling to cope. How many others suffered similarly and carried mental scars for the rest of their lives?

The heavy RAF fighter losses added urgency to the requirement for more Spitfires. With no British aircraft carrier up to the task, Churchill appealed directly to President Roosevelt for the loan of the American carrier USS *Wasp*. FDR's response was immediate and positive.

Goering's promise to Hitler was Malta would be 'Coventrated'. The weight of bombs dropped on the island in April was the equivalent of thirty-six times the devastating bombing experienced by Coventry. Throughout that hellish month, nearly 6,000 bombers attacked the island, 1,638 in a single week. Even though the assaults were concentrated on the airfields and Grand Harbour, the surrounding residential areas suffered grievously.

At the beginning of April, King George VI assumed the Colonelcy-in-Chief of the Royal Malta Artillery. This was a clear signal Britain did not intend Malta to fall. On 15 April 1942, the King awarded the George Cross to Malta. This award, and its timing, was a master stroke. There was no better symbol of Malta's will and endurance.

As Sybil Dobbie recalled, 'it was meant to include everyone on the island. There was not an old countrywoman, barefooted and wearing a *faldetta*, not a *dghaisa*-man rowing across the harbour, not a messenger, not a Gozo fisherman, not a girl in an underground office, or bombed shop, but felt that the King had understood his or her sufferings and had included him or her personally in the award. We almost felt as though we had each been mentioned by name.' From then on, Malta was known as George Cross Island and all who lived and served there were delighted with the distinction. Many pilots on the island began to wear Maltese crosses sewn on their right-hand pockets. But as Sybil also reflected, 'a medal will not feed the hungry, or shelter the homeless, or comfort the bereaved.' By the end of April, 85% of the houses in Floriana and 75% of those in Valletta had been destroyed or damaged.

Elsewhere in the Mediterranean, the situation remained grim for the Allies. Rommel's success continued and the British Army fell back, leaving Tobruk isolated, eventually stopping the *Afrika Korps* just sixty miles short of Alexandria. Malta was on the verge of starvation with no convoys having successfully unloaded their cargo since the previous November. The RAF's ability to mount a credible defence from the island was now questionable and very few RAF bombers remained able to interfere with Axis convoys. The only factor limiting Kesselring's attacks on the island was the weather.

With only a handful of RAF aircraft available, many of their crews teamed up with their army colleagues to fill sandbags and build blast pens to help protect the remaining aircraft. On some days the fighter strength was reduced to ten, then six, then sometimes four. Once the fighter strength was down to less than four, they were kept on the ground with all efforts devoted to building numbers back to a dozen or more. The artillery defences were little better. The majority of the guns, except those very close to the airfields, were limited to fifteen rounds per day. Sir William Dobbie stressed the need for a strong force of fighters and more supplies. He was advised a convoy in April was out of the question. The very worst must happen if stocks were not replenished, he said. It was now a question of survival.

On 12 April, Air Marshal Sir Arthur Tedder, the Air Officer Commanding-in-Chief Middle East, visited Malta from Egypt to see personally the conditions which had brought the RAF to its knees. From the veranda of the Xara Palace Officers' Mess in Mdina, he watched *Luftwaffe* fighters strafe RAF Ta' Qali; some aircraft actually fired at the Xara Palace itself. Tedder asked if Kesselring had been asked to lay on a show for his benefit. Later he visited Luqa minutes after it was bombed. He saw at first hand the combined efforts of airmen and soldiers as officers and other ranks, aircrew and ground crew, swarmed onto the airfield to fill craters left by the enemy bombers. 'That is the spirit of Malta,' he said. The morale of the RAF personnel was one of the most stimulating experiences Tedder had ever come across.

Soon afterwards, Churchill agreed it was time for a change of Governor. After two years in post, Sir William Dobbie had done more than enough. Exercising such responsibilities in such an environment for so long would have stretched the very best of men. He was to be succeeded by Viscount Gort, the man who saved the British Army at Dunkirk.

It was now a desperate race to re-supply Malta with Spitfires before Kesselring's glider sites were ready. On Malta's airfields, urgent measures were undertaken to build more dispersal points. Soon there were over 600 connected by forty-three miles of taxi track. Very little of this was possible without the support of the army.

On 20 April forty-six Spitfires arrived from the USS *Wasp*. Within twenty minutes, there was massive retaliation from the *Luftwaffe* which had carefully tracked the incoming aircraft on radar. The following morning, twenty-seven

Spitfires were available; by the evening, seventeen. Forty-eight hours after the reinforcements arrived, only seven Spitfires were flyable. This was Malta's nadir and, once again, the island was left virtually defenceless, bereft of adequate air defences.

To make matters worse, photographic reconnaissance revealed 1,500 glider strips ready in Sicily for an airborne assault. Matters were coming to a head. HMS *Upholder,* under the command of David Wanklyn, VC, was lost with all hands on its twenty-fifth mission. This was a bitter blow. *Upholder* had sunk almost 130,000 tons of enemy shipping, almost twice as much as any other submarine operating from Malta. The Royal Navy's submarines were now forced by weight of enemy air attack to quit Malta.

Tamara recounted that: 'On the 24 April, a Friday, pay day, Aida called for me and we went across to Accounts. The night before we had slept at her place in Hamrun and she was full of high spirits as by lucky coincidence her brothers, sisters and young nephew aged fourteen months, were there on a visit. We had a lovely quiet evening sitting round the fireplace and chatting. Usually everyone was scattered and with the everlasting air raids, visits were short-lived. Aida was particularly glad to have seen her nephew of whom she was very fond. She played with him all evening and insisted on feeding and putting him to bed.

'Just as pay-parade was over, a 200 plus raid warning was given over the Rediffusion. I wanted Aida to come with me to the shelter but she wanted something from the office she said and promised to join me at St Andrew's Scots Church as soon as possible. The raid, one of the heaviest Valletta had experienced, was over and Aida had not come in yet. I was getting quite uneasy, cursing inwardly her foolhardiness. I was sure she had gone to Hastings Gardens to watch the raid and stamp with joy at every machine shot down. She was blessed with the best eyesight of anyone I knew. At the All Clear, I rushed as far as headquarters to find her. Aida was not back at work yet. No one had seen her.

'The shelter next to the gardens had received a direct hit and the entrance was a mass of ruins. Some of the airmen, who had taken cover there, were in the sickbay. Aida was not amongst them. I asked a few fellows who knew her well whether they had seen her. The reports as to whether she had been in the shelter all the time were contradictory but they tallied at one point; she had rushed to take cover as soon as the aircraft started their dive. One of the airmen went as far as to say that he had heard her call out "Mother".

'I went back to the scene of the disaster. The ARP workers were busy carrying out wounded on stretchers and in ambulances. I asked Flight Lieutenant Vousden for permission to go as far as the ARP HQ. I ran all the way down Merchants Street with my heart in my mouth, praying that nothing may have happened to Aida. The ARP Centre, a large building reeking of iodine, was full of casualties lying on stretchers or on the floor. I asked the first warden I saw whether a girl and I gave Aida's description, had been brought in. "No," he said, he could not remember. He looked at a list he had in his hand. "No," he said again, her name was not on the list but there were many unidentified bodies, did I want to look at them? The incertitude I was in was too horrible to bear. "Yes," I said, "I will look at them."

'Our trek on sights, which I shall never forget as long as I live, began. I wished I had with me the pilot who had cold-bloodedly, in broad daylight, dropped his bombs on what he must have known was not a military target. Some bodies were so frightfully disfigured as to be unrecognisable. The only thing one had to go on was the clothes they wore. Aida had been wearing a grey skirt and a light green jumper. I searched on. I was feeling horribly sick and faint but I forced myself to look at every casualty. Aida was not amongst them. She was bombproof, she had told me that over and over again. I wondered whether she was at the club and made my way there. A few control room officers I knew well were sipping coffee in the lounge. I asked my eternal question: had they seen Aida? The answer was in the negative. They had just come up from duty. They did not even know she was missing. I told them the whole ghastly happening; they advised me to try the hospitals.

'There were about three civilian hospitals where casualties were carried to, according to their condition. Back at the office, I sat by the telephone until I had made sure from each one of them that no girl of Aida's description had been taken there during the last five hours. My last hope was to go and see whether she was at her aunt's who lived near the headquarters. As soon as I told her that Aida was missing she started crying and moaning. Dead, she was dead, she knew it. She took everyone within hearing distance as a witness. How many times had she told her to take cover? "Aie, aie, the wonderful girl, what harm had she done to meet such a horrible end?"

'She started tearing her hair in anguish. I found myself comforting her, I who needed all the comfort I could get. I left her as soon as her daughter came in. Black despair gripped me. I, who was so cautious in my affection, seemed to be fated to lose all my friends. There still remained Aida's people to see. They came to me as Aida and I had been living together. But what was I to tell them? I did not know any more than they did. Aida had disappeared. A couple of days later, her handbag was found amongst the ruins of the shelter.'

This shocking and terribly sad day finally forced Tamara to make up her mind: she had endured enough and agreed to Ronnie's urging to leave the island. The loss of such a truly loyal and supportive friend made her realise she no longer had sufficient courage to stay on Malta. Over the next few days Tamara began to gather her few possessions. Christina also invited her to come to tea and to collect the sewing machine Christina had borrowed. It had only been about a week since she

Vincenti Buildings, Floriana, summer 1942. Christina's apartment is on the top floor, left-hand corner. *(via Frederick Galea)*

had been to Christina's flat in Floriana, yet when she got there Tamara could hardly recognise the place.

'All around *Pietro Floriani* Street, only Christina's house was standing. "Standing" is a euphemism, her flat being on the fourth floor; it looked more like the Leaning Tower of Pisa than the real thing itself. There were four small craters in front of the door and a couple more round the corner. I could not imagine why Christina still insisted on living in it.'

'Just as tea was brewed, an air raid warning sounded. We took the machine down to Vincenti's shelter but Christina insisted on our going somewhere else. There was no reason for not staying there, we had used that shelter many times before, but Christina said she had a hunch and was adamant that we should leave. We took cover in another shelter a few yards down the road. In the middle of the raid, amongst other horrible sounds, we heard the hair-raising note of crashing masonry. When finally the raid ended, Vincenti's shelter was no more. My machine and Christina's few treasured possessions lay buried under a mountain of stones. Christina's sixth sense saved our lives.' This was the second time Christina's intuition saved them, the first being immediately before the attack on *Illustrious*.

There was still an ever present danger: a danger of starvation. Rations could hardly be cut further. Mid-August was estimated as the starvation date, but without relief, surrender would come earlier. This was the effect of the loss of March's supplies. But if it came to surrender it would not be addressed by Sir William Dobbie.

The Dobbie's were required to make their preparations to leave secretly. There were no goodbyes only a recorded broadcast to be transmitted after they had gone. Sybil Dobbie later wrote: 'This stipulation was a bitter blow to us. We felt that we and the garrison and the islanders had been through so much together. We had shared fear and elation, anxiety and relief, victories and defeats, danger and escapes. My father and mother (I came later) had faced those unknown perils with the men and women of Malta when they realised they would be the first community in the British Empire to endure heavy bombing and had little experience to guide them. Together we had endured the increasing pressure of the war and the growing shortage of food. Together we had all won the George Cross. And now, while things were apparently at their worst, while raiding and privations seemed still on the increase, we were leaving our friends without a word. We trusted enough in their affection for us to be sure that they would not think we had done so willingly, but we hated to do it, all the same.'

The Dobbie's departure was postponed until 7 May. Sybil said, 'I went up on the roof on the last evening and looked over scarred and battered Malta, where I had passed such an eventful time, and felt I would have given much to have been staying on, seeing things through to the end. We as a family had had the thread of our lives twisted up with that of Malta, with the warp and the woof of her suffering and her courage, and I could scarcely bear to see that thread cut. There was a heavy raid going on at a little distance, and I watched it for a time with a pain in my heart for the people must go on enduring things when I had got to safety. Then I resolutely turned my back on my last clear view of the island, with its purple twilight shot through with gun flashes, and went down to do some of the thousand-and-one jobs still outstanding.'

Viscount Gort flew in on 7 May, his arrival arranged so quickly he was unable to bring Malta's George Cross; it was sent later. Nevertheless, the impact of the award of the small silver cross was dramatic, a perfect symbol of King George VI's regard for the island and its people. Nothing could better illustrate Malta's place in history. From that day forward the *Times of Malta*, which had never missed an edition, carried an illustration of the George Cross on its front page. It still does.

Gort was well aware of Malta's precarious position, the tenuous nature of its supply lines and its vulnerability to air assault. That vulnerability was brought home within minutes of his seaplane landing. As he stepped ashore, a bomb landed uncomfortably close and a number of people assembled to meet him fell flat on their faces. In the middle of the ceremony to swear him in - held in the battered home of Kalafrana's station commander - more bombs fell. A number of officials hid beneath chairs and tables. Gort blanched at such behaviour. Only a few minutes earlier, the Dobbies had left. For Sir William it was always a case of job done, rank or position did not matter, and he and Lady Dobbie had done their very best for Malta at a particularly important time. Looking back, Sybil Dobbie said: 'As far as raids were concerned, we left Malta just when the night was darkest and the dawn nearest.'

On the afternoon of 30 May, at 5.00 pm, Tamara received the order she was to leave Malta at 10.00 pm that evening. 'Day by day, two years of the most gruelling experience in my life had drawn to a close. I packed two very meagre suitcases, had a last party at Captain Caruana's bar and at ten o'clock sharp we were at Luqa aerodrome where the Lodestar I was to embark on was warming its engines. Christina and my husband had come to see me off. I left with the feeling that I should have been braver and stayed to the end.'

Tamara wrote to Christina from Egypt urging her to join her but Christina felt that her place was in Malta. 'I did not want to be a Ratcliffe deserting a sinking ship and besides, after having gone so far, I wanted to stay and see things through.'

On the day Aida Kelly went missing, three unidentified people were confirmed killed in the blast at St John's Tunnel - *Mina s-Sewda* - in Valletta. The stark official report includes the following: 'Remains of a female adult of unidentifiable age, crushed body from fallen masonry due to an air raid, on April 24, 1942, at 10.45 am, at *Mina s-Sewda*, Valletta - buried April 26, at 10.45 am., in Division East GA-C-9.' This was a plot reserved for unidentified casualties within *Santa Maria Addolorata* cemetery in Paola.

This was almost certainly the 'tall, dark, lovely and so unalterably cheerful' Aida Kelly, a loyal and supportive friend to Tamara Marks and a gallant lady from the RAF headquarters.

Chapter 10

Spitfire Summer

Sunday, 10 May 1942

Christina had no idea yesterday would turn out to be such a great day, although, like everyone else, she had been very excited at the prospect of what might happen. It had been an absolute joy to place on the plot no less than sixty-one Spitfires heading through '*M*' for *Monkey* to Malta, all launched from the USS *Wasp* hundreds of miles to the west. This time, they arrived ready to fight. The boys had them refuelled and rearmed in no time at all, each aircraft manned by a fresh, Malta-experienced fighter pilot and ready to scramble in minutes.

It was now the morning after, and Christina wondered if their precious aircraft survived the night before, so many were usually destroyed on the ground. At one stage, they weren't able to place a single fighter on the plot. They had nothing to stop the hordes from the north, nothing except the guns. But even the anti-aircraft ammunition was rationed like everything else.

As soon as she reported for duty in the Hole, Christina discovered she needn't have worried - the Spitfires had been well-protected and well looked after. She focused on her duties on this new day, the day after the long-awaited Spitfire summer began. She had little to do organising the girls; they were always ready and well-practiced in playing their parts. They were the back-room girls, well-hidden under Valletta's fortress walls, far removed from the harrowing scenes in the city and skies above. But they were often touched by what happened up there; that was where they lived and where they might die, just as poor Patricia had done only a few weeks before.

The last few months had been totally one-sided; so many air boys they knew had bought it. Thank goodness Warby was well out of it. She often recognised their voices over the radio and it was heartbreaking to hear them say one of theirs had 'gone in' and there was no 'chute. She felt numb when it happened. Her task was then to remove that particular plot from the table. She recognised the voice of Bert Mitchell, a New Zealander with 603 Squadron. He called up on the radio just before he hit the water saying: 'So long Woody, I've had it.'

Recently, the days had been fraught, busier than ever before; relentless. Ever since January, there had been raid after raid, even when the weather was poor, and every time the boys were sent up against terrible odds. And every day their numbers were less than the day before. The girls grew weary of the same story day after day, week after week:

'Fifty plus bombers approaching the island.'

'Visual on hostile fighters now crossing Gozo.'

'One hundred plus milling up over Comiso.'

There were always too many one-way tracks on the table, too many hostile plots pointing at their tiny isolated island.

Then came today; day two of their early Spitfire summer. Things began to happen quickly, but they were ready, each and every one of them. It was as if a magic wand was waved over the Ops room. Within minutes, the cavern was a hive of activity, with an amount of traffic on the plotting table never seen before. Two pairs of hands were not enough to cope with the mass of plots on the painted sea between Sicily and Malta, and a helper was positioned at each end of the table to rake off old tracks and set up fresh blocks. There was no time to change over or be relieved; those at the main plotting table had to stay where they were. Those involved in the vital task of gun liaison, or in the all-important direction finding room, had to stay at their places too. It was a case of all hands on deck and there was no time at all to powder one's nose or make a brew.

High above her on the shelf, the faces of the chaps-in-the-gods radiated delight as they went about their duties with renewed vigour and enthusiasm. There was

an exultant note in the deep, powerful voice of Wing Commander Bill Farnes, the Controller, idol of the plotters, as he shot out a volley of orders over the radio. Handsome, rugged, ruthless, Farnes could raise a girl up or cast her down, reduce her to tears or induce her to laughter - it all depended on his mood. He was one of their finest controllers; that's what mattered.

Sitting next to him was Guy Westray, Ops B, with a telephone glued to each ear talking constantly to the airfields. All eyes were focused on the table, but how Bill Farnes could make head or tail of the chaos was beyond the comprehension of many. Hostile and friendly plots mingled with each other in what seemed one grand and glorious muddle. Yet the scene on the table was an accurate reflection of the picture in the sky above. It looked like the

Wing Commander Bill Farnes, Senior Controller D Watch Lascaris April-December 1942. (*Cara Egerton/Nick Farnes*)

outside of some fantastic wasps' nest, with aircraft milling about in a clash of colonies.

Among all the happy faces on the shelf, none beamed quite as brightly as Woody's: Group Captain Woodhall, the officer-in-charge of the Ops room, complete with his monocle held firmly in place as if by magic. Woody was in a class of his own. He now had squadrons of Spitfires manned by experienced pilots to put up against the Hun. Only Christina and her fellow plotters knew of the dozens of dummy runs he had staged over the radio with imaginary airborne squadrons. Once Woody put a Canadian with an unmistakable voice on the microphone at a stand-by radio set, then proceeded to give him dummy orders. The Canadian replied just as if he was flying his fighter. This resulted in two enemy fighters enthusiastically shooting each other down without any British aircraft airborne. Woody said to mark two 'kills' down to Pilot Officer Humgufery. Today there was no need for any such hoax.

'As instructions from the filter room came one upon the other into my headphones and I feverishly pushed out plot after plot to their positions on the table, I grew increasingly proud of the fact that my efforts, small cog in the big wheel though they might be, were of the utmost importance to the Controller above. I regarded it as a wonderful stroke of luck that my Watch, D Watch, should be on duty this great morning. And the girls themselves, by now all Maltese, were grateful for the opportunity to show their mettle, to explode the myth they would panic when really put to the test. They carried out their tasks so well that Woody, during a lull in the storm, came down from the Shelf and thanked each plotter personally for "the very fine show" she had put on.

'It was not until afterwards, when big Bill Farnes added his own special blooms to the verbal bouquet that the girls went to pieces - and then there was swooning all round! Had my heart not belonged to somebody else, like the rest of them, I might well have measured my length at the feet of that fascinating *homme fatal*.'

This latest Spitfire delivery marked a turning point in the air battle, although the desperate situation for the population continued. For some reason, after the Spitfire arrival the previous day, Kesselring did not unleash his bombers when the Spitfires were at their most vulnerable, within the first twenty-four hours. This gave the RAF time enough to prepare for the scene that unfolded on 10 May; the scene in which Christina and D Watch played such a useful part:

'The life-and-death struggle for supremacy between two air forces provided a never-to-be-forgotten experience for those who were able to watch. Shelter seekers and others who did not see the "show" got a good idea of what they had missed from the next morning's *Times of Malta*. "Axis Heavy Losses" screamed the big black headlines. "Spitfires Slaughter *Stukas* - Brilliant Team Work of AA Gunners and RAF - 63 Enemy Aircraft Destroyed Over Malta Yesterday."

'All Malta went wild with joy at this great turn of events. Fresh hope sprang into the hearts of the people. Spitfires, for which we had been crying out for so long, were now here to defend us, shoals of them.'

However, the Spitfires would not have been enough but for a lone Welshman: HMS *Welshman*. The day after the Spitfires arrived she docked after an incredible journey from Gibraltar. The scene she met was one of near total desolation. Wrecks were scattered left and right and masts of sunken ships pointed accusingly skyward. On the various wharfs, rubble reached the water's edge. Lord Gort was on hand; his presence felt everywhere offering help and encouragement. *Welshman* was soon surrounded by lighters, and working parties quickly unloaded the ninety-six precious Spitfire engines. By then her 100 RAF passengers, all Spitfire specialists, were safely ashore.

The Germans soon launched a ferocious attack. It was met by a vital part of the ship's cargo, the contents of six dozen crates of smoke-making compound. Soon the ship was hidden by artificial smoke. The attackers were also met by the newly-arrived Spitfires. Over French Creek, eighteen German aircraft were shot down. A few minutes after the raiders departed, Gort boarded *Welshman*. He found her listing, with holes above the waterline and her decks covered with debris. But her cargo was on land and she was still seaworthy. That evening, she cast off to steer between burnt-out and sunken hulks to a ring of cheers from the bastions of Valletta and Senglea and the singing of *Roll out the Barrel*. She was back in Gibraltar two days later. This lonely ship served Malta well.

The battle had indeed been furious, although the number of Axis aircraft destroyed - published in the *Times of Malta* - was exaggerated. On the evening of 10 May, Air Headquarters estimated twenty-three enemy aircraft destroyed, and a further twenty-four damaged, all for the loss of one Spitfire and one pilot missing. That evening, Rome Radio announced the loss of thirty-seven Axis aircraft against the destruction of forty-seven Spitfires. This was a huge success for Malta's defenders, but that evening Hugh Lloyd found the atmosphere amongst the fighter pilots subdued. They knew their enemy, and they were all aware of the previous short-lived successes. Famine was not far away and many pilots harboured doubts about their ability to hold on to the day's advantage.

Surprisingly, Kesselring reported to Berlin his task of neutralizing Malta as an offensive base was now complete. His premature and ill-judged comment reveals the inadequacy of Germany intelligence gathering. He then reduced *Fliegerkorps II* in order to increase support for Rommel's planned offensive in North Africa. Although it was not known at the time, Hitler postponed the invasion of Malta until after Rommel captured Tobruk. Kesselring, who always advocated the capture of Malta in order to guarantee supplies to the *Afrika Korps,* later wrote that the abandonment of the project to capture Malta was the first death blow to Germany's whole undertaking in North Africa.

Gort's first task was to ensure Malta did not starve its way to surrender. He took a firm grip and introduced more stringent rationing. Nutrition experts, along with dehydrated foods, were flown in. Gas, electric and water supplies were badly affected across the island. In fact, Valletta was without these services for five

Christina collects her daily supply of water from a street tap. *(via Frederick Galea)*

months. Hot drinks were a thing of the past. There was rarely enough fuel for pumps to draw water from underground wells which resulted in little for drinking and even less for sanitation.

Schools were closed, as were places of entertainment. Many streets were blocked by thousands of tons of stone. Nevertheless, the determination and loyalty of the Maltese did not waiver.

With a black market rife it was essential there was some control of supplies. Lord Gort expanded communal eating and Victory Kitchens, or VKs as they were known, were opened in every town and village. Some judged VKs were established 'in order that no one starved before all starved'. Christina was later involved in publicity photographs promoting the VKs. She recalled: 'When rabbit stew was offered one did not ask what had become of the cat.'

Eddie Cuell was 12-years-old at the time. One of his most vivid memories is of queuing, queuing for everything. 'Whether it was raining, or hot and sweaty, we queued for milk, which was one-pint bottle for eight of us per day.

'For kerosene I took a wine or spirit bottle to fill and that was on a first-come, first-served basis. Many times I was so far back in the queue that none was left.

'Mum always picked me to do these chores, except when we had to collect our food rations which were issued fortnightly; my sister Joan and my brother Wallace came and helped me.' Whatever it was for, the Maltese queued and so often it was the children doing the queuing, waiting patiently for things that quickly ran out.

174

A milk queue. *(via Frederick Galea)*

A paraffin queue. *(via Frederick Galea)*

'Then it got worse and we had the Victory Kitchens saga. Taking pots and dishes to be served in, many a time anything given to you hot was cold by the time you got home and then I was told off for being late. Then my mother, God bless her, had the task of warming it up somehow and having to serve it evenly between eight of us. I wondered where the rabbit and goat meat was coming from as dogs and cats were getting scarce. What were we being fed?' Eddie's elder sister Helen recalled: 'Like most Maltese we suffered the pangs of hunger, in fact probably we suffered more because we could never stomach the Victory Kitchen meals with the possible exception of tinned tuna. We never got any food from the service people; I think they were as badly off as the rest of us.'

As the siege continued with little prospect of relief the VKs came into their own. By May there were forty in twenty-three locations with 4,000 people registered to use them. With the lack of oil for cooking, people in their tens of thousands brought what little food they had to the VKs where it was cooked in bulk, saving precious supplies of kerosene. By the end of 1942 the VKs catered for the majority of the population with 170,000 people registered. The expansion of communal feeding was masterly and there is little doubt the population owed its survival to the VKs through some very grim days. Even stocks available on the black market gradually reduced.

Michael Longyear sometimes shared the troops' lunch at Floriana barracks. 'It consisted of a large ladle off batter mixture deep-fried in olive oil and nothing else.

Queuing at one of the Victory Kitchens. *(via Frederick Galea)*

I had one and it was really good batter, but there was nothing in it; just the same as the troops were given. One thing I liked was to chew the locust bean, normally fed to horses, which was sweet and tasty.'

Arguably more stringent rationing introduced much earlier might have alleviated the desperate situation. Yet it would only have delayed matters, it would not have relieved them. There were many occasions when the supply of flour was only enough for ten days, but then the lonely *Welshman* arrived and the situation eased. Over the next two months, she successfully ran the blockade twice more. She was only a single ship but the stores she delivered were crucial. After her third trip, her captain and twenty-one members of her crew received gallantry awards. Nevertheless, even Gort realised, without a significant re-supply effort, the outcome for Malta was inevitable - surrender.

The Air Historical Branch later recorded the first eight months of 1942 as the heaviest and most sustained bombardment in the history of air warfare. Throughout this period, photographic reconnaissance was the work of two or three pilots. At the beginning of the year, those pilots were Warby and Johnnie Walker flying Beaufighters. After Warby left, the recce effort was largely in the hands of newcomer Harry Coldbeck flying a Spitfire.

Despite having more Spitfires, Lloyd continued to direct Woody to be selective. To begin with, whenever the Axis sent over fighters, or 'little jobs' as Woody preferred to call them, Lloyd kept the Spitfires on the ground despite a clamour from his pilots to scramble. When the bombers were detected - 'big jobs' - then the Spitfires were released. Gradually the Spitfires asserted their authority and began to push Axis aircraft further north, intercepting enemy bombers out to sea by forward interception long before they could unload their lethal cargo.

Malta's radar operators, the controllers and the ladies of Lascaris were in their element. The RAF could now pick and choose when and where to give battle, using every tactical advantage available. The Axis was dogged and tenacious but was met in equal measure. One newly arrived Spitfire pilot said the tempo was indescribable: 'It all makes the Battle of Britain and fighter-sweeps seem child's play by comparison.' May 1942 marked the turning point in the air battle of Malta - Kesselring simply could not afford the casualties. Lloyd estimated 154 Axis aircraft destroyed that month, while the tonnage of bombs dropped reduced from over 500 in the first eight days to just over 100 in the remainder of the month.

While the Spitfires were essential in winning the air battle, the island could only be truly saved by a convoy; only time would tell whether the island could win the war against starvation. This was a distinct possibility which concerned Gort greatly. With rationing tightened yet again, the plight of civilians and servicemen alike was distressing, although most remained cheerful and complaints were largely good-natured. The relatively high morale was down to the success of the Spitfires which many could see overhead every day. 'With the coming of the Spitfires, the disappearance of the *Luftwaffe* and the tonic touch of springtime, the spirits of the islanders rose up and scraped the sky. People began to enjoy themselves again. Letting their hair down to hip-level, they flocked in their thousands to what places of entertainment were still left standing. The whirl of social life was stepped up to a fast and furious tempo, nobody caring a damn about the Italian Air Force.

'Confidence in our defenders was such that when the siren went there was no more scurrying to earth like frightened rabbits and foxes. In the cinemas, audiences sat through the picture they had gone to see without recourse to the "Rock Shelter on Premises" - a tag which had become as much a part of a film advertisement as the names of the stars and times of showing. At home, in the streets, in shops and offices, people got back their nerve and faced up to life with fresh courage.

'Once again *Strada Reale* in Valletta became the promenade of the evening stroller; the happy hunting ground of the lover for his lass. Up and down, between the ancient gates of the city and the Palace Square, the light-hearted crowds surged to and fro, gossiping and laughing - relaxing for the first time in many months. And relaxing with them in their leisure hours, were the Spitfire pilots. Attired in an outrageous combination of flying kit uniform and civilian dress, they were a great attraction as they ambled the street - often followed by gangs of small boys eager to get a close-up view of their new-found heroes.

'Not unmindful of the charms that lay beneath the bastions of Lascaris, the air boys displayed a lively interest in the work carried on at Fighter Control. Bunches of off-duty crews could be seen hanging round the entrance to the Ops room like so many stage-door Johnnies. If they could think up some excuse to get inside, so much the better, and as can be imagined, with the influx of all this manhood-in-flower the private life of a plotter became a thing of joy.

'A girl didn't need to be pretty to get a date - it was enough just to be feminine. Faces that normally would not get the Sliema Ferry off its moorings could now launch a thousand ships. There was a gleam of hope in Plain Jane's eye as invitations came in by the conveyor belt: meet me tonight at the Premier; let's roller skate at the Rockyvale; see you at eight in the Monico.

'It is doubtful whether the Union Club in Valletta will witness again such scenes of revelry and wild abandon as were enacted between its stately walls at the Saturday night dances. The premises had been converted into a club well over a hundred years ago, a strictly exclusive club that in normal times was frequented mainly by senior offices of the services and pedigree members of the civilian community. These days it was also a meeting place for the air boys and their girlfriends and many a half-breed and mongrel got mixed up with the poodles and Pekes. But nobody seemed to mind.

'On Saturday evenings, the Ladies Lounge, famed far beyond the shores of Malta as the "Snake Pit", was cleared of its furniture and carpets and a rollicking ragtime band moved in to charm the serpents. You wouldn't have known the place. Rank and position went by the board as stuffed shirts and staid old colonels cavorted with the rest of us in such frivolities as *Boomps-a-Daisy*, *Hokey-Kokey* and *Knees up, Mother Brown*.'

Godfrey Caruana was proprietor of Captain Caruana's, a small tobacconist's shop and bar on Kingsway. He also owned a cinema which he kept open as long as possible in spite of the bombing. Woody remembered him fondly: 'Godfrey, plump and always smiling, welcomed one as no one else can and when he sang his "Raspberry Song" for you, you knew that he had really taken you to his heart. In times when liquor was very scarce and profiteering was often met, Godfrey always sold the real stuff at something under the controlled price. When any of his RAF friends left the island he would open a bottle of his precious champagne and this would be "on the house".' Godfrey was a brave, generous and resourceful friend and always offered a warm welcome in a way few could.

Starvation date was calculated as mid-August; surrender date would be earlier. These were the facts and there was no escaping from them. Two convoys tried in June, one from the east and one from the west. The one from the east was forced to turn back. Only two ships from the west, two very battered, damaged merchant ships made it, greeted by thousands of people in silence, almost in reverence, given what they had endured. That was it, two out of six, but what they delivered was vital. It was a great achievement to get even two ships through and although the quantity of stores was relatively small, it saved Malta from starvation for a further two to three months. Nevertheless, rationing now reached its peak, the hunger of both garrison and population growing worse. Hugh Lloyd later commented: 'Had we taken serious notice of our supply situation in 1941, and had we taken a strong line and brought the Maltese fully into our confidence, we should not have been reduced to our very parlous state in the spring of 1942.' The cost of both operations was the loss of eleven ships and eleven more damaged; the RAF lost at least forty aircraft. But more time, very valuable time, was bought by the lives of Allied sailors and airmen. Meanwhile, Churchill pressed for another re-supply run.

News from North Africa was bleak. Tobruk, which held out so well when isolated in 1941, fell to Rommel on 21 June 1942 with over 35,000 taken prisoner. Churchill considered its loss a disgrace. Rommel continued relentlessly into Egypt. Kesselring then renewed his assault on Malta at the beginning of July, timed to coincide with the *Afrika Korps'* advance. A few days later, the Germans began a new offensive in Russia aimed at the Caucasus.

Luqa was hit time and time again but repaired quickly. Delayed action bombs were a constant menace and there were many casualties as well as acts of courage from personnel on the ground. The air fighting was relentless, but the Spitfires continued to enjoy significant success with superb controlling by Woody. Axis control was heard at one stage to say: 'Look after that 88 in the sea,' to which a German fighter pilot replied 'which one'. Kesselring kept up the pressure but he knew he was losing. The RAF suffered losses too, but there was a constant stream of reinforcements. One was Squadron Leader Lord David Douglas-Hamilton and he considered Woody to be Malta's outstanding fighter controller who, 'was absolutely tireless, and always considered the pilots first. During practically every big raid he controlled the fighters from the operating room. It was a miracle how he stood up to the strain, but every pilot was extremely grateful that he did; for nothing was better calculated to inspire confidence during a big battle than 'Woody' giving instructions on the R/T in his calm friendly voice.'

It was clear from the reduced attacks and the unwillingness of Axis aircraft to fully commit, the air battle of Malta was almost over. In the first thirteen days of July, Hugh Lloyd put the total of Axis aircraft as destroyed at 102 against the loss of 25 Spitfire pilots killed or missing. He estimated the figure of Axis aircraft shot down in the previous year at 693. By mid-July, 'Smiling Albert' Kesselring was no longer smiling; he had had enough.

On the island, many key personnel were exhausted. Air Vice-Marshal Keith Park arrived to take over from Hugh Lloyd. Park wanted to retain Woody but Lloyd insisted he be relieved. Woody left in July after his third successive tour as a senior controller. Lloyd departed to join Tedder's staff in Egypt having commanded the RAF in Malta for fourteen months. Two weeks later Lloyd was knighted.

Keith Park developed further the forward interception policy often credited with winning Malta's air war, but this was won by Lloyd in the hard-pressed days of April and May. With the RAF growing ever stronger, Malta's offensive roles could now be sharpened and made more deadly. It was time for Warby to come back.

Warby's second so-called 'rest period' from March had turned out much like his first. He was determined to get back onto operations, but first took some leave. Of great significance for Warby was a short flight from Heliopolis in Egypt in a photo recce Spitfire. From then onwards he mostly flew recce Spitfires.

Rommel's *Afrika Korps* appeared unstoppable with Cairo and the Suez Canal seemingly within reach. Defeat stared Britain in the face. In the battle for supplies, the Axis was winning. Rommel's advances were evidence of that, whereas Malta was still being strangled. It took General Auchinleck to stop Rommel at a little known railway halt only sixty miles from Alexandria. Hitler again postponed the invasion of Malta in favour of Rommel's advance, against his own High Command's advice. Hitler's decision would be judged at that railway halt: it was called El Alamein.

Operation Pedestal August 1942

In Malta the situation was on a knife-edge. A major re-supply run, Operation Pedestal, was planned in August. There was little point in secrecy as it had to sail through the narrow straits at Gibraltar in full view of many pro-Axis Spanish eyes. The armada comprised of fifty-nine warships supporting fourteen merchant ships. Three aircraft carriers carried seventy-two aircraft for defence and another carried forty Spitfires destined for Malta. Eleven of the merchant ships were British and two were American. The largest, American-built and British-manned, was the modern oil tanker *Ohio* of 14,150 tons, the most vital and most vulnerable of all. A single hit could easily turn her into an inferno. The combined crews of those sailing under the Red Duster and the White Ensign numbered 10,000.

On 11 August, the aircraft carrier HMS *Eagle* was hit by four torpedoes; she capsized and sank within eight minutes, taking all her aircraft with her except four which were airborne. Remarkably, only 160 of her crew of almost 1100 perished. The following day the merchant ship *Deucalion* was hit and abandoned. That evening the carrier HMS *Indomitable* was badly damaged and the destroyer HMS *Foresight* was left listing with engines stopped; she was scuttled the following day. The convoy still had 250 miles to go. Overnight, HMS *Nigeria* was hit by a torpedo and came to a halt. Within a minute, HMS *Cairo* was torpedoed and began to sink. The *Ohio* was hit two minutes later and also stopped. The *Santa Eliza* was damaged by a bomber in the very last minutes of daylight. *Empire Hope* was the first to go that night, torpedoed and abandoned. Next was *Clan Ferguson,* hit twice by torpedo-aircraft about fifteen minutes later. An ammunition ship, she lasted all of thirty seconds before blowing up. *Brisbane Star* was then hit, and headed for Tunisia.

Glenorchy was sunk in the early hours of 13 August; no survivors. *Almeria Lykes* was hit fifteen minutes later, and abandoned. *Santa Eliza* was sunk an hour later. At about the same time *Wairangi* went down. Now two cruisers and seven destroyers escorted *Rochester Castle, Wainarama* and the *Melbourne Star.* Meanwhile, *Ohio* and *Port Chalmers* tried to catch up. The cruiser, HMS *Manchest*er, disabled overnight, was scuttled. Another cruiser, HMS *Kenya,* was torpedoed, but was able to continue. *Wainarama* was hit by a dive bomber, exploded and sank immediately. HMS *Dorset* was then hit and disabled. She was finally sunk that evening. They were still many miles from Malta but now, at last, they were within range of the Spitfires. The bombing slackened off.

Christina enjoyed a free morning on Wednesday, 12 August; D Watch was not on duty until that afternoon. She had a new job, still at Lascaris in the Ops room, but she had now been appointed Assistant Controller. She also had a new home, her apartment in her very own leaning tower of Floriana having been declared uninhabitable. Her landlord, Gustav Vincenti, a wealthy architect, owned many properties and he rented her another apartment within a block also known as

Vincenti Buildings, but in Valletta itself. It was just up the street from the Whizz-Bangs' first rehearsal venue, the Victoria on Strait Street.

That morning, Christina couldn't settle. She had woken early, before dawn, and as usual her thoughts were full of the man she missed so much. It was five months since he had flown off in his pale blue Beaufighter, not into the sunset, but into the sunrise, east to Egypt and she earnestly hoped to safety, at least for a while. She was glad he had been sent away. The bombing had become truly awful and the air boys had been decimated. These days she never saw a 69 Squadron Maryland on the plot. No doubt Warby would be up to his usual tricks in Egypt. Whatever his bosses said, they couldn't keep him on the ground. Surely he would be safer there than over Sicily or Italy, or even on the ground in Malta. Please keep him safe.

As soon as it got light, things began to happen outside. There was a constant buzz of aircraft overhead. They had to be ours, she thought, these days were blitz-free; well, not quite, but the bombing was all relative to what had gone before. The arrival of the Spitfires in such numbers in May had made such a difference, but even they had been thinned out since. This morning sounded different, with a constant coming and going of Spitfires overhead. They were definitely Spitfires; she was well-capable of recognizing the sound of their Merlin engines and there were very few Hurricanes now; they had done their job well.

Christina just had to know what was happening. She tried to busy herself and even went up on the roof to see what was going on. That was something she wouldn't have contemplated a few weeks earlier. There was definitely something up, with Spitfires getting airborne and heading north-west out to sea. Maybe a convoy was coming in. Heaven knows they needed one.

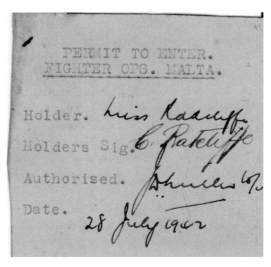

Christina's identity card. (*Miriam Farrugia*)

Time dragged by. Long before the start of her shift at 1.00 pm, Christina set off for the short walk to Lascaris. She turned right out of her apartment block then left onto Britannia Street, following it across Kingsway and Merchants Street and passing the Victory Kitchens she used so often. By then she was behind the *Auberge de Castille*. She crossed St Paul Street before turning right into St Ursula Street. Ahead of her was Upper Barracca Gardens. A few yards short, she turned left into Battery Street making for a very tall doorway. The top entrance, protected by sandbags standing eight feet tall, was guarded by Maltese soldiers. Having shown her pass she headed down the many steps leading to her very secret world. The journey usually only took a few minutes but that afternoon she completed it in record time.

Christina could foresee a busy time but she didn't care, she knew it would be interesting and she just loved being in the know, being in the centre of things. Once down the steps, she walked quickly down the long, dimly lit corridor.

'As soon as I opened the Ops room door I could sense something of a Tenth of May atmosphere about the place. There was the same air of excitement in the room. The same undercurrent of suspense. And from the serious expression on every face something out of the normal run of duty was afoot. Members of the off-going watch dallied about, seemingly reluctant to leave.

"What's the matter?" I asked the supervisor.

"Convoy," he replied, pointing a finger to the left.

"From the UK. And there's a hell of a scrap going on out there."'

After signing her name in the register, Christina climbed the narrow stairway to the platform, the Shelf, and pushed her way through the crowd of spectators to the front row of benches to take her place amongst the chaps-in-the-gods.

Now she had been elevated to the lofty position of Assistant Controller, did that make her a 'chap'? The thought made her smile, but only on the inside, she had very serious work to do this afternoon.

The 'chaps-in-the-gods' overlooking the plotting table. *(via Frederick Galea)*

Her place was next to Guy Westray, Ops B, in a seat of honour near Bill Farnes, the Senior Controller. Her new job involved more than just plotting. She recorded each new track as they came up with its grid position and whether it was friendly or hostile. She then had to note the time each plot was removed from the table. It was something of an optical feat, keeping one eye on the plotting table and the other on the hands in front of the blue, yellow and red triangles of the clock face. Somehow she also had to write everything down longhand in the hardbacked log book. Her job needed total focus.

Having been given the log by her opposite number on C Watch, Christina sat down. She surveyed the scene below to try and take in what was a complicated plot with a lot of activity as the girls surrounding the table, all wearing their headsets, moved their long rods to and fro. On the plotting table itself, there was the usual array of red, blue and yellow arrows, most of them on the left-hand side of the *M* for *Monkey* square. This covered the area through which any ships approaching Malta from the west, from Gibraltar, would come. Amid the thick of the aircraft plots, Christina noticed the dark blue discs they only used rarely to plot ships. There was also something on the table that looked almost alien, a cigar-shaped yellow indicator which she had never seen on the table before.

"'What's that yellow thing there?" I asked Ops B.

"The *Ohio*," he answered. "An oil tanker of the convoy. She's been hit and seems in pretty poor shape. Look out now - that's a new plot there up north. Thirty plus over Comiso."'

Christina quickly entered the northerly plot in the log and once again felt something mounting inside her, the pleasure of being on duty on yet another thrilling occasion; it was just like that memorable day in May.

Malta was now providing air cover for the remnants of a once mighty fleet that had fought hard to reach their beleaguered island and right now, right in front of her, a ding-dong battle was being fought out between their Spitfires and the attacking *Luftwaffe*. The *Regia Aeronautica* was involved too. The Germans and the Eyeties had turned their attention onto the ships endeavouring to save their agonised island, attacking with a new and strengthened determination to beat them into submission by starvation. Given everything they had lived through, everything they had suffered, Christina was convinced they wouldn't let them win.

She gradually picked up from Guy and from Bill Farnes something of the drama that had befallen the convoy called Pedestal. Of the fourteen ships that had set sail from Britain, only five had survived a terrific pounding. Only five had survived, so far. The suffering endured by the crews of merchant ships and warships alike was unimaginable. Now it looked as if the American-built tanker *Ohio,* with her precious and desperately needed cargo of oil, was to be beaten even as her goal came into sight. She had been hit many times Guy explained and was making only very slow progress towards them.

Everyone present was aware their lives depended on those remaining ships. Do or die, they just had to reach harbour. The air attacks on the island may have lessened but they were still at the height of the siege and far from safe. Food stocks were almost non-existent and they were desperately low on fuel and ammunition. Christina thought about the VKs. They weren't at all popular in the beginning but now everyone recognised how important they were. Even so Malta could not hold out much longer. The aircraft and guns were using ammunition at an alarming rate. As for fuel, no one knew how much was left, but there couldn't be much, especially with the number of aircraft she knew staged through every night.

'The plotter below pushed out another arrow to its grid position in the north-west corner of *N* for *Nuts*. She made a sign to the controller and pointed her stick to the plot:

"Another hostile plot, sir; twenty plus."

"Okay. Scramble Red Section."

'Ops B passed the order down the 'blower' to Luqa.'

As the minute hand on the large Ops room clock slowly ticked by, the plots on the table came up thick and fast. When she listened to the loudspeakers and heard the excited 'natter' of the fighter pilots over the radio, Christina often felt she was up there too, high up above the deep blue sea watching the action unfold beneath her. Some of the action had been described to her by Warby, but he only focused on the good bits, or the bits he thought funny. He did have an odd sense of humour sometimes. But Christina knew the reality of what those brave boys were doing up there and sometimes it was heartbreaking. She had heard that on the radio too. And so had her girls, some as young as fourteen. It touched them all. But they kept on doing their job, total professionals. It would hit them when they were off-shift, yet it was not something they could ever share with family or friends. What they did down here stayed down here in their own secret world.

Spitfires took off and others landed. They were refuelled and rearmed in a matter of minutes and were off again with a fresh pilot. There was no respite, not for anyone, pilots, airmen, Ops room staff - all were working as if their lives depended on what they did that day. And they did.

The afternoon wore on. It was getting warmer. The ventilation couldn't cope at the best of times, but with so many more people in the Ops room it was much worse than usual. After a staff visit earlier in the year, all the hangers-on were banned; now there was a notice on the door saying no unauthorised person was allowed to enter. For the most part it worked, but inevitably when something special was going on, the numbers on the shelf increased. People from neighbouring sections sometimes vested themselves with authority and bluffed their way in. Bill Farnes could clear the shelf in an instant with one or two well-chosen words which made some of the girls blush, but today he was simply too busy; there was too much going on to notice the hangers-on.

There were 'No Smoking' orders and signs everywhere. That was a laugh, as the atmosphere was heavily charged with the fumes of 'V for Victory' cigarettes. Issued free to troops, they were regarded in the smoker's world as the next best thing to army socks. Like everything else, even they were at a premium as non-smokers bartered their ration of the evil-smelling weed or sold them to addicts for a princely sum. While the fumes of 'Victory' were usually nauseating, they did have one advantage that hot, stifling afternoon in that crowded place so deep beneath Valletta's protective walls. They disguised, but only now and again, the ever-present smell of sweat and soap-starved khaki drill coming from the bodies all around.

As it approached quarter-to-four, Christina remembered nostalgically in happier times they would have been sipping a refreshing cup of tea and working through that ever popular product of the NAAFI, a wad. Tea and buns, both alas well up on the list of things that used to be. The heat and the oppressive atmosphere began to get to Christina; she felt faint. 'The blue, yellow and red triangle on the clock face merged into one other and a merry-go-round of colour spun before me. I was floating about in the clouds. The haze cleared and the clock resumed its normal position on the wall.

"It's either the heat or the hunger," I thought, "or both."

'I longed for a draught of cool clear air, a stimulating cup of tea, but it was like wanting the moon. Another wave of giddiness came in to attack, the clock did a couple of somersaults and I went back into the clouds ...

'Came a thud. A large brown-paper parcel fell into my lap. A hand gripped my shoulder tightly. Turning, I saw a handsome, bronzed face leaning over close to mine. I looked into a pair of brilliant blue eyes, laughing at me from beneath the battered peak of an old familiar cap.' Warby was back after more than five months away.

'Of all the emotions I experienced during those few moments, predominant was a sense of something very near to disappointment. There had been an eternity of waiting for this. All the weeks Warby had been away I had schemed and planned for his homecoming. Much of my sleeping time had been taken up with dreams of a wonderful reunion. It had certainly not been like this that he would return - unheralded, unexpected and bang in the middle of a battle.

'Fighting down a desire to go on gazing into Warby's blue eyes, I returned my attention to the plotting table. Warby understood.

"See you after six - in Captain Caruana's", he whispered, and slipped away.'

Despite the drama of a long, exciting afternoon, Christina couldn't wait for her shift to end. She hurried down the long corridor and climbed the many steps up from Lascaris into Valletta. She headed for Godfrey Caruana's bar in Kingsway. It was just the sort of cosy place where you could forget your troubles for a little while and put aside all thoughts about a horrid war. But without the war, she wouldn't have been in Malta and she certainly wouldn't have met Warby.

No one knew quite how dear Godfrey, bless him, could still provide anything in the way of 'genuine' drinks and heavens knows how he was still able to charge pre-war rates, unlike some. Godfrey had some special magic but whenever he was asked how he did it, he just smiled. He was a very warm human being. Most of the local bars put up their shutters long ago, or charged extortionate rates with many resorting to selling '*Stuka* Juice' - as the airmen called the local wine. Yet Godfrey could still produce a very good Scotch and soda, and there was nothing the least bit phoney about his Horse's Neck, Pink Gins, Green Goddesses and White Ladies. Horse's Neck! She smiled broadly at the memory of that frightening ride so long ago. They had laughed so much about it, afterwards. She stopped smiling immediately as she wondered what had become of those horses.

'The place was crowded when I arrived. After a quick glance round I saw Warby at the far end of the room, completely walled in by a mob of air boys. I had to steer a course with my elbows and tread over a carpet of shoe leather to reach him.

"Wotcher, Chris."

"Wotcher, Warby."

'He might never have been away.

'While Warby was giving his order to the barman I remembered the parcel I had been nursing since I left the Ops room, and I began to untie the knots.

"Open carefully," Warby warned, turning around.

"Treat me for shock," I gasped, as all the wrappers came down and all the splendour of the Middle East lay revealed before my eyes: a tube of toothpaste, toilet soap, a facecloth, a jar of cold cream, cards of hair-grips, several bundles of curlers. There was a comb too. Not that I hadn't a comb, but this one had a full set of teeth. A box of face powder, a lipstick and a small bottle of Coty's *L'Aimant* perfume completed the fabulous treasure.

"How did you guess?"

"I met your friend Tamara one day in Heliopolis. She said you were running rather short of these things."

'Rather short. But then thank goodness for Tamara. Now three months after she had left it was getting almost impossible to minister unto the needs of one's toilet, and such things as lipsticks, face powder and cold cream had already become memories of a bygone age. For hair curlers, I had managed pieces of blitzed telephone wire, salvaged from the ruins providing a rough but ready enough substitute.

"Then next time I'll load up the kite with curlers," Warby said with a laugh.

'I felt my heart beating somewhere down near my feet.

"Next time?"

'He laughed again.

"Come on, drink up and let's go to the Monico to see good old Tony. Then we must eat."

'He patted his tummy significantly.

"Big eats," he said.

'The man was crazy.

"Eat? Didn't Tamara tell you? We don't eat around here anymore. That was in the good old days."

'I explained to him all the restaurants had been closed by order since April. That we had to make do with the offerings of the Victory Kitchens and what we could get from the black market. Big eats had become the lightest of light snacks.

'Warby put his arm around my waist and helped her down from the bar stool. He held me close for a second and then ran his hand low across my ribs. He gave a low whistle.'

Warby had arrived on 11 August, the day Operation Pedestal's torture began. He flew two missions the following day and reported no sign of the main body of the Italian fleet putting to sea. It was after his flights on 12 August that he 'dropped in' on Christina. He flew twice more on 13 August and, that evening, three survivors of Pedestal - *Rochester Castle, Melbourne Star* and *Port Chalmers* - all damaged, entered Grand Harbour. The following day, they were joined by *Brisbane Star.* What about the *Ohio*?

Disabled and abandoned once, when there was a chance of being towed, the whole crew volunteered to go back. They fought desperately to make headway despite further bombing. Progress was painfully slow, the tow wires often parting with the tanker getting lower and lower in the water. By dawn on 14 August, *Ohio's* freeboard was less than three feet. Then the bombers came back. One dropped a 1000lb bomb

Christina with members of the RAF Gang. *(via Frederick Galea)*

behind the ship's stern tearing away her rudder, allowing water to gush in through a large hole. There was a great risk the tanker would break in two. Progress was at a snail's pace, a destroyer secured on both sides, and another at the bow. At 8.00 am on 15 August, *Ohio* entered Grand Harbour. It was the Feast of *Santa Maria*.

When she came in sight the loud cheering from everyone slowly subsided until there was absolute silence. Men removed their hats and women removed their black hoods and cloaks. From Fort St Angelo, a bugler sounded *Still*. Not a soul moved.

Of the fourteen merchant ships assembled off the west coast of Scotland two weeks earlier, nine were lost, along with an aircraft carrier, two cruisers and a destroyer. Over the next few days, Warby and others conducted sea searches between Tunisia and Sardinia only to find wreckage; by then the remnants of a once vast convoy were safely in Grand Harbour. The remnants were enough - just. A total of 55,000 tons of supplies delivered to a beleaguered Malta at great human cost - the cost of Malta's salvation. From the day of its arrival Pedestal became known as the *Santa Maria* convoy. Its seamen were deservedly applauded on the island, including at the Manoel Theatre, where a special performance in honour of the ships' crews was put on by the RAF Gang.

Pam Longyear married Hugh Nettleton on 12 August 1942 as the last survivors of Operation Pedestal came within sight of Grand Harbour. She and Hugh were both 21 years of age. As Michael recalled years later, 'the wedding breakfast was rather meagre but my father managed to get a scrawny chicken from somewhere. She was lucky to have a wedding coach. The plumes and harness were changed to black for funerals. The honeymoon was spent at the Riviera Hotel near Ghajn Tuffieha.' Hugh was soon posted to Egypt and Pam was evacuated to England via South Africa. That left Michael and his sister Pauline living at home in Pietà.

With Malta much more secure, the bomber force was re-built in order to develop further Hugh Lloyd's earlier approach of taking the attack to the enemy. With fuel and ammunition also delivered, Malta could now hit out at Rommel's supply lines from a base under a protective umbrella. The timing was

Pauline Longyear flanked by Michael and their mother in 1943.
(Michael Longyear)

vitally important for the whole Allied strategy in North Africa. Everything depended on supplies and if Rommel's supply lines could now be cut, even temporarily, he would be hard-pressed to hold the line against the 8th Army in the east and what was planned to come from the west. Rations were increased, not to normal levels as stockpiles were still low, but to a level which provided adequate nutrition.

A decimated 69 Squadron was also expanded and re-equipped. It needed a capable officer, a proven recce pilot, one who would lead from the front: Warby. Over the coming weeks, under Warby's command, 69 Squadron developed into an unusual and unique squadron with three flights each operating a different type of aircraft: Baltimores, PR Spitfires and Wellingtons. This was a huge challenge for a newly-promoted squadron leader. His approach was typically unique, although it didn't suit everyone. He let the Baltimore and Wellington flight commanders run their flights, although he sometimes flew in their aircraft as second pilot and a couple of times as a gunner. The Spitfire flight commander was Harry Coldbeck, who had been running the Spitfire recce flight since March. He was almost certainly miffed by Warby's appointment. A methodical programmer, his irritation increased markedly as Warby took little interest in running the Spitfire flight, but flew in aircraft without giving Harry a great deal of notice while keeping things close to his chest

On one early occasion, Harry was about to depart on the pre-planned midday flight. While strapping into his aircraft, Warby climbed onto the wing and told Harry, without explanation, he was taking the aircraft. He then asked Harry to go to an address in Valletta to meet Christina, whom Harry didn't know, and accompany her to lunch with Captain Riley, the master of the *Brisbane Star*. On arrival at Christina's apartment, she immediately feared the worst; Harry reassured her. She said they were too late for the luncheon engagement but instead invited Harry in for a cup of tea. It was Harry's first ever experience of tea laced with whisky and it was one he enjoyed. But it hardly dampened his feelings of irritation toward his new commanding officer.

Immediately on taking command, Warby adopted the style that was so successful in the past, communicating directly with the AOC or his deputy and debriefing them personally immediately after landing. Such an approach could be portrayed by some as by-passing the normal chain of command but it had been the 'norm' in Malta during Warby's two previous tours. Indeed it had been Hugh Lloyd's preferred way of doing business and even Harry Coldbeck could hardly have been surprised as he himself had often been tasked directly by Lloyd.

Sandy Johnstone arrived at Luqa in September, the beginning of the better times. Despite that, Sandy long reflected on a great sense of loneliness he felt. Morale was high but it was impossible not to feel isolated with the odds still stacked against Malta's survival. Their nearest friends were over 1,200 miles away. Lack of food was a constant worry and lack of heat in winter made life difficult. At one stage there was a serious epidemic of scabies amongst the ladies of Lascaris, which resulted in a tragedy for Sandy and his friends: they had to give up their very last bottle of whisky to be used to disinfect the Ops room telephone.

On 13 September, amidst the ruins of Palace Square Valletta, Viscount Gort formally presented the George Cross to Sir George Borg, Malta's Chief Justice, who accepted it on behalf of the Maltese people. The Longyears felt privileged to witness the presentation, standing as part of the great crowd on the side of the square immediately in front of Greenburgh Bros Ltd, military tailors.

Chapter 11

Warby's World

Over the Mediterranean Sea, north of Tripolitania - Wednesday, 14 October 1942

How many more times was he going have to do this? This was stretching even his famed 'luck'. Couldn't they see what he was trying to do, asking them to follow him? Yet all they wanted to do was blast him out of the sky. He jinked left and right changing his height to avoid the flak, yet trying to maintain a recognisable orbit around the ships. The tracer was deceptive. It seemed to rise slowly at first, arcing gently upwards before accelerating rapidly, missing his cockpit by what seemed like inches. 'Flaming onions', René called them. Poor gallant René. Those 'flaming onions' were getting damnably close! The Italian gunners were becoming more accurate each time he came back. And there were machine-gun bullets he couldn't see. The shell-bursts from the heavier guns looked to be harmless white puffs, almost like a cluster of mini-cumulus clouds. Up close though he could feel their violence before his right hand teased the elevators and ailerons to calm his aircraft. Given his constant jinks, he hoped his flight path was proving difficult for the gunners to predict.

He didn't have a choice; he needed to convince the captain of the Italian warship he was sending a message - a life or death message. After the third orbit he flew a straight course in the fervent hope they would follow him. So far that damned Italian captain didn't seem to have cottoned on? He had of course.

Warby rolled his aircraft's wings level once more. The well-harmonised controls responded crisply. They were beautifully balanced. No matter how often he flew the Spitfire he always got enormous pleasure from such a thoroughbred, a world-beater. He loved the freedom that came with being a recce pilot. The role was perfectly designed for him, the loner. A lonely warrior.

He headed north-west again. 'Please, please follow me,' he thought. After a couple of miles, Warby looked back. The warship still seemed to be ignoring him, still following in the wake of the cargo ship heading at full steam for Tripoli. Rommel would be pleased. But the Italians weren't ignoring him.

Warby had had to try again - it was ingrained in his nature not to give up. He also knew he was their only hope. They were definitely alive, but they had no hope of rescue without his help.

The day had begun like many others. The mission was routine. Three Beaufighters from 227 Squadron were tasked against the 2,000-ton Italian merchant ship *Trapani* escorted by a single warship the *Giacomo Medici*. They were somewhere off the coast of Tripolitania, one of three provinces in Mussolini's Italian Libya. The Beaufighter was a great aircraft but Warby loved his PR Spitfire, its solitude and its majesty. He could outrun anything the Axis could throw at him, providing he saw them coming of course!

They all hoped death, when it came, would be sudden, but often it wasn't. Sometimes it was slow and painful; you might see it coming yet be powerless to do anything about it. Warby hoped when his end came, as he knew it would, he would not fall into a sunless sea far from shore and out of sight of friends. As a recce pilot he suspected he would die alone. Chris would mourn his passing but he couldn't let himself dwell on the thought. It wasn't going to happen on this flight. Yet he knew it would, one day.

The three 227 Squadron crews were experienced and confident. The lead aircraft, *Q* for *Queen,* was being flown by 22-year-old Squadron Leader Peter Underwood, awarded the DFC only a few days earlier. All Warby had to do was photograph a successful strike and they could all head home for tea and medals.

It hadn't quite worked out that way. The Italian crews saw them coming in the clear blue sky. As the Beaus performed their graceful, insanely low, coordinated attack the anti-aircraft fire was intense and accurate. Whether *Q* for *Queen* was hit wasn't clear. Having attacked the *Trapani* with cannon fire, its bombs hung up. It exploded in the air only yards past the ship, and toppled into the sea in a great ball of flame, vividly red, horribly black, and terminal. Peter and his navigator 21-year-old Ivor Miller would have known for a second or two they were about to die.

Maybe the shocking loss of their leader put the others off. The second aircraft, *Y* for *Yorker,* straddled the ship's deck with cannon fire, but its bombs overshot. It departed to the north-west trailing smoke. *H* for *Hotel* also attacked with cannon fire and Warby observed hits on the ship's deck. No bombs were dropped. *Hotel* made a second run but the bombs undershot. It could do little except exit stage right at speed and make its escape.

The mission was an abject failure. There was little left for Warby to record on his cameras except the *Trapani* turning for Tripoli with its valuable cargo intact, destined for the *Afrika Korps.*

Warby turned away, saddened by the deaths of friends. He gradually overtook poor *Yorker* trailing smoke, thickening smoke as the mortally wounded Beau got lower and lower. They hadn't a hope. By now they were too low to parachute. Ditching was their only option, a hazardous manoeuvre at best. John Bryce did very well getting his dying aircraft down onto the water in one piece. Warby saw John and his navigator, young Cole, clamber into their small dinghy before *Yorker* slipped beneath the waves. They were left on their own bobbing about in a tiny two-man dinghy, with a lone PR Spitfire circling helplessly above and little hope of rescue. Now what? They were much too far away from Malta and there was no possibility of any friendly ship this far south. The Beaufighter crew's deaths would be long and lingering. Unless …

Surely life in an Italian prisoner-of-war camp was preferable to a slow death at sea? Could he get the Italians, so recently fighting for their own lives, to follow him and save the lives of their former assailants?

He had circled the *Giacomo Medici* three times before setting course for the dinghy and then he flew round the dinghy three times, slightly higher and in sight of the Italians before returning to the warship to do the whole thing again. So far his efforts were to no avail. His fuel was now critical. This attempt had to be his last.

Three times more he circled, ducking and weaving, before setting course for the Beaufighter crew. After a mile or so he looked back. Hurrah! The Italian warship was at last following him! He flew low over the dinghy for the final time, waggling his wings and saw them waving. They knew he had found help. He just hoped they would not be too disappointed when they recognised the shape of their rescuer. Warby pulled up into a wide orbit as the Italians got closer. He hung around for a little longer until he saw the Beaufighter crew hauled safely aboard the *Giacomo Medici*. At least the Eyeties had stopped shooting at him! But there was a reason for that.

Suddenly six Italian *Macchi* fighters swooped towards him. Warby had misjudged the game. He had not given the Italian captain enough credit. He had played his hand well, knowing all along what Warby was doing, simply trying to keep Warby loitering until he summoned the cream of the *Regia Aeronautica* from the Italian airbase at Homs, east of Tripoli.

The Italian fighters approached fast. They would have done better to have swung wide around him out of sight, to get between him and Malta. Maybe their numbers made them overconfident but with six they were still a threat. The *Macchi* was the best fighter the Italians had but it was no match in combat against a Spitfire: a normal Spitfire. Alas Warby wasn't flying a normal Spitfire. The price his PR Spitfire paid for its extra speed, very high ceiling and extended endurance, was to have no guns, no armament of any kind. Not even any armour-plating. It relied on speed and agility, and a good pair of hands. He would need all of these qualities if he was to make good his escape. Four fighters got onto his tail but they struggled to close the range and Warby's powerful Merlin engine soon accelerated him out of trouble. Once clear he began a cruise climb, throttling back gently as he didn't have a great deal of fuel. He kept a wary eye on his six o'clock.

Warby then lit a cigarette. It was his way of unwinding and he often smoked in the cockpit even though it was against the rules. He always made sure the oxygen was switched off first though! The lads who serviced his aircraft didn't seem to mind when they found his cigarette butts stuffed under his parachute. He reassured the airmen they were 'out' before putting them down there. That usually made them laugh; he had always got on well with his ground crew. They were a brilliant bunch. Not for them a posting to Egypt for a rest. When they arrived in Malta they were there for the duration and for much of their time it was hell on earth.

He finished his cigarette, carefully stubbed it out and pushed it easily beneath his parachute. He rarely did up the straps of his parachute anyway; there never seemed to be much point on a low-level mission.

He was going to be late. Chris would be worried. It was her Watch on duty at Lascaris: D Watch. She had been working at Lascaris without a break for sixteen long months and was now Assistant Controller. Like everyone else in the Hole, she would know he was overdue and that two of the Beaufighters had 'bought it'. He knew she worried about him. There was not a lot he could do about that. He often said to her he was safer in the air while everyone 'copped it' on the ground. He worried about Chris; she was desperately thin.

Soon he was within range of Malta and in answer to his call he heard the reassuring voice of Bill Farnes. He would soon be home; Chris would now relax as she moved his marker across the plot. Home for tea and medals. Would there be any tea, he wondered?

Chapter 12

Autumn

October 1942 - October 1943

Sergeant J. Deakin, a War Office photographer, took a series of photographs in Malta in order to demonstrate to people in Britain and the USA that life was carrying on despite the siege. Christina was chosen to feature and Deakin followed her as she went about her daily business when off duty. There were fifty photographs in three series: *A Fighter Control Girl, Malta GC, has 24 hrs leave*, *Wearing the* Faldetta and *Christina rehearses her dance*. The images offered a fascinating insight into the life of a young lady on an isolated island at war. They were widely circulated with some featured in magazines such as *Illustrated* and *Life* on both sides of the Atlantic.

That autumn Warby undertook a series of 'special flights' photographing the Sicilian coastline. Most of his sorties when in command of 69 Squadron were in Spitfires.

The Axis embarked on its final blitz of Malta over a ten-day period in mid-October after which the bulk of the *Luftwaffe* in Sicily was transferred to North Africa. From then on, raids tapered off and by the end of the month, daylight bombing had virtually ceased. The *Luftwaffe's* defeat was complete. It had cost the Axis an estimated 1,378 aircraft lost between June 1940 and October 1942.

The switch of the *Luftwaffe* came too late for Rommel as the Battle of El Alamein had already begun. It was the first major offensive against the Germans since the European war began. On 3 November the Allies broke out and Rommel ordered a full retreat. Four days later, the Allies landed in Algeria and from then on the Axis was squeezed on two fronts. Montgomery fully recognised Malta's vital role in his victory. Attacks on cargo ships destined for the *Afrika Korps* proved decisive, Rommel later admitting he lost the battle of supplies by a wide margin. Malta had the lives of many Axis soldiers on its conscience, he said.

El Alamein could not have taken place without Malta being held and everyone involved in its defence and re-supply contributed enormously to the Allied victory. Without Malta on the offensive, at great cost, the *Afrika Korps* would rapidly have built up its strength, probably seizing all of Egypt. Now the threat to the Suez Canal was over and the Axis was denied Middle Eastern oil once and for all.

Warby often flew back to Egypt for intelligence briefings, although some suggested he was simply re-stocking Christina's larder or obtaining alcohol and cigarettes for the airmen. That his aircraft was invariably packed with items on his return was a huge bonus for the airmen who remained devoted to him. On 3 November, the citation for Warby's third DFC was published in the *London Gazette*:

> Since August, 1942, this officer has completed numerous operational photographic sorties, many of them at low altitudes and often in the face of opposition from enemy fighters. His work has been of the utmost value. In October 1942, his gallantry was well illustrated when he directed an enemy destroyer to a dinghy in which were the crew of one of our aircraft, which had been shot down. Although he was fired upon by the destroyer and engaged by Italian aircraft, he remained over the area until he observed the drifting crew were picked up by the destroyer.

Christina's needle had more work to do. A few days later there was deserved recognition for Harry Coldbeck, 69 Squadron's Spitfire flight commander, with a DFC recommended by Warby. A few days later Harry was shot down. After more than 150 recce missions from Malta in six months, Harry spent the remainder of the war in captivity. But at least he survived.

Misfortune for 69 Squadron continued with another pilot shot down two days later. Then, on 15 November, Warby went missing over Tunisia. D Watch was on duty at the time. Sixteen year old Marion Gould said when the news came through they were all on edge and many were upset, Christina was in great distress but carried on. All of the girls were aware of Christina and Warby's relationship. That he was missing was also the subject of an article in the *Times of Malta*.

Warby had been heading home when he was attacked by two German fighters. He crash landed at Bône, captured a day or two earlier by the Allies. Warby then made his way to Gibraltar with a string of adventures on the way. Air Headquarters Malta was duly notified their favourite son was alive and well. Bill Farnes sent a note to Christina:

> I suppose you will have heard that Adrian Warburton is on the map once more - at Gib?

Later he sent another:

> Miss Ratcliffe: S/L Warburton flying in from Gib: Tomorrow. Farnes.

Newly-promoted
Wing Commander
Adrian Warburton
on the roof
of Christina's
apartment,
November 1942.
(RAF Museum)

Bill Farnes was clearly well aware of their relationship.

Warby had borrowed a Spitfire in Gibraltar and flew back via Bône to retrieve his undamaged camera magazine from his crashed aircraft. On arrival at Luqa on 21 November, where few were aware he was safe, he was met by Luqa's station commander, who asked Warby where he had been. Warby explained, apologising for being late. He was then told he had been promoted to wing commander. There was more work for Christina's needle. Warby was 24-years-old and had spent less than three months as a squadron leader. He took his film to be developed six days after taking off on the original mission.

On the surface, Warby's promotion didn't affect him. Previously, when asked by his ground crew when he would replace his old and shabby cap, he said 'when I'm a Wingco.' But he couldn't ever bear to part with it. In the remainder of that remarkable week, Warby flew another nine sorties. Neither orders, nor his new rank, could keep him on the ground. A posting to a ground appointment within Air Headquarters might have done the trick if Keith Park was concerned about the amount of flying Warby was doing. On the other hand, Warby was quite obviously

'The most valuable pilot in the RAF' and 'Christina of George Cross Island'.
(via Frederick Galea)

doing a remarkable job both individually and in leading his unusual squadron. The reality was, despite Warby biting enormous chunks out of his renowned luck, he was most valuable to the war effort when in the cockpit.

It was discovered two anti-aircraft gunners on one of the Pedestal ships were US Navy sailors. This was a perfect opportunity for morale-building publicity. Who better to include but Malta's own recently promoted recce hero, just returned from the dead, and the photogenic Christina? By then they were a well-known couple on Valletta's streets and recognised as an important part of Malta's story. Photographs were taken with the sailors on the roof of Christina's Strait Street apartment. This resulted in the only official photograph ever showing Christina and Warby together.

Stocktaking indicated Malta could hold out until December, but even so, the population had been put back on near starvation rations from late September. The predicted limit of Malta's endurance was the beginning of December.

Sandy Johnstone joined Bill Farnes at Lascaris as a controller. With the Axis well and truly on the back foot, Sandy and Bill took a leaf out of Woody Woodhall's book in keeping them there, sometimes with false transmissions from non-existent RAF squadrons heading toward Sicily. It was very satisfying for the ladies of Lascaris to move plots of Axis fighters to and fro over Sicily trying to intercept elusive, but actually non-existent, RAF raiders.

The siege of Malta was effectively raised by a convoy in mid-November. Before entering harbour, the flotilla formed line ahead and bands played on the decks of the escorting warships, so reminiscent of the 1930s when the Mediterranean Fleet was in Grand Harbour. The ships were welcomed by thousands of Maltese lining the bastions and the Barracca Gardens. They were joined by many members of Malta's garrison and everyone cheered and waved flags as each ship entered harbour.

Sandy Johnstone witnessed 'frenzied outburst of tears, laughter, and loud unrestrained cheering. Young boys and girls leaped and screamed, while their parents roared themselves hoarse as they watched the long-awaited convoy gliding in to safety. Old and young hugged and kissed each other; a few people just stood quietly, the tears of relief rolling unashamedly down their cheeks.' The much-needed supplies were landed at dusk on 20 November, the same day Benghazi fell to the British 8th Army. The Germans sent a small force of bombers to disrupt unloading; they were all shot down and there was no damage.

It had taken a valiant defence and an incredibly resilient people to see Malta through incessant bombing, the most prolonged, the most severe, endured anywhere throughout the Second World War. The skies above the besieged island also saw the most ferocious air-combat of the war. The more famous Battle of Britain lasted four months whereas the air battle of Malta lasted two and a half years. Throughout those hard months, the Maltese people faced near starvation. Yet they demonstrated resilience even greater than was shown against the Turks almost 400 years earlier.

The Ministry of Information included the following in *The Air Battle of Malta*: 'Blue water lapped against the wreckage of many gallant ships in Grand Harbour. Great mounds of broken masonry disfigured the streets of stairs and the alleys in towns and villages. The airfields were unlovely with thousands of old wounds. Upon the steep hill of Bighi, overlooking the harbour, the churches and the streets, a shapely tree flowered magenta against the cypresses and firs shading the resting place of the airmen who fought and died upon this battlefield of rock and sky and sea.'

That autumn Mary Longyear, daughter Pauline and son Michael were evacuated. They left their Pietà home in the early hours and embarked at Luqa in a Liberator bomber named *St Anthony*. All the passengers were women and children. They sat on wooden benches on either side of the bomb bay for take-off and landing; there were no seats or safety belts. The flight took all day, flying south deep into the Sahara Desert to get beyond the Allied and Axis armies still locked in combat. Then they flew west, then north over the Atlas Mountains before landing at Gibraltar, a hazardous event at any time. Michael felt: 'No excitement at our first flight, no anticipation of going to a new country, no fear of what was to come, no relief on leaving Malta and the bombing and no wonder about the present circumstances. Perhaps our senses had been dulled by continuous stimulation for a long period.'

Evacuation offered an escape to safety. A few days before the Longyears made their escape, on Saturday, 31 October, twenty-four Malta fighter pilots, many wounded, including Wing Commander Arthur Donaldson and the already famous Malta ace 'Screwball' Beurling, joined ten civilians on another Liberator bound for the UK via Gibraltar. Two of the civilians were babes in arms. Including the crew, there were thirty-nine on board the converted bomber.

One of three brothers, all fighter pilots, Arthur was an admirer of Diana Tonna. Knowing he was being evacuated on the same flight as a close friend of hers with her baby, Diana asked Arthur to look after her. Said Arthur, 'Next to me was a beautiful Maltese girl called Bella; she had a son of about one year with her and she was going home to join her husband, a FAA [Fleet Air Arm] pilot'.

In the midst of a storm, the aircraft landed too far down Gibraltar's short runway. The pilot attempted to go round again but the aircraft stalled at about forty feet in the air and dived into the sea, sinking like a stone. Those sitting unstrapped in the bomb bay had little chance. There was nothing Arthur Donaldson could do. While he survived, Bella - Mrs Isabella Josephine Aston and her baby son Simon - did not; nor did the other mother and child - Mrs Edna Chase and her son Thomas. A total of fourteen passengers perished. They had survived the very worst the Axis had thrown at them, only to die in the most tragic of accidents.

Michael and Pauline Longyear spent two weeks in Gibraltar housed in the military hospital, but separated from their mother. Their voyage to England on board HMT *Empire Pride* took three weeks. From Liverpool they journeyed to Exmouth to join the Longyear's eldest daughter Doreen. Pauline joined the WAAF as soon as she was sixteen and became a plotter once more, this time in uniform and at RAF Boscombe Down near Salisbury. She and Michael had had quite a childhood.

Victor Longyear returned to England to take part in the invasion of Europe and fought through Belgium and northern Germany eventually stopping at Hannover at the war's end.

Pauline Longyear with a WAAF friend in 1944. *(Michael Longyear)*

Back in Malta, with hunger receding, the issue of four candles and eight nightlights to every family before Christmas demonstrates just how short everyday items were. From then on, the task of the authorities changed as Malta became a springboard for the invasion of Southern Europe. For everyone at Lascaris, life became even busier with their surroundings the scene of frantic activity as a new combined services headquarters was excavated further down the tunnel. The engineers went to great lengths to disguise the construction by distributing excavated stone amongst ruined buildings. The new war rooms were expected to be ready to start operations early in 1943 for use in the invasion of Sicily, scheduled for July.

December brought Warby a dose of influenza but that didn't stop him flying seventeen missions in nineteen days. On 19 December, he was granted ten days hard-earned, local leave. But he was up to something, planning a rather special, totally unofficial flight, one completely in character and completely against the rules.

Always conscious of the airmen's lot, Warby made every effort to learn about their tasks. He went much further than the norm for a senior officer, establishing close, often informal, working relationships with his men. Most crews signed over their aircraft immediately after landing and left the ground crew to it; Warby often helped clean his aircraft out. His reputation simply grew and grew. He was also well aware the majority did not get the benefit of rest tours in quieter locations. Many ground crew simply carried on under immense pressure and dreadful living conditions until the war was won. The concentrated bombing on Malta's airbases had often resulted in intolerable stress for many.

Warby persuaded some of his very willing technicians to rebuild a damaged Wellington from the many wrecks on the airfield. One night while on leave, he took off in the 'non-existent' Wellington and flew to Cairo where it was filled with food and 'goodies' as well as Christmas booze. He returned at night, the cargo squirreled away. Warby's reputation peaked. There is little doubt senior officers knew, or quickly learnt about this escapade, but they turned a blind eye. Before Christmas dinner for the airmen, traditionally served by their officers, Warby invited some ground crew to his office for a glass of champagne, first introducing them to the various group captains present.

Ken Rogers, a pre-war regular, got to know Warby well. He thought Malta the ideal place for Warby; it allowed him to express his individuality, which would have been smothered in the UK. He said Warby needed both Christina and Malta's informal atmosphere.

Inevitably, some changes in Warby impacted on his relationship with Christina. They were both living and working under great pressure and, although Warby benefitted from two rest periods in Egypt, Christina had been on the island since March 1940. She worked tirelessly through the harshest period of Malta's long siege and saw the area surrounding her home devastated by bombing, even her own flat becoming uninhabitable. Now Warby was back, she suffered yet more stress ever fearful the man she loved was putting himself at tremendous risk every time he flew. When he went missing in November, the strain and worry must have been unbearable, but she carried on doing her duty. Now the siege was over, the bombing greatly diminished, and everyone realised the war in North Africa was drawing to a close. This was the very moment when pressure on Christina should have eased. Instead she saw her precious Warby taking on more and more. By then, maybe she knew the pressure came from within him. Inevitably this led to tension. Warby knew no other way and even his love for Christina could not diminish his determination to lead his squadron in the only way he knew how, from the front.

It was also time for the curtain to fall for a final time on the troupe who had been so important to Christina and many others on the island: 'At the end of December, the Whizz-Bangs disbanded after two-and-a-half years. They had made the boys laugh when there was nothing to laugh at. They had risked their lives to entertain and one member of the party, Gwen Regent, had been killed.'

Two Canadians, 'Mac' Brown and Ed Maloney, joined 69 Squadron and soon became Warby's deputies and two of his greatest admirers. They described Warby as one of the greatest men they ever met, a total professional and a superb example to his pilots. They were mature and serious, older than Warby, and they had a positive effect on him.

A new Warby had now emerged, very much more mature in relation to his duties, and well aware of his responsibilities. His longer than regulation hair was gone, as was his flamboyant dress, at least on the ground. His leadership was seen by many as inspirational. His ground crew would sometimes even 'bully' or 'berate' him if he brought back a damaged aircraft. But they worried about him, perhaps far more than he worried about himself, and they never gave up trying to persuade him to do up the shoulder straps of his seat harness; he rarely bothered. His habit of pushing the remains of his cigarettes underneath his parachute was constantly remarked upon. Eventually an ashtray was fitted to the Spitfire he flew most often.

The Meadowbank Hotel on Tower Road in Sliema was acquired for all 69 Squadron aircrew and Warby was required to live there with his men. He shared a room with the two Canadians. Mac often accompanied Warby socially and soon found himself seconded as a dance partner to Christina. Warby claimed he could only dance to the tune *Jealousy* and orchestras often played it when he made an appearance. Even then his dancing skills were hopeless. Mac and Ed described Christina as glamorous and were both envious of Warby's monopoly of her. Mac later described Warby as a wonderful man who did not know fear;

nothing seemed to upset him. He thought Warby, with his typically dry English sense of humour, well-disciplined and highly regarded by everyone. Ed said there was nothing in the least bit phoney about Warby who treated everyone as gentlemen.

By February 1943, 69 Squadron was enormous and the decision was taken to split it into three separate squadrons, the Spitfire flight becoming 683 Squadron with Warby its first commanding officer. Warby was then granted some UK leave.

In North Africa what was left of the *Afrika Korps* was squeezed between Montgomery's 8th Army from the east and the Americans and British advancing from the west. Tripoli had fallen on 23 January and the remaining German and Italian troops were contained within a shrinking perimeter around Tunis.

In the spring Warby met Elliot Roosevelt, son of the American President Franklin D. Roosevelt. Elliot commanded all US photo-recce units in north-west Africa and a close friendship developed between the two. Elliot was an unconventional character with 'clout' and he soon developed a deep admiration for the equally unconventional Wing Commander War*bur*ton, as the Americans pronounced his name. They responded well to Warby's example and to his no-nonsense, get-the-photographs approach, listening carefully to what he had to say. His laid back attitude and involvement with American enlisted men was warmly welcomed, as was his very broad interpretation of rules and regulations. As far as the Americans were concerned, Warby was one of the good guys.

The end for the Axis in North Africa came on 12 May 1943 when all Axis resistance ceased; over 240,000 prisoners were taken. The next main event was Italy. Prior to that, Warby played a key role in the capture of the small, heavily-defended island of Pantelleria. Of strategic importance because of its location between Tunisia and Sicily, Warby flew all four recce missions personally. One of his pilots later remarked Warby was the only pilot he ever heard of who was fired at by anti-aircraft guns from above. Warby photographed the complete shoreline, as well as all the defences and coastal batteries, allowing Allied planners to pinpoint every defensive location, all of which were subjected to a merciless bombardment. As soon as the invading force was sighted, the defending garrison surrendered. The Americans acknowledged Warby's work saved many lives.

On 26 May 1943, at her home in Vinc nti Buildings Valletta, Christina received a formal letter from the Air Ministry. It was addressed to 'Miss Christina Ratcliffe, BEM.' She had been awarded the British Empire Medal. The letter read:

Madam,

I am commanded by the Air Council to inform you that on the occasion of the Birthday Honours List, 1943, His Majesty the King has been pleased to approve the award to you of the BRITISH EMPIRE MEDAL in recognition of your meritorious service and devotion to duty during the period of the heavy air bombardment of Malta. The award will be published on the morning of Friday, 4th June.

The Air Council wish me to convey to you their warm congratulations on this mark of His Majesty's favour.

I am, Madam,

Your obedient servant,

The letter was signed by the Permanent Under-Secretary of State at the Air Ministry in London.

Five other 'Ladies of Lascaris' received similar letters that morning: Irene Arnold, Irene Cameron, Marigold 'Pickles' Fletcher, Phyllis Frederick, and Carmela Galea. Bill Farnes, D Watch's very able Senior Controller, was appointed as an Officer of the Most Excellent Order of the British Empire - OBE. Bill had actually received a Mention in Despatches at the beginning of the year. To have received two decorations for his time at Lascaris demonstrates the measure of the man.

The British
Empire Medal
(Civil Division,
ladies).

Christina's citation read:

> Miss Christina Ratcliffe has been employed as a plotter in the operations room at Air Headquarters, Malta, since 15th June 1941. She was in charge of her watch and throughout the heavy air attacks on the island, never once failed to report to duty on time. She lived a considerable distance from the headquarters. When raids were in progress there was no transport, but she walked to work regardless of bombs and shrapnel. During one raid her home was destroyed, but she carried on her work with her customary coolness and efficiency. Throughout, her work was of a high standard and her brave and cheerful demeanour were an inspiration to those who served under her.

This image was published in the *Times of Malta:* 'Christina of George Cross Island: Bright sunlight lends an added dignity to the bombed streets and squares in which Christina is walking.' *(via Frederick Galea)*

Christina had lived in Malta from before Italy declared war, through and beyond Malta's most trying days sharing the risks and the rations and working tirelessly to entertain troops. For six months, she combined her work with the Whizz-Bangs with duties as a plotter, before becoming Captain of D Watch at the height of the air battle, and then Assistant Controller. Like other civilians, she could have opted for evacuation. Christina's award was richly deserved and entirely on her own merit. The following day, she received a telegram of congratulation from Warby's mother, Muriel, saying how glad and proud she was to hear of Christina's decoration. It seems Warby's mother was well aware of their relationship.

At dawn on 20 June, HMS *Aurora* made her way into Grand Harbour. The identity of a passenger was so important it was kept secret until 5.00 am that morning. The visitor was King George VI. Every vantage point around Grand Harbour was thick with cheering people as *Aurora,* flying the Royal Standard, passed the breakwater at 8.00 am. The King stood on a special platform built in front of the bridge so people could see him. Everyone went wild with enthusiasm. When the King stepped onto Maltese soil, all the bells in Malta's many churches began ringing. The King made an extensive tour of the island and later lunched at Verdala Palace with the recently promoted Field Marshal Viscount Gort. This was the first visit of a reigning Sovereign to Malta since 1911. The visit produced the most spontaneous and genuine demonstration of loyalty and affection many had ever seen.

On 683 Squadron, Warby remonstrated with one of his young pilots for taking photographs lower than the assigned height, the individual having done so to stay below cloud, exposing him to ground fire. Warby told the pilot, who was 23-years-old, he was too young to die and Warby had no wish to inform his wife she was now a widow. The pilot concerned was utterly deflated. A few minutes later Warby congratulated him for producing excellent photographs which delighted the interpreters. Warby was two years older than the 'young pilot' and had been doing exactly the same, taking risks to bring back the goods, for the best part of three years.

Others were noting changes in Warby. He was long overdue a genuine rest and there were signs he was becoming weary and edgy. He was less of a loner and drank more than before, being more inclined to party. He may have been more conscious of his increased attractiveness to ladies, many of whom were drawn toward him. Warby and Christina were still very much a couple, but she was aware of what was going on and had concerns. She would have known better than anyone that Warby was in desperate need of a prolonged rest. She must have been torn by such thoughts, as a rest tour would take him away from Malta, this time back to England. As always though, Christina was more concerned about Warby's welfare, which she put above all things. She too was under immense strain.

Planning was well underway for the Sicily landings - Operation Husky - for which 683 played its part. Despite his rank, wide responsibilities, and discouragement from Air Headquarters, Warby photographed the beaches personally. This caused some irritation amongst his pilots. He covered the area from Gela to Syracuse from a height of 200 feet on four missions. Hugh O'Neill flew fighter escort and commented that Warby was undeterred by the flak, simply smoking a large cigar as he went about his task. Once again Warby's photographs exceeded expectations and he received numerous letters of congratulation. The C-in-C Middle East, General Harold Alexander, signalled Malta asking that Warby be personally thanked. He said the pictures were as technically perfect as if taken on a peacetime exercise. They offered a complete picture of the enemy's dispositions and movements.

Warby was then tasked with photographing the actual beach landings as they took place. He was particularly concerned about the American tendency to shoot at any aircraft near their ships so he took pains to ensure they were well briefed about his mission. Nevertheless, his Spitfire was hit repeatedly by friendly fire and he only just made it back to Malta. His ground crew were horrified at the damage. As Warby climbed down from the aircraft ignoring a large hole in his wing, he said laconically to the waiting airmen that the radio didn't work. Later the same day, Warby borrowed a fighter Spitfire and accompanied three experienced Spitfire flight commanders on a fighter sweep over Syracuse to vent his frustration on the enemy.

When Marion Gould entered the Lascaris Ops room for her night shift at 11.00 pm on the evening of 9 July, she was astonished to find General Montgomery, Lord Louis Mountbatten and many other well-known 'top-brass' seated on the dais. They were overseeing the largest scale amphibious and airborne landings ever attempted. The table was alive with plots of ships and aircraft all heading for Sicily. Marion said: 'It was one of the most exciting nights of my life seeing history unfold before my eyes.' The following morning, as she crossed Marsamxett Harbour to go home after her shift, she looked out to sea at a huge armada of ships destined for Sicily. She didn't see her boyfriend Eric for three days, he having set up a first aid medical centre to receive the wounded who were soon pouring in.

The atmosphere in Malta had changed again. Now there were seven Spitfire squadrons at Luqa, four at Hal Far and five more at Ta' Qali. With Qrendi also an operational fighter base and a newly-constructed US base on Gozo, there were nearly 500 Spitfires and twenty-two fighter squadrons on the islands. This was a far cry from the days of *Faith*, *Hope* and *Charity*.

By late July, 683 Squadron was operating in and out of captured airfields in Sicily. In the same month, Warby was awarded a bar to his DSO; there was more work for Christina's needle. To others Warby appeared casual, almost indifferent, about the honours he had earned. By then he was wearing the DSO and bar and the DFC and two bars; the bars being shown as a rosette on the medal ribbon. One pilot said it looked as if his medal ribbons were riveted onto his tunic. The citation for his second DSO was published on 6 August. If Christina hadn't been fully aware of what Warby had been getting up to in the air, all was now revealed:

> Wing Commander Warburton has commanded No. 683 Photographic Reconnaissance Squadron since its formation on 8th February, 1943 and prior to the formation of this squadron he commanded No. 69 Squadron.
>
> This officer has flown a total of 375 operational sorties involving 1,300 hours flying. From Malta he has completed 360 sorties with a total of 1,240 hours. During his tour of duty in Malta, he covered all the Italian and Sicilian targets continuously, invariably obtaining 100% cover with his photography.
>
> In recent months, since he commanded No. 683 Squadron, he has continued to operate on all the routine sorties required from pilots of the squadron, selecting for himself the sorties which have been considered of a most dangerous nature.
>
> On a recent operation, one camera became unserviceable. In order to ensure that full photographic coverage would be obtained, he covered every target, including Taranto, three times being continuously chased by Me109s.
>
> On 15th November 1942, Wing Commander Warburton was despatched on a photographic reconnaissance of Bizerta. He was attacked by Me109s and his aircraft being damaged he force landed at Bône. From there he went to Gibraltar, returning to Malta a few days later in a fighter aircraft. He encountered two Ju88s on his return journey which he engaged, destroying one and damaging the other.
>
> On December 5th, this officer carried out a photographic reconnaissance of Naples. In spite of intense flak and enemy fighter opposition he covered the whole of the target area at 4,000 feet.
>
> On May 18th, he took low level obliques of the whole of the Pantellaria coastline from a height of 200 feet. He was fired on continuously by the AA coastal batteries but succeeded in obtaining results which proved extremely valuable in the eventual invasion of the island.
>
> Wing Commander Warburton has destroyed a total of nine enemy aircraft when flying armed reconnaissance aircraft and three on the ground.
>
> The importance of the results obtained by this officer in spite of intense enemy opposition and in all weathers cannot be too highly estimated. The success of operations carried out from this Island, the

safe arrival and departures of convoys are largely dependent on the accuracy of photographic reconnaissance.

Wing Commander Warburton is to a great extent responsible for this successful reconnaissance. His personal enthusiasm for operations, his courage and devotion to duty have set the highest example to all with whom he has associated.

By then Christina was well aware Warby was driven. Even his love for her wasn't enough to curb that drive. He of course knew better than anyone the glory days of independent operations from Malta were over. He was looking for more.

An RAF North African photo recce wing was about to be formed and Warby wanted to command it. He made yet more trips to Tunisia. Christina knew this was a difficult time for Warby. There were quarrels and Warby's more outgoing behaviour was bound to have been a factor. The quarrels always ended with reconciliations but Christina was becoming increasingly worried she might be losing her man. They both must have been near the end of their tether. They needed time together but there was none. Others commented Warby appeared to be war weary, but he always seemed to be ready for another mission. Yet he was still warm and caring about others, though often seen as serious, even sad.

During the summer of 1943, the war artist Leslie Cole undertook a series of paintings of scenes of devastation in Malta, as well as portraits of Maltese children, housewives and some of the island's personalities. One portrait was of Air Vice-Marshal Keith Park; another was of Christina. The war photographer J. Deakin, now a lieutenant, who completed the series of images of Christina the previous year, was again on hand for publicity purposes and photographed Christina in early August at Leslie Cole's studio.

On 3 September, Air Vice-Marshal Park presented the one surviving Gladiator, *Faith,* to the Maltese people. Two days later, Italy surrendered. At long last, everyone had something to celebrate. Church bells rang out and the streets were quickly festooned with bunting and flags as the whole island went wild with joy. Crowds not seen since June 1940 gathered everywhere, with people singing and dancing; all except Christina. The one person she wanted to share victory with wasn't there and she had received no word. She walked the streets they had walked together many times - *Porto Reale* up to Merchants Street, then left down Britannia Street back to Kingsway. She continued down the steepening slope to Strait Street, but instead of going home she turned left to meander back to the city walls.

After all Christina and Warby had gone through together, it seemed she was destined to celebrate Malta's victory on her own, miserable and feeling more alone than she had done before. After an hour she turned into South Street and headed for the Monico. Perhaps she should just go and get sloshed, she thought.

'And then suddenly I saw him coming towards me, running down the street, with his arms outstretched: "Chris, I've been looking all over the bloody place for you."

'It was the first time I'd heard him swear and I loved it. Right there in the middle of South Street he went down on his knees and pleaded forgiveness. I wept buckets of tears. Passers-by must have thought we were nuts.'

Warby paraded with 683 Squadron for the final time a week later. He left Malta on posting in October having been in command of a photo-reconnaissance squadron on continuous war operations for fourteen months.

Christina never saw Warby again.

Chapter 13

Pour que tu me n'oublie pas completement

October 1943 - 1952

Warby flew to Tunisia and then to England for three weeks' leave. Christina would have known of his plans but is unlikely to have heard from him until he arrived back in North Africa at the RAF airfield at La Marsa near Tunis. He became the first commanding officer of 336 (PR) Wing declared operational on 1 November 1943. It comprised of 683 Squadron, still in Malta, 682 Squadron, also with Spitfires, and 60 (South African Air Force) Squadron operating Mosquitos. Warby's recce wing was part of an Anglo-American organization commanded by Elliot Roosevelt.

Many pilots ended up physical or nervous wrecks after less than six months of operations from Malta. Yet Warby had continued for nearly two and a half years with only very short breaks in between tours. His final tour of fifteen months in command of 69 and 683 Squadrons was unusually long in wartime. Nor could his rest tours be described as such and attempts by senior officers to curb his flying were cursory. More could have been done to keep him on the ground but he would have fiercely resisted any attempt. But selecting him for yet another demanding command appointment was hardly likely to reduce the pressure on him. Despite his leave, Warby must have been affected by stress and it would have been obvious to all concerned he would drive himself hard. Perhaps it was a case of needs must and having the best man for the job regardless of the cost to the individual.

Christina heard about Warby via Lascaris and then by letter. She knew he would hit the ground running at La Marsa. She would also have learnt what was going on through their mutual friends on 683 Squadron, which didn't move from Malta to La Marsa until mid-November. Soon after that, it was announced President Franklin D. Roosevelt had conferred the US DFC on Warby. This was his sixth gallantry award - 'Six-medal Warburton' - all earned for operations from Malta. The citation read:

> While on a mission to obtain urgently needed photographs of the coastline of Pantelleria on Jun 3rd, he distinguished himself through

his resolute courage and calm efficiency under fire. Flying over the island at two hundred feet, within easy range of every type of anti-aircraft battery and drawing fire of even large coastal guns, Warburton photographed virtually the entire shoreline, gaining information of inestimable value to the allied Force which later invaded the island. His proficiency as pilot and photographer, and his selfless devotion to duty reflect great credit upon him and the armed forces of the United Nations.

The next news was grim: Warby had been in a road accident. Initially taken to hospital in Carthage, his injuries were serious and included a broken pelvis. He was transferred to No. 2 RAF General Hospital at Maison Carée, Algiers. He wrote to Christina from there. He was expected to be hospitalised for at least three months with the lower part of his body encased in plaster. At least he was alive. Warby would be grounded for months, or so Christina and the RAF thought.

Warby's wing, 336 Wing, moved from La Marsa to San Severo on the Foggia Plain in Southern Italy, 683 Squadron being the last to complete the journey on 20 December. By then Warby had received the news he must have anticipated but which would have been devastating: he lost command of 336 Wing.

In mid-January he wrote to his father, having been bedridden for seven weeks, with around five more to go. In his letter Warby said Elliott, meaning Elliot Roosevelt, was moving on and he hoped to accompany him. For obvious reasons, he said nothing about the likely destination, which was San Severo. Warby also said if he was able to follow Elliot, he might be able to settle with his friend once and for all. Did Warby tell that to Christina? She was only thirty minutes flying time from San Severo.

Bill Carr, a 683 Squadron pilot, described what Warby then did: 'Growing tired of being bedridden he climbed out of the window, "borrowed" a vehicle and made his way to the airport. There he located some old friends and they cut off his cast. He borrowed shorts and a shirt and a Mark IX Spit from a friendly squadron commander and flew to see us of his old squadron, now located in Italy. While he had a parachute, he had no maps and the aircraft had no oxygen. In due course he found us, and among other things en route had flown over a weather front that topped out at 25,000 feet. Lesser mortals in the best of health would not have survived such a flight, yet, the following day, he visited us at dispersal in San Severo and allowed that he must be getting old because he felt too tired to share a few noggins with us that evening.'

After that Christina probably heard only snippets and rumours until Warby was back in England in February. Letters to and from Malta would have been infrequent, even if they used RAF friends to pass on mail and messages. But she would have learnt he did join his American friends at RAF Mount Farm near Oxford, close to the RAF photo recce hub of RAF Benson.

One of Warby's South African friends back at San Severo in Italy said Warby visited San Severo *after* being appointed liaison officer to the US 7th Photo-Reconnaissance Group (PRG) at RAF Mount Farm on 1 April. Warby let it be known he would be back on about 12 April and asked for a party to be laid on. Others on 60 Squadron at San Severo also said Warby was expected on the same date. That was the day Warby disappeared.

Christina found out soon afterwards when, 'an airman at Regional Control where I was then working said to me quite casually: "I suppose you've heard about your old friend Wing Commander Warburton?"

'He brought me a copy from the filing cabinet. It was a request for news of Warby, missing on a flight from England. To begin with I was not unduly worried. Nor was anyone else. He had been missing before and, anyway, nothing could ever happen to Warby. But each time I went on duty my first question was: "Any news about Warby?"

'There was none. All sorts of rumours began to run around. Warby had been shot down. Then from another source: "No, Warby had crashed into the Alps". I wrote to his mother and she told me that Warby was missing and had last been heard of over Lake Constance. My belief is that he had an engine failure while actually over the lake.'

The request for news came from Elliot Roosevelt. He said Warby, flying an American P-38 Lightning, went missing in action on 12 April 1944 when on an operational shuttle run mission to Italy. The signal said Warby's destination was either Alghero or San Severo. The news Warby was missing was met with disbelief. Signals were sent to various RAF bases, including Malta, asking if he had landed there. It took the RAF nearly three weeks, until 1 May, before they notified Warby's mother. Even then the long-dreaded telegram raised doubts as the Air Ministry asked to be advised if she heard news of Warby from any other source. Evidently there were some who believed he would still turn up. Christina was one of them.

Her belief about Warby going down into a lake was pure speculation as she was convinced Warby could never have been shot down. Many questions were asked about his last flight to try and work out where he might have been lost. Some insisted Warby's destination was Alghero, but the commanding officer of the 7th PRG, as well as Elliot Roosevelt who approved the sortie, said it was San Severo. Some suggested Warby may have been heading for Malta to see Christina, others that he crashed in Switzerland. Most thought his aircraft had come down in the sea or into a lake, but there was no evidence either way. Others questioned Warby's state of mind. Although he became increasingly fatalistic as the war progressed, there were no indications he harboured a death wish.

Jack Vowles, the young airman Warby befriended on Malta, summed up many peoples' thoughts about Warby the legend: 'We never thought he would not come back.' Christina would have been one of many who thought that. He never did come back. She probably often looked at the note Warby wrote to her much earlier, long before he left Malta:

Tout mon amour, pour que tu me n'oublie pas completement.

Of course Christina would never forget Warby. But, just as she had when he went missing in November 1942, she kept her emotions hidden. Part of her still hoped he would somehow turn up.

The headmistress of Christina's old school, Manchester High School for Girls, had written to Christina congratulating her on the award of her British Empire Medal. Christina was invited to visit the school to talk to the girls about her wartime experiences. She replied to the school in late 1944 or early 1945, and her letter was published in the school magazine in May 1945:

> It is extremely nice of you to send both your own and the school's congratulations on my award of the BEM. There are possibilities of my being able to visit before the autumn, though everything depends on the course of the war, for I am still working at RAF headquarters here and cannot get away for leave in England until the war in Europe is over. I have been in Malta for almost five years - the most eventful five years of my life - so you can well imagine how I am longing to get back home. Your invitation to come and tell the school of my experience would be accepted with pleasure. I think I should really enjoy telling the girls about the adventures I have had in Malta.

With Malta's siege over, and southern Italy soon in Allied hands, the war gradually moved north away from Malta. Things on the island slowly began to return to normal. One visible sign of normality was the re-opening of places of entertainment, including the Morning Star. There were still many troops based on the island and in transit, and many former entertainers and cabaret artistes returned to Valletta's nightclubs and music halls. Christina continued to work for the RAF. It also seems she went back to Gianni Fiteni's establishment for a while working in cabaret. This would have been an ideal way to fund a potential trip back to England.

Lisa Mallia née Debattista lived in Valletta. She was one of seven children. Her mother ran a shop which stocked toiletries and other items not far from the Morning Star. The shop was on *Strada Ospedale*, not far from *Strada Stretta,* and a number of the barmaids employed there paid for their purchases by instalments which Lisa sometimes collected. Lisa would walk up *Strada San Giuseppe*, turn the corner and step into the Morning Star. Lisa said Christina sang there and immediately took a liking to Lisa, for whom she bought sweets. Lisa remembered Christina fondly and considered her a great friend. She last saw Christina shortly before she left Malta to visit her family in England. While such a visit would have been far from straightforward to arrange, Christina's continued work with the RAF would have helped, especially as she had been employed by the RAF since June 1941. She certainly would have been entitled to leave.

While relatively little is known about what Christina got up to after the war, it is highly likely she visited her family in the autumn of 1945. While in England she would also have tried to find out what had happened to Warby. She had previously been in touch with Warby's mother but Muriel would not have been able to offer anything new. Christina may have tried to contact many of her and Warby's mutual RAF friends. She knew Warby had stayed for a time with his close friend, the Australian Tich Whiteley, who had been based at RAF Cranage near her parents' home in Cheshire. Tich certainly knew Christina. Did she get in touch with him?

But no one would have been able to offer Christina anything other than speculation and she had heard most of that in Malta. She probably realised by then that Warby was not coming back. She would have continued to listen in hope to all the wild rumours but there was no certainty, and there would never be any closure. She would have hoped he would simply turn up unannounced. But in her heart she must have known he had 'bought it', been 'bumped'. A light went out of her life.

By then Christina had decided to make her life in Malta. She also had a business venture in mind and she may well have discussed this with her parents. She also had some shares she sold. This may have been to help fund the venture she had in mind, to run in parallel with her job with the RAF. She did not return to the Morning Star, which continued in business until the mid-1950s when it and other surrounding properties were demolished to make way for residential apartments.

The task of clearing debris and rebuilding in Malta was immense. Christina's landlord, Gustav Vincenti, was an influential architect and it wasn't long before her original apartment in Floriana, the one with the amazing views, was ready for her to move back into. This was where Warby first stayed in 1941. It became Christina's home for the rest of her life. She continued to work for the RAF, becoming a civilian secretary to successive station commanders at RAF Luqa, and she stayed in this role for many years.

Like many others who suffered material loss through bombing, Christina submitted a claim for the possessions she lost when Shelter No. 2, Vilhena Terrace, was destroyed. Her claim was for just over £94. It was over three years after the war's end before her claim was paid, although for some reason Malta's War Damage Commission deducted just over £5 from the claim.

In 1946 there came an immense shock for Warby's family and for the RAF. That shock may have extended to Christina. Mrs Eileen Warburton, Warby's wife, came forward to claim his medals and decorations. She was duly invited to Buckingham Palace for the investiture.

Warby had married in secret in October 1939 shortly after war was declared and almost a year before he came to Malta. There was much publicity at the time of the investiture and headlines in British newspapers of 'Medals but no Bread'. This referred to the lack of any allowances - marriage or widow's - for Mrs Warburton.

Eileen, known as Betty, was 26-years-old when she married Warby; he was 21-years-old at the time. They had met in Gosport where Betty worked as a barmaid in The Bush public house - 'Betty of the Bush'. They had known one another for only three or four weeks when they married. The marriage was over within days, with them never actually living together. In later years, Betty even expressed doubts about whether the marriage was ever consummated. Betty also had a 9-year-old daughter from a previous marriage, who was living with her parents. Did Warby know of her before the wedding?

Regardless of the unusual nature of the short-lived marriage, Betty and Warby never divorced, although Betty had intended to serve papers but never did. The marriage was a fact. There would have been inevitable headlines in Malta about Warby, Malta's very own hero. There would also have been a great deal of speculation, and Christina would have been plagued with requests to enlarge on her friendship with Warby. She said nothing.

Christina was in touch with her friend Tamara, who had earlier urged her to join her in Egypt, but Christina always said her place was on the island. Tamara wrote several letters to Christina but never returned to Malta despite invitations to do so. Maybe there were too many unhappy memories: the horrors of the bombing, the tragic loss of her friend Aida Kelly and of course her own attempted suicide. Tamara may also have fallen a little in love with René Duvauchelle. Maybe falling in love in a siege was all too easy.

As Christina later reflected about René and Jacques, 'they never lived to see the liberation of their country, the victory for which they had risked so much to attain.' The two Frenchmen were buried near Catania in Sicily before being moved to the French military cemetery in Rome. In 1949, René was appointed as a Knight of the Legion of Honour, a Companion of the Liberation and awarded the Croix de Guerre with Palm. In 1950, he was brought home to France and buried at Vaux-le-Penil in Saint-et-Maine.

Christina opened a small café in Valletta - The Café Christina - which she ran when off-duty from the RAF. On the left-hand corner just beyond Old Mint Street, it was around the corner and a short walk from Christina's former apartment on Strait Street. It was also close to many of the bars and restaurants she and Warby had known well. How long she kept the café is unknown. Maybe she dreamt Warby might find her there one day. Christina later wrote a short story about the café. She called it *Threepence Charity*:

> It was an autumn evening in 1947. Down at the 'Café Christina' in Britannia Street, Valletta, things were very quiet and peaceful, only the clicking of two pairs of knitting needles breaking the stillness of the empty bar. I did not like things so quiet, so peaceful; nor did Susie, the barmaid. Accustomed as we were to the hustle and bustle of a full house, the laughter, the gaiety, the jokes with the customers, we were not at all happy when business was slack. But business was always slack on a Thursday. It was the prelude to Friday's storm. Tomorrow was pay-day and the place would be packed out. We would be run off our feet; we would be half-dead with exhaustion at the end of the evening. So seated on beer crates behind the counter we persuaded ourselves that we needed the rest and got on with our winter sweaters. Suddenly there were footsteps in the deserted street. A customer?
>
> We got up from our beer crates, stuffed our knitting under the counter and looked hopefully towards the door. The footsteps came near. They stopped. There was a brief, almost eerie, silence. Then slowly the heavy tapestry curtains over the doorway was drawn apart, and into the bar stepped a man with the largest and quite the most grotesque nose I had ever seen.
>
> 'Susie. Who on earth is this?'
>
> 'Ssh. He's a beggar. I've seen him before.'
>
> The man approached the counter, holding out a little tin saucer. Face to face with him, I could see that the nose was false. It was made of *papier-mâché* and attached to the bridge of his horn-rimmed spectacles with a piece of tape. Susie reached for her handbag.
>
> 'No, don't' I said. 'Give him something from the till. Poor fellow, do you think he would like a drink?'
>
> The beggar smiled at me.
>
> 'Thank you very much madam. But I do not drink.'
>
> It occurred to me that for a Maltese of the beggar class he spoke English remarkably well. Susie took a threepenny bit from the till and dropped it into the saucer. A look of gratitude came into the man's eyes.

FALL IN. DOWN KINGSWAY TO BLACKLEY'S — MARCH.
HALT. LEFT TURN. 250 PACES DOWN THE SIDE STREET
— QUICK MARCH. YOU'RE THERE! WHERE?

THE CAFE CHRISTINA

66a, Britannia Street, Valletta.

AN ENGLISH BAR WITH A CONTINENTAL
ATMOSPHERE

SOFT LIGHTS — SWEET MUSIC — PALM TREES.

From the first edition of the *Luqa Lens* in April 1952. *(National Archives)*

CAFE CHRISTIN

66a, Britannia Street,
(3rd turning left after Kingsgate)

Valletta - Malta.

THE COSIEST LITTLE BAR IN TOWN

SOFT LIGHTS
SWEET MUSIC
PALM TREES
BLUE GROTTO
(See over)

A MALTE
ALLEZ
Au Café CRISTINA
66, BRITANNIA STREET, VALETTA.
(3ème rue à gauche après Kingsgate)

VOUS POURREZ Y BOIRE
DE DELICIEUX CAFÉS
DE LA BIÉRE, DU VIN,
DES ALCOOLS,
ET
TOUTES SORTES DE BOISSONS NON-ALCOOLIQUES

(ON PARLE FRANÇAIS.)

DOČI V MALTU
OBISKAT
Kafanu KRISTINA
66, BRITANSKA ULICA
(3a, Vogal Kraljeve Ulice)

DOČI VAMO TU JE NABOLJA
PIĆA KAFA PIVA
VINO I ALKOHOL
I DRJGE NAJBOLJE PIĆE

Advertisements for Café Christina. *(Miriam Farrugia)*

219

'Thank you, thank you so much ladies. Goodnight.'

He bowed politely and turned to go. As I did so I caught sight of his profile. To my amazement, I could see a distinct space between the artificial nose and the cheekbones. Behind the mask there was nothing - just nothing. From that evening onwards the man with no nose visited us regularly once a week. And regularly once a week he went away enriched by threepence from the till. But oddly enough he always came to the bar at opening time.

'He can't have much business sense', Susie remarked. 'Otherwise he would come when the place is full.

When I said, jokingly, that the beggar was shy I did not realise how near I was to the truth. But it happened that one evening, this time a Friday, our beggar turned up later than usual. When he arrived the tables were all occupied and there was a sizeable crowd round the bar. Obviously embarrassed and reluctant to come forward, he cut a pathetic figure as he hovered about the doorway nervously fingering his little tin saucer. Opening the tin drawer, I took a threepenny bit and beckoned him over. The people around the bar stopped talking. All eyes were focused on the man with the artificial nose. There were shudders of revulsion, looks of sympathy, a few sniggers. It was my turn to be embarrassed. As I handed over the threepence I felt like some Pharisee parading his almsgiving for all to behold.

To my surprise the beggar did not take advantage of the pay-day crowd. He merely pronounced his usual thanks and hurried away. On that particular evening among the customers at the counter was a certain gentleman whom I shall call Mr Knowall. Short and plump with a florid face, he was a well-known character in the Valletta bars, flitting as he did from one to another with the ease - if not the grace - of a butterfly on the wing. As might be expected, Mr Knowall on his peregrinations came into contact with a wide variety of people. And people absolutely fascinated him. So did their private lives, which he appeared to study with an almost unhealthy interest. He knew everything there was to know about people worth knowing, and a good deal more about those who were not.

'Soft. That's what you are, soft,' he told me when the beggar had gone.

'Fancy giving money to a bounder like that'.

'He's not a bounder,' Susie interrupted, 'he's a poor creature without a nose and no one will give him a job.'

'Serves him right. It's his own fault. Comes from a good family too.'

Christina and Café Christina
in Britannia Street, now Melita
Street, Valletta. (*Miriam Farrugia*)

The customers were all ears. Mr Knowall was in his element. There was nothing he enjoyed better than dispensing a nice bit of scandal over a pint of ale.

'Of course, you know what's wrong with the chap's nose, don't you?'

There were no suggestions.

'Well, I'll tell you. He's got a disease. And it isn't the sort you mention in drawing rooms. Nor in public houses for that matter.'

Having imparted this juicy piece of information, Mr Knowall quaffed down the remainder of his beer, wiped the froth from his lips with his coat-sleeve and made for the next port of call.

Came Christmas Eve. And with it a charming surprise. When Susie and I opened up the bar we found a Christmas card, addressed to me, lying on the doormat. Enclosed with the card was a small, neatly-written note, which read:

"Mrs, this is a small compliment by sending you a Christmas card for the trouble taken that every week you gave me 3d charity. Yours truly, A CARBONARA

NB. God will help you now and then."

To say that Susie and I were deeply moved would be to put it mildly. We wept unashamedly.

'You wait until Mr Knowall sees this' I said when I had dried my tears.

We had not long to wait. Mr Knowall was our first customer. I let him get settled comfortably on his barstool and then pushed the Christmas card and the accompanying note in front of him.

'Read that. It's from the man with no nose'.

Mr Knowall examined the card very carefully and read the little message. Meanwhile I studied his face intently, curious to see his reactions. I was hoping there would be a sign of remorse, some expression betraying shame for the unkind remarks he had made about the beggar. But I was disappointed.

'Touching. Very touching' he sneered. 'The crafty devil. Playing on your sympathy, that's what he is. I suppose next time he comes in you'll be soft enough to fork out sixpence.'

But there was no next time. Strangely enough the man did not come back, and Susie and I never saw him again. Months went by and the beggar passed out of our thoughts. Then one evening Mr Knowall rushed into the bar in a state of great excitement.

'What did I tell you?' he cried.

He dealt the counter a punishing blow with his fist.

'What did I tell you?'

Susie and I were perplexed. He told us so many things.

'That fellow without a nose. I saw him in Cook's this afternoon. He's going on a cruise. A cruise, mark you. I heard him, with my own ears, actually booking a passage'.

Mr Knowall paused to see the effect of his words. If a display of surprise was what he was after, he was well rewarded. We were flabbergasted.

'So you see,' he went on, 'that's what he was doing with all the money mugs like you were fool enough to give him. Saving up for a cruise.'

Astonished we certainly were, but we were not unduly distressed. After all, it was not as if we had been robbed of our lifetime's savings.

'Well, all I can say is: Jolly good luck to him!' was Susie's only comment.

I shared her sentiments. If the beggar was going on a cruise, which seemed to be the case, then so be it. And that, as far as I was concerned, was that. But there was more to come. The story had by no means ended.

It was 14 February 1949 - St Valentine's Day. I had been shopping for groceries and had returned home with some of my purchases wrapped in a local newspaper. I was about to throw the paper into the rubbish bin when something in it caught my eye. It was the heading, in heavy black type, of a news column reproduced from the *Daily Mirror* of February 7. Five little words that read: *TONY TWEAKS HIS NEW NOSE.*

Seized by a sudden curiosity, I straightened out the crumpled paper and began to read the column.

'Anthony Carbonaro is fifty years old,' it said, 'but he was like a child with a new toy as he sat on the edge of a hospital bed yesterday, tweaked the end of his nose with finger and thumb and said; 'It's wonderful. I can really feel it.'

The story went on:

'For the last thirty years - until yesterday - Anthony Carbonaro had never had a nose of his own - just a false one that was attached to the bridge of a pair of spectacles and fooled no one. He had been nineteen, a good-looking Maltese soldier fighting in the Dardanelles when a fragment of shrapnel severed his nose clean off.'

It was then explained that a few months ago the man without a nose, living on a ten shillings a week pension, was sitting in his garret room in Malta reading a magazine. In it he saw a photograph of Professor Pomfret Kilner, the plastic surgeon. Carbonaro wrote to the professor.

'You have helped many. Can you give me a new nose?'

In a few months it was arranged. The Government of Malta paid Carbonaro's fare to England and the operation was performed at the Churchill hospital at Oxford.

'You don't know how I've had to suffer in the last thirty years,' said Carbonaro. 'Everyone has shunned me. I would go into shops and they wouldn't serve me. Children would call unkind things to me as I walked down the street. But now - oh, it's so wonderful I could cry with happiness.'

I, too, could have cried with happiness when I finished reading the story. It was indeed wonderful to know that after so many years of suffering, Anthony Carbonaro could take his place once again in the world as a normal human being. Yet at the same time was it not shocking to think that the greater part of his suffering had been brought about by the unkind words and deeds of his compatriots of whom not the least blameworthy was that old gossip, Mr Knowall?

If only there had been a little more sympathy and understanding, a little more charity, how much misery and heartbreak could have been spared to a lonely, unfortunate man?

***

Marion Gould, the 16-year-old plotter Christina taught to dance, got engaged to Army medic Eric Childs. They planned to return to Britain together, Marion volunteering for the WAAF and Eric for the Parachute Regiment as a medic. Back in England in 1944, Marion found herself in yet another Ops room as a plotter, but this time in uniform. Unfortunately, Eric's parachute course was in the Middle East. He then served in Italy. They eventually caught up with one another in September 1944. Eric was later sent to help alleviate the desperate

Eric & Marion Childs, 1946.
(Margaret Biggs)

state of survivors of Bergen-Belsen and Auschwitz, an experience that would stay with him for the rest of his life.

Despite the war coming to an end in Europe, Marion wasn't quite done with volunteering; this time for security duties with the Special Operations Executive. She was based at Netheravon on Salisbury Plain, but also covered the flying boat base at Pool Harbour. Her duties were merely clerical, or so she says; she did not wear uniform. Marion and Eric married in November 1946 and she was demobbed a few months later in 1947.

On Monday, 20 February 1945, Gladys Aitken followed Christina with a move to Regional Flying Control, still at Lascaris. By then the family had moved back to a much safer Valletta, to 122A Old Bakery Street. Gladys and Mary continued to work for the RAF at Lascaris until the end of the Second World War.

Gladys had been courted for some time by RAF radio operator Joe Duddell. Gladys and Joe were married in April 1945. Gladys was held in high regard at Lascaris, her commanding officer saying 'she has proved herself to be keen, efficient, trustworthy and punctual' throughout her service. He went on to say: 'Her resignation due to her forthcoming marriage is greatly regretted.'

Gladys Aitken & Joe Duddell's wedding April 1945
Mary Aitken is on the extreme left, their father Alexander is between the
two girls. Their mother Mary is on the right. (*Sandra Patterson*)

Gladys and Joe moved into their own home in Old Bakery Street in June. By then she was expecting their first child, which set a pattern for their happy life together. They had ten children. With Joe later stationed at RAF Siggiewi, they stayed in Malta until May 1953 before moving to England eventually settling in Telford, Shropshire. Joe served in the RAF for a total of twenty-six years. One of his many deployments was to Christmas Island in the Pacific for the UK's nuclear tests in 1957 and 1958.

Mary Aitken became a nursing sister after her time as a plotter at Lascaris. She met and married a Royal Navy surgeon Alan Tooley. They had three children.

The two eldest Cuell girls, Agnes and Betty, made their homes in England. Helen stayed in Malta and was about to get engaged. Sadly, her would-be fiancé, a civilian who worked in intelligence, was killed as a pillion passenger in a motor cycle accident while on his way to ask Helen's father, Walter, for her hand in marriage. Helen never got over his loss. At some stage she transferred to RAF Luqa where she worked in the NAAFI.

The third of the Cuell sister plotters, Joan, married RAF Flight Sergeant Jock Watret; he went on to become a squadron leader. Brother Eddie, who had queued so long and so often, joined the Royal Malta Artillery as a gunner as soon as he was old enough. He was surprised to find himself undertaking a course at Lascaris in the very same plotting room in which his three sisters had worked. For four children of the same family to work at Lascaris is extraordinary. As for Ted Baker, who unsuccessfully courted all three of the Cuell aircraft plotters, when he returned to the UK Betty introduced him as a pen-pal to her young Aunt, Ester MacTavish. In 1947, Ester went out to Malta as a nurse to escape the terrible winter and rationing in Britain. She married Ted. So Ted found his girl after all.

Michael Longyear at long last enjoyed a period of stability and more conventional education in England. In 1946, with his mother, he was shipped from Tilbury to Cuxhaven to join his father in occupied Germany. They then travelled by train to bomb-torn Hannover to join a small enclave of British military families living in houses confiscated from Nazi party members. In 1947, Michael became a founder pupil of an experimental co-educational, comprehensive, British military boarding school. Prince Rupert School in Wilhelmshaven was in the barracks of the former German *Kriegsmarine* U-boat training flotilla. It was from there that *Korvettenkapitan* Günther Prien sailed in U-boat 47, entered Scapa Flow and sank HMS *Royal Oak* four weeks after the outbreak of the Second World War. All in all, Michael experienced quite an education.

Pauline Longyear was discharged from the WAAF in 1946 and re-joined her parents in Hanover. Sadly, her elder sister Doreen was soon a widow. Her husband, Hugh Nettleton, was demobbed from the RAF and entered teacher training. He contracted polio and died in 1947. Victor Longyear retired from the Royal Engineers in 1949 after a very long career having served in two world wars. A year later, the Korean War broke out. Victor promptly offered his services. His offer was declined.

Chapter 14

'Carved on my Heart'

1952 - 1988

Hugh Lloyd, Malta's former Air Officer Commanding, had a highly successful RAF career reaching the rank of Air Chief Marshal before retiring in 1953. He was also a screenwriter for the film *Malta Story,* produced by J. Arthur Rank and was a guest at the film's world premiere at the Odeon Theatre in Leicester Square on 25 June 1952.

Christina provided material for *Malta Story* which captures well the impact of war on the island. While characters' names were changed, the Jack Hawkins' character is undoubtedly based on Lloyd himself. The main theme is a touching love story between a photo-recce Spitfire pilot, played by Alec Guinness, and a Maltese civilian plotter working at Lascaris, played by Muriel Pavlov. While there are parallels between them and Christina and Warby, there are two other key characters in the film who are a much closer match. Anthony Steel plays a photo-recce squadron commander, the boss of the character played by Alec Guinness, and he is involved with a senior civilian aircraft plotter, perhaps a Watch Captain, played by Renée Asherson. The parallels between these two and Christina and Warby are striking.

Miriam Cassar, later Farrugia, was a little girl when she met Christina in the 1950s. Her family on her mother's side, the Portellis, had property in Bugibba near St Paul's Bay and spent vacations in a house facing the sea on Islet Promenade close to Angelo's Guest House. Miriam's family also owned the small house next door which was two doors from Angelo's. Christina rented this house and retained it for the rest of her life. At the time Bugibba was a very small community of about twenty families, many of whom only came for their holidays.

Christina was approaching her fortieth birthday when Miriam first met her, although Miriam thought she looked much younger: 'She was always a very friendly person, friendly with everyone; she would come to our place as if she was one of the family and join in with the various activities. *Fenkatas* [rabbit stew] were often organised and, with so little traffic, long tables were placed outside across the road; everyone was invited, it was like one big family.

Christina at her Bugibba home. (*Miriam Farrugia*)

'We were quite a big family; I was the eldest of five children. I remember Mum used to put my two brothers and two sisters to sleep in the afternoon, but I never slept. From when I was about six or seven years old Christina would come for me every day in summer at around two in the afternoon and ask my Mum if she could take "Mimi" with her to swim. We went to a place right opposite where we lived. She was the first woman I saw in a two-piece swimsuit here in Malta and I believe she was the first ever to wear one. I was always fascinated by her, she was so beautiful. I can still picture her lovely face; her blonde hair was shoulder-length with hanging curls. Always with impeccable hair, she was stunning. Everybody used to stare at Christina she was so lovely.

'I used to go to her place with her and she showed me pictures of herself and her friends. Once I did hear her say to my aunt who visited that she loved a man called Warby very much and now she would never get married. At the time I didn't know who Warby was. She was a very lonely person, even though she had quite a few friends coming over to stay during the summer months. She had an old convertible 1940s' car and she used to come for us to take us for a ride. I admired her a great deal, a vibrant and vivacious lady, and she liked me, always wanting me to be with her. Christina longed for company.'

From the late 1950s, Miriam's family didn't stay at Bugibba so often. Miriam returned there as a teenager but Christina's door was always closed. It was over twenty years before Miriam saw her again.

In April 1958, a fifteen-part series about Warby was published in *The Star* newspaper in the UK. Written by Roy Nash, it was called *The Unknown Air Ace*. It was followed a few days later by a five-part series written by Christina

228

herself called *One Woman Goes to War*. By then Christina was 44-years-old, still living in the Floriana apartment she had once shared with Warby. The articles are well written and describe Christina's childhood, early dancing career and then Malta and fighter control. She also talks about Warby but doesn't hint at any relationship other than friendship. That set a pattern in the years ahead, with a veil drawn over the true nature of their relationship. In the final article, Christina said she was still working as a secretary for the RAF in Malta where Warby had become a legend. 'But for me he still lives. He could come walking in tomorrow and I don't think I should be a bit surprised.'

But he didn't come walking in tomorrow or the next day, or the day after that. Missing, believed killed, nothing more. By then, Warby had been missing for fourteen years. Photographs of Christina were included with the articles,

Christina's living room in Bugibba.
(*Miriam Farrugia*)

one of which looked recent. It showed an older and still very slim Christina, very smartly dressed with her blonde hair curled to the shoulder. She is smiling and wearing her British Empire Medal, complete with bow, with great pride. Christina kept a scrapbook and increasingly pursued her hobby of writing, even making a start on her own story. She was approached often to tell her tale but declined all offers and tried to avoid attempts by journalists and authors to seek her out.

Christina was an attractive, outgoing, and charismatic lady who enjoyed company. She would have come into contact with many people in Malta after the war and with many RAF personnel through her work at Luqa. But she never met anyone to match Warby. She also had Maltese friends, especially from her Lascaris days, although most of her 'girls' were a lot younger. Inevitably, many married and had families of their own and her contacts with them gradually diminished. Christina had a dog which she called Isosceles. She called her open-top car 'The Flying Saucepan.'

In 1965, Tony Spooner's autobiography *In Full Flight* was published. It included a photograph labelled 'Christina' but with no surname, the caption simply said she served the RAF so well she was decorated for her work. There are no direct references to her by name in the text. Spooner said Warby lived in a flat in Valletta

Isosceles & 'The
Flying Saucepan'.
(*Miriam Farrugia*)

with a charming cabaret artiste; he made no link with the girl in the photograph.
Was he deliberately holding a veil over Christina's identity yet somehow felt
compelled to include a photograph knowing how important she was in Warby's
life? Perhaps he was aware she wanted to maintain a degree of anonymity over her
relationship with Warby.

Christina used the National Bank of Malta, later the Bank of Valletta, on
Kingsway where she was often seen by George Darmanin, the chief cashier.
George retired in 1968 and often spoke of Christina to his daughter Valerie and her
husband Frederick Galea who developed an increasing interest in Malta's air war.

It's uncertain how often Christina returned to England. She may have visited
as soon as the war in Europe was over and perhaps again when her father died
in September 1952. Her mother died in 1969 and Christina attended her funeral.
This may have been her last visit to England. How long she worked for the RAF
is also uncertain but it was long enough for her to become entitled to a pension.

Christina was committed to living alone. As she grew older she sought out
others by visiting places where she had experienced laughter and good company:
the small corner cafés and restaurants which are such a feature of Malta's towns
and villages. She ran one - The Café Christina - for a number of years. By then
the Monico and Cilia's on South Street were long gone. She became a regular at
Angelo's Guest House in Bugibba and at another in Floriana. The Green Shutters
was on St Thomas Street, Floriana, across the road from what was the Queen's Store
owned by the Mallia family who had looked after Christina and the Roches in their
hour of need in 1940. Christina recounted her stories many times, often showing
people her photographs and her medal. After she retired from the RAF she spent
more and more time in Bugibba. She enjoyed the company there and continued
to work on her writing. Inevitably she became withdrawn from a shrinking circle
of friends.

In 1974, a Maltese newspaper, now defunct, published a fifteen-part series written by Christina. By then Warby had been missing for thirty years. Yet she again avoided any reference to her feelings toward him, simply referring to him as a good friend. Later that year she wrote an article entitled *Food for Thought,* which was published in the *Times of Malta* in December 1974:

> The many and varied tempting dishes on the menus of hotels and restaurants, at present being advertised, have been conducive to my taking a trip down Memory Lane. Down the long, long trail a-winding to the war days of 1942 when Malta was on the verge of famine. When the daily bread given to each of us amounted to little more than a few crumbs; when fortnightly rations consisted of one tin of corned beef, one tin of sardines, two ounces of tea or coffee, either ¼ lb lard or ¼ lb margarine; when a small bottle of cooking oil was issued

Christina in front of the Britannia Street Victory Kitchens, Valletta, October 1942.
(via Frederick Galea)

every other ration period; when only on odd occasions did we get a little sugar. And then, 'in order that no one starved before all starved', the Government set up Victory Kitchens in every town and village.

At first the Victory Kitchens did not meet with much support, but as the siege continued and the prospects of relief from outside grew more remote, the kitchens came into their own.

It was not long before they were catering for almost the entire civil population. Indeed, it was due to these VKs, as they were dubbed, that the people owed their survival through those grim days of hunger. The black market was rife on the island and had there been no control of what supplies there were, no meting out of a fair share to all, however meagre, Malta might not have been able to claim that there were no deaths to starvation.

The one portion of food per person per day was served on a take-it-away basis in exchange for a small coupon, a booklet of which for a week's 'repasts' was to be had for the princely sum of three shillings! Among my wartime souvenirs is one such meal ticket (although why it was never used is beyond my recollection) and on it are printed the details: 'No. 639. Series B1. Monday 1 Lunch Cost 2d.' A typical menu was:

> Monday - *Minestra*
> Tuesday - *Balbuljata*
> Wednesday - One sardine with a few haricot beans
> Thursday - *Minestra* again
> Friday - A small helping of spaghetti
> Saturday - One sardine and beans again
> Sunday - Goat's meat in gravy

There were grumbles and complaints of course for the running of the machinery for feeding the community was not without its hitches. There was mismanagement, in some instances pilfering of the stocks by the employees themselves, and a shocking ignorance of culinary art was manifest in some of the dishes doled out for our consumption. *Balbuljata*, for example, which in normal times was a delectable Maltese speciality made with scrambled eggs, cheese, onions and tomatoes had nothing at all in common with the unappetising, powdered egg concoction masquerading under the name. But then, the making of a Beeton out of a bricklayer can at times be difficult and all were not domestic scientists who manned the Victory Kitchens.

The Editor of the *Times of Malta* was inundated with a flood of letters from correspondents with un-tickled palates, and from the sort of people who at the best of times like nothing better than a good old grouse. It seemed that there were those among us who having received their daily bread expected a lush layer of jam on it. Nevertheless, the moaners were allowed a free field in the paper to air their grievances and quite a number of the letters provided some entertaining reading.

One unrequited lover of *Minestra* wanted to know why the Victory Kitchens continue to serve out vegetable soup when we were perpetually requested to preserve our water supplies. Another person, no doubt a lover of animals, asked if it were quite fair that while *gharry* horses were being underfed to a point of starvation, large quantities of carob should be on sale for human consumption. He was referring to the beans of the carob tree, which were peddled in the streets at a penny for two pods.

A Sliema housewife described in detail her unsuccessful efforts to persuade the local Victory Kitchens staff to separate a portion of goat's meat from its gravy. Unable to eat 'the flesh of this little animal' she intended to give her share of it to a neighbour, keeping back the gravy to eat with her ration of bread. But her request was

Christina had written on the back of this image: 'Taken in the Victory Kitchen. (During siege when all food & vegetables collected by Government and issued as "meal" once a day to public.) We had to take our own dishes and carry the stuff home.' (*Miriam Farrugia*)

flatly refused by the manageress of the VK with the remark that orders from Head Office stipulated that the meat must be put in the sauce!

Another day the same housewife was queuing for the *plat du jour*, in this instance spaghetti, when a woman who had just been served had the misfortune to drop her basin. It broke and the contents oozed into a steaming sticky mess on the floor. But all was not lost - the spaghetti was speedily scraped off the floor by one of the employees and taken behind screens. 'Then', in the words of the correspondent, 'the one whose turn it was to receive his food next had to wait such a long time that he became suspicious of something going on and went to investigate. In the yard he found the kitchen staff busily washing the spaghetti that had been picked up from the floor - against which he strongly protested.'

The cries of the ill-fed population did not go unheeded. The Information Office issued a notice to the effect that the Government was aware that a section of the public did not like *Balbuljata* and that in some cases had refused to accept it. It was regretted, however, that there was nothing with which to replace this dish and arrangements would therefore be made for persons who preferred to go without it to pay for six meals a week instead of seven. But before taking such action members of the public were strongly advised to consider the fact that this form of food (dried egg), though new, was very nutritious and strongly recommended by the Ministry of Food and the Ministry of Health Departments in England.

The reaction to which was a V-for-Victory sign!

Christina's story *Three Pence Charity* was published a year later.

Salvatore Muscat, known as Salvu, lived in Mosta with his parents. He got his first full-time job when he was 19-years-old. It was in Bugibba, in Angelo's Guest House on Islet Promenade. He travelled each day by bus. Owned by the late Angelo Vella who lived above the premises with his family, both the owner and the restaurant were well-known locally. Angelo also owned the Seaview Hotel and later the Qawra Palace Hotel. Although the current bar and restaurant has changed a great deal, and the upper stories now house luxury apartments, it is still in the same location, owned by the same family, and run by one of Angelo's daughters. In 1981 Bugibba comprised mostly of rental apartments, very popular with British tourists in the summer, as well as some hotels and guest houses. Many Maltese families from Zebbug and Birkirkara also had their summer homes in the town.

Salvu worked from 9.00 am until 6.00 pm, including weekends. He was soon drawn towards the ever-smiling lady with the light grey hair worn to her shoulders. She always arrived alone. Christina was 67-years-old and had been one of the restaurant's most regular customers for years. She had a long established routine.

'On entering Angelo's there was a small bar immediately on the left and facing it on the right-hand side was the indoor restaurant. In the bar area there were two or three tables which weren't set for a meal, which was where Christina spent a lot of time while reading the newspaper, completing the crossword and writing. For lunch she moved into the restaurant and always sat at table 6 or 7. Angelo's had a beautiful beer garden at the back with a bird orchard. A large bar spanned the outside stone floor. Music was provided at weekends by a mobile disco. An important celebration at Angelo's was a replica wedding of Lady Diana on 29 July 1981 which spread into the streets. A local traditional band provided the music.'

Christina spent a lot of time in Bugibba from the end of the main tourist season in late September until early July the following year, travelling by bus from her Floriana home. She often came on consecutive days for weeks at a time, arriving at 2.00 pm for her daily meal. She usually stayed in the restaurant until the evening. Sometimes she slept over in the house she rented from Miriam Farrugia's family two doors from the restaurant but, on most occasions, she caught the last bus to Floriana from Bugibba Square at 8.00 pm.

She tended to be simply dressed Salvu recalled: 'I remember she used to love pink clothes and always wore a scarf. She carried a large handbag and wore a heavy coat in winter and a hat. Her hair was light grey and shoulder-length. She used to love her lipstick and always had her make-up bag with her. Sometimes she was heavily perfumed. If I remember correctly she used to wear some pin badges on her top, probably from the war days, but I can't elaborate on that, a pity.'

A few years earlier, probably in the late 1970s, Christina had fallen on the stairs to her Floriana apartment and broken her leg; it was some hours before she was able to summon help. During her recovery how she coped with the eighty-eight steps from her Vilhena Terrace entrance to her top-floor apartment is unimaginable. From then on she walked with a stick and that is how Salvu remembered her. He often picked up the walking stick when it fell from her chair or when leaning against the wall.

While Christina was always on her own when she arrived, and ate alone, she often spent a lot of time later in the afternoon talking to two other regular customers, both British and former military veterans who lived in Bugibba. They invariably arrived at 5.00 pm and drank pink gin, so were almost certainly ex-Royal Navy. 'Her favourite scotch was Dewar's White Label with soda (no ice). I remember that like yesterday.' Christina did speak some Malti: 'She always used the phrase *grazzi hafna* - thank you very much - on many occasions. She used other words too and we often laughed about how she pronounced them.'

Christina showed Salvu her British Empire Medal, which was always in her handbag. 'She used to read the *Times of Malta* and do the crossword, very much part of her daily routine, and then she would start making notes in a small notebook. She also carried a note pad too, which she often wrote in, and she said it would be her book when it was finished. She showed me some clippings of her articles from the *Times of Malta* and loads of photographs, especially one of a man in the RAF. You could see tears in her eyes when she got his photograph out.'

On 18 May 1982, Christina's article *The Merry Tenth of May* was published in the *Sunday Times of Malta* to coincide with the fortieth anniversary a few days earlier of the day that marked the turning point of the air battle of Malta. In the final paragraph Christina said: 'I just cannot believe that almost four decades have passed since the memorable Tenth of May. It is said that the older one grows the faster time flies so I am now left wondering what its speed will be like when I am a centenarian.'

Another of Christina's stories was published on 15 August 1982. *A Day of Rejoicing* coincided with another very important date for Malta, the fortieth anniversary of the arrival of the *Santa Maria* convoy. In this article, Christina offered the first and only glimpse into how she felt about Warby: 'There had been an eternity of waiting for this. All the weeks Warby had been away I had schemed and planned for his homecoming. Much of my sleeping time had been taken up with dreams of a wonderful reunion. Fighting down a desire to go on gazing into Warby's blue eyes, I returned my attention to the plotting table.' This was Christina at her most heartfelt. Had she decided the time was now right to reveal something of her true feelings for Warby nearly forty years after he went missing?

A number of Malta veterans returned that month for the anniversary. One was Tony Spooner, who had been working on a biography of Warby for twenty-five years since he read Roy Nash's articles. When Tony met Christina she would undoubtedly have welcomed his earlier discretion in his biography about her involvement with Warby. By 1982 it seems she was ready to talk and she would have enjoyed sharing their common experiences and talking about mutual friends.

Tony later wrote to Marion Could, now Marion Childs and living with her husband Eric, the former medic, in Raglan in Wales. He said: 'Christina is still going strong in Malta; drinking like a fish but otherwise OK. I found her to be a highly intelligent person'. This would suggest he had not previously met Christina. She was 68-years-old by then and had been on her own for nearly forty years. She may have been a verging alcoholic for some time.

Given the amount of personal information Tony included in his book, Christina must have cooperated fully. Did he mention to her the letter Warby wrote from hospital to his father in which he expressed the hope he would be able to settle with his friend once and for all? Tony was sure Warby meant Christina. If he did mention it to Christina, then she would have grasped it as confirmation Warby was planning to come back to her. It would have meant a great deal.

She was probably unaware of an underlying heart condition and her earlier reference to life when she was a centenarian suggests she anticipated many more years ahead, more than enough time for her to complete her story. Maybe when she met Tony she thought she could say a little more about her and Warby. Why had she waited so long to say anything about her involvement with Warby and nothing about her personal feelings toward him? Were they too personal, too private? Or had there been other factors at play? When did she learn Warby was married? Had he told her? Or did someone else? Or did she first find out in 1946 when Betty Warburton came forward?

When Warby introduced himself to Christina in the ERA Club in Floriana in January 1941, she would have been as unaware as everyone else he was married. Nor at that stage would she have cared a great deal. As far as she was concerned 'a Greek God' had just walked into her life only days after the devastating loss of her young Frenchman Jacques. Would Warby have revealed his short-lived marriage to the attractive blonde he had just met? No way.

Warby's closest friend at the time was the Australian Tich Whiteley. Tich was an honourable man and took it upon himself to sort out the torrid state of Warby's finances. Warby had been in a great deal of debt in England, reputed to have been one of the reasons why he was despatched to Malta in the first place. The other reason was vaguely referred to as 'woman trouble' although none in the RAF were privy to Warby's deception concerning his marital status. If Tich had known Warby was married he would have ensured an appropriate allowance went to Warby's wife regardless of the circumstances of the short-lived and quickly-regretted marriage on both Warby and Betty's parts. Tich knew of Christina and may well have met her as the war came to an end. Even as late as 1978 he was discreet about her relationship with Warby: 'Presumably someone still has Warby's log books - perhaps a lady whose name begins with C - perhaps his family. I hope they will in due course present them to the RAF Museum.'

When Christina's relationship with Warby began it was probably a case of carpe diem for both of them. Many had the same attitude and those few who became aware of Warby's marriage over time were unlikely to say anything. He was a popular hero and few thought he would survive the war. Live and let live was the attitude of many. Most would have wished them well, to enjoy what they had until the war intervened which it surely would.

Another factor was the attitude of the British military establishment to any hint of what they considered scandalous behaviour involving officers. With Christina soon employed by the RAF, Warby guarded his secret well. He may have explained things to her in 1942, but by then she was in too deep, very much in love, and any admission by him is unlikely to have made any difference to how she felt. She herself was no shrinking violet and was certainly not naïve about relationships. She was engaged once before and may have been very close to it a second time. Also her theatrical career may have broadened her perspective. Christina would have forgiven Warby many things and is unlikely to have held his rash decision in 1939 against him, given the circumstances; if she knew.

Regardless, it would be wrong to make a judgement seventy-five years later about people's attitudes and emotional responses when living under the conditions existing at the time in Malta. The island was under siege and death, serious injury or separation was around every corner and both Christina and Warby had been touched by them. There were different rules and expectations in those days. And love is a most powerful human emotion as well as being the most enduring.

When Betty Warburton appeared in 1946, if Christina had not known about her, she would have been shocked at Warby's deceit, perhaps even heartbroken. If that was the case, she would have closed that chapter on an exciting, very romantic, but ultimately sad aspect of her life and moved on. She certainly had the strength of character and resilience to do so and could easily have made another life. That she did not suggests she was not taken by surprise. For other reasons she chose to harbour what had long been in her heart, and to protect it.

The publicity surrounding Betty focused attention on Malta's very own hero and some of this may have reflected on Christina. Those who knew her well also knew of her involvement with Warby. Now was the opportunity for her to reveal all, to tell her story, but instead she chose to keep it to herself, refusing to be drawn, refusing to reveal her side of a story about one of the Second World War's most highly decorated airmen. And when she did write, she described Warby as a friend. It is not difficult to understand why.

Roman Catholic Malta has a clear attitude to marriage: it is for life. Divorce was illegal until 2011. Warby was well known on the island. To many people he was Malta's hero. If Christina revealed she had an affair with him, a married man, and they lived together for a time, this would have been damaging to Warby's reputation on the island which made him. She would wish to avoid doing that, knowing friends who knew the truth would respect her discretion. She chose to do nothing to tarnish the memory of a man applauded, almost revered, in Malta. She kept her memories to herself.

There was another factor. Christina continued to work for the RAF for many years after the war. She might have wished to avoid what some might consider scandal. Only in the 1982 article, long after she retired, did she offer a brief, almost tantalising glimpse of a relationship with Warby which went beyond friendship. Maybe she realised it was time to hint at their story. And it is a beautiful story.

Warby's disappearance hit Christina very hard. To begin with she covered her feelings but she felt his loss very deeply and over time it had a telling effect on her life. She never married, admitting she never found anyone who even came close to Warby. She held on to the memory of their happy times, hoping someone who had known Warby, or had news of what happened to him, might get in touch.

How much of Warby's life when he was away from Malta did Christina know? There were certainly letters between them and she would have been aware of his movements through mutual friends. While Warby was sustained by Christina, and he gave her his love, she also knew other women were attracted to him. She may have suspected he became flirtatious but there is no indication he had any serious involvement with anyone else. His remark in the letter to his father about being with his friend once more would have reassured Christina her love was reciprocated and Warby had hopes of a future together. But, in a postscript in the same letter, Warby refers to a 'Cairo BINT' with whom his father saw Warby in Cairo. Warby said the lady in question was, 'relaxation, needed sometimes'. Did Tony Spooner show Christina the full contents of the letter? He quoted it in full in *Warburton's War*.

Tony had heard talk about Warby's social life away from Malta and questioned whether Warby played the field. But he did not know Warby personally. Was what he heard accurate? Or was it hearsay based on crewroom gossip. Tony himself acknowledged it may have been what others expected. Squadron crewrooms are ideal for discussions about air tactics, but they are also notorious hotbeds of gossip.

Christina heard the rumours too and may not have been surprised. She may have wondered over the years whether Warby was faithful to her, or whether she was just one of many love interests. In *Warburton's War* Tony Spooner asked: 'Did she smooth the raw edges of his character and later pay the penalty by having him casually play the field as in Cairo and Tunisia?' Did Spooner reveal any of this to Christina? If he did not, and Christina had no inkling, then her cherished memories may have been shattered when *Warburton's War* hit the shelves in 1987. It would have been a popular read in Malta. If it was the first indication of Warby's possible infidelity, it would have come as a crushing blow. How would she then have reacted, drinking heavily, having kept a candle burning for Warby for over forty-three years? She was lonely and verging on alcoholism. She may also have been suffering from other ailments too. And whether she knew it or not, she had ischaemic heart disease. Was her heart now finally broken?

What became of some of the other ladies of Lascaris? Of Tamara Marks, sadly we know nothing more.

As for Pauline Longyear - Tuppence - perhaps the youngest Lascaris plotter of all, after staying with her parents in Hannover she returned to England, taking

Pauline Longyear, with the actor Bill Johnson. *(Michael Longyear)*

up clerical work in Portsmouth. She always had a keen interest in the stage, her brother Michael referring to her as being 'stage-struck'. But what chance did she have of not being so? Throughout her first ever job with the RAF at Lascaris, during very impressionable days for one so young, both of her Watch supervisors were members of the Whizz-Bangs, Christina and Pickles. Both were also subsequently decorated for gallantry. She was an active member of the Portsmouth Players, a serious amateur dramatics company to which she gave a lot of her time. In 1951 Pauline managed to get herself photographed with the actor Bill Johnson who played the lead in the original production of *Kiss Me, Kate* at London's Coliseum Theatre.

Pauline never married. Sadly, she died in 1978 of a family ailment, heart failure. She was only 50-years-old. Her younger brother Michael was called up for National Service in the British Army. Unsurprisingly he joined the Royal Engineers. He served in the Canal Zone in Egypt between 1951 and 1953, living through yet more harsh experiences of conflict. Afterwards he was posted to bomb disposal units having learnt the correct way of removing TNT from bombs.

Michael married, had a family and enjoyed a long career as a scientific officer involved in microbiology research. From his Hampshire home he indulged his love of cricket by playing in the Hampshire League until the age of sixty-one. In 2006 Michael wrote of his and his family's Malta experience. His memories of growing up within a family at war offer a fascinating and unusual perspective.

One particular passage touches on an aspect which affected many but was rarely written about. In describing the challenges of feeding a family Michael said: 'The stoicism shown by women in dealing with all of these problems was never realised at the time and probably is still not appreciated. To feed, clothe and keep clean a family with no running water, electricity, fuel, food or clothing, must have been a nightmare for them. In retrospect I realise that my mother (and no doubt many others) never communicated any panic or worries to the children. They always showed a brave face and did wonders with what little food there was.

Not once, as children, did we ever consider that we were underprivileged, could be killed, be under the jackboot, interned, or shipped away, and worse should the enemy be successful in taking the island. It just did not enter our heads but was probably at the forefront of our parents' minds. This I now put down to the stability and support given to the family during this testing period, particularly to my mother who never panicked or became despondent and my father who was always a tower of strength.'

What of the Cuell sisters? Betty, the first to become a plotter, spent the rest of her life in England. She and Mac had three children; sadly their first born, Patricia, died within a week. Their second daughter was Angela, known as Jane; she married John Passmore. Betty died in 2015 at the age of ninety-three.

In 1990, Helen Cuell took part in the BBC television progamme *Songs of Praise* presented by Martyn Lewis. It was filmed in Malta in August 1990 to coincide with the anniversary of the arrival of the *Santa Marija* convoy. It was broadcast in the UK on Remembrance Sunday, 11 November 1990. Helen would have been in her late sixties by then, an elegant and charming lady. At the time, the Lascaris operations room had just been refurbished and she visited there for the first time in nearly fifty years.

'It has to be, of course, so far down to be safe. It was damp but one felt very safe and I think it was ideal for what we were doing. I suppose at the time we didn't feel terribly important, it was just a job for us, but I realise now what a very, very important job it was we were doing.

'The messages for the table here used to come from the radar stations all round Malta, and we used to plot the aircraft on the little boards, their heights, the number of aircraft, enemy or friendly etc. One would feel very humble being down here and very, very fearful in case one made a mistake. Each Watch had about eighteen people in it. The atmosphere was very friendly indeed but in spite of this terrible bombing we still had some very jolly times. But I think it was the faith, the faith definitely. Whenever you went down to a shelter all you could hear was the Holy Rosary being recited over and over and over again, non-stop. It was Our Lady, the Rosary to Our Lady, which kept us safe.'

Helen spoke very well, easily recognisable as a lady of Lascaris in B Watch, 1942, despite the passage of time. As the programme closed against a backdrop of Grand Harbour, Helen was standing in the front row on the left of the crowd of islanders and holidaymakers standing behind Martyn Lewis.

Helen never married. She and her mother Carmella moved into 45 (later re-numbered 47) St Margaret's Street, Sliema, which was later bought by her sister Joan's son Andrew for them to live in for the rest of their lives. Helen looked after her mother until she died in 1971 and continued working at Luqa until the British withdrawal in 1979. Her youngest sister Mona joined her there, both working for the NAAFI. Helen later worked in a library and was known to be a very good seamstress; she was a popular figure in Malta. She drove a car, much to the concern of various nephews and nieces, as she enjoyed a tipple. After two of her Australian nieces visited they said, 'Auntie Helen often had a lot of gin beneath her tonic.'

Helen wrote of her wartime experiences and her story was published in 1998 in *The People's War Malta: 1940/43* by Laurence Mizzi. Helen said: 'Looking back, I feel that the Operations Room was a key factor in the defence of Malta and although everyone contributed his or her share to the war effort, I think Malta owes its survival mainly to the RAF.' Sadly, Helen did not live to see her words in print. She died on 20 January 1995 at the age of seventy-two. She was a very popular lady and there was a huge gathering at her funeral. There are obvious similarities between Helen and Christina: both were ladies of Lascaris at the same time; both lost the men they loved in tragic circumstances as they made their way toward them, and both ended up working for the RAF at Luqa. Neither got over the loss they felt, chosing to live alone for the rest of their lives, perhaps taking too much solace in alcohol. They now both rest in *Santa Maria Addolorata* cemetery in Paola.

The third Cuell plotter was Joan, only 15-years-old when she was recruited. She and her husband Jock eventually settled in England, Jock retiring from the RAF as a squadron leader. They had two sons, one of whom, Andrew, bought the Sliema house for his grandmother Carmella and his Aunt Helen. While Joan and Jock were courting they often visited The Premier, a bar in Queen Victoria Square, Valletta. Joan was a very good singer and whenever she and Jock arrived at The Premier, the resident Oscar Lucas Band would play especially for her. Joan died in Lincoln in 1997 at the age of sixty-nine.

Mona was the youngest of the Cuell girls, only 6-years-old when the war began. In the 1950s, she was courted by Gordon Hide, an RAF signaller working at Lascaris; he was lodging at the Cuell house. When it became apparent that Mona and Gordon were dating, Gordon was asked to move out - which he did. They were married in 1956 and their son, Adrian, was born at Mtarfa in 1958. On leaving the RAF, Gordon worked for Cable and Wireless in Malta, or so the family was told. This was a cover story, as he actually worked for GCHQ in Y Service at Lascaris intercepting signals. At some stage Mona joined her sister Helen at RAF Luqa employed by the NAAFI. Gordon died in 1989 at the age of sixty-six. Mona followed in 1993, only 58-years-old.

Eddie Cuell bought his discharge from the Royal Malta Artillery on 17 December 1954 and married Mary (Maria Paulina Rosario Carmella Lucia) Gatt two days later. They left for a new life in Australia just over a week later, celebrating their honeymoon en route. Eddie was following in the footsteps of his two brothers, Joseph and Wallace, who had emigrated the year before. Eddie and Mary lived in Canberra for thirty-six years before moving to Queensland. They have three daughters: Diane, Sandra and Kathleen. In 2017, at the age of eighty-seven, Eddie's memories of Malta remain clear and sharp.

Josephine Valetta, who married Welsh soldier Ted Roberts, made her home in Rhyl. In 2012, at the age of eighty-five and by then Josephine Barber, she and her son Paul Roberts made a poignant return visit to Malta.

Gladys Duddell, née Aitken, and her husband Joe were married for forty-six years until he died of non-hodgkins lymphoma in 1991 at the age of seventy-one. Joe and Gladys had been active members of the British Nuclear Test Veterans' Group. Gladys was initially denied a War Widows' Pension, but her eldest daughter Sandra Patterson successfully fought the case on her mother's behalf. Gladys died on 31 December 2015. Her ashes were spread in Malta in Upper Barracca Gardens directly above the RAF operations room at Lascaris where she and so many other heroes did such valuable work. Her younger sister Mary, another lady of Lascaris, died in 2017.

Marion Childs never returned to Malta. Her father Charles retired from the British Army in 1955 as a major, already in the early stages of muscular dystrophy. He then worked in the Royal Navy Dockyard in Plymouth until 1958. He died in 1961. Marion's mother Millicent lived a further twenty years. Marion and Eric's daughter Margaret was born in 1950 and another daughter Katherine came along in 1962. Sadly Katherine suffered from spina bifida; she was 3-years-old when she died.

Marion and Eric were married for sixty-four years until Eric died in 2010. In 2018, seventy-five years after leaving Malta, Marion still spoke of her time there with great pride. Few of Raglan's residents who know the quietly-spoken, polite lady who had worked in Boots the chemist in Monmouth for twenty-five years, could ever have imagined the life she experienced in Malta's greater siege and as a young lady of Lascaris. 'Everything happened to me before I was twenty,' Marion said.

There was one aspect of Marion's service which left her disappointed: All service personnel

Marion Childs, née Gould, about 1955.
(Marion Childs)

243

stationed in Malta during the Second World War were awarded the Malta Medal, but it was denied that brave band of civilian women, Maltese and British alike. They took the same risks doing exactly the same job but were denied the award. The paltry reason given was that they wore no uniform. They were offered copy medals instead. 'What an insult!' said Marion. No one would have worn such medals with more pride than the ladies of Lascaris.

Miriam Farrugia saw Christina in Bugibba in the 1980s. It was a Saturday afternoon and Christina was coming out of her Bugibba home. She had changed a great deal over the thirty years since Miriam had last seen her. Some changes were inevitable. Christina was also using a walking stick. But Miriam would have recognised her by her hair anywhere, even if it was a little whiter. 'I went over to speak to her and as soon as I told her that I was Miriam, she gave me a big hug and called me little Miriam. Later that night, coming from dinner, I saw her coming out of a bar, one of the bar and restaurants of Angelo's on Islet Promenade.' Christina was very unsteady. Miriam went over to her and helped her home. 'I helped her to bed and closed the door for her. That was the last time I ever saw Christina.'

Salvu Muscat moved to Bugibba after he got married in 1984. He still worked the day shift at Angelo's but also worked evening shifts too. Christina was still a regular for lunch, often every day. She always seemed to have money. Angelo's had a set menu for 1.95 Maltese Lira, and Salvu can still recall Christina's choice 'was soup or egg mayonnaise and roast beef or roast chicken for her mains and crème caramel to follow. She was a very good tipper as she always used to tip me one Maltese Lira every time after lunch, which for that time was a lot. I remember when my wife came into the restaurant with our new-born baby boy she gave her five Maltese Liri as a present for the boy.'

Christina would usually have a glass or two of wine with her meal and then during the rest of the day she would have around six whiskies with soda, without ice. She also smoked occasionally. As Salvu normally finished work at 6.00 pm, Christina may have drunk more afterwards. Others described how Christina would become 'happy' but never difficult. That was how Salvu remembered her, 'she used to get slightly drunk but not to extremes; she never annoyed anyone. Sometimes when I had an evening shift I would walk her down to her place as she used to struggle a bit; that's when she would normally sleep over.'

From the moment Christina retired she travelled by bus, the No 49, most days from Floriana to and from Bugibba. The roads were much less busy then, but the journey through Msida, Birkirkara, Balzan, Lija, Mosta, and Burmarrad to St. Pauls Bay and then to Bugibba would still have taken thirty-five minutes each way. She did that on a regular basis for about nine months each year. She only avoided Bugibba at the height of the tourist season. She probably loved those journeys through the towns and villages and countryside she knew well. She would have engaged with her fellow travellers making conversation easily in English or French and some Malti. She would have been in her element. No doubt as she disembarked she would say *grazzi hafna* to the driver, with a smile.

In Bugibba she was seen as a generous lady who enjoyed company. She was always willing to share her stories and show her newspaper cuttings and photos. At Angelo's Guest House, where she was known well, she had a regular routine of luncheon, reading, doing crosswords and writing. This is not a picture of a recluse who shunned people. Her drinking may have impacted on others, but not in any negative sense, she became happier.

In the winter of 1986/87, Angelo's closed for a lengthy refurbishment. During that period Christina used two other restaurants in Bugibba, Angel's Two and The Porthole, both of which were owned by the Vella family. In April 1987, Salvu got another job at Ta' Fra Ben restaurant in Qawra. 'I saw Christina around October 1987. She was waiting for the bus in Bugibba Square and was very happy to see me. That was the last time I ever saw Christina.'

Christina was a keen photographer and kept many images, some in albums, others in scrapbooks and envelopes. She also held onto some newspapers, all with a particular memory. One was the 12 September 1943 edition of *The Sunday Times of Malta*. It's easy to understand why she kept this one - it was the day newly-surrendered Italian battleships arrived in Malta, and only days after the tearful reunion she had with Warby, when he fell to his knees in front of her in South Street pleading forgiveness. That Sunday was also the day on which Warby paraded with 683 Squadron for the very last time before handing over command and leaving Malta for good soon afterwards.

The newspaper included an article which recalled the first Malta-launched landing in Italy in March 1941:

> Indifferent weather had prevented the taking of photographs of the objective, but on 9th February, Flying Officer (now Acting Wing Commander) A. Warburton, DSO, DFC, piloting a Glenn Martin, took good pictures of the target area.
>
> They disclosed the existence of two viaducts about 200 yards apart; that to the east, it was decided, was the one to be destroyed ...

This mission was flown only days after Warby came into Christina's life. Little wonder she kept that newspaper. Precious memories.

Christina also kept a cutting of an article from *The Sunday Express*, dated 21 February 1962. Entitled *There's much to marvel at in magical Morocco*, it was written by the British travel writer Lewis De Fries. Christina first travelled to Morocco twenty-five years earlier and took hundreds of photographs of her time there. More magical memories.

Precious memories: Adrian wearing his beloved Service dress hat, early 1941, lovingly repaired by Christina. A Glenn Martin Maryland is in the background. (*Miriam Farrugia*)

Happier days. (*Miriam Farrugia*)

Christina donated many of her photographs and a scrapbook and notes to the National War Museum in Valletta. Had she given up on the idea of writing her book? Did she know she was ill and unlikely to find out how quickly time passed 'when I am a centenarian?'

Having few links with the UK, Christina also donated her British Empire Medal to the museum. By then there was very little remaining of the decoration's red bow with the white edges, held often in her hands and shown to anyone interested, one of her few links with the life she had and the love she lost. Christina died a year later.

Chapter 15

The End of a Quest

Malta, November 2014

It was dark when we touched down at Luqa. There was little Jackie and I recognised. The modern terminal bore no resemblance to the one I looked at many times from my old squadron headquarters. The drive to Valletta didn't ring any bells either, so much had changed. I thought about the people who endured Malta's siege in the Second World War. I had met many through their own words and those of others. Nearly all the main players are gone now but there was one ghost I knew could only be found in Malta.

Would I be able to match old images to present-day locations? Would any of the wartime buildings still be recognisable? What about Christina's former homes, one in Strait Street and two in Floriana, including the one in which she died? Having visited Warby's grave in Bavaria, I was determined to find Christina's final resting place and pay my respects on the island she said was, 'carved on my heart'. What started out for me as accidental interest following a chance phone call was now a quest I was determined to see through.

We didn't recognise where we were until we approached *Porte des Bombes*, the scene of Malta's very first civilian deaths on Tuesday, 11 June 1940. The dual carriageway of the former *Strada Sant' Anna* was immediately familiar, as was the circular bus terminus in front of Valletta's curtain walls. Sadly, the famous old buses are long gone. We then entered the grounds of the Phoenicia.

From her Floriana apartment roof in 1940, Christina described the Phoenicia as unfinished. Today it is a magnificent hotel built by the Stricklands, well known on the island and within its politics. Mabel Strickland was the editor of the *Times of Malta,* which, despite its offices being in heavily-bombed Valletta, didn't miss a single edition throughout the Second World War. Afterwards, the newspaper offered occasional glimpses into Christina's world.

The hotel is charming and elegant and as welcoming as the island itself. And so are the people who work there. It was touching to recognise the fondness the Maltese staff have for the British, not just as guests, but as old friends. It takes

The Phoenicia Hotel, May 2018. In the right foreground is the First World War Memorial. Between it and the eternal flame is the Malta Memorial commemorating those airmen who were lost flying from bases in the Mediterranean who have no known graves. It names 2,301. (*Paul McDonald*)

a long time to grow an old friend. Many spoke with genuine affection about the Royal Air Force when it was based on the island.

Did Christina ever visit the Phoenicia? Did she sit on the balcony overlooking the gardens, perhaps smiling at a particular memory as she sipped a Horse's Neck? More probably she would have enjoyed a Dewars White Label and soda, no ice. Had she ever watched the sunset over Marsamxett Harbour and dreamt of a long-overdue Warby returning with a fantastic tale to tell? As I discovered later, Christina is certainly in the Phoenicia now.

Great Siege Road skirts Valletta on the Marsamxett Harbour side until it reaches Fort St Elmo. It is an ideal route to go 'by walk' and take in the scale of Valletta's immense fortress walls with bastion following bastion. Within the harbour is Manoel Island with Fort Manoel probably little different now from when it was built in the eighteenth century. There is nothing to indicate its wartime role as a safe haven for submariners as they lay submerged alongside at the height of the bombing.

Looking back toward the small headland of Pietà, which separates Msida Creek from Pietà Creek, Guardamangia Hill stands out. That's where we lived in August 1975. The house where we stayed was next door to the Longyear's home at the height of the bombing. Michael Longyear described how a bomb had fallen straight down the well in our garden and exploded underground. Many times he watched attacks on the Royal Navy's submarine base and on Grand Harbour from his perfect vantage point next to the hospital on the hill. Looking now at the sun-baked residential district, what Michael and his family experienced was unimaginable.

The majesty of Valletta can only be grasped from within Grand Harbour. For a first-time visitor arriving by sea the impression must have been awe-inspiring as it was for Christina and her friend Sheila, when they arrived on the SS *Knight of Malta* one spring evening in 1937. How different it must have looked to the sailors who fought their way to a bombed and battered island a few years later.

Dockyard Creek and Parlatorio Wharf are where a battered HMS *Illustrious,* such a symbol of survival, spent a few crucial days being made ready for a rush to safety. Opposite is the old Customs House on Barrier Wharf, Christina's last stepping stone on her journey to Malta. The ground rises steeply behind the wharf with Floriana on the left and the Phoenicia on the horizon. Further left are apartment blocks commanding magnificent views over the harbour. Were these Floriana's Vincenti Buildings from which Christina painted such a fascinating picture with her words? It was from there she looked in shock at what was left of the Three Cities after devastating bombing by the *Luftwaffe* trying to seek out HMS *Illustrious*. She also watched the appropriately named HMS *Gallant*, minus her bow, beached below Crucifix Hill. It was the *Gallant* which delivered Christina and the Rodney Hudson Girls from the horrors they witnessed in Spain.

Christina crossed Grand Harbour often. There were sad times, as on 17 January 1941, when she and Tamara Marks travelled to a scene of unutterable destruction in Senglea, but there were lots of good times too, and Christina would have been captivated by the magic of the harbour and the capital. In the late afternoon Valletta is an unforgettable site, its limestone buildings almost luminous as the light fades, with the many churches cresting high above the houses and immense walls as the city begins to fall quiet. Once the war was over and the extensive reconstruction began, there would have been much to remind Christina of the good times and the sad times. Wherever she went, she was never far away from the resting places of many she and Warby knew, friends with whom they laughed and danced, now resting among others in well-kept places.

All the characters in this story passed through *Porta Reale*, City Gate, beyond the ditch between Valletta's limestone walls. To the right is the entrance to the old railway tunnel in which hundreds of Maltese, as well as Christina and her friends Cecil and Babs Roche, found protection. Time, neglect and bombing took their toll on Valletta, yet the cobbled streets are still a haunting reminder of the Knights of St John. On Republic Street (*Triq Ir-Repubblika)*, formerly Kingsway and *Strada Reale*, is the Royal Opera House. For over seventy years since the evening of 7 April 1942 it served as a memorial to fascist aggression. A few years ago it was judged time to give the Maltese people back their beloved Opera House. It is now complete, though not totally rebuilt. The auditorium has rows of seats and there is a covered stage. The entrance is at the bottom of the original imposing steps, but the walls and pillars have only partially been restored, leaving most of the Opera House open to the elements. It is a telling reminder of darker days.

The Wembley Store, a shop Christina and Tamara favoured, and above which Pauline and Michael Longyear had their school lunches, is on the junction of Republic Street with South Street (*Triq In-Nofsinar*). The outer façade has changed little, apart from the addition of cash machines, but the cavernous interior is a delight to explore, a reminder of the old general stores and bazaars. The Monico bar on South Street is long gone, as is Cilia's, its former premises now housing a gent's outfitters. It was on South Street, on the evening of 8 September 1943, the day of Italy's surrender, a brooding Christina walked. Despite the bells and the bunting she felt miserable and alone until she saw Warby running toward her with arms outstretched. Oblivious to the stares of passers-by, he got down on his knees to plead forgiveness. Christina wept buckets. Midst the many tourists and passers-by, I found it difficult to picture the scene.

On the left on Republic Street is the National Museum of Archaeology, formerly the *Auberge de Provence*. A favourite port for the 'fishing fleet' to dock in 1930s Malta, the 'snake pit' is now full of exhibits. As the 'officers-only' Union Club, it was the scene of parties and many a fond farewell. Now there is no sense of what it was in those days. Did Christina and Warby spend their last evening together here or did they, like Tamara, prefer the more relaxed atmosphere of Captain Caruana's Bar? It too is long gone. Republic Square (*Misraħ Ir-Repubblika)* is the location of the Grand Master's Palace and the seat of the Maltese Government. On its wall are three plaques: The first contains Malta's George Cross citation, the second a message from President Roosevelt on 7 December 1943. The third is in Malti and commemorates independence from Britain on 21 September 1964.

A gradually steepening hill drops down toward Fort St Elmo. The former *Strada San Nicola* (St Nicholas Street) crosses at right angles but there was no door labelled '105', nothing to show the location of the Morning Star in another life. I could gain no sense of what this place must have been like seventy years earlier. Maybe something of the atmosphere still existed at night.

The old Drill Hall of Lower Fort St Elmo houses Malta's National War Museum which I knew was full of links to my story. Once there, maybe I would feel a connection. Run by Heritage Malta, the museum focuses on the contribution of the Maltese in two World Wars and especially under the appalling conditions of 1942. Close to the entrance, there are displays devoted to Christina and Warby.

They include items donated by Christina, including her British Empire Medal. It is mounted in a frame along with a photograph of Christina next to the plotting table at Lascaris. To my eye, the ribbon looked slightly odd, although it could have faded with age. It was the civilian version, without the light-coloured stripe

Christina Ratcliffe, BEM, the National War Museum, Valletta. *(Fiona Vella)*

down the middle, and it was hung on a ribbon rather than a bow, which would have been normal when the honour is awarded to a civilian lady. But, mounted behind glass, like many exhibits in a museum, it felt cold; it was impossible to get a feel for the lady in the photograph. I needed to find something else. I wasn't sure exactly what.

The museum describes Malta's war well. There is the last remaining Gladiator of the famous three, the wreckage of a Spitfire and an Me109 recovered from the seabed. And there is the last survivor of a forlorn hope: a black-painted boat used by Italian sailors in their ill-fated assault on Grand Harbour. In pride of place is a replica George Cross famously awarded to the Maltese people in 1942 and still proudly emblazoned on the Maltese flag. It was easy to lose track of time in the museum. The photographs of the destruction and bomb damage have great impact and the extent of rebuilding needed must have been extraordinary. Toward the exit I paused to look at a display dedicated to the many Maltese who gave their lives fighting valiantly on the island and elsewhere. Many were in the Royal Malta Artillery, so resolute in defence; many more served and died in the dockyards and on board ships sailing under the White Ensign and the Red Duster. I left for the Lascaris War Rooms hoping to find a connection with my ghost on the way.

I headed for the infamous Gut. It was deserted. Even by night I suspect it would be the same. No faded charm here; just faded. Boarded up windows and long locked doors. There were one or two signs of its past but few would look closely. For most of its length there was no activity, commercial or otherwise, a dusty run-down forgotten street. When I got up the hill toward Old Theatre Street (*Triq It-Teatru l-Antik*), the 'officers and civilians only' part, it was different with smart cafés, up-market restaurants and shops. I hoped to find my connection a little further on, where Strait Street (*Triq Id-Dejka*) widened into a smart residential terrace.

Half-way down I stopped, and turned to face Christina's apartment block in Valletta's Vincenti Buildings. She moved here in 1942. It was mostly office accommodation, but acting on an impulse, I entered and climbed the many steps until I faced the top-floor apartment Christina occupied; it was still a private residence. I went through a nearby open door onto the roof. It was here Christina and the girls of D Watch, all Maltese, practiced dancing against an amazing skyline.

Christina and some of the ladies of her Watch dancing on the roof of the Strait Street apartment she shared with Warby. Christina is second from the left; Gladys Aitken is second from the right. (*Miriam Farrugia*)

And it was here in the late autumn of 1942 that the only official photograph of Christina with Warby was ever taken.

On leaving, I followed the footsteps Christina would have taken on her way to Lascaris. I turned right out of her front door then left onto Britannia Street, now Melita Street. Having crossed Kingsway, as she would have known it, I continued across Merchants' Street. Nearby is a reminder of the Victory Kitchens, a small sign beneath a specially placed street light on the left just beyond Clarks Shoes. Christina was photographed here in October 1942 having collected her midday meal.

I then passed directly behind the block which contained the *Auberge de Castille,* crossing St Paul Street before turning right into St Ursula Street. Ahead of me was Upper Barracca Gardens, but a few yards short I turned left into Battery Street, making for what would have been the sand-bagged and guarded entrance to the RAF headquarters at Lascaris. The very high walls were still there but without the eight-foot tall sandbags; but I could imagine the efficient Maltese soldiers standing guard. Here, Christina would have shown her pass before hurrying down the many steps as she had done on 12 August 1942. On that day she completed the journey in record time anxious to find out what was going on. Seventy-two years later, I hurried too, entering the tunnel, before turning left into what had been No. 8 Sector Operations Room. I entered Christina's world.

With the departure of British forces in 1979, Lascaris was simply locked up. There were attempts to open it as a tourist attraction but none were long-lasting. When access was gained to the combined operations room, a large map of the Mediterranean showing Soviet buoys and moorings of the 1970s covered an entire wall. The map had not weathered well and fell apart when touched, revealing an astonishing oil painting dating back to 1943. The painting's condition is superb, and it shows the map used for the Allied invasion of Sicily. Overlooking the room are offices used by Eisenhower and his three single-service commanders, Cunningham, Alexander and Tedder. Each had a single telephone, the main method of communication apart from coded signals and despatch riders. It is difficult to imagine how they kept control of their forces, including 160,000 troops in North Africa, from these tiny offices.

The Lascaris War Rooms were finally opened to the public in 2010. Run by the Malta Heritage Trust (*Fondazzjoni Wirt Artna),* my Maltese guide told the story of the air battle very well. He brought the place alive. The fighter control room is fascinating and I could visualise the girls surrounding the plotting table, moving the various plots as instructions came through their headsets.

Was that 16-year-old Marion Gould using the long rod to move a block indicating an incoming raid? Looking down on them from the shelf were the chaps-in-the-gods, Wing Commander Bill Farnes, the Senior Controller sitting centre stage with Flight Lieutenant Guy Westray, Ops B, in the next chair. Next to him was the Assistant Controller, a totally professional Christina Ratcliffe. Where would Woody have been, Group Captain Woodhall, wearing his monocle? What about Air Vice-Marshal Hugh Lloyd? Maybe he was lurking unobtrusively, holding his cigarette holder, keeping his eye on things, letting his team get on with their job. Yes, this was better; there was a real feel about this place despite the passage of time, an atmosphere kept alive by enthusiastic and knowledgeable staff. It was easy to imagine the atmosphere, if not the noise, the oppressively hot working conditions and the smell, for those who served long hours here between 1940 and 1943.

I paused to look at the photographs adorning the walls. There was one of Christina. It shows her and a young girl carrying a large container of water, their daily supply, collected from a street tap. The caption simply says: 'Street in Valletta, corner with Law Courts.' There is nothing to identify the blonde lady with the apron over her dress. Taken in October 1942 the original caption read: 'One of the most important things of the day is to get your supply of water from the tap in the street; this she does with the help of Lisa, the little Maltese girl from the next flat. When Christina is on her day shift Lisa gets the water and her dinner from the Victory Kitchens for her. Despite the fact that they have to carry these heavy buckets filled with water up five flights of stairs they think nothing of it. It is in the simple everyday things that one realises how truly wonderful is the spirit of the people living in Malta with all their deprivations and hardships, they just take it in their stride and hardly give it a thought.' Christina would have been thrilled to be back at Lascaris.

On leaving the War Rooms, I turned left, exiting the tunnel - the Hole - into the Ditch beneath Valletta's inner and outer walls towering above. Hugh Lloyd's office, with its corrugated iron roof, was located here. There is a long-disused, single-story stone building with a corrugated iron roof beneath one arch of the viaduct high above. Could this have been his office? Was this where Carmela Galea worked long hours as Lloyd's secretary?

Another left turn took me into a short tunnel which exits beneath Upper Barracca Gardens into Herbert Ganado Gardens overlooking Grand Harbour. Before Christina was forced to move from Floriana, she would have followed a similar path after an arduous shift, perhaps in an air raid sprinting from slit-trench to slit-trench, or hurrying to get home in advance of the curfew, or picking her way carefully through the rubble in the blackout. Maybe she had a Whizz-Bangs performance to go to or a date with Warby. No doubt they walked this path many times together, with ruins all around, to them unseen. It felt very real.

The exit from the gardens in Floriana is opposite the war memorial and next to another devoted to the Royal Malta Artillery. Vilhena Terrace is on the left and I was convinced the apartment blocks facing me were Vincenti Buildings. I couldn't help wondering about the twists and turns that brought Christina here, to a siege and a life she never could have imagined and a love she barely had.

Vilhena Terrace faces Valletta and the apartment blocks were indeed those I had seen from Grand Harbour. Christina's flat from autumn 1940 was on the top floor of one. From her description, her balcony must have looked, at least in part, toward the former George V Gardens facing Grand Harbour and the Three Cities. She was forced to leave in 1942 because of bomb damage but returned immediately her flat became habitable. She lived there until she died.

Vilhena Terrace and *Triq Pietro Floriani* are parallel streets running at right angles from the former *Strada Sant' Anna* toward Grand Harbour. I walked the length of *Triq Pietro Floriani* down to the open square on the left. Was this Gunlayer Square (*Piazza Miratore*)? If so I was standing next to the apartment block in which Tamara and Ronnie Marks had their home until they were bombed out. Luqa's station commander, Wing Commander Robert 'Jonah' Jonas and his wife Gina also lived here in 1940 and 1941.

The large apartment blocks between both streets form squares with entrance doors on each of the four sides but there was nothing I could find to identify any of them as Vincenti Buildings. This area was badly damaged and much rebuilding had taken place. In *Triq Pietro Floriani* I asked an elderly Maltese gentleman if he knew of Vincenti Buildings. He pointed to both of the blocks facing me. The opposite side of them was Vilhena Terrace, also the wartime location of the Engine Room Artificers' Club, the scene of many a dance, with its very own air raid shelter. The gentleman then asked who I was looking for and I said an English lady who lived there from the war until she died over twenty-five years earlier.

'What was her name?' he asked.

'Ratcliffe,' I replied.

The name meant nothing to him. I then said: 'Christina.'

'Oh, yes, Christina,' he said.

'I often saw her on this street. She lived up there.'

He pointed to a top floor corner balcony. I was dumbfounded. So this was where Christina lived and where she died all those years ago. I hadn't even needed to find her address; the first Maltese man of whom I had enquired actually knew Christina by sight.

'It is the flat with the darker coloured balcony,' he said.

He indicated a balcony on *Triq L-Imhazen* connecting *Triq Pietro Floriani* to Vilhena Terrace. The entrance was round the corner. She always opted for top-floor apartments despite the many steps. Of course she was young and fit in those days and her home commanded the views she loved. It was cheaper too of course. It is understandable why she moved back here as it was the first home in Malta she could call her own and it was the first she shared with Warby. But the stairs must

Christina's Floriana apartment. *(Paul McDonald)*

have become increasingly difficult as she grew older and a terrible struggle when she had to walk with the aid of a stick.

The Maltese gentleman went on to say the enclosed wooden balconies, so typical of Maltese homes, were replaced after Christina's death. When access was gained to her apartment, there were lots of tins of cat food, he said. Christina must have been in the habit of feeding the strays around the streets and in the gardens across from her front door. Maybe she felt an affinity with their lonely lives. I found myself visualising a very sad situation. In a touch of irony, an apartment in the building next door was now the home of the Italian Ambassador representing the very country whose action caused Christina to be stranded in the first place. As I made my way back to the Phoenicia, I reflected on a remarkable coincidence: the very first person I had spoken to in Malta about Christina remembered her from twenty-five years earlier.

The following day we drove to Ta' Qali. Only the Nissen huts pointed to the airfield's wartime past. What I was looking for was in a quiet corner: the Malta Aviation Museum set up and maintained by dedicated Maltese enthusiasts. It houses many exhibits about the Royal Air Force and the Fleet Air Arm. There is also a display dedicated to Warby. On leaving the museum, I recognised a Maltese gentleman coming in, although we had never met. I was slightly shocked. If I was right, this was yet another coincidence. He looked embarrassed, aware I was staring at him as he approached.

'Mr Galea?' I asked.

'Yes.' He said.

'Frederick?'

He again said yes, although he was clearly taken aback by this unexpected approach from a complete stranger. I recognised Frederick from his photograph on the cover of his books. Our conversation soon turned to Christina. I queried her British Empire Medal ribbon in the National War Museum. Frederick said when she donated the medal only a few threads remained. He recovered what he could, matching it locally so the medal could be displayed mounted on a single ribbon - a lovely gesture. That explained the absence of a bow.

As we left the museum, I reflected on another remarkable coincidence, meeting the one man who knew more about Christina than anyone. He and his wife Valerie played hugely important roles on her behalf after she died. Without Frederick's later work editing and publishing Christina's story, and that of Tamara Marks, their tales would probably never again have seen the light of day. Still, I was saddened by what Frederick told me: Christina's life seemed to have ended badly after many years of living on her own. I questioned whether I was likely to uncover anything positive.

Forty years earlier I was familiar with the roads to and from Luqa. They were the same roads the Whizz-Bangs old bus followed, but much had changed, with villages expanding and merging one into another. Christina would have driven past the Malta Sports Club at Marsa many times in 'The Flying Saucepan' on her way to work at RAF Luqa. It is easy to imagine her with shoulder-length blonde hair, probably beneath her characteristic straw hat. She may have laughed in the open-topped car as she passed the racecourse where she had hung on to a horse's neck for dear life. What had been RAF Luqa was now an industrial estate. There were some wartime Nissen huts still in use, yet others were relics of war, untouched for decades. The former Officers' Mess was as we remembered it but it was of post-war construction, built on the ruins of what had gone before. There was nothing I saw at Luqa that touched my tale.

Later I visited Upper Barracca Gardens beneath which is the Lascaris operations room. Next to the gardens is the Saluting Battery which still resonates twice daily. The fountains and flowers frame magnificent views of Grand Harbour. Looking south-west, the ground slopes down toward Floriana and I could easily make out what I now knew was Christina's top-floor apartment with the dark green, enclosed balcony. In fact the apartment is visible from all along the wall which traverses the Sciberras peninsula to Hastings Gardens where Aida Kelly lost her life. The view of Christina's last home reminded me of the painting of *The Laughing Cavalier* whose eyes are said to follow the viewer from every angle.

I was beginning to think that about Christina: everywhere I went there was something to remind me, something to draw me back to her story. Did she want it told? I again followed the route she would have walked from Lascaris back to her Floriana home. Despite the daylight, the traffic and the tourists, it felt real.

When the Whizz-Bangs was formed, a rehearsal room was needed. By then Strait Street, or 'The Gut', famous and popular amongst sailors for decades, was meant to be 'off limits', but many still found their way there. It is now home to some very smart restaurants and also to a branch of Marks and Spencer. As we exited the store, we faced an old theatre with a public convenience on its left. Surely not, I thought, not after seventy-four years? On the corner with Old Theatre Street, my wife Jackie pointed out a faded advertisement high up on the wall. This was the very place where the Whizz-Bangs had their origins. Was there no escape from Christina's story?

We turned left walking down Old Theatre Street until we came to the Manoel Theatre where Christina played *Cinderella* in the Whizz-Bangs Christmas pantomime in 1940. Belying the dusty, faded exterior, the interior has been tastefully restored and is quite magnificent. It was easy to imagine the concert party playing to a packed house full of laughter.

Later that evening I went into the Phoenicia's Club Bar to enjoy a Cisk, a fine Maltese beer. The walls of the bar are adorned with photographs from the 1930s and 1940s. I sat near the French doors that open onto the balcony overlooking the hotel gardens, with Marsamxett Harbour beyond. As I looked up, on the wall opposite was a photograph of Christina which I immediately recognised. I walked across to look more closely. Could I not get away from this lady? It was another taken in October 1942 and shows her sitting in bed in her Valletta apartment, already wearing make-up. The original caption said, 'She reads the *Times of Malta* and lets her tea go cold.' But there was no caption on this image, nothing to identify who she was for those who did not know her story.

Turning round, I got another shock. There was yet another photograph of Christina immediately above my chair. It showed her sitting on the Valletta-Sliema ferry holding her straw hat and wearing gold bangles on her right forearm. Underneath, it was signed: 'Christina, Fighter Control, RAF'.

Was there no escape from this lady, dead for over quarter of a century? Were these simply coincidences or was a hidden hand guiding me, pushing me toward finding Christina, urging me to tell her story? I had certainly felt her presence many times, a haunting ageless presence, but not haunting in any negative way.

I was determined to revisit Floriana and find out more about the district and the home in which Christina spent most of her life. The following day I walked toward *Porte des Bombes*. These days Floriana is a town of faded Baroque beauty, dominated by the church of St Publius. I asked a local man if he knew of the Green Shutters. He confirmed it still existed and pointed me in the right direction. It was on the corner of St Thomas Street (*Triq San Tumas*) and St Francis Street (*Triq San*

Christina in October 1942, displayed in the Club Bar of the Phoenicia. *(Paul McDonald)*

Franġisk) but was closed with tables and chairs stacked inside ready to be placed on the pavement.

Christina's first home on the island in 1937 was a room in a house in Floriana, owned by Gianni Fiteni, which she shared with Sheila and the other four girls who formed the troupe performing at the Morning Star. When she returned in 1940, she shared the same house with Cecil and Babs Roche who worked in another of Gianni's nightspots.

On the evening of 10 June, after Mussolini had declared war, Christina described how she walked up *Strada Capuccini (Triq Il-Kapuccini)* at the top of which a huge

'Christina, Fighter Control RAF.' (*Paul McDonald*)

wooden cross mounted on a ten-foot plinth stood silhouetted against the sky. I walked the same route. The plinth is still there but the wooden cross has now been replaced by another marking the entrance road that leads to a Capuchin Monastery. After the first bombing raid, Christina looked from her balcony toward St Francis Barracks and talked to a soldier there. I knew the barracks from the 1970s as the NAAFI and a medical centre. The houses facing the barracks are on *Pjazza Robert Samut* and one of them was Christina's home in 1937 and later in 1940, although I didn't know which. Many have iron grills on the front footpath beneath which are cellars, and a number have open balconies facing the barracks. I could imagine her sitting on her balcony with Cecil and Babs watching the sun set behind the high ground around Mdina trying to work out what the future might hold for them.

I headed back to the Green Shutters. It is a pleasant corner café, typical of many in Malta. I could well imagine old men sitting in similar bars some years earlier talking about Miss Christina and a dashing RAF pilot, symbols of Maltese resistance.

On the other side of the road was the former Queen's Store owned by the Mallia family who looked after Christina and the Roches when they were without food in the opening days of the war. I then walked slowly down St Francis Street (*Triq San Franġisk)* before turning right into *Pietro Floriani* (*Triq Pietro Floriani)*, then left into the short cross-street leading to Vilhena Terrace. I could easily imagine Christina doing the same. She would have been on her own, walking in the dark to an empty apartment with only the stray cats in the gardens over the road for company and memories of a short, intense period in her life and her lost love. I didn't feel alone; I felt I was walking in the footsteps of her ghost - but a smiling ghost in a straw hat.

I had made contact with Ingrid Scerri, a Maltese lady now living in Christina's former apartment; Ingrid was the very next occupant after Christina and she very kindly agreed to allow me access to the apartment block.

Christina said there were eighty-eight steps up to her top-floor apartment. There were two more immediately off the street. They were quite a climb, perhaps easy for a young fit dancer but I found them a real challenge. There were another two flights of steps up to the roof but the views when I got there were well worth the effort and exactly as Christina described in the autumn of 1940. The Phoenicia Hotel could just be glimpsed to the left and then an amazing panorama takes in Valletta and its approaches with the imposing *Auberge de Castille* in the centre. The Barracca Lift, now in use once more, and the Upper Barracca Gardens are clearly visible atop Lascaris Bastion. And to the right are magnificent views of Grand Harbour and the Three Cities, long recovered from the devastation wreaked upon them. It was a privilege to take in the views Christina enjoyed.

Ingrid had clear memories of the quiet English lady who lived just around the corner from where she had grown up and she had heard of the English officer, the 'English colonel' she called him, with whom Christina was involved. Ingrid said Christina invariably wore a straw hat and smiled at everyone. She would often see

Valletta's skyline from the roof of Christina's apartment. *(Paul McDonald)*

261

her with her dog. As I slowly made my way down those many stairs, down which Christina had often run helter-skelter, I needed to find my quiet, ever-smiling ghost and say hello in person.

It was only a short drive to Paola and the cemetery of *Santa Maria Addolorata*. The high spire of the church was visible from some distance. The large car park was almost empty with cars outnumbered by flower sellers' vans and trailers. The cemetery is large, built in a fan-shape with the point beginning at the car park and the fan opening up the steep hill toward the church. There were thousands of graves in the stony ground. Many had ornate headstones, some had photographs. In the absence of soil and the impossibility of keeping grass alive through Malta's long hot summer, the graves were each covered with stone or concrete slabs. There were also many shared plots; originally Christina rested in one of those.

Thinking it would be straightforward to find her grave, I walked up the left-hand side, East Division, trying to locate the letters identifying each section. There were some single letters on the kerbstones and on adjacent walls, but many were missing or not visible from the footpath. Near the church, in what I thought might be the right section, I walked up and down looking at each grave, but to no avail. Many rows were confusing and after about forty-five minutes of fruitless searching, I was hot and tired and getting nowhere. I then skirted the church to the left to find it was only half way up the cemetery, not at the top as I first thought. The cemetery continued beyond, less steeply, widening left and right. This was proving difficult and a much longer task than I anticipated.

I headed back to the office, which is where I should have called in the first place. There I met a young man called Eman Bonnici. I said I was trying to locate the grave of an English lady who died over twenty-five years earlier. 'Ratcliffe?' he asked. I was again lost for words, finding someone who instantly thought of Christina. Eman was the cemetery's archivist and very helpful. He knew much of Christina and Warby's story.

I bought some red silk roses which I hoped would last through the coming winter and into the summer. I also wrote a message on a card, but not from me. I figured not many who came to pay their respects would also have had the opportunity to have done the same at Warby's grave in Bavaria. I climbed the slope once more, passing the church heading for the far left corner of the graveyard. Christina's grave wasn't difficult to find; it was within a few yards of the boundary and faced the morning sun.

According to the post-mortem, Christina died between September and October 1988, one to three months before she was found. Her apartment was sealed after her burial until next-of-kin were located. Jack Downs, a Scottish uncle on Christina's mother's side was found. He knew of no relatives in the Manchester area so placed an advertisement in local newspapers. Martin Ratcliffe, a nephew, came forward.

About two years after Christina's death, Martin, who had met Christina only once around the time of her mother's funeral in 1969, travelled to Malta to settle Christina's affairs. The apartment was still sealed having been left untouched. Everything was now covered in a layer of grey fumigation dust. Christina's bed still bore the indentation of where she had lain for so long.

Martin later wrote to the *Times of Malta* to see if Christina could be reburied in a grave of her own. His enquiry was passed to Frederick Galea, by now well-known as a historian and author and an active member of Malta's National War Museum. Frederick and his wife Valerie took up the request, contacting various agencies to have Christina re-buried. This was not a straightforward task given the shortage of burial plots on the rocky island and the waiting list of over 4,000 whose families sought individual graves for their loved ones. Frederick persisted and his efforts were eventually rewarded. It was through Valerie's father that Frederick had first heard of Christina and he and Valerie were happy to do what they could.

With money available from Christina's estate, Frederick sourced a marble headstone and arranged to have a photograph mounted with an inscription beneath. It was Valerie who kept company with Christina when she was disinterred nearly five years after her passing.

The *Times of Malta* carried a short article on Monday, 19 April 1993 under the heading *New Resting Place for War Heroine:*

> The remains of war heroine Christina Ratcliffe are being re-interred at the *Addolorata* cemetery on April 28.
>
> Miss Ratcliffe, BEM, who died in Floriana in 1988, is buried in the government section at the *Santa Maria Addolorata* cemetery. A private grave has been purchased and adorned with its own headstone.
>
> Miss Ratcliffe was an English cabaret dancer who formed a troupe with others to entertain army, navy, and RAF personnel, calling themselves the Whizz-Bangs. She later answered a call for English-speaking girls to man the telephone switchboard in the RN/RAF underground Operations Room, becoming subsequently assistant to the Fighter Controller.
>
> The re-interment of her remains on April 28 will be held at 10.30am.

The short re-burial service was taken by a Capuchin friar. It was attended by Jack Downs, Martin Ratcliffe and his family, and by Frederick and Valerie Galea, as well as a few well-wishers and a representative of the British High Commission. Thanks largely to Frederick and Valerie, Christina now rests in Grave No 4,

Section MA-D East Division of *Santa Maria Addolorata* cemetery only a few miles from where she lived and died. The cemetery is well named - Our Lady of Sorrows. When visiting family graves there, Frederick and Valerie always walk a little further up the hill and pay their respects to Christina. They are often pleasantly surprised to find flowers on her gravestone. She hadn't been forgotten.

As I walked up the hill I reflected on what I had learnt about Christina. As she grew older she became withdrawn from her shrinking circle of friends. Years earlier, when she found herself alone on the evening of Italy's surrender in 1943, she thought the only thing to do was to go and get sloshed. Since then, and having been alone for so long, had alcohol become her solace, her only comfort? Was that how she tried to ease the increasing loneliness she suffered and her sense of loss? Was that loss made worse when *Warburton's War* was released in 1987 because of the questions it raised over whether Warby truly felt the same as she? For over four decades she lived with no closure, maybe she then faced doubt. And then she died. I struggled to correlate the picture of a vivacious, outgoing, intelligent girl who took pride in her appearance, with an image of a sad and lonely recluse.

When I got to the top of the cemetery it wasn't difficult to find where she lay. The enamelled photograph of Christina looking directly at the camera could have been taken yesterday. She would have been thrilled to read the words,

Christina's final resting place in Paola. *(Paul McDonald)*

'Christina of George Cross Island' on her headstone. There were some faded flowers on her grave; she was remembered. Hopefully, her spirit is now in a happier place.

Miriam Farrugia, the young Maltese girl Christina befriended in the 1950s, summed up the situation movingly and well: 'I think it was a very sad story, loving someone and waiting for him to come back, and for him never to return. I think it is a very sad story to love somebody and you can't be with him. And then as she grew older she started drinking a lot. I think that people that drink, they are sad when they drink a lot. Christina Ratcliffe didn't deserve to die this way because she died all alone and with no one to take care of her. Christina was a lovely, lovely woman.'

When Christina arrived back in Malta in 1940, she was 26-years-old and a very worldly-wise lady. I am sure she, like many others in the Second World War, lived for the moment, not knowing what the future held. She was only 31-years-old when the war ended and she must have realised Warby wasn't coming back. Yet she was still the same intelligent and confident lady she had always been, well capable of handling herself and making her own choices and decisions as she had always done. She chose to remain in Malta.

Her life with Warby was terribly short, totalling about two years. No one can ever be sure about the true nature of their relationship but few could doubt their love for one another. By saying nothing in public and avoiding journalists, Christina protected Warby's reputation on the island where he was revered. Equally no one will ever know with absolute certainty Warby's intentions on 12 April 1944. But I think he planned a future with a girl from Cheshire whom he left behind on an island in the sun. It is only sad she never knew for certain.

Perhaps like many others in wartime, Warby was like a flame that flares up and burns brightly before being snuffed out. *Carpe diem;* seize the day, take no thought of tomorrow. For many thousands, tomorrow never came. For others who were touched by them, tomorrow proved to be long and lingering.

I left Christina's graveside on the hillside in the sun. She now rests in a place of honour thanks largely to Frederick and Valerie Galea. In the background, to the right of Christina's headstone, is the beautiful church of *Santa Maria Addolorata* with its unusual spire which looks almost English.

I slowly walked down the long hill through an almost empty cemetery leaving behind some silk roses and a note sent on behalf of someone far away.

On my way down the hill I began to revise my thoughts. Christina Ratcliffe was a very strong-willed woman, certainly strong enough to deal with loss and move on. That loss did not drive her to drink. Her lifestyle had always involved drinking, although living alone may have resulted in her drinking more. And she did move on, alone. That was her choice. She ran Café Christina and worked for the RAF for many years, eventually spending more and more time at Angelo's

Christina's grave. *(Paul McDonald)*

Guest House in Bugibba overlooking St. Paul's Bay. And she wrote, and wrote. Between 1958 and 1982 more than two dozen of her articles were published in newspapers in Britain and in Malta. Is this a picture of an unhappy, reclusive alcoholic? I don't think so.

Christina was a generous lady who enjoyed company. In her own way I think she was happy with her memories, her writing and her conversations with people

266

she met, even strangers. But it is still sad to think she had so many years living on her own and she certainly didn't deserve to die alone and unnoticed. Christina Ratcliffe should be well remembered on the island whose suffering she shared and to whose victory she contributed.

When I got back down to the office next to the cemetery entrance I thanked Eman Bonacci, as well as the flower seller; perhaps they thought me rather odd. Maybe I was, allowing myself to get caught up in an old story, the main players in which had left the stage long ago.

It's a near certainty Christina read *Warburton's War* when it was released in 1987. Was she surprised or disappointed by any of its content? With the story she herself was writing left unfinished, was the time now right to try and offer another perspective, one with the balance only the passage of time can bring? On my visit to Malta almost everywhere I turned there were links with Christina. I often felt unnerved, disconcerted. Did she want their story told? When I returned home to North Yorkshire, I was hooked.

Christina had guarded the reputation of the man she loved and lost, and continued to do so long after he was presumed dead. She was an honourable lady and, for her work in the long years of the air battle of Malta, she was very much a hero too. She described herself as a 'back-room girl', but she was a great deal more than that. Although she never 'hit the headlines as a prima ballerina' and was never to enthral 'an audience at Covent Garden or even the Manchester Opera House', Christina Ratcliffe danced beneath the spotlights in some of Europe's capitals, lights soon dimmed as Europe marched blindly toward the catastrophe of another war. She saw some of the latter days of French Colonial Africa and found herself on the steps of Valletta's Customs House. Arguably her many dozens of performances with the Whizz-Bangs were worth far more to her audiences than any in Covent Garden and their shows outran many staged in the West End. She had a string of adventures, dancing across Europe and North Africa and down to Dakar, waltzing 'in and out of the Spanish Civil War and, finally, to take a last curtain call in the battle and siege of Malta. All of which was not bad going on a pair of wooden legs.'

Yet Christina did hit the headlines, although not in the manner she could ever have imagined. As 'Christina of George Cross Island', Mary Christina Ratcliffe, BEM, from Dukinfield in Cheshire, was a symbol of heroic resistance and resilience. She too should be remembered, and not just in Malta.

Chapter 16

Star of Strait Street

2016 - 2018

Christina Ratcliffe was one of six ladies of Lascaris recognized by the award of the British Empire Medal in King George VI's Birthday Honours of July 1943. She was selected for the honour because of her work as an aircraft plotter for two years from June 1941. However, her overall contribution to Malta's war went a great deal further spanning five years.

In July 1940, a year before she was recruited by the RAF, she helped found the Whizz-Bangs concert party. She performed with them for eighteen months, the latter six while she was also working shifts as a plotter. Following her promotion to become Captain of D Watch in December 1941, she gave up performances with the troupe, although she made occasional guest appearances with the RAF Gang.

Christina was later appointed as Assistant Controller within No 8 Sector Operations Room. After she was decorated she remained at Lascaris for another two years until victory in Europe. She then moved to RAF Luqa. Importantly, much of what we have learnt about the work of the ladies of Lascaris and their contribution to the Allied victory comes from Christina's very own words, hers being one of very few first-hand accounts of those days of drama and great tension.

After many years of living on her own, Christina's life ended unnoticed and in tragic circumstances. That is a fact and there is no avoiding it. Yet her contribution to Malta's war should not only be remembered, it should be applauded. But how can any story of her life be told without focusing on the sad circumstances of her death?

When I visited her grave in 2014 at *Santa Maria Addolorata* cemetery, a few lines from another Christina came to mind. From Christina Rossetti's *Remember*:

> Yet if you should forget me for a while
> And afterwards remember, do not grieve
> For if the darkness and corruption leave

A vestige of the thoughts that once I had,
Better by far you should forget and smile
Than that you should remember and be sad.

The last two lines seemed to sum up the situation perfectly. Remember and be sad? Christina would rather be forgotten altogether. She was a happy person who lived life to the full, a buoyant, vibrant lady who engaged with people. 'Always impeccable hair, she was a lovely, lovely woman', said Miriam Farrugia. Christina Ratcliffe was a lady who raised a smile for strangers even after years of living on her own. That's how she would wish to be remembered, smiling. And perhaps by doing what she had always wanted to do since childhood, singing and dancing on the stage. But how on earth could such a thing be possible?

In September 2016 I was contacted by the playwright Philip Glassborow. He too had become intrigued by Christina's story and was considering creating a theatrical entertainment about her. Although based in England, Philip had the germ of an idea about writing a musical play to be performed in Malta, with Christina played by an actress friend Polly March. Could this be the opportunity for Christina's story to have a happier ending some thirty years after her passing?

Philip Glassborow,
writer and producer of
Star of Strait Street.
(Philip Glassborow)

At the time, the Maltese authorities were in the process of reinvigorating Strait Street in Valletta, the *Strada Stretta* concept. Was there any chance of some sort of production in the very street where the Whizz-Bangs conducted their first rehearsals? Surely there could be no better place. I readily agreed to Philip's request to act as an advisor and source for material. I was happy to help in any way possible.

Much would depend on the support of those involved in the concept, the artistic director of which was Dr Guiseppe Schembri Bonaci. It was his task to coordinate the efforts of the team tasked with regeneration. The focus was on 2018 and the celebrations to mark Valletta's selection as European Capital of Culture. Coincidentally, Dr Schembri Bonaci is related to Gianni Fiteni, the owner of the Morning Star in which Christina performed seventy-eight years earlier.

Restoration within Strait Street has accelerated over recent years. The narrowest street in Valletta, it is also one of the longest at 665 metres. When Jackie and I last visited we noticed how much it had changed, although at the time those changes were mainly between Old Theatre Street and the city walls, in what had often been referred to as the 'posh end'. From Old Theatre Street down the hill to Fort St Elmo - The Gut - relatively little had been accomplished. The focus for 2018 was to turn the whole street into a hub of social life and creative activity. One of Dr Schembri Bonaci's objectives is to regenerate music and cabaret, theatre and urban culture. It was this aspect on which Philip Glassborow focused. A musical play performed in Strait Street seemed an ideal way to contribute to the 2018 celebrations. With eighteen months to prepare, Philip had plenty of time to turn his ideas into reality.

However, another opportunity quickly presented itself, an opportunity too good to miss, although it was one that turned Philip's thoughts about a measured and relatively gentle timescale upside down. Malta was to take over the Presidency of the European Union in 2017 and celebrations in Valletta were rightly planned. Could Philip put together a production in very short order for a performance in 2017?

A 'workshop' production in a suitable venue within Strait Street might be possible, perhaps in one of the old bars being brought out of retirement. This would attract interest in the *Strada Stretta* concept as a whole and the work of regeneration. It might also be a good way to trial and promote a short musical with a full production in 2018 still being the target. Was such a thing possible in such a timescale? The answer was maybe. Then the timescale was shortened even more. To fit in with the 2017 Valletta celebrations, Philip was asked to have something ready by early April. And he was in England. And he needed a Malta-based team.

Thankfully Philip has great skill and experience to fall back on. He also has some key connections in Malta which would prove vital in the months ahead.

First among them was Polly March. Born in Malta, and now living on the island, Polly was good friends with Philip and they had worked closely together in the past. Not only was Polly a fine actress in her own right, but she was also an accomplished director and was ideally placed to coordinate matters on the island as the production came together, reaching back to Philip in England with whom she was in constant touch.

Philip first worked with Polly when acting professionally with the Globe Players Shakespeare Company & Children's Theatre. Afterwards he began writing for the stage, radio and television, notably for the BBC's *Play Away*, *The Sunday Gang* and *Jackanory Playhouse*. As a writer, his theatrical musicals include *The Great Big Radio Show!*, a musical version of J.M. Barrie's *Peter Pan*, and *A Kid for Two Farthings* (book and lyrics), based on the novel by Wolf Mankowitz. His musical play *Welcome to Terezin* was presented at the Mill Studio, Guildford, and the Edinburgh Festival.

Philip has dramatized and directed many classics for radio. They include *Billy Budd, Sailor, Christopher Himself* with David Suchet, Adam Godley and Bernard Cribbins, *At the Back of the North Wind* starring Juliet Stevenson and Joss Ackland, *Silas Marner* starring Michael Williams, Jenny Aguter and Edward Woodward, *The Secret Garden* starring Dame Joan Plowright and Prunella Scales, *Les Miserables* with Brian Blessed, Toyah Willcox, Geoffrey Palmer and Tony Robinson, and *Christmas Day at Kirby Cottage* with John Rhys-Davies, Julia McKenzie and Finty Williams.

For television and radio, Philip has devised and scripted documentaries including *Charlie Chaplin, Composer,* which he co-presented with Josephine Chaplin, *Laurel and Hardy's Music Box*, and the BBC's tribute to *Gene Kelly* presented by Leslie Caron. He wrote and presented the BBC's acclaimed drama-documentary *The Gory Details,* which featured David Suchet and Frank Langella.

Polly March had demonstrated her wide talent by directing Philip's production of *The Great Big Radio Show* at the Manoel Theatre in Valletta. Philip visited Malta for the first time for the show and fell in love with Valletta and the islands, and with the Maltese people. He immediately recognised the island's talent base of gifted actors and singers. A key individual in the show's success was the talented Welsh musician Geoff Thomas, on stage throughout the performance.

Polly was educated in England and then trained at Guildhall. She has worked in most theatres in England, playing everything from Queen Victoria to a parrot, via any number of Ray Cooney farces and Agatha Christie thrillers! She had actually created the role of Myrtle, in Philip's cult pastiche 1930s musical before directing it in Malta. She has also worked extensively on radio. Two of her solo shows won awards and *Beauty and the Bounders*, her solo performance as Lilian Baylis of The Old Vic, was commissioned by the BBC. She was then appointed Artist in Residence at New York University. Since settling in Malta, Polly has appeared in

Polly March, actress,
in a performance
of *Much Ado
about Nothing.
(Polly March)*

a number of plays for the Malta Amateur Dramatic Club and FM productions, and
has directed several major productions.

The partnership of Philip in England and Polly in Malta was to prove the key
ingredient in what followed. They were both fascinated by Christina Ratcliffe's
true-life love story set against the background of the Second World War and
recognised it immediately as a great subject for a musical play. With Christina
having been an entertainer at the Morning Star, just off Strait Street, there was an
opportunity to incorporate some of the wonderful swing music of the 1930s and
1940s which she would have performed.

Three weeks after being contacted by Philip, and a week before he flew to
Malta to discuss the project with Polly, he sent me a first draft of some early pages
of the script. He called the production *Star of Strait Street* and intended to write it
principally around just two actresses; a young wartime Christina, and an older self
in the 1970s. The latter would be played by Polly. I thought Philip's script captured
Christina perfectly, while the songs he intended to include were particularly
evocative of the period.

One of the early meetings in Malta was with Dr Schembri Bonaci who quickly became a key supporter of the project. By late November, Philip and Polly's embryonic play was added to the *Strada Stretta* concept calendar for a workshop performance in Valletta in early April 2017. But time was desperately short, even for a workshop performance. Also some form of financial support was needed.

Philip applied for sponsorship to the Mackintosh Foundation, a charity set up by the well-known theatrical impresario Sir Cameron Mackintosh. Amongst other things the Foundation promotes and develops theatrical, musical and dramatic arts. Philip was aware Sir Cameron Mackintosh had links with Malta, but until he heard back from Sir Cameron's brother Nicky he was unsure what those links were: Their 98-year-old mother, the former Diana Tonna, was Maltese. In another remarkable coincidence in an amazing story, Diana had also known Warby in Malta. She was now one of only a handful of people who were young adults in Malta during the Second World War.

In the same month, Polly met Charles Azzopardi, General Manager of the Phoenicia Hotel and Rob Bruno, the Business Manager. The Phoenicia too had connections with Christina and the hotel played an important role in setting me off on my quest to find out more of her story. Charles and Rob were very interested in the play. Not only did they agree to sponsor the production, but they said they would consider hosting a performance in the Phoenicia ballroom during the Valletta 2018 celebrations. That would certainly be a special date to include in my diary.

The Mackintosh Foundation offered rehearsal space in their London headquarters. To have been able to work in the atmosphere of the fabled 'hit factory' would have been magical but logistical and budgetary constraints meant Philip couldn't realistically bring over the cast and crew from Valletta.

By then there were also hopes of a TV documentary about the making of the play, set against the background of Malta today. Malta Television was certainly keen and Sky Arts expressed an interest in acquiring the production for broadcast. While working all hours to complete the script, Philip also got in touch with film producer Pete Doherty to explore filming options.

Central to Philip's plans was the scheme to revitalise Strait Street which had been such a vibrant hub for entertainment in the past. There had been clubs and bars and cafés with live music catering for servicemen with many visiting singers. Strait Street may have been the 'red-light district' of Valletta for a time, but it also provided regular work for many musicians and performers. Much of Philip's time was spent considering how best to incorporate the swing music of the era within his script.

There was still a vital decision to be made. Who should be cast as the younger Christina? An actress was needed of proven ability, a singer and dancer who could tell a love story with Malta at its heart; a story that also celebrated the gallantry of dozens of Maltese and British ladies working together, the ladies of Lascaris.

Larissa Bonaci. *(https://m.facebook.com/larissabonaciactress)*

And all set against a scene of suffering and resilience that became the stuff of legend. Larissa Bonaci (https://m.facebook.com/larissabonaciactress) fitted the bill perfectly.

Well-known in Malta for her television and film work, Larissa trained at the prestigious American Academy of Dramatic Arts in Los Angeles. She won the award for best performance for her role in *Don't We All* at the Malta Cine Cinema National Film Competition in 2013. She featured in *Saul: The Journey to Damascus* in 2014 and in *A Dangerous Arrangement* in 2015. She also played a CIA agent in the film *13 hours* in 2016. A dancer with fourteen years' experience in ballet and a classically trained soprano, she has performed in various plays and musicals at the Manoel Theatre. Larissa was the perfect choice to play the younger Christina alongside Polly.

Music was to be a key ingredient in the production. Although intended to be a relatively short musical play, Polly and Larissa would be on stage throughout. They would be accompanied by a pianist who was also likely to be on stage for the whole performance. Someone with great versatility was needed. Another key connection had been made during the Valletta production of *The Great Big Radio Show*.

Geoff Thomas is a Welsh musician whose wide career in music made him an ideal choice. Not only is he a gifted musician, he has also been involved in teaching, composing, arranging, accompanying, adjudicating, and examining. His

Larissa Bonaci, actress. *(Justin Mamo)*

long career included eleven years as a schools' music inspector during which he demonstrated that music teachers needed carrots, not sticks. Throughout, Geoff found time to be involved in practical music at all levels and worked with amateur operatic societies in many parts of the UK.

Geoff was musical director of the award-winning opera *Gogledd Cymru*, and was invited to conduct in Kazakhstan. He moved to Malta in 2013, and has been involved in music of all kinds in Malta and Gozo. In 2018, he will be chorus master for both *Don Giovanni* and *Aħna Refuġjati*, a new Maltese opera written especially for Valletta 2018. Together with his wife Julie, he wrote a musical in Malti which played to packed houses in Gozo in May 2017. All in all, Geoff was a perfect choice as musical director to work for a second time with Philip and Polly.

January was a hectic month. In Malta a host of supporting players was needed. An accurate historical timeline had to be established both for the script and for the film documentary. At the same time, Polly and Larissa needed to get 'inside' their character if they were to do Christina justice. And Philip needed

Geoff Thomas, composer and musician. *(Geoff Thomas)*

to complete the script! With everyone involved living in two separate countries, there were many challenges. Polly asked for my suggestions about Christina's key character traits:

> Outgoing, adventurous, not content with routine; longed to go on stage.
> Determined, resilient, enthusiasm for travel and thirst for adventure.
> A romantic with guts, inner steel and a sense of humour.
> Attractive and charismatic.
> Gregarious, worldly-wise.

Miriam Farrugia's summing up of Christina became an essential guide for the two actresses: 'I will always remember Christina as a very vibrant and vivacious lady and she should be pictured that way'. Polly and Larissa made arrangements to meet Miriam.

Rehearsals were scheduled for the end of March with workshop performances at The Splendid on Strait Street in early April. More work was done developing the background material and the historical context against which the play was set, not only for the script itself but also for the associated publicity material as well as the theatre programme. Initially, three performances were scheduled for the evenings of Tuesday, Wednesday and Thursday, 4, 5 and 6 April 2017.

Within a few days Philip sent me his first draft of the full script. It was an amazing piece of work. He captured Christina's nature and determination perfectly and had recreated great drama and tension. Above all, despite the intention to use a single stage set, he had cleverly created atmosphere. Philip and Polly had decided not to use a male actor to play Warby, although his character, played by Polly, does make a few brief appearances from time-to-time. For decades Warby has been something of an ethereal character, a man of mystery and not because of the manner of his disappearance. In the play, he remains shadowy to everyone except Christina and she makes it clear, just as she did in real life, she has no intention of lifting the veil. Philip also dealt with the issue of Warby's marriage extremely well. To have avoided it would not have been right. For anyone who knew anything of the story, it is the elephant in the room. Philip dealt easily with whether Christina knew of Betty Warburton and in doing so built in the important American connection.

Polly and Larissa became immersed in the story of Malta's siege. Polly remarked on 'the quite extraordinary resilience and courage of the people of the Maltese Islands who, under heavy, continual bombardment, worked ceaselessly to keep the island free from occupation. They had very little food, fuel and ammunition - and yet they fought on. This little musical has, at its heart, a love song. A love song for the people of the Maltese Islands, whose courage and unquenchable spirit shone brightly at a time of terrible danger and privation. Warby was a recce pilot and away a lot; that they were in love was plain to all. She had to continue doing the concert party gigs and working at Lascaris, whilst he was flying missions. And sometimes, of course, she was on duty when he was flying. The tension must have been unbearable during those moments.' With Polly playing Christina in the 1970s, she remembers the high points of her life, and conjures up her younger self. Larissa, as 'a romantic with guts, inner steel and a sense of humour', takes the audience through the good times and the bad, the joys, the tears and fears.

Larissa was very much hoping the play would bring back some of the 'buzz' in Strait Street, some aspects of the life that had been known there in years gone by. The Malta theatre scene is constantly active but is quite small. More collaborative work involving writers and actors from Malta and abroad would be a good way of expanding, she said. In particular Larissa hoped the new production would move their audience with a true story very much at the heart of Malta. Everyone involved in the production was confident Larissa was right.

Geoff Thomas added occasional male voices to the play while a former colleague of Philip's from the BBC, Chris Carnegy, added RAF 'official announcements'. Dave Arnold added the American voice. Throughout the script, Philip's choice of songs was terrific; the atmosphere created allowed both girls to link perfectly on stage together, albeit thirty years apart. I was staggered not only about how much Philip had been able to put together in such a short timescale from his home in England, but also by the number of people who stepped forward to help. There was a unique Malta story here to be told and lots of people wanted to be part of it. Erica Muscat was Assistant Director and Emma Loftus choreographer. Jason Masini offered lighting and technical assistance. The music associates were Elizabeth David, ARCM, and Helen Williams, wardrobe was looked after by Laura Bonnici, and Paula Fleri-Soler was the media consultant. All the publicity photographs were taken by Justin Mamo and he also covered the dress rehearsals too. Many were used by journalists and reviewers of the play. A host of volunteers also came forward to help: Elizabeth Micallef, Sonia Bezzina, Katel Delia, Melanie Erixon, Jennifer Icao-Calleja, Lizzie Glassborow, Moira Davies and Vladislav Ilich.

A vital contributor to the show was Jackie Grima, one of the foremost movie make-up artists in the business, and not just in Malta; her skills are in demand worldwide. Jackie loved the story so much she agreed to do the period make-up and hair styling as a gift. As Polly said, 'the period look is of the essence'.

John Rhys-Davies, actor.

278

Much progress was also being made in developing the documentary. Pete Doherty had agreed to direct and the Welsh actor John Rhys-Davies, who admired Malta and the Maltese a great deal, offered to co-produce with Philip, as well as doing the commentary. Both intended to be in Malta for the opening of the play.

In late March it was a privilege for me to meet Diana Mackintosh, and she filled me in with a great deal of Malta background. Her memory of those days was remarkable. She also offered the startling information that she had been walking out with Warby up until the point he met Christina. At the time, Diana's elder brother was an officer in the Royal Malta Artillery and he knew both Warby and Christina. Later, Diana met a British Army officer, Ian Mackintosh. In due course Ian left Malta for Italy as the Allies moved north. Diana followed him and they were married in Florence soon after the war ended. Cameron was the first of their three sons. In 2017, seventy-six years after having been walking out with Warby, Diana could still recall an utterly charming, handsome young man with slightly crooked front teeth. There were so many connections within this story. Diana also confirmed that she and her son Nicky intended to fly to Malta to see *Star of Strait Street*.

April was a very good choice for the opening of the play as it marked seventy-five years since the award of the George Cross to Malta and its people. Given such a coincidence, and the fact that the British High Commission was fundamental in initiating the investigation which resulted in Christina being found, I suggested Philip invite the British High Commissioner His Excellency Stuart Gill, OBE, to a performance. He readily accepted.

Rehearsals began on 20 March and they went well. In fact, demand for seats was such that people were invited to the dress rehearsal and both technical rehearsals too. With such interest in the play two additional performances were added on the Tuesday and Thursday evenings. Over the next few days there was much publicity on the island advertising the opening of the play; even the *RAF News* in the UK carried a feature. As a result, a press preview performance was also added to an already busy schedule.

On Thursday, 23 March, the *Times of Malta* carried a feature under the title *A love story in midst of raging war*. The excellent article, written by Sarah Carabott, included photographs, one of which I knew well: Christina sitting in bed reading the *Times of Malta*. Sarah also wrote two further articles seeking information from anyone who had known Christina.

Following the press day performance when she met the cast, Veronica Stivala wrote a feature entitled *A Star for the Times*, published in the *Sunday Times of Malta* on 2 April, two days before the play opened:

> It's nostalgic, it's about love, and beautiful people, but it's also about strength and courage and serves as a window into life in Malta during

the war. Veronica Stivala meets the cast and creatives as she too falls in love with *The Star of Strait Street*, who also, like her, wrote for *The Times* (of Malta).

The beautiful Christina Ratcliffe came to Malta in 1937, with a three-month engagement at The Morning Star, just off Strait Street in Valletta which was extended to six months. Malta had become part of her, and she loved it, body and soul. Returning in 1940, she stayed on throughout the war, working in the Lascaris War Rooms, and creating the Whizz-Bangs, a troupe of entertainers who toured army camps, air bases, forts and clubs. And that's how she met Adrian Warburton; at twenty-six the most decorated pilot in the RAF, eccentric, crazy, gallant beyond belief. How could she not fall in love with him? Like him, she was attractive, charismatic and adventurous and with their personalities, zest and determination, they were to become living symbols of the island's unconquerable spirit. The relationship lasted until 1944, when Warby failed to return from a reconnaissance mission.

The writer, Philip Glassborow, also fell in love with Malta when he visited for a previous production which he also wrote, *The Great Big Radio Sh*ow. He explains this sad love story which he wrote, and which will soon come to life in the very street where this story took place - Strait Street, early next month.

The site-specific two-hander sees Christina in the 1970s (Polly March), looking back over her life in the 1940s (Larissa Bonaci) as she worked as an entertainer during the war. This gave Glassborow the opportunity to make use of a 'marvellous treasure-trove of wartime hit songs to include in the show as well as to write some new songs in period style.'

Indeed the war plays an important role in this play; in Polly's words, it is 'paramount' to the story: 'It was the war that brought Christina and Warby together, and it was the Maltese friends she made during that time and later that sustained throughout the rest of her life. The story could not have happened without the war.'

Polly explains how the character she plays is 'looking back, still, somehow, wanting to believe that her golden boy would fly back for her. She remembers those glorious, terrifying days of the bombing, knowing, as everyone did, that this day could be their last, and she remembers the friends she made among her Maltese neighbours, and those who cared for her, and looked after her in the later years.' In 1943, Christina was awarded the British Empire Medal. 'She was a woman of spirit and courage and humour; the life of a young dancer/entertainer in the 1930s and 1940s was even tougher than it is now,' comments Polly as she explains more about her character. Post war, Christina wrote articles for this newspaper, then *The Times of Malta*, and she opened The Café Christina, in Melita Street. She stayed on in Malta, until her death, living in Floriana.

Adding to this, Larissa Bonaci stresses how the woman's love for the island is 'evidently seen through all the great work she did in Malta.' Larissa is over the moon to be able to play such 'a strong woman who was not only a hopeless romantic, but who worked hard to push women forward in society, breaking through that glass ceiling.'

Another important protagonist is the music that features in the play. Musician Geoff Thomas explains how World War II was the first major conflict during which popular music was accessible to a wide audience:

'There were ballads, marches, big band dance numbers and patriotic ditties. You had Gracie Fields, Vera Lynn, George Formby, Glenn Miller, and Anne Shelton. And, of course, there were parodies and pastiche. In this musical play, the music reflects the era and the world of Christina Ratcliffe.' To achieve this, notes Thomas, Glassborow complemented some songs of the period (*Ship Ahoy*, *I Double Dare You*, etc) with some original pieces which evoke the atmosphere of Strait Street and, in particular, The Morning Star. 'The music is used at key moments to reflect on the past, to create the atmosphere of the club itself, and to add extra pathos to the ending. So, prepare for more wartime classics such as *Welcome to Valletta* and *When Your Heart Found Mine*.'

The story has caught the attention of a documentary production company who will be following the creation of the piece and which none other than John Rhys-Davies (Gimli in *Lord of the Rings*) will be presenting. It will be aired on Maltese TV and also on networks in the UK and USA.

The first two official public performances took place on Tuesday, 4 April, with the world premiere at 7.00 pm and a second show at 9.00 pm. An additional performance was added on Wednesday, making six over three nights.

Frederick Galea attended the first show, and the audience were told of his ground-breaking work documenting Christina's story. Filming of the documentary also began.

The *Times of Malta* carried a review by André Delicata called *Singing amid the sirens:*

Philip Glassborow introduces *Star of Strait Street* to the audience. *(Justin Mamo)*

The Splendid goes back to its roots as a stage for a WWII story of life, love and bravery.

The fascinating history of the Maltese islands during the tumultuous World War II has been documented countless times, but it is always the humanity behind the factual textbooks which keeps tugging at our heartstrings and inciting our curiosity.

Nowhere better than Strait Street to revive a love affair between a chorus girl and an RAF officer, which eventually turned into the young girl's love affair with the island itself.

Strada Stretta Concept, led by artistic director Giuseppe Schembri Bonaci, under the auspices of the Valletta 2018 Foundation, have facilitated the production of a new short musical sponsored by The Phoenicia Malta and The Mackintosh Foundation.

Star of Strait Street, written and directed by Philip Glassborow, centres around the life and love of Christina Ratcliffe, a British chorus girl whose dreams of getting a lucrative performing engagement and touring the world, led her to Malta in the late 1930s - an island which stole her heart, along with that of the dashing and highly-decorated Wing Commander Adrian Warburton, one of the RAF's most prominent aces and crucial in the defence of Malta.

In a two-hander featuring Geoff Thomas as musical director and onstage pianist, the weight of the roles are played by Polly March as an older Christina Ratcliffe living in Malta in the 1970s, reminiscing about her prime during the war years, and Larissa Bonaci as the young Christina. The latter takes the audience on a musical journey which traces her relationship with Malta from 1937 on her first six-month performing engagement, onwards into the outbreak of war and her life then - from changes in priorities and her involvement at Lascaris War Rooms as a plotter to rallying the troops with her own cabaret troupe, the Whizz-Bangs.

Glassborow's script is based on the writings of Ratcliffe herself, who spent the rest of her life in Malta, till her death in the late 1980s, as well as the historical book on Warburton by Paul McDonald.

Ratcliffe's on and off love affair with Warburton is the romantic gold in terms of storytelling but what emerged the most was her strength of character and resilience during some of the most terrible times which Malta ever endured - as well as her love for the island and its people.

In a preview presented last Saturday, March was great in her portrayal of a feisty older woman who has seen the world change and lived through history - transmitting charm and that British stoic spirit which makes everything bearable with sharp wit and good humour.

With light choreography by Emma Loftus, March's Christina introduced us to her younger self - a naïve and earnest young woman played sensitively by Bonaci. Both women took on various other roles, filling in for friends, colleagues and Warburton himself, but Glassborow's clever little script managed to weave in these reports and reveries into Christina's conversations with herself.

For indeed, the performance ran as a dialogue between maturity and youth, all the while revealing the strength of the characters involved without relinquishing the importance given to the setting.

Part nostalgia and part artistic reimagining of the people involved, *Star of Strait Street*, set at The Splendid, which fills in for Christina's real cabaret venue The Morning Star - a cabaret bar originally owned by the artistic director's family during the war - highlights the 'small world' coincidences which make Malta so familiar and which in part stole Ratcliffe's heart, after the war broke it.

A highly enjoyable show which traces the human elements of Malta's wartime past, while showcasing quality talent and a story which is both intriguing and endearing. Definitely one to watch.

Stuart Gill, the British High Commissioner, said on Twitter: 'Just seen *Star of Strait Street* by Philip Glassborow. A gem. Catch it if you can. With brilliant Polly March and Larissa Bonaci.'

On Thursday, 6 April, the *Times of Malta* ran another feature written by Philip Leone Ganado. This followed a visit to the newspaper by John Rhys-Davies, Diana Mackintosh and her son Nicky, as well as Philip Glassborow and the team involved in the film documentary.

During the visit John talked about the special bond that exists between Britain and Malta. 'We are partly documenting the story of the play, but it becomes more of a celebration of love in a time of war and about the love the English had - and have - for Malta. They came to Malta for all sorts of different reasons, with all sorts of class and racial assumptions. But Malta seduces them.' John's father-in-law was based in Malta during the First World War and he still treasures his writings from his time on the island. John also feels 'love' for the island, describing the Maltese as 'magical': 'You are who you are because you have assimilated six or seven thousand years of history into the very dust of Malta; it is part of you. It's unique and remarkable.'

On 7 April, the day following the six highly successful performances, the team was hosted by Frederick Galea at the Malta Aviation Museum at the former RAF fighter station at Ta' Qali where filming for the documentary continued. By then, bookings had also been received for a performance at the Malta Amateur Dramatics Club in Santa Venera on 26 May. Coincidentally, this was the day Christina Ratcliffe was informed she had been awarded the British Empire Medal in 1943. Another booking was received for a performance at the Royal Malta Golf Club in June and a later one at Naxxar.

On 21 May, *Malta Today* ran an article by Teodor Reljic called *The Romance that rocked Strait Street*. Theodor described the play as a 'true and bittersweet wartime romance'. By then *Star of Strait Street* was recognised as a huge success.

Two performances were sold out at the *Teatru Salesjan* in Sliema on 23 February 2018. 'We had such a fabulous evening Polly. You were magnificent. I would urge everyone, if they get the opportunity, to experience *Star of Strait Street*. Thank you to all involved for a great show.' 'An extremely good show, well done to all.' 'The two lead actresses were incredible, so talented and complemented each other beautifully. Congratulations to all involved in the performance - superb evening, thank you!' 'Really enjoyed the show Polly! Thank you and well done to you and everyone involved in the show.' 'Such a fabulous night!!! Thank you to all involved for such a great show.'

By then Jason Micallef, Chairman of Valletta 2018, had confirmed the show would be part of the official 2018 festival to celebrate Valletta's selection as cultural capital of the Europe. This was confirmed in the official programme for Valletta 2018 with performances at the Phoenicia Hotel on 15 May 2018.

STRAIT STREET – also known as "The Gut" by the sailors on shore leave...

The bars, cafes, dance halls and restaurants of Strait Street were a magnet for visiting servicemen during WW2. It was a vibrant hub of entertainment, featuring artistes from abroad (like the African-American dancer Levy Wine and his Spanish wife Dorothy) alongside popular local stars like the female impersonators 'Bobby' and 'Sugar Ocello', and contortionist 'The Sparrow'.

Front cover for the programme of the world premiere of *Star of Strait Street*.

At the stage door: Two 'Christinas' outside The Splendid. *(Justin Mamo)*

Larissa. *(Justin Mamo)*

Larissa as Christina. *(Justin Mamo)*

Larissa & Geoff in rehearsals. *(Justin Mamo)*

Polly as Christina. *(Justin Mamo)*

Geoff Thomas, musical director of
Star of Strait Street. (Justin Mamo)

Polly. *(Justin Mamo)*

'Christina' in the 1940s, with 'Christina' in the 1970s in the background. *(Justin Mamo)*

Aircraft plotters. *(Justin Mamo)*

Taking the salute. *(Justin Mamo)*

The wine glass. *(Justin Mamo)*

Looking back. *(Justin Mamo)*

Shock at a revelation. (*Justin Mamo*)

The finale. (*Justin Mamo*)

Two 'Christinas'. *(Justin Mamo)*

The published reviews were all very positive. However, the personal impact the production had on some members of the audience was astonishing. Len Moscrop was brought up and educated in Malta and knows the island well. Soon after the show he wrote to Polly and Larissa:

> I was fortunate enough to attend the Premiere of the *Star of Strait Street* last night. It was for me and my friends a theatrical experience beyond anything we had expected; grown men do cry! You both brought Christina to life and placed her into the hearts of many present. Set in the perfect location of her Floriana apartment (although goodness knows how you got a piano up the 96 steps to her flat!) the whole feel of the Splendid evoked an air of the very nostalgia, love and slight seediness which embraces the whole story. Christina's life became our life for that all too brief and precious hour last night. Pouring out of the Splendid to walk amongst the ghosts of Strait Street as we made our way back to the hotel last night I could almost smell the dying embers of the Strait Street I knew as child nearly fifty years ago. The two of you and your fellow artists involved in the gift you gave us all last night should be very proud indeed of what you achieved as the sun went down on Strait Street.

Christina, whose grave we visited yesterday, would have blushed I'm sure at the attention being heaped upon her at the moment but the both of you would I'm sure know that; you both 'carved Christina on our hearts'.

Break a leg tonight and for the rest of the run and thank you, thank you, thank you.

Larissa Bonaci described Christina as having 'worked hard to push women forward in society, breaking through that glass ceiling.' She was not alone. All the ladies of Lascaris did that. It is good that what they did, as well as their sacrifice and courage, is being so well remembered seventy-five years later. Their long overdue encore is well-deserved.

Christina Ratcliffe, BEM. *(Paul McDonald)*

Postscript

We arrived back in Malta on Tuesday, 8 May 2018, nearly six years after my quest first began. This time our visit was to coincide with *Star of Strait Street's* performances in the Grand Ballroom of the Phoenicia Hotel in Floriana. Our first few days were spent relaxing in the Xara Palace Hotel in Mdina where, seventy-six years earlier, the then Air Officer Commanding-in-Chief Middle East, Air Marshal Sir Arthur Tedder, watched *Luftwaffe* fighters swooping down to strafe RAF Ta' Qali.

Over the next few days we visited many of the places associated with Christina. The Old Vic Theatre on Strait Street itself is now well disguised as a street café, while the 'convenient' location next door is rather grand. In fact, changes on the former *Strada Stretta* are gathering pace with more small restaurants opening beyond Old Theatre Street toward The Splendid, where *Star of Strait Street* opened in April 2017. One enterprising owner had a sign outside his premises saying, 'The Gut is open for business! Tourists welcome.' And they were, with much laughter and music and a wide variety of places to eat and drink. There's more to do to bring the old places back to life but at least a good start has at last been made.

A hectic few days followed with Philip and Lizzie Glassborow. We also met Polly March, who had been very supportive in putting the last pieces of Christina's story together. There was some excellent publicity promoting the play and Christina and Warby's story. Edwin Ward wrote a superb piece which now features on the Phoenicia's website (Appendix B) and the talented journalist Sarah Carabott, already familiar with the story and the play, contributed a two-page spread in the *Times of Malta* on Saturday, 12 May (Appendix C).

I had long-awaited the play's performance, but first I was privileged to be a fly-on-the-wall at the final rehearsal. To see such professionals, actors and supporting players working together, solving a myriad of challenges with lighting, sound, props, seating, programmes, display material etc., etc., while actually rehearsing at the same time was simply astonishing. The two performances later that evening were to packed audiences which included the US Ambassador and the British High Commissioner. The shows were superb. Polly, Larissa and Geoff, combined to tell a beautiful story that had joy, sadness and much poignancy. This was a true Malta story.

Within an hour of the second performance, if any of the audience had looked in they would have seen the cast and their supporting players, including a playwright and an author, packing up props and posters. The very next day the cast cast-off, en route to Australia to perform in front of yet more packed houses in Sydney, Melbourne and Adelaide. London is calling too, in November.

It was a whirl of a few days and truly heart-warming to see the play so well received by so many people. At talks Philip and I gave, and at the Phoenicia performances, we noted that Maltese of a younger generation were in the majority. I hope what they saw and heard added to their knowledge of the remarkable endurance and achievements of their parents and grandparents all those years ago.

After the shows, a pleasant task was to revisit the Club Bar at the Phoenicia - where my quest for Christina truly began after seeing her photographs on the wall. Philip and I were glancing through the many other pictures, at the request of the hotel staff, to see who else we could identify. There was a splendid shot of the actor/director Noel Coward with Lord Gort... evocative pictures of ships in Grand Harbour... so many other stories to tell!

There was one final visit I had to make before leaving Malta. At the entrance to *Santa Maria Addolorata* cemetery I asked the lady flower seller for real flowers this time:

'A colourful display for a lady who rests here,' I said.

'For your mother?' she asked.

'No,' I said, 'for a lady who passed away thirty years ago.'

'Oh,' she said, and gave me a slightly quizzical look.

Then she said: 'In that case, here's a sunflower from me to her.'

Annex A

Ladies of Lascaris - 1 June 1942

Civilian Lady Aircraft Plotters:

A Watch (15)

Mrs Jackson, Watch Captain, Valletta
Mrs Jane Ashman, Sliema
Miss Clews, Pietà
Mrs Cox, Floriana
Miss Dilley, Sliema
Miss Hartley, Sliema
Mrs Jones, Floriana
Miss Mifsud, Gzira
Miss Nash, Sliema
Miss Owens, Sliema
Miss Poulton, Gzira
Miss Robinson, Valletta
Mrs Taylor, Valletta
Miss Winifred Turk, Pietà
Miss Whear, Gzira

B Watch (13)

Mrs Margaret 'Pickles' Fletcher, Watch Captain, Floriana, founder member of the
    Whizz-Bangs, awarded British Empire Medal July 1943
Miss Gladys Aitken, St Georges, later Mrs Gladys Duddell
Miss Helen Cauchi, Birkirkara
Miss Elizabeth 'Betty' Cuell, Casalpaola, later Mrs Betty MacTavish
Miss Grech, Sliema
Mrs Lillian Griffiths, Floriana
Miss Marjorie Hedley, Floriana
Miss Doris Hersey, Sliema, later Mrs Doris Caldwell
Miss Margaret Hersey, Sliema
Mrs Doreen Lardeaux, Floriana

Miss Carmel Smith, Sliema
Miss Priscilla Tomlin, Sliema
Miss Rosemary Tomlin, Gzira

C Watch (13)

Mrs Gray, Watch Captain, Floriana
Mrs Brightman, Floriana
Miss Irene Cameron, Floriana, member of the Raffians, awarded British Empire
    Medal July 1943, later Mrs Irene Clark
Miss Drake, St Georges
Miss Maria Falzon, Floriana, later Mrs Maria Warren
Miss Hart, Sliema
Mrs Hitches, Msida
Mrs McConnell, Hamrun
Miss Murray, St Georges
Mrs Josephine Roberts, née Valetta, Floriana, later Mrs Josephine Barber
Mrs Melita Rustage, Floriana
Miss Spanton, Spinola
Miss Storace, Floriana

D Watch (12)

Miss Mary Christina Ratcliffe, Watch Captain, Valletta, founder member of the
    Whizz-Bangs, awarded British Empire Medal July 1943
Miss Cox, Floriana
Miss D'Arcy, Floriana
Miss Doris Grimstead, Birkirkara
Miss Phyllis Hoyle, St Paul's Bay
Miss Pauline Hadcroft Longyear, Pietà
Miss Mutter, Pietà
Miss Rapinett, Valletta
Miss Josephine Roebuck, Msida
Miss Teeling, Hamrun
Miss Turner, Valletta
Miss Worley, Floriana

Between 1940 and 1945

Miss Mary Aitken, St Georges, later Mrs Mary Tooley
Carmen Borg
Miss Anne Button

Miss Mary Patricia Cameron, Floriana, killed 1 March 1942, 18-years-old
Carmel Caruana
Miss Peggy Christie
Miss Helen Cuell, Casalpaola
Miss Joan Cuell, Casalpaola, later Mrs Joan Watret
Miss Sarah Darmanin Demajo
Sarah Ellul
Mrs Phyllis Frederick, Sliema, awarded British Empire Medal July 1943
Miss Helen Gauchi
Miss Marion Gould, Sliema, member of the Whizz-Bangs, later Mrs Marion Childs
Miss Hayes
Jane Hayston
Miss Zoe Meade
Miss Mary Raynor
Mary Vassalo
Stella Vella
Nanette Williams
Miss Catherine 'Kay' Xuereb, later Mrs Catherine Cussins
Julie Xuereb

Civilian Lady Cypherines 1 June 1942 (11):

Miss Irene Arnold, Sliema, awarded British Empire Medal July 1943
Miss Jessica Barber, Tarxien
Mrs Budd, Sliema
Mrs Sheila Davies, St. Julians
Miss Derby, Sliema
Miss Mae Edwards, Sliema
Miss Kluge, Sliema
Miss Larchin, Valletta
Miss Lewis, Valletta
Miss P. Scott, Sliema
Mrs Southwick, Sliema

Secretary to the Air Officer Commanding (Malta) 1 June 1942:

Miss Carmela E. Galea, St Julians, awarded British Empire Medal July 1943

Clerks:

Miss C. Bencini, Hamrun
Mrs Bony

Miss C. Briffa, Sliema
Miss M. Cavarra, Sliema
Miss Cole, Sliema
Miss J. Grech, Hamrun

Employed in the RAF Headquarters between 1940 and 1942

Miss Aida Kelly, Hamrun, killed in an air raid 24 April 1942, age 26 years
Mrs Tamara Marks, Floriana

Annex B

Malta's Love Story: Casablanca replayed at The Morning Star

By Edwin Ward, CEO Ogilvy Malta,
Saturday, 12 May 2018.

In Mediterranean lore, 'The Morning Star' is a planet, especially Venus, when visible in the east before sunrise. As Adrian 'Warby' Warburton spots his Venus, Christina Ratcliffe, from the cockpit of his Spitfire, a war had begun to rage that would ignite personalities and passions, and derail one of the biggest attempted land grabs in history. We learn all this within a few seconds of meeting former RAF Group Captain Paul McDonald, who has now transitioned to professional author having penned *Malta's Greater Siege* which inspired Philip Glassborow to pen *Star of Strait Street*.

Warby, Wing Commander Warburton, became legendary in the RAF for his role in the defence of Malta. A son of Malta, Warburton was christened on board a submarine in Grand Harbour, Valletta. The flying ace was educated at St Edward's School in Oxford, where Sir Douglas Bader was also educated. The famous pilot took some incredible risks; prior to Admiral Cunningham's surprise Taranto night attack, he circled Taranto harbour several times, then his cameras failed. Undeterred, Warburton then flew so low, his observer was able to read off the names of the battleships as they flew past. Guided by this intelligence, the Fleet Air Arm launched its devastating attack that night.

One important source for McDonald was meeting Maltese author Frederick Galea, whose *Carve Malta on my Heart* revealed a great deal of Christina and Adrian's story. Someone else who has given a voice to hero Warby, is the voice given full force in Philip Glassborow's musical *Star of Strait Street*. Warby was a star in the sky. The star who is the title of 'The Morning Star', is Christina Ratcliffe. She helped turn The Morning Star in *Strada San Nicola* into the most popular cabaret and club of the entire Mediterranean Fleet.

To help the war effort, Christina volunteered as a plotter, air traffic monitoring that played a vital role in World War II, quickly becoming a Captain of a team of

18 plotters hidden deep in the tunnels below Valletta, listening to the radio traffic of the pilots, even when many of them had close personal relationships with the pilots. Christina championed the recruitment of Maltese girls, who became an essential part of the war effort. Christina was promoted to Assistant Controller and awarded the British Empire Medal.

For those wanting to know what Christina looks like, two photos of her hang in The Phoenicia's Club Bar, and the performance of *Star of Strait Street* will be performed in the hotel's Grand Ballroom next week, a venue which was not available when Christina and her troupe 'The Whizz Bangs' formed in order to entertain the troops. This pin-up girl of the Fleet fell for her reconnaissance pilot in a period where love meant a few stopovers between missions.

Christina was an author, who, according to McDonald, is 'historically important'. If the kind of history that Warby was making had the British High Command issuing praise then Christina's memoirs are given a value beyond her daily life, and she was decorated for her wartime contributions. The two heroes had a few short periods together between January 1941 and November 1943, when Warby took orders for a flight to North Africa, but sadly was never able to return, and soon after disappears without a trace after receiving orders from Elliott Roosevelt, son of President Franklin D. Roosevelt and First Lady Eleanor Roosevelt.

As colonel of the Northwest African Photographic Reconnaissance Wing during this period, a sub-command of the Mediterranean Air Command, Elliott worked on the shuttle bombing project with the USSR, which is what probably got Warby killed flying a secret mission in a special US 8th Air Force reconnaissance plane. Why was Warby sent and not a US pilot? That's an intriguing question, but Warby's status for pulling off critical missions was by this time unparalleled.

Military aviation combat almost began with reconnaissance, which has always fed into military strategy. It's no coincidence that young Warby was interested in contributing to that vital element for military command, his father had been a high-ranking naval officer. Marshal of the Royal Air Force Lord Tedder considered him 'The most valuable pilot in the RAF' having flown 395 operational missions mostly from Malta to provide information that ultimately stopped the Axis powers from taking the Suez Canal.

The Siege of Malta in the Second World War was a military campaign in the Mediterranean Theatre. For Tedder to attribute Warburton so highly, it was this campaign that saved the Allies from a loss that would give Europe and the world a distorted shape. Malta helped stop the world from falling to the Axis powers. That Siege was based on General Erwin Rommel, in de facto field command of Axis forces in North Africa, recognising its importance quickly. In May 1941, he warned that 'Without Malta the Axis will end by losing control of North Africa'. In fact, for 28 thunderous months it was the most bombed place on planet earth.

McDonald's reconnaissance compiling *Malta's Greater Siege* has led to the idea for another book, which will tell the story of the heroine plotters, to be called *Ladies of Lascaris - Christina Ratcliffe and the Forgotten Heroes of Malta's War*. We look forward to welcoming Paul back to The Phoenicia as he researches and writes his next book due to be published in November.

Christina waited for the rest of her life for her love Adrian Warburton to return. She never knew his fate. He was shot down by the Germans over Bavaria, his body undiscovered for 58 years until found in a field outside Munich and later laid to rest at the Commonwealth War Graves there.

Christina indeed chose to spend the rest of her life in Malta, the island she grew to love, and passed away here in the 1980's still waiting for her beloved Warby to return. During her time on the island, the English newspaper *The Star* carried a five-part article penned by Christina herself on her wartime experience in Malta, called *One woman goes to war*. In 1974, the Maltese newspaper *Malta News* expanded this story, under the heading *Carve Malta on my heart*, in a series of fifteen parts. Ms Ratcliffe wrote five articles for the *Sunday Times of Malta*, which appeared in 1974, 1975, 1980 and 1982. Those articles no doubt helped Christina to conjure up her flamboyant flying ace and feel him closer for a few brief moments before her death.

Annex C

Strait Street cabaret performer Christina Ratcliffe celebrated in new book

Words that come Strait from the heart
By Sarah Carabott, Times of Malta, Saturday, 12 May 2018.

A former RAF pilot has written a book about a wartime decorated cabaret performer whom he never met, but whose spirit lives on in the memory of several Maltese people, roads and archives.

Christina Ratcliffe, believed to have been the lover of pilot Adrian Warburton, is remembered mostly for her charming and resilient nature as a financially independent young woman who first landed in Malta in the late 1930s as a cabaret performer.

'Warburton was pretty unusual - he was a gallant, brave man, but after my research on Ms Ratcliffe, it seems like her life was more extraordinary. She was a very determined woman, who left industrial northwest England in her 20s, and travelled Europe as a singer and dancer,' Paul McDonald, OBE, 69, told this newspaper.

Ms Ratcliffe never planned on remaining in Malta, but her departure was delayed with Italy's war declaration on Britain. She went on to cheer the troops with her own cabaret troupe the Whizz-Bangs, and eventually worked as a plotter at the Lascaris War Rooms.

She spent the rest of her life in Malta, till her death in the late 1980s. Sadly, Mr Warburton disappeared while in action over Germany in 1944, and his remains were only found a few years ago.

'Warburton's disappearance in the war remained a great mystery - no one knew what had happened to him and some wondered whether he was trying to come back to Malta to see Christina. His remains were only found 60 years after his disappearance, in the wreckage of his aircraft in Bavaria.

'Back then I was based in Germany, and I was told that he was a photo-reconnaissance pilot. This was the first in a series of surprises, because when I was based in Luqa in the 1970s, I formed part of a photo-reconnaissance squadron,' Mr McDonald said.

The spirit of Ms Ratcliffe and Mr Warburton seems to have followed Mr McDonald on a following trip to Germany and later to Malta. While on holiday, he located the Floriana apartment where Ms Ratcliffe used to live. A person who pointed him in the right direction remembered her, even though she had passed away some 25 years earlier.

'I was stunned. People still remembered her by name,' he said.

'Later on, as I came out of a shop in Valletta, I was shocked to see the Old Vic theatre, which hosted the very first rehearsal room for the Whizz-Bangs.

'Everywhere we went there was some connection. I met, by chance, Frederick Galea who has researched her story extensively and was very instrumental in providing a memorial to her.

'Then one day, a couple of nights before returning home, I was sitting at a bar at the Phoenicia Hotel, and right in front of me I saw a framed photo of Christina Ratcliffe reading the *Times of Malta*. I stood up to take a closer look, but as I returned to my seat, I realised that there was another photo of her right above my head. That was it. I knew I had to write a book.'

Later on this year, Mr McDonald will be publishing a book called *Ladies of Lascaris: Christina Ratcliffe and the Forgotten Heroes of Malta's War*.

Mr McDonald was based in Malta with the RAF between 1975 and 1978 and both his children were born here. He was speaking to this newspaper ahead of a discussion at Lascaris War Rooms on Monday. The following day, snippets of Ms Ratcliffe's life will be retold in the musical play *Star of Strait Street*, which will be performed at the Phoenicia Hotel.

The discussion between Mr McDonald and British High Commissioner Stuart Gill, entitled *A Lascaris Lady and a World War II Enigma*, will be held on Monday at 7pm at the Lascaris War Rooms in Valletta. Entrance is free, however space is limited and pre-booking by email on gabriel@witartna.org is advisable. The discussion will be moderated by Philip Glassborow, writer of *Star of Strait Street*, which debuted at the Splendid under the auspices of the Valletta 2018 Foundation.

On Tuesday, *Star of Strait Street* will be performed twice at the Phoenicia Hotel in Valletta, ahead of a tour of Australia. Both performances are sponsored by the Mackintosh Foundation and the hotel itself. Polly March, Larissa Bonaci and Geoff Thomas will be performing in Sydney, Melbourne and Adelaide.

Bibliography & Sources

Books

Brookes, Andrew J., *Photo Reconnaissance* (Ian Allan Ltd, Shepperton, Surrey, 1975)

Cameron, Ian, *Red Duster, White Ensign* (Futura, 1959)

Coldbeck, Harry, *The Maltese Spitfire* (Airlife, 1997)

Cull, Brian, and Galea, Frederick,

Gladiators over Malta, 2008 (Wise Owl, Malta, 2008)

Marylands over Malta (Wise Owl, Malta, 2014)

Dobbie, Sybil, *Grace under Malta* (Lindsay Drummond, London, 1944)

Douglas-Hamilton, James, *The Air Battle for Malta* (Mainstream Publishing, Edinburgh, 1981)

Galea, Frederick R.,

Call-out (Malta, 2002)

Carve Malta on my heart and other wartime stories (Malta, 2004) *Women of Malta* (Wise Owl, Malta, 2006)

Johnstone, Sandy, *Where No Angels Dwell* (Cedric Chivers Limited, Bath, 1974)

Lloyd, Sir Hugh, *Briefed to Attack* (Hodder & Stoughton, London, 1949)

Longyear, Michael, *Malta 1937-1942* (2006)

Lucas, Laddie, *Malta: The Thorn in Rommel's Side* (Penguin, London, 1993)

McDonald, Paul, *Malta's Greater Siege & Adrian Warburton DSO* DFC** DFC (USA)* (Pen and Sword, Barnsley, 2015)

Mizzi, Laurence, *The People's War*, (Progress Press, Valletta, 2002)

Schofield, John and Morrisey, Emily, *Strait Street Malta's 'Red-Light District' Revealed*, (Midsea Books Ltd, Valletta, Malta, 2013)

Shores, Christopher, Cull, Brian, Malizia, Nicola, *Malta: The Spitfire Year 1942*, (Grub Street, London, 1991)

Spooner, Tony,

Supreme Gallantry (John Murray, London, 1996)

Warburton's War (Crécy, 1994)

Woodhall, Woody, *Soldier, Sailor & Airman Too* (Grub Street, London, 2008)

Documents, Magazines, Newspapers, Online Articles, Periodicals
Callaway, Tim, *Adrian Warburton (Aviation Classics, Issue 14)*
Carabott, Sarah, *A love story in midst of raging war* (*The Times of Malta,* 23 March 2017)
Delicata, André, *Singing amid the sirens* (*The Times of Malta,* 3 April 2017)
Ganada, Philip Leone, *Actor Rhys Davies talks of special bond between Britain, Malta (The Times of Malta,* 6 April 2017)
Ministry of Information, *The Air Battle of Malta* (*HMSO*, London, 1944)
Nash, Roy, *The Unknown Air Ace Star* (*The Star*, 3-18 March 1958)
Ratcliffe, Mary Christina,
A Day of Rejoicing (*The Sunday Times of Malta*, 15 August 1982)
Food for Thought (*The Sunday Times of Malta,* 22 December 1974)
One Woman goes to War (*The Star,* 14-18 April 1958)
The Merry Tenth of May (*The Sunday Times of Malta,* 18 May 1980)
Three Pence Charity (*The Sunday Times of Malta,* 26 October 1975)
Reljic, Teodor, *The Romance that rocked Strait Street* (*Malta Today*, 21 May 2017)
Rhyl woman relives her wartime experience in Malta (*Wales Online*, 22 February 2012)
Stivala, Veronica, *A Star for the Times* (*The Sunday Times of Malta,* 2 April 2017)
Vella, Fiona, *Love in Time of War*, (2014)
Whiteley, Earnest, *Warburton and PR from Malta, 1940-41* (*RAF Quarterly, Volume 18, No 1* (1978)

Unpublished Sources:
Memoirs of Air Cdre Robert Jonas (RAF Museum)
National Archives, Kew, London:
AIR 20/7866 - *Luqa Lens* - Copies of RAF Luqa magazine
AIR 23/5556-5575 - No 8 Sector Operations Room Ops B logs 1942 and 1943

Interviews/Personal Recollections/Other Sources
Eman Bonnici, archivist, *Santa Maria Addolorata* cemetery
Heidi Burton (née Cox), photographer
Tim Calloway, historian and Editor *Aviation Classics*
Lieutenant General William Keir 'Bill' Carr, CMM, DFC, CD
Marion Childs, née Gould
Edward Cuell
Cara Egerton
Peter Elliot, Curator *Emeritus*, RAF Museum, Hendon, London
Nick Farnes
Mario Farrugia, Chairman and CEO Malta Heritage Trust (*Fondazzjoni Wirt Artna*)
Miriam Farrugia

Frederick R. Galea
Valerie Galea, née Darmanin
Gwen Hobson, archivist Manchester High School for Girls
Christine Joy, former archivist Manchester High School for Girls
Gordon Leith, Curator, RAF Museum, Hendon, London
Michael Longyear
Salvatore Muscat
Sandra Patterson
Martin Ratcliffe
Pam Roberts, archivist Manchester High School for Girls
Ingrid Scerri
The late Jack Vowles

Index

INDEX